# ELEGY FOR AN AGE

# ELEGY FOR AN AGE

## The Presence of the Past in Victorian Literature

But now the whole Round Table is dissolved
Which was an image of the mighty world,
And I, the last, go forth companionless,
And the days darken round me, and the years,
Among new men, strange faces, other minds.'

Tennyson, 'The Passing of Arthur'

## John D. Rosenberg

Anthem Press
London

Anthem Press
An imprint of Wimbledon Publishing Company
75–76 Blackfriars Road, London SE1 8HA

or

PO Box 9779, London SW19 7QA
*www.anthempress.com*

This edition first published by Anthem Press 2005

*British Library Cataloguing in Publication Data*
A catalogue record for this book is available from the British Library.

*Library of Congress Cataloging in Publication Data*
A catalog record for this book has been requested.

1 3 5 7 9 10 8 6 4 2

ISBN   1 84331 156 9 (Hbk)
ISBN   1 84331 154 2 (Pbk)

Typeset by Footprint Labs Ltd, London
*www.footprintlabs.com*

Printed in India

To MOSES HADAS (1900–1966) and
GEORGE E. JONAS (1897–1978)

Incomparable Teacher and Secular Saint—
My Mentors in all the best that I later became

Frontispiece: J. M. W. Turner, *The Fighting Temeraire*.

# CONTENTS

# LIST OF FIGURES

# ACKNOWLEDGEMENTS

The insights of generations of my students have contributed significantly to the evolution of this book. I am also indebted to the fine work of my research assistants, most recently Donna Hobbs, Donna Fusco, Leticia Sanchez, Tianhu Hao, Suzy Shedd and Patricia Akhimie. Dr. Elliott Zuckerman, dear friend and critic of my writing for half a century, offered valuable suggestions on the Tennyson, Ruskin and Pater chapters. Professor Joseph Connors kindly critiqued my Ruskin chapter. Professor Gerald Monsman generously shared his annotated edition of Pater's *Gaston de Latour* with me in advance of its publication.

Fellowships from the John Simon Guggenheim Foundation, The American Council of Learned Societies and The National Endowment for the Humanities sustained me during various stages of my research and writing. My thanks are also due to the reference librarians of the Columbia University Library, the Vermont State Library in Montpelier, to Bob Jolly of the Peacham, Vermont Library, and to Michael Roche and Greg McCandless of the Northeast Regional Library of Vermont.

To the astute and sympathetic prodding of Tom Penn and Robert Douglas-Fairhurst, my editors at Anthem Press, I am indebted for a more unified and shapely book than I initially submitted to them. Their early enthusiasm for the project was vital to me. But my greatest thanks are due to my wife, Maurine, and to my former student – now colleague – Jill Muller. Whole chapters have vanished because of their insistence on thematic continuity, and those that remain glow more brightly for their scrutiny. Scarcely a page of the manuscript has passed their keen eyes without gaining in clarity of argument or economy of expression.

Peacham, Vermont
August 2004

# 1

# THE AGE OF ELEGY

In the first days of the century just passed, the British buried their Queen with an empire's lamentation. Plump but diminutive, aged and wasted by disease, Victoria was lowered into a casket crowded with memorabilia: bracelets, rings, lockets of hair, plaster casts of the hands of those she loved, the dressing gown of her long-mourned Albert. Her coffin was as cluttered as the mantelpieces of her subjects, whose compulsion to collect expressed their need to grasp at stability in a world in radical transformation.

The Victorians who speak to us most urgently today thought of themselves as living not in an age of peace or progress but, in John Stuart Mill's phrase, in 'an age of transition,'[1] caught between a vanishing past and an uncertain future. Such an unsettled cultural climate provided rich soil for the flourishing of elegy. The Gothic Revival embodied this nostalgia in stone. When the ancient Houses of Parliament spectacularly burned to the ground on the night of 16 October 1834, the nation chose to rehouse its government in an edifice that looked back longingly to the Middle Ages. Oxford, the home of lost causes and itself a kind of medieval Eden of cloistered spires and chiming bells, gave rise to the Oxford Movement, which sought to revive the fervor and ancient rituals of the medieval Church, a movement that led in time to the conversion to Catholicism of two of our most greatly gifted elegists, John Henry Newman and Gerard Manley Hopkins. Tennyson's once immensely popular *Idylls of the King*, set in medieval Britain, commemorates an idealized world that never was but that has haunted the English imagination for over a millenium.

Waking daily to newness in all its forms – new sciences and intellectual disciplines, new and vastly more rapid modes of transportation, new political and social institutions, vast new acquisitions to the Empire, new relations between the classes and the sexes, sprawling new cities in which machines were housed with far more care than the 'hands' that worked them – the Victorians felt, in Matthew Arnold's phrase, like wanderers

...between two worlds, one dead,
The other powerless to be born.
                              ('Stanzas from the Grande Chartreuse,' ll. 85–6)

Faced by such a dizzying present, connecting with their past became for the
Victorians a sort of survival strategy. For the present was both exhilarating
and menacing, like the vertiginous landscapes that rushed past them at
unprecedented speed outside their railway carriage windows. They sought
points of purchase, as it were, in an imagined past that appeared more stable
than the present. It is no accident that the Victorians were obsessed with
origins, with history and the new sciences of philology and archaeology – a
literal unearthing of the buried past. The *Oxford English Dictionary* (1881–
1928) traces the pedigree of every word in the language back to its first usage
in print. The most revolutionary book of the period, more a muffled denotation
than an elegy, Darwin's *Origin of Species* (1859) deconstructed the narrative of
Genesis and opened up frightening temporal vistas reaching back to a remote,
pre-human past.

Darwin is something of an anomaly in the company of my elegists. In his personal
life, he formed deep and lasting ties and mourned their severing in death. He
grieved for decades over the early death of his favorite child Annie and wrote a
singularly beautiful prose elegy on her passing (see p. 126, fn). But as a scientist
he voyaged beyond the attachments and vicissitudes of human time. He
measured time not in years or decades but in the aeonian rise and subsidence
of continents, for he had a capacity to hold time in his head akin to holding
one's breath under water for months on end. This ability to sense with his
intellectual pulses the ticking of an immeasurably slow cosmic clock is the
grand peculiarity of his mind. The ruins of the Parthenon or of Carthage, the
unearthing of a warrior buried since the last ice age, aroused in the Victorians
nostalgia tinged with a sense of distant kinship. But the gigantic fossilized
skull of a long-extinct Megatherium that Darwin unearthed on the coast of
Argentina and shipped to England awakened only astonishment in its
beholders. Like so many of his contemporaries, Darwin was at bottom an
historian, but the story he tells is of the time before human time, and hence
lacks the nostalgia of elegy.

Histories of all kinds, factual and fictional, became bestsellers. History, the
study of public time, found its complement in the flourishing of autobiography,
the research into the origins of the self in private time. Wordsworth's *Prelude*
(1805; 1850), an epic about the origins of the poet's self, uncovers the roots of
his creative powers in early childhood 'spots of time.' The *Prelude* is an elegy to
the discovery and eventual fading of Wordsworth's genius.[2] In *Apologia Pro
Vita Sua* Newman traces the origin of his believing self back to the child who
crossed himself on entering a darkened room. Wordsworth's disciple, Ruskin,

revisits the same formative territory in *Praeterita* as a child who meets his aboriginal self beside the banks of the River Tay and the Springs of Wandel. In his brief autobiographical 'Child in the House,' Pater discovers the self he later inhabits in the perfume of sensations that 'toss and fall' about him as he sits beside his mother on a long June afternoon. The best Victorian autobiography is intrinsically elegiac, a turning inward and backward to the Child who is, in Wordsworth's phrase, 'Father of the Man.'

Tennyson's *In Memoriam* articulates a unique mix of intensely private grief over the death of Arthur Hallam and the larger cultural shock of a world in which faith has yielded to doubt; Wordsworth's trust in a benevolent God and a benign Nature has been usurped by a Darwinian 'Nature, red in tooth and claw' (Section 56, l. 15). As the century progressed, looking back at the fading of a cohesive past gave way to anxiety over a menacing future. In 1886, just after Tennyson completed *Idylls of the King*, he foresaw 'a mighty wave of evil' poised to break over Western civilization 'in the next fifty years. All ages are ages of transition, but this is an awful moment of transition.'[3] Elegy yields to Apocalypse in the blighted earth and smog-shrouded sun of Ruskin's *Storm Cloud of the Nineteenth Century* (1884) and in the terrified self-alienation of Hopkins's late Sonnets of Desolation:

> O the mind, mind has mountains; cliffs of fall
> Frightful, sheer, no-man fathomed.
> ('No Worst, There Is None,' ll. 9–10)

As attuned to the cultural moment as Hopkins felt alienated from his, Tennyson surveys a nightmare landscape at the end of 'The Passing of Arthur,' where the King fights his 'last, dim, weird battle of the West' in

> A land of old upheaven from the abyss
> By fire, to sink into the abyss again;
> Where fragments of forgotten peoples dwelt (ll. 82–4)

– a wasteland where one would not be altogether surprised to meet Yeats's rough, messianic Beast slouching toward Bethlehem.

2

In writing about a century of English elegy, my imagination has been most compelled by the particularities of certain writers' lives and the words they put on a page, rather than by generalities about the Victorian period. At the end of his *Apologia Pro Vita Sua* (1864–5), Newman remarks that arguments in proof of God's existence make no buds unfold within him nor cause his moral being to rejoice. So it is with me when I avert my eyes from the lives and words of my elegists, with whom I have, perhaps, a natural affinity, having written all my adult life, without realizing it, elegies in the guise of literary criticism. In this I resemble Molière's M. Jourdain, who awakens one day to the realization that he has been speaking prose all his life. Fortunately for me, much of the most moving literature of the English nineteenth century is one long song of mourning, and this book is perhaps best read as a rehearsal of that song in prose. Of course, the very words I linger over, like the daily experiences of those who composed them, lived and moved and had their being in a particular time and place. Such words reflected, and also shaped, a unique cultural moment. But I am more comfortable when writing of Victorian elegy through the lens of particular elegists than in hazarding panoramic generalities.

In this I remain true to Coleridge's insistence that, although elegy may treat of any subject, it must remain 'always and exclusively' personal.[4] Classical elegy could address any subject, provided it was written in elegiac metre (alternating lines of dactylic hexameter and pentameter). Yet elegy as I understand it is a mode of expression that transcends all restrictions of genre. By my lights Virginia Woolf's *To the Lighthouse* or J. M. W. Turner's *The Fighting Temeraire* are as quintessentially elegiac as Tennyson's *In Memoriam*.

Elegy requires a fine equipoise between remembered joy and present regret. If the pleasure implicit in the recollection of loss becomes too predominant, elegy slips into the sentimentality of unresisted regret; if present pain wholly occludes recollected pleasure, elegy aborts itself in tears or breaks down into Lear's thrice repeated 'howl' of pain over Cordelia's corpse. Tennyson discovers in *In Memoriam* 'a use in measured language,' which like 'dull narcotics,' numbs pain, (Section 5, ll. 2, 4), as do the comforting cadences of the great Anglican service for the Burial of the Dead: '...earth to earth, ashes to ashes, dust to dust...' But elegy can suffocate under the cloak of ritual. It must, I believe, center on personal loss, although that loss may be of places or beliefs as well as persons, and the person may be imaginary, as in Wordsworth's quintuplet of elegies to Lucy Gray. Newman, Arnold and Hopkins mourn their departure from Oxford as keenly as Tennyson mourns the death of his friend Arthur Hallam and of Hallam's surrogate, Arthur the King. From this perspective, the most famous of English elegies – Gray's 'Elegy Written in a Country Churchyard' – is less a song of mourning than a talented and pleasing simulacrum of grief. The dead are ever plural and anonymous. They elicit the poet's 'passing tribute of a sigh' (l. 80). We never hear the anguished note that Wordsworth sounds for the young Lucy:

> But she is in her grave, and, oh,
>     The difference to me!
>                     ('She Dwelt Among th' Untrodden Ways,' ll. 11–12)

Gray's Elegy appeared exactly a century before Tennyson's *In Memoriam* (1850). The commanding difference between them – between decorously dropped tears and the deeply personal language of a poet shocked into grief – is due above all to Wordsworth, who made the poet's own sensations and recollections the dominant subject of his poetry.

Yet grief is a ventriloquist who speaks in many voices. Although the greatest elegies spring from personal loss, they also arise from the ashes of elegies past. *In Memoriam* pays homage to classical elegy and to Milton's 'Lycidas.' To cross the Atlantic for a moment, Walt Whitman commemorates a national tragedy in a voice as uniquely his own as the scent of lilacs. But at the center of 'When Lilacs Last in the Dooryard Bloom'd' lies a trope as ancient as elegy itself, the strewing of flowers over the dead. As the funeral train winds through countryside and cities draped in black, Whitman lays a broken sprig of lilac on Lincoln's coffin. Late in *In Memoriam*, when Tennyson's work of mourning is mostly over, he wreathes a bouquet for Hallam out of his tears:

> ...and my regret
> Becomes an April violet,
> And buds and blossoms like the rest.
>
> (Section 115, ll. 18–20)

The long history of English elegy is a pouring of fresh tears into ancient vessels. The germinative lines of 'The Passing of Arthur,' which Tennyson composed immediately on learning of Arthur Hallam's death in the autumn of 1833, echo the greatest of Anglo Saxon elegies, 'The Wanderer.' Bedivere, Arthur's last surviving knight, mourns for himself and for his dying King:

> And I, the last, go forth companionless,
> And the days darken round me, and the years,
> Among new men, strange faces, other minds.
>
> ('The Passing of Arthur,' ll. 404–6)

The lines articulate perfectly the wrenching sense of personal loss and alienation that Tennyson expresses elsewhere in letters and poems occasioned by Hallam's death, most hauntingly in the seventh section of *In Memoriam*, where he stands alone at night, 'like a guilty thing,' outside the doors of Hallam's house in a drizzling London rain. But here, in 'The Passing of Arthur,' through the words of Bedivere, Tennyson objectifies that grief in a remarkable distillation of 'The Wanderer,' in which the mourner, a lordless and homeless exile, bereft of his companions, embarks alone on seas of wintry desolation.

From its shadowy beginnings onwards, English elegy is a laying to rest of ghosts. The voice of Virginia Woolf's deceased mother sounded obsessively in her head until she wrote the last words of *To the Lighthouse* (1927),[5] an act of exorcism at whose center she placed the radiantly beautiful and compassionate Mrs. Ramsay, a remarkable likeness in body and spirit to her mother Julia Stephen. Just before setting words to paper she searched for 'a new name' for her books to supplant the word '"novel." A new _____ by Virginia Woolf. But what? Elegy?'[6] The final scene of her archetypally Modernist novel contains an unmistakable allusion to the close of Tennyson's 'Passing of Arthur.'[7] The artist Lily Briscoe, surrogate for Virginia Woolf the novelist, stands on the shore, straining to see on the vanishing horizon a little boat that carries Mr. Ramsay, his son James, and a sock that Mrs. Ramsay long ago knitted for the crippled son of the lighthouse keeper. In the final lines of 'The Passing of Arthur,' Bedivere, having consigned Excalibur to the 'Lady of the Lake,' cries out to his departing King,

> Ah! my Lord Arthur, whither shall I go?
> Where shall I hide my forehead and my eyes? (ll. 395–6)

Arthur recedes into the distance, until the boat

> Looked one black dot against the verge of dawn,
> And on the mere the wailing died away. (ll. 439–40)

Likeness emerges from unlikeness in the infinitely receding horizons at the end of both novel and idyll. Lily Briscoe cries out silently, 'Oh, Mrs. Ramsay,' to the ghost she sees sitting beside the vanishing boat. Excalibur, the potent instrument of Arthur's power to subdue the primal chaos lurking just beneath the surface of civilization, becomes in Woolf's feminized elegy a homely sock, a sword metamorphosed into a sheath. Like Arthur, Mrs. Ramsay is a keeper of the light, the sock an emblem of the fragile fabric of civilization that she knits together for her family but that was blown to pieces, along with her son Andrew, in the trenches of the First World War.

A ship itself is the subject of J.M.W. Turner's great elegy in oils, *The Fighting Temeraire*, painted in 1838, the year after Victoria ascended the throne. Turner was in his sixty-fourth year when he saw at sunset, from the shore of the Thames, the 'Temeraire' in tow of a steam-tug pulling the great hulk upriver to be broken apart for salvage. The painting is a memorial to the desecration of a national treasure, for the demolition of the 'Temeraire' struck a collective chord of outrage and grief over the passing of a great ship and of a heroic age. Thackeray likened the painting to a performance of 'a magnificent national ode.'[8] Ruskin wrote of it as a 'funeral march,' the richest in pathos of all paintings not directly depicting human pain.[9] As Ruskin suggests, Turner's *Temeraire* is a requiem with no visible mourners. Not a single human soul appears on deck or on shore. The ship is as pale and inert as a ghost, a buoyant hulk. Neither tug nor ship appears to cast a proper wake as the fire-belching tug steams like a flaming arrow toward the viewer.

Decades before the painting was first exhibited, the 'Temeraire' had fought with conspicuous bravery alongside Nelson at Trafalgar in 1805, her triple decks of massive cannon firing into the French fleet. The ship had been five years in the building; over five hundred oaks had been felled for her keel, hull, deck and masts.[10] But in the painting her cannons have already been stripped for scrap, and she seems to ride weightless and impotent in the water, bereft of guns, sails, crew and the ensign of the Royal Navy. Turner's all but audible indignation breathes through the last words of his title – The Fighting Temeraire tugged to her last berth to be broken up, 1838 – and seems to color the painting itself. The wide reaches of the Thames are dead calm; the chilling, desolate blues of the deep channel in the left foreground contrast with the preternaturally lurid sunset. The setting sun on the right horizon marks the end of an epoch, prophetic, perhaps, of the setting of the sun on the British Empire. But the startling, blood-red sunset marks more than the end of the day or of an era. It suggests an impending and unholy sacrifice, in this instance the imminent dismemberment of the great ship itself.

A sense of shattered majesty lies at the heart of elegy. It dominates every detail in Turner's painting, as it dominates the closing moments of Tennyson's *Idylls of the King*. Arthur lies mortally wounded, his head in the lap of the tallest of the Three Queens, a Tennysonian *Pietà*. A few lines later Tennyson repeats the famous choric line that frames the beginning and end of *Idylls of the King*: 'The old order changeth, yielding place to new.'[11] Turner's almost exactly contemporary elegy mourns the displacement of the age of heroism by the 'new order' of steam and coal, of iron and industry.

Figure 1: A.W. N Pugin, *Catholic Town in 1440, The Same Town in 1840.*

The Victorians felt keenly both the novelty of the age and their own sense of belatedness. Turner renders this experience in the contrast between a steam-driven tug and a towering ghost ship. A.W.N. Pugin, the great Catholic apologist and architect of the Gothic Revival, published in 1836 a work whose title itself is *Contrasts*.[12] The book contains paired, exquisitely engraved plates juxtaposing medieval buildings with their stunted, nineteenth-century counterparts. In the first – 'Catholic Town in 1440' – a broad, clear river flows through a city of delicate spires and gabled houses; behind them rises an idyllic landscape that frames an urban paradise. In 'The Same Town in 1840' Pugin's Catholic Camelot seems to have darkened into the smoke-belching Coketown of Dickens's *Hard Times* (1854). The church spires have been truncated into smokestacks, a gas-works rises over the ruins of an ancient abbey, and a huge, windowless, octagonal prison dominates the once pastoral foreground.

Carlyle structures *Past and Present* (1843) around a Pugin-like series of contrasts. An elegy to a vanished England, the book is also an angry indictment of the present. Emerson called this seminal work of social criticism an 'immortal newspaper,'[13] a fusion of the timeless and the topical, often on the same page. Two structures dominate the opening pages: the Workhouse at St. Ives, 'a Poor Law Bastille' (the inmates were incarcerated for the 'crime' of poverty and allowed fewer calories than were convicted felons), and the ruins of the once-thriving Abbey of St. Edmundsbury, a twelfth-century monastic community whose daily life Carlyle reconstructs with astonishing circumstantiality from the chronicle of one of its monks. The two walled communities are Carlyle's contrasting emblems of ancient community and modern alienation, of hope and hell.

Carlyle the social critic lies beyond the purview of this book; Carlyle the elegist is the subject of my next chapter. For Carlyle spent a lifetime writing elegies in the guise of history, which he conceived of as the struggle to behold, piously and passionately, 'the faces of our vanished Fathers.'[14] The young Carlyle had lost his Calvinist faith in God the Father but discovered in 'the Prophetic Manuscript of History' a more credible account of the past and future than in Scripture itself. He is the most articulate example of a most common Victorian phenomenon – the religious temperament severed from religious belief.[15] T.E. Hulme famously defined Romanticism as 'spilt religion'; much of early Victorian elegy is an attempt to gather up that spill. But the greatest of the late Victorian elegists, with the single exception of Hopkins, have all let go of past certainties. Pater worships beauty and welcomes the new relativism that Carlyle, Ruskin and Arnold despised. His *The Renaissance* (1873) discreetly undermines Ruskin's elegy to Gothic in *The Stones of Venice* (1851–3). To the shock of his contemporaries, Pater disavowed the old Judeo-Christian moral and sexual constraints and celebrated instead the ancient Greek worship of male beauty, in which he found a more compelling object of adoration than the Christian God of Love. Swinburne caricatures Tennyson's 'Morte d'Arthur' as the 'Morte d'Albert,' yet his 'Ave Atque Vale: In Memory of Charles Baudelaire' is one of the finest elegies of the century. And in 'The Leper' he succeeds in fashioning a moving elegy out of the lament of a necrophiliac monk over the remnants of his lady. Yet aesthetes such as Pater, Swinburne and Wilde lean heavily on their older contemporaries. Wilde would be virtually witless were it not for the earnest pieties of his predecessors.

Victorian elegy wears both a public and a private face, the one expressive of the loss of a sustaining culture, the other of personal loss. Tennyson is unique in voicing both before so wide an audience, for his performances as a public bard were at least as popular as his more personal lyrics. His laureate poems, though of less interest to us than to Victoria's contemporaries, echo well into the twentieth century. Mr. Ramsay in *To the Lighthouse* repeatedly recites a line from 'The Charge of the Light Brigade' – 'Some one had blundered' – a blunder magnified on a horrific scale in the trenches of the First World War, the true terminus of the Victorian age.

Heroism rather than a poet's grief sounds in the opening lines of Tennyson's majestic 'Ode on the Death of the Duke of Wellington':

> Bury the Great Duke
>   With an empire's lamentation,
> Let us bury the Great Duke
>   To the noise of the mourning of a mighty nation...
>
> Lead out the pageant: sad and slow,
>   As fits an universal woe... (ll. 1–4, 13–14)

More an anthem than an elegy, the Ode cries out to be set to music by a Victorian Handel. Consciously archaic, it harks back in its unabashed nationalism to James Thomson's 'Rule Britannia.' But it also celebrates a present of imperial greatness, as befits Tennyson's first publication as Victoria's Poet Laureate. The empire mourns, not the poet; the woe it commemorates is collective, not particular.

In most of the essays that follow I am drawn to elegy as an expression of personal loss. But in the most powerful Victorian elegies, the private and the public coalesce. Matthew Arnold's 'Dover Beach' (1867) is set in the intimacy of a bedroom where two lovers gaze out at the calm, moonlit waters of the Dover Straits. But the slow, tremulous tides recall

> ...the turbid ebb and flow
> Of human misery... (ll. 17–18)

and the drying up of a once full 'Sea of Faith,' whose 'melancholy, long, withdrawing roar' the poet hears echoing in the distance. Arnold here touches on a chord of feeling common to many of the Victorians, anguish over God's withdrawal, here registered with quiet Arnoldian regret, but as pure panic in *In Memoriam*, where the poet portrays himself as

> An infant crying in the night:
> An infant crying for the light:
> And with no language but a cry. (Section 54, ll. 18–20)

Arnold expresses his more controlled anxiety in perhaps the saddest (because so impersonal) plea for love in the face of uncertainty in all of English literature:

> Ah, love, let us be true
> To one another! for the world...
> Hath really neither joy, nor love, nor light,
> Nor certitude, nor peace, nor help from pain.... (ll. 30–4)

Arnold composed 'Dover Beach' in the summer of 1851, immediately after his marriage. A generation later human ties seemed even more difficult to sustain. In the 'Conclusion' to *The Renaissance* (1874) Pater wrote that all human experience 'is ringed round for each one of us by that thick wall of personality through which no real voice has ever pierced....' Our solid sense of self is an illusion, for the self is a mere 'design in a web, the actual threads of which pass out beyond it.' Pater does not mourn the passing of stability and certainty but insists on the illusoriness of the very world itself, a fiction invested with reality only by language, but in fact a mere congeries of vanishing 'impressions, unstable, flickering, inconsistent.'[16]

   This seems, and *is*, strikingly modern. But so too, I would argue, is Tennyson's *Idylls of the King*, long misread as a Victorian Gothic fairy tale but in reality one of the gloomiest elegies on the failure of idealism in our literature. The fall of Camelot is foreseen from its very founding, and Arthur's illusory 'city built to music' ('Gareth and Lynette,' ll. 272–3) collapses in the fratricidal discord of his Last Battle, a cacophony of

> Oaths, insult, filth, and monstrous blasphemies,
> Sweat, writhings, anguish, labouring of the lungs,
> In that close mist, and cryings for the light,
> Moans of the dying, and voices of the dead.
> ('The Passing of Arthur,' ll. 114–17)

This is the same Apocalyptic landscape that concludes 'Dover Beach,' a 'darkling plain'

> Swept with confused alarms of struggle and flight,
> Where ignorant armies clash by night. (ll. 36–7)

The age of elegy was also the age of anxiety.

## 3

In my final essay I turn from particular elegists to a common experience that touched the lives of them all – the displacement of the older idea of the earthly city as a New Jerusalem by the rise of a new image of the Victorian city as an industrial Inferno, a wasteland of sprawling towns and of rivers so polluted that they caught fire. Dickens is the pre-eminent explorer of this urban labyrinth. Joe, the starving crossing-sweep in *Bleak House* (1854), looks up at the cross of St. Paul's but sees only 'the crowning confusion of the great, confused city…so high up, so far out of his reach' (Chapter 19).

A century later St. Paul's was enveloped in the smoke and flames left by waves of German bombers. One of their bombs gutted the Bloomsbury home of Leonard and Virginia Woolf. At the time Woolf was struggling to complete 'A Sketch of the Past,' her intimate elegy to the passing of her parents and of the Victorian age. The ghosts of Wordsworth and Pater haunt her pages. She transfigures Wordsworth's 'spots of time' into her own 'moments of being,' Pater's 'thick wall of personality' into the 'sealed vessels' of ourselves, 'afloat upon what is convenient to call reality.'[17]

The last dated entry in 'A Sketch of the Past' is November 1940, one of the darkest moments of World War Two and in the life of Virginia Woolf. Twice in her lifetime she had seen 'a mighty wave of evil' break over Europe. But she ends with a radiant elegy to her life before the deaths of her parents, and of so many of her generation in the killing fields of the First World War. The year is 1900, the place 22 Hyde Park Gate. Nowhere else do we come so close to breathing the very air, sitting in the very rooms, of the Victorians:

> I remember…the ceremony of our visits to great men. For father and mother were equally respectful of greatness…. I remember Meredith dropping slices of lemon into his tea. I remember that [G.F.] Watts had great bowls of whipped cream; and a plate of minced meat. 'I kissed him,' said mother, 'before he dipped his moustache in the cream.' He wore ruffles at his wrists, and a long grey dressing gown. And we went to Little Holland House always on a Sunday morning. I remember that Lowell had a long knitted purse, constrained by two rings; and that a sixpence always slipped out of the slit. I remember Meredith's growl; and I remember the hesitations and adumbrations with which Henry James made the drawing room seem rich and dusky. Greatness still seems

to me a positive possession; booming; eccentric; set apart; something to which I am led up dutifully by my parents. It is a bodily presence; it has nothing to do with anything said. It exists in certain people. But it never exists now. I cannot remember ever to have felt greatness since I was a child.

Four months after writing these lines, on 28 March 1941, her pockets weighted with stone, Virginia Woolf drowned herself in the rain-swollen waters of the River Ouse. A century earlier, Tennyson desperately longed to believe that in the fullness of time he would again clasp the hand of Arthur Hallam, and Arthur the King passes in the hope of his second coming. Virginia Woolf had no faith at all in her eventual return; yet, like Tennyson, she shaped out of her desolation a consummate elegy to the end of an age.

# 2

# CARLYLE: HISTORY AND THE
# HUMAN VOICE

For Carlyle the contrary of history is not fiction but oblivion, the unraveling of the collective human memory that holds civilization together. History is not a record of civilization; it is civilization itself, the past speaking to the present and to the future through the voice of the historian. Without that animating voice, we would have neither history nor elegy – only gibberish and unmarked graves.

History and the human voice, life and speech, are virtually one in Carlyle's mind. His moving reminiscence of his stonemason father, begun while the body still lay above ground and finished just after it was laid in the grave – an elegy so spontaneous as to be the diary of the mourner as well as a portrait of the dead – is above all a tribute to James Carlyle's powers of speech. 'Never shall we again hear such speech as that was,' Carlyle writes, the purest 'of all the dialects I have ever listened to,' a 'full *white* sunlight.'[1]

James Carlyle died in 1832; three years later, on the occasion of another loss that Carlyle took at least as hard, his father returned to him in a dream. Carlyle had gone to sleep late on the night of 6 March, 1835, after John Stuart Mill, pale and shaken, had told him that the entire first volume of *The French Revolution*, which Mill had been reading in manuscript, had been inadvertently burnt. The following morning Carlyle wrote in his *Journal*:

> The night has been full of emotion; occasionally sharp pain (something cutting or hard – grasping me round the heart) occasionally with sweet consolations. I dreamed of my Father and sister Margaret alive, yet all defaced with sleepy stagnancy, swoln hebetude of the Grave, – and again dying, as in some strange rude country: a horrid dream!

Like the dream itself, in which Father and Sister die a second death in a strange country, Carlyle dies twice as he relives their deaths and, in the unvoiced language of the dream, the death of his book. Much of the horror of the dream and all of its poignancy lie in its *wordlessness*. The dead are clearly seen – their bloated features emerge all too visibly – but they cannot hear or make themselves heard: 'How I longed for some Psalm or Prayer that I could have *uttered*,' the *Journal* entry ends, 'that my loved ones would have joined me in! But there was none: Silence had to be my language.'[2]

The journey into the past is for Carlyle always a double journey, backward in time and downward into the self, a descent simultaneously to the underworld of the historical past and to his own interior life. While working on his history of Cromwell, he wrote to his friend John Sterling that he was doing 'mole's work, boring and digging blindly underground; my own inner man is sometimes very busy (too busy) but the rest is all silence.'[3] The allusion to Hamlet's excited trafficking with his father's ghost[4] captures Carlyle's sense of dread and shame at being too close to the untouchable dead, an emotion that colors his letter of the same period to Emerson: 'I have again got down into primeval Night; and live alone and mute with the *Manes*, as you say; uncertain whether I shall ever more see day. I am partly ashamed of myself: but cannot help it.'[5]

On these fertile descents into 'primeval Night' Carlyle brought along as little baggage as possible, taking only the sparsest of notes and storing his research in his prodigious memory. He composed in a strange, self-induced state of hyper-alertness and somnambulance, a kind of feverish semi-consciousness: 'Partly I was busy,' he wrote to Emerson on completing *On Heroes*; 'partly too, as my wont is, I was half-asleep.'[6]

However eccentric, Carlyle's mode of composition is as old as that of the Hebrew prophets and ancient Bards, for whom memory did its labor of sorting and synthesizing in a state of inspiration or semi-trance. Carlyle's great works of imaginative synthesis – *Sartor Resartus, The French Revolution, Past and Present* – are shaped not as reasoned arguments but like controlled dreams in which recurrent symbols do the work of discursive logic. Writing, particularly the writing of history, always necessitates for Carlyle a kind of willed fellowship with the dead. 'Dryasdust' is the desiccated archivist Carlyle fears he may become, but beyond Dryasdust – or beneath him – lies the miracle-working mole Carlyle deliberately turned himself into in order to resurrect the past. Midway through his research on *Cromwell* he complained to Emerson of having burrowed his way through mountains of dreary rubbish, but the complaint is tinged with a nervous gaiety again reminiscent of Hamlet in the company of ghosts and graves:

> I even take a gowlish kind of pleasure in raking through these old bone-houses and burial-aisles now; I have the strangest fellowship with that huge genius of DEATH...and catch sometimes, thro' some chink or other, glimpses into blessed *ulterior* regions, – blessed, but as yet altogether silent.[7]

*Silent* because the heaped mounds of unsorted archives have not yet begun to speak to Carlyle, and hence he cannot yet endow them with life. His struggle to bring his hero to life figures centrally in the prologue to *Cromwell*, in which he takes his reader on a mythic voyage to the underworld of the British Museum. Some fifty thousand pamphlets and folios lie mouldering in labyrinthine corridors, a 'shoreless chaos,' unindexed, unedited (6:2).[8] No one has more vividly evoked the stagnant backwaters of archival research, the sheer inchoateness of the unreconstructed past:

> But alas...what is it, all this...inarticulate rubbish-continent, in its ghastly dim twilight, with its haggard wrecks and pale shadows; what is it, but the common Kingdom of Death? Behold here the final evanescence of Formed human things...changing into sheer formlessness; – ancient human speech itself has sunk into unintelligible maundering. This is the collapse, – the etiolation of human features into mouldy blank; *dis*solution; progress towards utter silence and disappearance.... (6:10)

This haunting passage marks the return of Carlyle's 'horrid dream' on the night his manuscript had sunk into the wilderness of things once alive. But the dream of personal loss has widened into a collective nightmare of human oblivion, a shadowy sunken continent, 'trackless, without index, without finger-post, or mark of any human foregoer' (6:3). In this Carlylean underworld of Anti-History, presided over by the plutonic Dryasdust, the human past has been all but eradicated under mounds of successive errors and mindless commentary. The sound of the fifty thousand pamphlets 'is not a *voice*, conveying knowledge or memorial of any earthly or heavenly thing; it is a wide-spread inarticulate slumberous mumblement, issuing as if from the lake of Eternal Sleep' (6:3).[*]

Despite his own great powers of recall, Carlyle repeatedly stresses the importance of *forgetting* in the writing of history. In the prologue to *Cromwell* he contends that the historian rises above a mere Dryasdust and becomes a

---

[*] Carlyle's evocation of the voicelessness of the unreconstructed past is itself voiced by the main speaker of the prologue to *Cromwell*, more than half of which is set off in quotation marks and imagined as spoken by a character other than Carlyle. The point would not be worth making were it not that Carlyle's editors and critics, by omitting his indications of direct and indirect discourse, have in effect been misquoting him for over a century and a half. Passages often cited as 'straight' Carlyle are in fact spoken by one of his many quirky impersonations – Dryasdust, Smelfungus, Sauerteig, Teufelsdröckh, Plugson of Undershot, Sir Jabesh Windbag. To obscure the identity of the speaker is to lose half of what is said, for, in Carlyle's view, no thought exists apart from the voice that utters it, just as no historical text exists apart from the contending chorus of voices that enacted it.

sacred poet as much by virtue of 'wise oblivion' as by 'wise memory' (6:8). And in 'On History Again' (1833), he compares Memory and Oblivion to Day and Night, each essential to the other's existence (28:173). In part he is pointing to the principle of selective omission, without which history could not be written. But he is also stressing the necessity of cultivating the unconscious mind in recovering the collective past, as Wordsworth had made its cultivation essential to the recovery of the individual past. 'A like unconscious talent of remembering and of forgetting again,' Carlyle asserts, is indispensable to the writing of history and of autobiography (28:173). For Wordsworth the self preserves its continuity and sanity through a return to those early, formative experiences in nature when it first came to consciousness. The self remains open to such experiences through a 'wise-passiveness' (the equivalent of Carlyle's 'wise oblivion') that puts to momentary rest the conscious, ratiocinative mind. The epic journey inward into autobiographical time that Wordsworth began in *The Prelude* finds its analogue in the epic journey backward into historical time that Carlyle began in *The French Revolution*.

It is above all as memorialists – the one, of the continuities of the self in nature; the other, of the continuities of human society in time – that Wordsworth and Carlyle distinguish themselves in a century that was obsessed with history. Wordsworth's term for the 'binding' that holds the self together is 'natural piety';[9] for Carlyle we must invent an equivalent term such as 'historical piety.' The defining note of this piety is a piercing love of the past, a backward-glancing search by those who, in Carlyle's phrase from the *Cromwell* prologue, 'struggle piously, passionately, to behold, if but in glimpses, the faces of our vanished Fathers' (6:3). For Wordsworth, the search is for the face of his vanished self, reflected in the still waters of his past, where he can glimpse 'The Child [who] is Father of the Man.' The genius of Wordsworth and Carlyle, divergent in so many ways, coincides in the drive to escape the prison-house of time and reach those islands of consciousness in which the past coexists with the present.

Wordsworth described such privileged moments in the grainy phrase 'spots of time,' and his best poetry evokes them. Carlyle's finest passages are built upon spots of historical time, uncanny moments of temporal montage in which the remote past breaks through the grid of the present, or the once-present collapses into the past, as when in *Past and Present*, the ancient chronicle of Jocelin of Brakelond, 'suddenly shorn-through by the scissors of Destiny, *ends*' (10:125), and the reader is plunged back again into the noise of the nineteenth century. *Past and Present*, as its title suggests, is a gallery of these montages. History for Carlyle is the half-magical science of celebrating this 'wondrous...contiguity and perpetual closeness [of] the Past and Distant with the Present in time and place; all times and all places with this our actual Here and Now' (5:160–1).

Here we confront the grand peculiarity of Carlyle as a memorialist of the past: all other elegists station themselves in the foreground of the present and look back longingly at a vanished world, from the lament of the Anglo-Saxon warrior grieving for his lost lord to the mature Wordsworth in quest of his lost boyhood self near the ruins of Tintern Abbey. Carlyle obliterates all middle distance separating past from present. He steps through the temporal frame, as it were, and plunges his reader into the vanished world he depicts; he inhabits the world of the dead as if they were living, and, in one astonishing passage in *Past and Present*, through the medium of Jocelin's chronicle, *touches* the very toes of the disinterred St. Edmund. The result is a kind of estranged or inverted elegy, in which the past usurps the present, and the present appears phantasmal or unreal.

However much Carlyle feels a Tennysonian tenderness for vanished faces, he drops no idle tears over a past that he austerely refuses to romanticize. 'No age ever seemed the Age of Romance to *itself*,' he writes at the start of 'The Diamond Necklace,' his first historical work: Roland de Roncesvalles rode in bad weather and good, chewed on tough beef, 'was saddle-sick, calumniated, constipated….Romance exists…in Reality alone' (28:327, 329). Carlyle casts no soft haze over the distant past precisely because, for him, it is not distant but present and needs only our heightened consciousness to recognize its proximity. He practices a kind of hard-nosed mysticism, moving back in time in order to obliterate time. In Carlyle's eyes the past does not 'progress' in measured steps towards the present but is eerily contiguous with it, like the drowned man of Wordsworth's childhood, recalled years later, who bobs up 'bolt upright' in the heightened present of his mature recollection.

Carlyle's insistence on the matter-of-factness of the past has the paradoxical effect of investing it with extraordinary mystery and vitality. His description of twelfth-century England in *Past and Present* begins in an almost palpable prosiness of ditches and cattle, but Carlyle's pictorial realism proves to be the thinnest of illusions; within a few lines we look not at but *through* the picture to the timeless world that lies behind it:

Behold therefore, this England of the year 1200 was no chimerical vacuity or dreamland, peopled with mere vaporous Fantasms…but a green solid place, that grew corn and several other things. The Sun shone on it; the vicissitude of seasons and human fortunes. Cloth was woven and worn; ditches were dug, furrow-fields ploughed, and houses built. Day by day all men and cattle rose to labour, and night by night returned home weary to their several lairs. In wondrous Dualism, then as now, lived nations of breathing men; alternating, in all ways, between Light and Dark; between…hope reaching high as Heaven, and fear deep as very Hell. (10:44)

The passage spans in miniature the great Carlylean circuit linking the mundane to the cosmic. The brief, repetitive cadences echo the lesser rhythms of daily life – ditches dug, fields plowed, cloth woven – until the lesser cycles compose one macrocosmic cycle, cattle linked to men in their rising at dawn and in their return at night to their 'lairs,' day joined to night, season joined to season, all pivoting on the great axis that joins the habitations of men to the Heavens above and the Hell below. Carlyle's insistence on the prosaic reality of the twelfth century produces some of the finest poetry of the nineteenth, a poetry of visionary realism whose proper medium is prose.

Into this charged ambience of ditches and stars rides Richard Cœur-de-Lion, 'not a theatrical popinjay with greaves and steel-cap on it, but a man living upon victuals' (10:44). The jolting awkwardness of the writing and the plebeian 'victuals,' like Roland's tough beef and constipation (a problem that also plagued the porridge-eating Carlyle), are meant to shock the reader out of the dreamy world of historical fiction and into the world of historical fact. A few lines later Carlyle wonders what sort of 'breeches' King John wore on the occasion of his visit to the Abbey of St. Edmund. Carlyle's source is Jocelin of Brakelond, a monk whose *Chronicle* of daily life under the rule of Abbot Samson was published by the Camden Society in 1840. 'These clear eyes of neighbour Jocelin,' Carlyle writes,

> looked on the bodily presence of King John; the very John *Sansterre*, or Lackland, who signed *Magna Charta* afterwards in Runnymead. Lackland, with a great retinue, boarded once, for the matter of a fortnight, in St. Edmundsbury Convent; daily in the very eyesight, palpable to the very fingers of our Jocelin: O Jocelin, what did he say, what did he do; how looked he, lived he; – at the very lowest, what coat or breeches had he on? Jocelin is obstinately silent. Jocelin marks down what interests *him*; entirely deaf to *us*. With Jocelin's eyes we discern almost nothing of John Lackland. As through a glass darkly, we with our own eyes and appliances, intensely looking, discern at most: A blustering, dissipated human figure, with a kind of blackguard quality air, in cramoisy velvet, or other uncertain texture, uncertain cut, with much plumage and fringing; amid numerous other human figures of the like; riding abroad with hawks; talking noisy nonsense; – tearing out the bowels of St. Edmundsbury Convent (its larders namely and cellars) in the most ruinous way, by living at rack and manger there. Jocelin notes only, with a slight subacidity of manner, that the King's Majesty, *Dominus Rex*, did leave, as gift for our St. Edmund Shrine, a handsome enough silk cloak, – or rather pretended to leave, for one of his retinue borrowed it of us, and *we* never got sight of it again; and, on the whole, that the *Dominus Rex*, at departing, gave us 'thirteen *sterlingii*,'

one shilling and one penny, to say a mass for him; and so departed, –
like a shabby Lackland as he was! 'Thirteen pence sterling,' this was
what the Convent got from Lackland, for all the victuals he and his
had made away with. We of course said our mass for him, having
covenanted to do it, – but let impartial posterity judge with what degree
of fervour! (10:45)

The paragraph opens with the double frame of Carlyle's observing the clear-
eyed Jocelin as Jocelin observes King John. It ends with the reader drawn
through the frame and into the picture. Like Carlyle, the reader ceases to
observe Jocelin and begins to think Jocelin's bitter thoughts, to watch shabby
Lackland through Jocelin's eyes. The transition occurs about two-thirds through
the paragraph, within the sentence that starts, 'Jocelin notes only....' By the
time the reader reaches the italicized 'we' a few lines later, he must cast himself
in the role of the resentful Jocelin if the passage is to make any grammatical
sense. Carlyle has moved, imperceptibly but decisively, from medieval Latin
chronicle to a kind of dramatic monologue in prose. Throughout the paragraph
Jocelin functions not as an inert 'source,' but as a vocal presence within the
events he narrates. Although long dead, he is still 'our neighbour' [neahgebur,
nigh-dweller], for even though he lived next door in time and place to King
John, he is also, because of the 'wondrous contiguity' of past and present,
neighbor to the whole company of Carlyle's readers, living and dead. He is
near to us but deaf to our entreaties; the power of the passage depends upon
Jocelin's ghostly proximity. However passionately the historian implores his
monkish source – what did Lackland look like? how did he live? – Jocelin of
course cannot utter an iota of fact beyond what he has already recorded. Time
may be an illusion for Carlyle but mortality is not; Jocelin rejoins the long-
dead in the pause between Carlyle's insistent questioning and his own firm
answer: 'Jocelin is obstinately silent.' The obstinacy, of course, is not Jocelin's
but Carlyle's. In repeatedly interrogating the dead monk, Carlyle seems to
awaken Jocelin's stubborn resistance, like a sleeper tossing and struggling to
hold onto his dream. All verbs up to this point have been in the simple past.
The disruptive shift from past to present – 'Jocelin marks down what interests
*him*; entirely deaf to *us*' – is doubly disorienting. It piles the weight of seven
centuries on Jocelin's grave and at the same time brings him and shabby Lackland
back to disconcerting life. Past and present reverse themselves along with voice
and point of view, as Carlyle enacts, in virtual dumb-show, Jocelin pointing to
what interests him, Carlyle beckoning in the other direction, twelfth-century
chronicler and nineteenth-century editor gesturing across the ages.

The King John who rides like an incarnate apparition through Carlyle's
paragraph is not of course the King of Jocelin's *Chronicle*. For in Jocelin's clear
but unreflective eyes, the King is as yet untinged by the medium of time. Carlyle

knows he cannot portray in the nineteenth century the King John who
appeared in the twelfth century; yet in forcing us to confront the great gap in
time, he seems almost to obliterate it. He portrays with absolute fidelity not
King John Lackland but his own painterly efforts to visualize the King through
the flickering medium of time and of Jocelin's words. The resulting picture is a
piece of pure impressionism, precise yet triumphantly amorphous, as if Turner
had painted King John by torchlight. We see a rough confusion of colors and
textures, fringes and plumes, with an equestrian figure in red velvet, clusters
of men in noisy motion, and only one hard detail, more heard than seen, the
'thirteen *sterlingii*' whose hollow jingle signals the departure of King Lackland:

> And in this manner vanishes King Lackland; traverses swiftly our strange
> intermittent magic-mirror, jingling the shabby thirteen pence merely;
> and rides with his hawks into Egyptian night again.... How much in
> Jocelin, as in all History, and indeed in all Nature, is at once inscrutable
> and certain; so dim, yet so indubitable; exciting us to endless
> considerations. For King Lackland *was* there, verily he; and did leave
> these *tredecim sterlingii* if nothing more, and did live and look in one
> way or the other, and a whole world was living and looking along with
> him! There, we say, is the grand peculiarity; the immeasurable one;
> distinguishing, to a really infinite degree, the poorest historical Fact
> from all Fiction whatsoever. (10:45–6)

Here we strike the bedrock of sheer wonder that underlies Carlyle's historical
writing. It is a strange emotion, this seemingly redundant astonishment that
whatever happened did indeed happen. Yet in Carlyle's 'vague shoreless
Universe,' in which we are buffeted by the 'ever-fluctuating chaos of the Actual'
(2:9, 10), it *is* astonishing that anything ever condenses out of the aboriginal
flux long enough to fix itself in time, space, or human consciousness. In this
shifting, illusory world, Carlyle clings to the elusive solidity of fact as if it were
the last credible miracle. Hence his amazement that 'King Lackland *was* there,
verily he.' The other side of Carlyle's 'green solid' England of the year 1200 is
that perhaps it exists only as a picture in the historian's mind. So, too, although
King John is 'palpable to the very fingers of our Jocelin,' the shadow he casts –
like the shadow of Tennyson's King Arthur – is more real than his substance,
just as Jocelin's obstinate silence is more expressive than his words.

Carlyle's power of endowing the past with extraordinary 'presence' is
enhanced by his complementary genius for undermining the actuality of the
here and now. He is the poet of the insubstantiality of the 'real' and the reality
of the phantasmagoric, the one always heightened by the other. The two are
deftly juxtaposed in Carlyle's portrait of the dying Louis XV at the start of *The
French Revolution*. The death-scene opens in a miasma of putrid odours,

whispered intrigues, thick tapestries. But the heavy-textured realism dissolves into the starkness of a medieval morality drama as Carlyle turns to the Do-Nothing King and ushers him out of life with an elegy to a cipher.

> Yes, poor Louis, Death has found thee. No palace walls or life-guards, gorgeous tapestries or gilt buckram of stiffest ceremonial could keep him out.... Thou, whose whole existence hitherto was a chimera and scenic show, at length becomest a reality: sumptuous Versailles bursts asunder, like a dream, into void Immensity; Time is done, and all the scaffolding of Time falls wrecked with hideous clangour round thy soul: the pale Kingdoms yawn open; there must thou enter, naked, all unking'd.... (2:20)

As always in Carlyle's most charged moments, the actual and the spectral change places. Foreground fades into background, 'reality' dissolves into the dream it mirrors, and the chimerical King, more substantial in death than in life, slips out of time into eternity. Much of Carlyle's poetry is in the phrase 'scaffolding of Time,' with its image of Time as the flimsy prop of actuality, the skeletal lattice of illusion around which we structure our fleeting lives. But the prop is weighty and crashes to earth with the clang of armor; it falls with the ring of allusion, too, for this least heroic of modern kings, a mere 'Solecism Incarnate' (2:21), dies to an ancient Homeric formula – 'He dropped forward on his face and his armor clattered upon him.'[10] Carlyle's irony is too austere to be mistaken for the mock-heroic, his compassion too controlled for sentimentality. The perspective is at once close-up ('poor Louis') and distant – a eulogy spoken from Olympus – as it ranges across the narrow circuit of Louis's chamber to a whole spectrum of times and conditions, naked and exalted, ancient, medieval and modern.

Carlyle's sense of the illusoriness of reality goes back to his earliest childhood and gives a haunting quality of doubleness to the world he grasped through his senses and reflected in his books. The feeling is epitomized in lines from *The Tempest* to which Carlyle attached special importance and which he first saw, as a young boy, on a bust of Shakespeare hawked in the streets of Ecclefechan by a vendor of images:

> We are such stuff
> As dreams are made on, and our little life
> Is rounded with a sleep. (IV. i. 156–8)

The thirty volumes of the works of Carlyle are an extended gloss on these lines. His sense of the insubstantiality of matter was always most keen when he was absorbed in the anxious labors of composition. Soon after beginning research on *Cromwell* he recorded in his *Journal*:

> As I live, and have long lived, death and Hades differ little to me from the earth and life. The human figure I meet is wild, wondrous, ghastly to me, almost as if it were a spectre and I a spectre.[11]

In the same spectral temper Carlyle wrote *The French Revolution*, especially those early chapters which he forced himself to rewrite with the double anxiety of having to begin again what had gone up in flames. The sense of unreality that haunts the great death-scene of Louis XV at Versailles haunted Carlyle himself no less keenly in London as he wrote by day and, like Dickens, walked the streets at night:

> The world looks often quite spectral to me; sometimes...quite hideous, discordant, almost infernal. I had been at Mrs. Austin's, heard Sydney Smith for the first time guffawing, other persons prating, jargoning. To me through these thin cobwebs Death and Eternity sate glaring. Coming homewards along Regent Street, through street-walkers, through – *Ach Gott*! Unspeakable pity swallowed up unspeakable abhorrence of it and of myself. The moon and the serene nightly sky in Sloane Street consoled me a little.... Woe's me that I in Meshech am! To work.[12]

The alienated Scotsman in London easily slips into the idiom of the Hebrew Psalmist lamenting his sojourn amid alien people. Louis XV dying at Versailles, Paris during the Revolution, early Victorian London – Carlyle bathes them all in the same phantasmal glow, sees them all through the same visionary eyes. The night-walk through London combines the circumstantial and the spectral in a way that recalls the *Inferno*, which Carlyle had begun to study only a few days before describing his 'almost infernal' walk. The force of Dante's vision makes itself felt as strongly in *The French Revolution* as in the 'Unreal City' of *The Waste Land*, where 'death had undone so many.'

All through the summer of 1835 Carlyle was in a 'detestable state of enchantment' as he rewrote the first volume of *The French Revolution*.[13] The agony of composition was 'like a Nessus's shirt' and threatened to burn him 'into madness.' He rewarded himself on completing the volume with a visit to Scotland, but the return to the site of his earliest associations only heightened his sense of estrangement. 'I flew to Scotland and my Mother for a month of rest,' he wrote to Emerson, but rest 'is nowhere for the son of Adam. All looked so "spectral" to me in my old-familiar Birthland; Hades itself could not have seemed stranger; Annandale also was part of the Kingdom of TIME.'[14]

In a letter to his wife Jane occasioned by the same visit, the Scottish countryside at first glance seems solid enough, but Carlyle's perspective elongates as his sentence lengthens, until the rolling hillside in the foreground all but vanishes into the cosmic distance:

> ...I saw the 'Sweet Milk Well' yesterday; flowing (for the last four thousand years) from its three sources on the hillside; the origin of Middlebie Burn; and noted the little dell it had hollowed out all the way, and the huts of Adam's Posterity built sluttishly on its course; and a Sun shining overhead, ninety millions of miles off; and Eternity all round; and Life a vision, dream and yet fact, – woven, with uproar, on the Loom of Time![15]

Nothing is more characteristic of these cosmic pastorals of Carlyle than their lack of any middle-distance, any fixed anchoring in time and place. Although he is on the actual spot and sees the brook with his own eyes, he beholds it not in his own time but in the inhumanly elongated perspective of four thousand years. And he observes on its banks not the farmers of Annandale but 'Adam's posterity', as if huddled there under a distant sun since the Creation. In the course of a single sentence, the 'I' of Thomas Carlyle has become the Eye of Eternity surveying the 'dream and yet fact' of man's life in time.

Two years later, in the exhausted pause after completing *The French Revolution* in 1837, Carlyle again returned to Scotland and his mother. 'There is no idler, sadder, quieter, more *ghost*like man in the world even now than I,' he wrote from his parents' farm at Scotsbrig to John Sterling. There follows one of the most beautiful passages in all of Carlyle's letters. The ghosts of his father and sister, who had risen to haunt his dreams on the night he learned of the destruction of his manuscript, are here at last laid to rest. In place of the menace of his night-walks in London he conveys an unearthly serenity like that of Wordsworth's 'A Slumber Did My Spirit Seal':

> Scotsbrig, Ecclefechan,
> 28th July, 1837—
>
> ...[T]he old Brook, Middlebie Burn we call it, still leaps into its '*Caudron*' here, gushes clear as crystal thro' the chasms and dingles of its '*Linn*'; singing me a song, with slight variations of score these several thousand years...I look on the sapphire of St. Bees Head and the Solway mirror from the gable-window; I ride to the top of *Blaweary* and see all round from Ettrick Pen to Helvellyn, from Tyndale and Northumberland to Cairnsmuir and Ayrshire.... One night, late, I rode thro' the village where I was born. The old 'Kirkyard Tree,' a huge old gnarled ash, was rustling itself softly against the great Twilight in the north; a star or two looked out; and the old graves were all there, and my Father's and my Sister's: and God was above us all.[16]

The passage haunts us by its very silence. The only sound is the speechless song of the immemorial brook and the soft rustle of the churchyard ash. The union of living and dead, of earthly and eternal, is perfectly caught in the elegiac close: the stars 'looked out,' the old graves 'were all there,' like half-animate presences gathered into a company. Carlyle's father and sister are in some strangely indeterminate state, syntactically suspended in the final phrase following 'all there.' Carlyle sees their graves, but the haunting capitals carry the suggestion that he also sees them. In the world of time, father and sister are beneath the ground and Carlyle above it. But in the last clause – and God was above us all – the perspective shifts, in a twinkling the distinction is obliterated, and James, M0argaret, and Thomas are all seen, side-by-side, under the eye of God.

In December 1853 Carlyle returned to the farmhouse at Scotsbrig and kept vigil by his aged mother's bedside. On Christmas Day she died. That night he slept in the room next to hers, 'her Corpse and I the only tenants upstairs.'[17] The following day he buried her beside his father and sister, in the ancient Ecclefechan churchyard, in the same grave in which he now lies.

2

I have dwelt on Carlyle's expressive silences, but he is in fact the most insistently *vocal* of writers, scarcely capable of composing a page without impersonating the voice of one or another of his characters, invented or historical. History, for Carlyle, is virtually synonymous with the spoken word. *The French Revolution* is a veritable 'Whirlpool of Words' (2:101) – speeches, eulogies, decrees, long-lost love-letters, shouts of execration, epigrams voiced at the foot of the guillotine. The most sustained of Carlyle's many vocalizations is the 'Voice of France,' first heard as an incessant buzzing of the people in the streets of Paris and in the countryside night and day, gathering in chorus to protest the abuses of the *ancien régime*, rising into the roar that fractures the stones of the Bastille, and culminating in the shriek of Robespierre at the moment of his beheading.* Overriding these multiple voices is the narrator himself, who functions as a kind of chorus within *The French Revolution*, the eulogist of the deaths he witnesses. 'Pity them all; for it went hard with them all' (4:120), he exclaims in requiem for all the unnamed dead.

If we recall our embarrassment over similar passages of authorial intrusion in Victorian fiction, we can appreciate the remarkable freedom Carlyle has

---

* A.J.P. Taylor comments memorably on the dramatic quality of *The French Revolution*: 'You do not read his books; you *experience* them, and what you experience in them is the storm of the world…. *The French Revolution* is the only work in which the past is not merely narrated, but recreated.' 'Macaulay and Carlyle,' in *Essays in English History* (Harmondsworth, Middlesex: Penguin, 1976), pp. 60–1.

won for the narrator in *The French Revolution*. Unconstrained by the need to create a verisimilar world (he begins with the 'real' world of history), he can impersonate Louis XVI or eulogize a lone hand sticking up from a tumbril above the heaped embrace of its brother corpses, 'as if in dumb prayer, in expostulation *de Profundis*, Take pity on the Sons of Men!' (4:42). The ghostly hand is an emblem of the hopes of mankind awakened by the Revolution and smashed by the Reign of Terror.

The disembodied hand points mutely to a passage some hundred pages later, where the most eloquent of the Voices of France, the Girondists, stand at the foot of the scaffold on the morning of 31 October 1793. On the previous night, after hearing the verdict of the Tribunal, the lawyer Valazé stabbed himself in the court-room, but his suicide fails to thwart the guillotine:

> On the morrow morning all Paris is out; such a crowd as no man had seen. The Death-carts, Valazé's cold corpse stretched among the yet living Twenty-one, roll along. Bare-headed, hands bound; in their shirt-sleeves, coat flung loosely round the neck: so fare the eloquent of France; bemurmured, beshouted. To the shouts of *Vive la République*, some of them keep answering with counter-shouts of *Vive la République*. Others, as Brissot, sit sunk in silence. At the foot of the scaffold they again strike up, with appropriate variations, the Hymn of the Marseillaise. Such an act of music; conceive it well! The yet living chant there; the chorus so rapidly wearing weak! Samson's axe is rapid; one head per minute, or little less. The chorus is wearing weak; the chorus is worn *out*; – farewell for evermore, ye Girondins. Te-Deum Fauchet has become silent; Valazé's dead head is lopped: the sickle of the Guillotine has reaped the Girondins all away. 'The eloquent, the young, the beautiful and brave!' exclaims Riouffe. O death, what feast is toward in thy ghastly Halls! (4:199)

This remarkable *diminuendo* is itself 'an act of music,' Carlyle's requiem for the silencing of the eloquent voices of France. The rapid run of clauses – 'Samson's axe is rapid.... The chorus is wearing weak; the chorus is worn *out*' – mimics the tempo of Samson's axe. Into this final silence obtrudes the final horror: the beheading of the already-dead Valazé. The redundance of the act is mimed in the internal rhyme of the subject ('*dead head*') and the apt passivity of the predicate ('*is lopped*'). In its intransitive sense *lop* means *to hang limply, to droop*, and Valazé's lifeless head offers no resistance to the blade. One lops dead limbs from a tree, a sickle lops tall grass; all flesh is as grass, Carlyle reminds us, for the blade of the guillotine makes a grim '*sickle*' that '*reaps away*' the Girondists in a harvest of Terror.

A small band of Girondists survives in hiding in the south of France, but the last two are found in a wheat field, their bodies half-eaten by dogs. The narrator's eulogy, borrowed whole from the opening lines of the *Iliad*, gives a new twist to the old Greek horror of posthumous mutilation: 'So many excellent souls of heroes sent down to Hades; they themselves given as a prey of dogs and all manner of birds!' (4:201). We are now late in the calendar of the Revolution and at the end of the book entitled 'Terror,' the mythic Underworld of *The French Revolution*. As befits such a world, the epigram that closes the book is spoken posthumously by the just-beheaded Vergniaud. The epigram now does double duty as epitaph: 'As Vergniaud said: the Revolution, like Saturn, is devouring its own children.' (4:201).

The force of Vergniaud's epigram lies not in its literary grace but its literal and monstrous truth. Throughout the narrative, metaphors become literalized as stark realities, and stark realities, like the uprisen Hand, are transformed into symbols. The placards paraded by an angry Paris mob pursuing the brutal Bertier de Sauvigny – 'He devoured the substance of the People – He drank the blood of the widow and orphan' – read like pure political hyperbole. But the rhetoric quickly turns into grim retributive reality when the mob tears out Sauvigny's heart and parades his head on a pike (2:207–8).

It is a cliche of writers sympathetic to the Revolution that the *ancien regime* 'lived off the sweat' of the people; for Carlyle the cliche conceals a more pertinent and primitive reality: the *ancien regime* devoured the flesh of the people,[*] the Revolution then devoured the *ancien regime*, and finally in Vergniaud's words, the Revolution devoured itself.[18]

The final cannibalizing act of the Revolution is the beheading of its head, Robespierre. But the association of the Revolution with cannibalism has been implicit from the beginning, where Carlyle describes a forty-foot gallows that towers like a 'grim Patibulary Fork' over the starving peasantry (2:34, 58). The gallows of the old order is replaced by the insatiable guillotine of the new, its huge axe rising and falling 'in horrid systole-diastole' (4:193). Imagery of gorging and disgorging, of eating and being eaten, is so prevalent as to suggest that, for Carlyle, revolution is the politics of aggression by ingestion: the 'least blessed' fact on which society rests, he contends, appears to be the 'Primitive Fact' of 'Cannibalism: That *I* can devour *Thee*' (2:55). This is Carlyle's version of aboriginal social sin, his 'anti-social contract'; fittingly, it appears in a chapter that satirizes the naïve optimism of Rousseau ('Contrat Social').

Fraternity may be the most desirable of social goals, but Carlyle insists that it is scarcely 'natural' and never lasting. The louder the nation 'swears Brotherhood,' the sooner it will revert to Cannibalism, he says ominously of

---

[*] Early in *The French Revolution* Carlyle cites an ancient law, fallen into desuetude but remaining on the books, that allowed a lord returning from the hunt 'to kill not more than two Serfs and refresh his feet in their warm blood and bowels' (2:12).

the Festival of Federation (3:70). All the great *fêtes* of the Revolution – the Festival of National Federation, of Reason, of the Supreme Being – Carlyle calls '*feasts*,' not '*festivals*,' as if to underscore by his very literalism the primitive and ritual origins of Jacques Louis David's elaborately staged pageants of popular enlightenment.

That revolution involves a 'reversion' to 'Primitive Fact,' an overthrow that is both renewal and regression, lies at the heart of Carlyle's understanding of the upheaval of 1789. Revolution is cyclic, thus in large measure inevitable; and it is inherently generational and familial, like the archetypal revolt of the sons of Uranus against their father. 'That *I* can devour *Thee*' is Carlyle's aggressively ingestive metaphor for class warfare. It is also his Malthusian update of an old story: Cronus castrates his father Uranus and, with the aid of his brother Titans, seizes the throne of the world. Fearing usurpation by his own children, Cronus devours them all except Zeus, by whom he is in turn overthrown.

At the end of *The French Revolution* Carlyle reminds us of the Human Tannery at Meudon, where breeches were made from the skin of the freshly guillotined, and he prays that 'there be no second Sansculottism in our Earth for a thousand years' (4:313). In this context *Sansculottes* – literally, *without knee-breeches* – suddenly stares at us as *without skin*; the term, all along a synecdoche for the revolutionary underclass, now suggests the perennial and frightening vulnerability of the human condition. Is civilization only a 'wrappage,' Carlyle had asked in the chapter on Meudon, a cover only skin-deep through which our savage nature 'can still burst, infernal as ever?' (4:247).

How could the children of the Enlightenment have fathered such a state? *Because* they were children of the Enlightenment, Carlyle grimly replies. True to its Enlightenment origins, the Revolution enthroned Reason, but it also unleashed the Furies; it worshipped Liberty but institutionalized Terror; it proclaimed universal brotherhood yet devoured its own children. In so doing, the Revolution, as Carlyle understood it, was neither inconsistent nor hypocritical. He found much irony but no contradiction in celebrating the Festival of Reason – the Goddess was enthroned with great fanfare at the high-altar of the Cathedral of Notre-Dame, renamed the Temple of Reason – on the eve of the worst atrocities of the Revolution, the fusillades at Lyons and the mass drownings at Nantes.

## 3

I close with the most dramatic scene in *The French Revolution*, the beheading of the incessantly verbal Robespierre. In the finest irony of the book, Robespierre becomes most human when rendered speechless, first by his own suicidal hand, then by Samson the Executioner.* In the weeks before his execution, Robespierre appears rarely in public. Carlyle describes this period of withdrawal as Robespierre's 'forty-days' during which he 'sits apart' and meditates in solitary places (4:274). These glancing allusions to Jesus's forty days in the wilderness and to the agony in Gethsemane[19] mark a new dimension in Carlyle's portrait of Robespierre and prepare us for the extraordinary scene to come, which he aptly calls 'our fifth-act of this natural Greek Drama' (4:283). The stress falls on *natural*, for Carlyle wants to contrast the genuine pity and terror of Robespierre's death with the contrived theatricality that preceeds it, including the 'Seagreen Pontiff's' performance at the Feast of the Supreme Being.

The scene opens in a tumult of shouting from the Convention floor that drowns out Saint-Just and Robespierre and ends in their arrest. Besieged within the Hôtel de Ville, Robespierre's brother Augustin and the Jacobin commander Henriot leap from a window, only to land alive in a mess of masonry and sewage. This Dantesque 'fall' is prelude to the discovery of Robespierre, who for the first time in one thousand pages is depicted as utterly speechless:

> Robespierre was sitting on a chair, with pistol-shot blown through not his head but his under-jaw; the suicidal hand had failed. With prompt zeal, not without trouble, we gather these wrecked Conspirators; fish up even Henriot and Augustin, bleeding and foul, pack them all, rudely enough, into carts; and shall, before sunrise, have them safe under lock and key. Amid shoutings and embracings.
>
> Robespierre lay in an anteroom of the Convention Hall, while his Prison-escort was getting ready; the mangled jaw bound up rudely with bloody linen: a spectacle to men. He lies stretched on a table, a deal-box his pillow; the sheath of the pistol is still clenched convulsively in his hand. Men bully him, insult him: his eyes still indicate intelligence; he speaks no word. 'He had on the sky-blue coat he had got made for the Feast of the *Être Suprême*' – O Reader, can thy hard heart hold out against that? His trousers were nankeen; the stockings had fallen down over the ankles. He spake no word more in this world. (4:284–5)

That the eloquent Robespierre should have shattered his own jaw is a bit of natural symbolism Carlyle neither overlooks nor needs to underscore.[20] Given the hostility of his earlier portrait of Robespierre, it is remarkable that he can now portray Robespierre's execution as a moving sacrifice; it is virtually

---

* Samson appears only rarely in *The French Revolution* but always to dramatic effect. A figure of towering strength, he is a sinister version of his biblical namesake, who is also a kind of executioner. Charles Henri Sanson (Carlyle's misspelling of the name is surely significant) was the public executioner of Paris from 1788 to 1795. He inherited the family business from his father and in turn bequeathed it to his son.

miraculous that, without an iota of comedy or blasphemy, he can persuade us that Robespierre's death, like that of Louis XVI, partakes of elements of the sacrifice of Christ. Only Carlyle could create a death-scene of high tragedy out of a self-mutilated pedant in silk trousers and a sky-blue coat. Just when the reader might be moved to mockery, he is asked, instead, if his 'hard heart' can keep back its tears. Carlyle focuses on the blood-stained linen, the keen intelligence still animating the eyes that look out from the shattered head and register every instant of the protracted agony. But most of all we are moved because we are made to witness two martyrdoms enacted simultaneously, the one before our eyes, in 'an anteroom of the Convention Hall,' the other, in the wings of our recollection, where 'the soldiers led him away into the hall, called Praetorium.... And they clothed him with purple.... And they smote him on the head.... And when they had mocked him, they...led him out to crucify him.'[21] Robespierre's silence before his accusers – a reiterated silence, for Carlyle twice says that Robespierre spoke 'no word more' in this world – echoes Jesus's refusal to answer the chief priests and Pilate – 'he answered to him never a word.'[22] The emphasis on Robespierre's silence is especially significant because so gratuitous: he could scarcely be expected to speak. The silence heightens the horror to come, when, instead of 'My God, my God, why has thou forsaken me?' we hear a shriek of pain.

After a night and day of public display and humiliation, Robespierre, along with some twenty others, is led to the Place de la Revolution. It is late in the afternoon of 28 July, 1794. This is the last of the great processions of *The French Revolution*, 'the very roofs and ridge-tiles budding forth human Curiosity,' and it evokes all previous processions – Louis XVI to the same spot only eighteen months earlier, the grand convocation of the Estates-General on 4 May, 1789, and a millennium before that, the ghostly procession of the long-haired Merovingian Kings, 'slowly wending on their bullock-carts through the streets of Paris' (2:7). Along the route an unidentified woman leaps onto Robespierre's tumbrel to curse him, a real-life, latter-day Fury[23] who serves to remind us that this is the last act of Carlyle's 'natural Greek Drama':

> All eyes are on Robespierre's Tumbril, where he, his jaw bound in dirty linen, with his half-dead Brother and half-dead Henriot, lie shattered; their 'seventeen hours' of agony about to end. The Gendarmes point their swords at him, to show the people which is he. A woman springs on the Tumbril; clutching the side of it with one hand, waving the other Sibyl-like; and exclaims: 'The death of thee gladdens my very heart, *m'envire de joie*'; Robespierre opened his eyes; '*Scelerat*, go down to Hell, with the curses of all wives and mothers!' – At the foot of the scaffold, they stretched him on the ground till his turn came. Lifted aloft, his eyes once again opened: caught the bloody axe. Samson wrenched the

coat off him; wrenched the dirty linen from his jaw: the jaw fell powerless, there burst from him a cry; – hideous to hear and see. Samson, thou canst not be too quick! (4:285)

The whole gathered power of *The French Revolution* compresses to a single point in that shriek of Robespierre. The Revolution had begun in words: first the words of the *philosophes*, then a rising tide in the streets of Paris and the halls of the National Assembly. Robespierre had mastered those words and for a time became the articulate intelligence of the Voice of France, 'the Chief Priest and Speaker' of the Revolution, as Carlyle calls him (3:246). Speech had been fine-tuned into slogan and decree and epigram; even the phlegmatic Louis XVI arrived at the scaffold prepared to speak his final piece, until the drummers and Samson cut him short. But in this last act of Carlyle's drama, death lapses into pure savagery, the Revolution cannibalizes itself, and, fittingly, speech degenerates into an aboriginal scream. The cries of the self-blinded Oedipus, the howls of Lear, are not more chilling than the shriek of Robespierre.

One wants to put this painful scene aside, but meanings unfold within meanings, like wounds hidden within wounds. Samson's wrenching off the sky-blue coat and the bandage is an act of pure malice: neither coat nor bandage could resist the axe, which Robespierre's still-sentient eyes see poised above him. In Matthew, when Jesus is mocked, the soldiers bedeck him in a scarlet cloak; in Luke, with a robe of royal purple, which is taken from Him before the Crucifixion.[23] We now see why Carlyle pauses over the nankeen trousers, the sky-blue coat, the brutal stripping on the scaffold, just as he had earlier paused over the dividing of the beheaded King's puce coat and the dipping of handkerchiefs in blood. The very unlikeness of Robespierre to Louis and of both to Christ enables Carlyle to pile resemblance upon resemblance without the parallel rising to consciousness or collapsing into parody. The gruesomeness of the narrative further impedes such recognition, but on the deeper level where dream meets reality and symbols take on flesh, the full power of the scene discloses itself. Robespierre's execution-crucifixion is a narrative enactment of the question posed at the Human Tannery: is civilization 'only a wrappage,' a clothing that conceals our savage nature? The central symbol of *Sartor Resartus* – clothing – and the central question of *The French Revolution* return in the guise of a soiled coat and a bloody bandage, 'wrappages' both, emblems of desecrated humanity. At the end of *The French Revolution*, in the farewell to the reader, Carlyle speaks of man as 'an incarnated Word' and of human speech as a living, sacred fountain. He was perhaps recalling his first letter to Emerson, in which he announced his intention to write a book on the French Revolution and remarked that at bottom 'there is *nothing sacred*, then, but the *Speech of Man* to believing Men!'[24] Seen in this light, Samson's act is the ultimate blasphemy, a mutilation of the 'incarnated Word' within man.

Robespierre's scream of animal terror is also the cry of the stricken god: 'Jesus, when he had cried again with a loud voice, yielded up the ghost.'[25]

Until his humiliation and death, Robespierre had figured as a 'Seagreen Formula' for whom words had usurped realities. But now Carlyle's compassion for the mute, mutilated human being overcomes his contempt for the ideologue. His eulogy for Robespierre begins in grudging admiration and then rises to something much greater:

> O unhappiest Advocate of Arras, wert thou worse than other Advocates? Stricter man, according to his Formula, to his Credo and his Cant, of probities, benevolences, pleasures-of-virtue, and suchlike, lived not in that age. A man fitted, in some luckier settled age, to have become one of those incorruptible barren Pattern-figures and have had marble-tablets and funeral sermons. His poor landlord, the Cabinet-maker in the Rue Saint-Honore, loved him; his Brother died for him. May God be merciful to him and to us! (4:285–6)

The cadences of the liturgy for the dead – 'Lord, have mercy upon us; Christ, have mercy upon us' – first heard faintly at the King's execution, now ring clearly through the final sentence, as if Carlyle were conducting a burial service in the presence of the insulted body. That *we* are present among the mourners and beside Carlyle follows from the wording of the closing prayer: 'May God be merciful to him and to *us*!' In our long journey through *The French Revolution* ('O Reader!—Courage, I see land!') [4:288], we are close to that final moment when Carlyle will move still closer and call us Brother.

The simplicity, clarity and beauty of Carlyle's farewell to the reader has the ring of the spoken word, as befits an utterance about the sacredness of human speech:

> And so here, O Reader, has the time come for us two to part. Toilsome was our journeying together; not without offence; but it is done. To me thou wert as a beloved shade, the disembodied or not yet embodied spirit of a Brother. To thee I was but as a Voice. Yet was our relation a kind of sacred one; doubt not that! For whatsoever once sacred things become hollow jargons, yet while the Voice of Man speaks with Man, hast thou not there the living fountain out of which all sacrednesses sprang, and will yet spring? Man, by the nature of him, is definable as 'an incarnated Word.' Ill stands it with me if I have spoken falsely: thine also it was to hear truly. Farewell.

# 3

# STOPPING FOR DEATH: TENNYSON'S
# *IN MEMORIAM*

Within a week of his father's death, Tennyson slept in the dead man's bed, 'earnestly desiring to see his ghost, but no ghost came.'[1] Years later, recalling his failed effort to conjure his father's spirit, he remarked that 'a poet never sees a ghost.'[2] Tennyson's comment is at least as strange as his disquieting act. For it could be said that he saw nothing but ghosts; his greatest poetry is about absence rather than presence, about vanished persons and shadowy places, particularly the long and vivifying shadow cast over his life by the passing of Arthur Hallam.

Hallam and Tennyson met as undergraduates at Trinity College, Cambridge, and the four years of their friendship, until Hallam's death at the age of twenty-two, marked the 'most emotionally intense period he ever knew.'[3] There is no reason whatever to doubt this judgment of Robert B. Martin, the best of Tennyson's modern biographers, or to question Sir Charles Tennyson's account of his grandfather's devastated response to the 'brutal stroke [that] annihilated in a moment a love passing the love of women. The prop, round which his own growth had twined itself for four fruitful years, was suddenly removed.'[4]

Hallam died of a cerebral hemorrhage in Vienna on 15 September 1833. The bad tidings reached Tennyson and his sister, Emily, to whom Hallam was engaged, in the first week of October. His body journeyed more slowly to England, where it was buried on 3 January 1834, nearly four months after his death. A letter from Henry Elton, Hallam's uncle, announced the death and the projected homeward journey by sea:

> Your friend Sir, and my much loved Nephew, Arthur Hallam is no more–…. He died at Vienna on his return from Buda, by Apoplexy, and I believe his Remains come by sea from Trieste.[5]

That last clause struck deeply into Tennyson's imagination, for within a very few days of receipt of Elton's letter, Tennyson drafted the earliest composed section of *In Memoriam*, lines of tender address to the

> Fair ship, that from the Italian shore
>    Sailest the placid ocean-plains
>    With my lost Arthur's loved remains,
> Spread thy full wings, and waft him o'er. (9.1–4)[6]

'My *loved* Arthur's *lost* remains,' Tennyson might as easily have written, given the intensity of his attachment and the depth of his anxiety over the safe transit of Hallam's body. Written so early in the long course of the composition of the poem, and so soon after Tennyson learned of Hallam's death, the 'Fair Ship' sections are remarkable for their hushed tranquility, combining in equal measure the cadences of prayer and lullaby:

> Sleep, gentle heavens, before the prow;
>    Sleep, gentle winds, as he sleeps now
> My friend, the brother of my love. (9.14–16)

In a poem as profoundly strange as *In Memoriam* – a strangeness masked by Tennyson's use of the conventions of elegy and by his occasional banality – it is especially strange that he should pray for the well-being of a corpse. The exquisite calm of the 'Fair Ship' sequence conceals an anxiety so deeply displaced that it would rather imagine Hallam suffering a second death by drowning at sea than dwell upon his actual death in a Vienna hotel room. And so Tennyson fears that his friend's corpse might not be laid to rest beneath English earth but, instead, be engulfed by a raging storm

> Fathom-deep in brine;
>    And hands so often clasp'd in mine,
> Should toss with tangle and with shells. (10.18–20)

The ghastly clarity of the lines serves to remind the poet, as it reminds us, that he is twice removed from his beloved friend – severed by death as well as by distance. The agitated, to-and-fro motion of Hallam's hands stresses their lifelessness, their remoteness from Tennyson's once-frequent clasp, indeed their disjunction from Hallam's body; his hands are reduced to bones entangled with seaweed and shell. The sense of touch, central to all that is most passionately felt in *In Memoriam* –

> Doors, where my heart was used to beat
>    So quickly, waiting for a hand,
> A hand that can be clasp'd no more (7.3–5)

– is here weighted with repugnance, the primitive chill of touching a corpse.

Intensity and banality alternate throughout *In Memoriam*. Through a kind of systole and diastole, they mimic the rituals of mourning, re-enacting our contrary need to hold on and to let go, to embrace and to bury the dead. 'Drowning in sorrow' is the unstated commonplace that underlies *In Memoriam* from its opening through Section 19, in which Tennyson describes Hallam's burial in Clevedon Church, within earshot of the sea. 'Let Love clasp grief lest both be drowned,' he writes in Section 1, anticipating the once-clasped hands that now toss with tangle and shell. Section 6 confesses its own triteness in the thrice-repeated 'common' of its opening: 'Common is the commonplace' that 'Loss is common to the race.' The three vignettes of domestic sorrow that follow depict in miniature the human family in grief – a father, a mother, a maiden awaiting her lover, each at the moment tragedy strikes. The maiden's fiancé is drowned: an unwitting mother prays for the safe return of her sailor son as

> His heavy-shotted hammock-shroud
> Drops in his vast and wandering grave. (ll. 15–16)

Tennyson's language, with its weighty alliterative compounds, evokes a whole brief life from cradle to grave in 'hammock-shroud,' and its allusion to Clarence's dream of drowning in *Richard III* (I iv. 39) all but overwhelms the 'keepsake' style of Section 6. At this point in *In Memoriam*, beneath its surface triteness the reader senses a deadlier undertow: all bodies at sea are Hallam's body, adrift and condemned to a wandering grave, like those anxious, unburied shades in Homer, or Virgil's helmsman, Palinurus, who slips wordlessly beneath the waves.

The close kinship of sleep and death is the subject of Section 11. Its five stanzas constitute a single sentence, the quiet shock of whose close arises from the dormant metaphor in the phrase 'dead calm':

> Calm is the morn without a sound,
>   Calm as to suit a calmer grief,
>   And only thro' the faded leaf
> The chestnut pattering to the ground:
>
> Calm and deep peace on this high wold,
>   And on these dews that drench the furze,
>   And all the silvery gossamers
> That twinkle into green and gold:
>
> Calm and still light on yon great plain
>   That sweeps with all its autumn bowers,
>   And crowded farms and lessening towers,
> To mingle with the bounding main:
>
> Calm and deep peace in this wide air,
>   These leaves that redden to the fall;

> And in my heart, if calm at all,
> If any calm, a calm despair:
>
> Calm on the seas, and silver sleep,
>    And waves that sway themselves in rest,
>    And dead calm in that noble breast
> Which heaves but with the heaving deep. (ll. 1–20)

I cannot read these lines without overhearing the hushed breathing of the poet, an insistent rhythm that comes to a deathly stop with the 'heaving deep' of the last line. The word 'calm,' repeated eleven times, pulses like a muffled heartbeat that soothes and disquiets. Tennyson achieves the illusion of movement over vast spaces virtually without the aid of verbs, extending the copulative 'is' of line 1 through all five stanzas. The poem opens in morning sunlight (the gossamer webs twinkle in the early light) and closes in moonlight ('silver sleep'), but this particular pastoral is redolent not of burgeoning but of decay, the falling leaves signaling mortality. The eye of the poet rises from the foreground woods of the opening to the uplands (the 'high wold') of the second stanza. From this vantage the distant sea emerges beyond the inhabited plain, a prospect that in fact is visible from the Lincolnshire wolds of the poet's Somersby home, where Tennyson and Hallam once walked together through landscapes later memorialized in Sections 89 and 95. Midway through the middle stanza, the poet soars above any landscape perceptible to a mortal eye, traverses the 'wide air' of the penultimate stanza, and comes to rest at sea, beside the undulant body of Hallam. The rocking, lullaby-like cadences of Section 9

> – Sleep, gentle heavens, before the prow;
>  Sleep, gentle winds, as he sleeps now –

return in the closing lines of Section 11, but now chilled by the touch of death. The placid sea sleeps, the waves, with a will of their own, negate their own motion, as if momentarily stilled by the deeper stillness of Hallam. But his is a calm that can never be broken, a 'dead calm'[7] that 'heaves but with the heaving deep,' as earlier his nerveless hands tossed to and fro on the ocean floor.

The most startling effects of In Memoriam all have a transgressive quality, a crossing of borders that normally separate the living from the dead, the natural from the supernatural, one sex or species from another. Death in In Memoriam, especially in the darker, earlier sections, is not so much the cessation of life as a displaced activity, corpses in motion or embraces underground:

> Old Yew, which graspest at the stones
>    That name the under-lying dead,
>    Thy fibres net the dreamless head,

Thy roots are wrapt about the bones.

....................................

And gazing on thee, sullen tree,
  Sick for thy stubborn hardihood,
  I seem to fail from out my blood
And grow incorporate into thee. (2.1–4, 13–16)

The poem opens conventionally enough with a bow to Gray's 'Elegy' and the perdurable associations of yew trees with country churchyards. But Tennyson's tree has mortal longings and a will of its own as it grasps at the gravestones and, penetrating still more deeply, entwines itself around the bones of the dead. This embrace of the living and the dead, of the vegetable and the once-human, both macabre and beautiful, is an oblique measure of the intensity of the poet's need to touch his friend.[8] The tree's grasping roots are tentacular, finger-like, as is seaweed, and in the entwining of root and bone, like that of 'tangle' and hand in Section 10, we find another trope for hands once clasped that can be clasped no more, or clasped only transgressively. Both the tree's will to grasp the dead and the power of the stones to name them contrast with the utter inertness of those beneath, whose heads are speechless and 'dreamless.' In the immediately preceding section, the words 'clasp' and 'behold' prepare us for the invasive tactility of Section 2: the coarser roots enwrap the bones; the finer, lace-like fibres net the head, encasing it as in a winding sheet. In such a context we do not, I feel, go beyond Tennyson's intention in detecting the word 'corpse' in the 'incorporate' of the final line. Reaching into the worlds of the living and the dead, the tree can possess Hallam in a way that Tennyson no longer can. But in becoming, as it were, one flesh with the tree – growing 'incorporate' into it – the poet can embrace the dead at one remove. This, I believe, is the undermeaning of the final quatrain, alongside the more obvious sense that the poet envies the yew's hardiness in the face of the vicissitudes of the seasons. The marriage celebrated in the Epilogue to *In Memoriam* is only the last of a series; this is the first and one of the strangest, between a poet and a tree.

If a corpse is encoded into Section 2, so a ghost is lodged in Section 7, in which the poet lingers at daybreak outside Hallam's deserted house. This bleakest of all lyrics in *In Memoriam* is remarkable for its brevity, its distillation of utter desolation into twelve lines. Yet the 'Dark House' section was one of the last composed, virtually an afterthought. The currents of feeling released by Hallam's death ran more deeply and erratically than a mere calendar of shocked loss and slow recovery might suggest. Mourning, like joy, has its surprises: hence the serene expectation of the first composed 'Fair Ship' section, and the anguish of Section 7, written long after we might suppose the work of mourning to have been done.

In *Memoriam* is a love story; it is also about Tennyson's release from bondage to a dead person. It is autobiographical, but it is not, as T. S. Eliot contended, 'a diary.'[9] I am reminded of Tennyson's remark to his son, Hallam:

> This is a poem, not an actual biography.... The different moods of sorrow as in a drama are dramatically given...'I' is not always the author speaking of himself, but the voice of the human race speaking thro' him.[10]

Here, as so often when commenting on his own poetry, Tennyson is defensive, distancing himself from readings that strike him as too literal or too personal. Yet Section 7 is intensely personal and vulnerable, and it is so precisely because Tennyson can 'do grief' in many voices, dramatizing his grief through the words of Luke and Shakespeare, Milton and Wordsworth. No reader doubts that it is indeed Alfred Tennyson who stands, ghostlike and guilty, on the wet pavement outside Hallam's door:

> Dark house, by which once more I stand
> Here in the long unlovely street.
> Doors, where my heart was used to beat
> So quickly, waiting for a hand –
>
> A hand that can be clasped no more –
> Behold me, for I cannot sleep,
> And like a guilty thing I creep
> At earliest morning to the door.
>
> He is not here; but far away
> The noise of life begins again,
> And ghastly thro' the drizzling rain
> On the bald street breaks the blank day. (7.1–12)

The house is dark because it is night, because lights are dimmed in sign of mourning, because the house is a body from which the spirit has departed, an emblem of the absent Hallam's grave. In standing beside it 'once more,' the poet confesses to his repeated, pained visitations, a measure not merely of the duration of his grief (he had been mourning for seventeen years when he wrote the lines) but of the compulsive repetitiveness of mourning itself. While haunting Hallam's house at night, Tennyson is himself haunted by another premature death that bore singular poetic fruit, the death by drowning of Edward King, also a Cambridge student memorialized by a Cambridge classmate, the first line of whose elegy begins with a repetition that Tennyson himself reiterates: 'Yet once more, O ye Laurels, and once more.' Violent storms at sea late in 1833 gave Tennyson good cause for concern over the safe return of Hallam's body.[11] But death by drowning would not, I believe, so preponderate in the early sections of In Memoriam if Tennyson were not feeling the strong undertow of 'Lycidas.'

The long unloveliness of the London street reflects the pastoral bias built into all English elegy. But Wimpole Street, where the Hallams resided, is in fact long and, despite its Georgian housefronts, appeared unlovely to the Victorian eye ('flat, dull, spiritless,' Disraeli calls it in *Tancred* [1847]).[12] Here, as always, Tennyson prided himself on the accuracy of his descriptions, and we do well to look hard and precisely at what Tennyson looked at, before we drift into freer associations. True, the poet's wretchedness casts a pall upon the street, but city streets are unlovely in a drizzling rain at dawn, especially if you are alone in front of the closed doors of a dark house. This particular street is doubly unlovely because Love itself, in the form of Hallam, is absent: the poet stands before his empty tomb.

The outstretched 'hand' that closes the first stanza awaits, but never clasps, the hand that opens the second, a gulf of white space keeping them forever apart.[13] The 'no more' of line 5 echoes and mournfully negates the 'once more' of line 1. So too the tactile 'clasp'd' of line 5 reaches forward to 'Behold me' of line 6, disclosing, in addition to the imperative sense of 'Look at me,' the imploring sense of 'hold me.' But who does the poet command to look at him, or beg to embrace him? What I had always taken to be a uniquely Tennysonian lyric in fact imitates one of the many classical genres Tennyson deploys throughout In Memoriam, in this instance, the *paraclausithyron*, or the song of an excluded lover who 'stands outside the house of his mistress and laments that the door is bolted against him. He addresses the door and holds it responsible for his rejection.'[14] This is not very promising, certainly not in a modern, highly personal love poem, but gifted poets ring remarkable changes on tarnished tropes. The syntax of the stanzas compels us to read all that precedes the dash at the end of line 5 as addressed to the doors of the dark house; our heart tells us otherwise. In Memoriam straddles many worlds, ancient and modern, public and private, conventional and idiosyncratic. In Tennyson's words, 'altogether private grief' in In Memoriam 'swells out into thought of...the whole world.... It is a very impersonal poem as well as personal.'[15] For Tennyson's learned audience, 'Behold me' is addressed to a pair of doors. But for most of Tennyson's readers, from the Queen to the men and women in the Victorian street, 'Behold me' was addressed directly to them, silent auditors of their Laureate's grief, witnesses of his progress from suicidal despair to troubled faith. But it is also and most intimately addressed by a ghost to a ghost, by a poet who has strayed outside the limits of normal waking life in quest of his dead friend. 'Behold me' is Tennyson's impatient, anguished cry to Hallam – 'see me and clasp me' – but it goes unanswered in front of doors now closed but once open, like the valves of a once-beating heart.[16] And so 'like a guilty thing' he creeps away at dawn, a perilous time for ghosts, who fear light as the living fear darkness. So, too, the ghost of Hamlet's father is startled by the daybreak and vanishes 'like a guilty thing / Upon a fearful summons.'[17] Yet even if we are deaf to the echo of the ghost in *Hamlet*, we feel the psychological rightness of the poet's guilt as he fashions some of his finest lines out of the raw material of his grief, turning loss into gain and surviving the young friend – also a poet – whom he always believed to be immeasurably his superior in grace and intellect.[18] Much later in *In Memoriam*, just before the poet marries Hallam's spirit in Section 95, he returns to Cambridge and hovers, ghostlike, outside his friend's former rooms. He hears songs and revelry coming from within, but 'Another name was on the door' (87.17). The scene evokes many others in Tennyson's poetry in which the poet stands alienated from the social group, a posthumous figure of Death-in-Life, peering through windows, eavesdropping at doors, revisiting a former life where

> all hath suffered change:
> For surely now our household hearths are cold:
> Our sons inherit us: our looks are strange:
> And we should come like ghosts to trouble joy.
>
> ('The Lotos-Eaters,' ll. 116–9)

These memorable lines, almost opulent in their articulation of desolation, contrast starkly with the four flat monosyllables of loss that open the last stanza of Section 7: 'He is not here.' How could Hallam possibly be present? The force of the words lies in the utter aptness of their superfluity. For with each recognition of loss comes the shock of first recognition, the need to reiterate what is already known but cannot be believed. Beyond the aptness of the words there are echoes, as if from the grave, of a text far more familiar to Tennyson's readers than to us – the 'He is not here' spoken by the angel at the empty tomb of the risen Christ. The distance between the dead friend and the living God is nowhere greater than here, as the poet waits unwelcomed before the vacant house. The daybreak is 'ghastly' because colorless, a corpse-like gray in the drizzling rain; but also because 'ghastly' comes from the same root as 'ghostly' and does double duty, like the 'corpse' incorporated into Section 2. In this dismal context, the sounds of the emergent day make a distant discord, a mere renewal of noise. The deathfulness of the dark house seems to spill out onto the bald, featureless street and the blank day, void of event because void of Hallam. Some two thousand lines later, the 'blank day' of Section 7 broadens into the 'boundless day' that closes Section 95. The dead friend of Section 7 undergoes a gradual apotheosis that renders him, by the end of the poem, indistinguishable from the 'Immortal Love' of its first line.

## 2

I have foreshortened a very long journey much of whose meaning lies in the simple fact of its length, as the importance of a funeral is sometimes measured by the number of cars or coaches in the procession. *In Memoriam* is a slow, winding procession that, like mourning, circles back upon itself even as it progresses. It is six times longer than 'Adonis,' fifteen times longer than 'Lycidas.' At once highly conventional and transgressive, *In Memoriam*'s first transgression is against genre, its inordinate length. But Tennyson's excesses, being Tennysonian, are measured excesses. He strains the generic seams of elegy to the bursting point, yet he remains eminently Victorian in mourning at such elaborate length. Edward FitzGerald expressed the minority view in complaining that his friend Tennyson had written a 'volume of poems – elegiac – in memory of Arthur Hallam. Don't you think the world wants other notes than elegiac now? *Lycidas* is the utmost length an elegiac [poem] should reach.'[19] Victoria was never more Victorian than in her inconsolably protracted mourning over Albert, and the bonds of respect and affection between the Queen and her Laureate derived in part from their being world-class mourners, the most celebrated of their century.* The corpse of Prince Albert was laid to rest inside five coffins, as if to underscore the redundant abundance of his widow's grief. Hallam's embalmed and eviscerated remains were disembarked at Dover, drawn across England in a massive coffin by sixteen black Hanoverian horses followed by three mourning coaches (one of them, the family coach, contained an empty seat reserved for Tennyson), before being at length laid to rest in Clevedon Church. As Peter Sacks observes, the coffins and hearses of the period, like its elegies, 'seemed designed almost to detain the remains of the dead.'[20] Tennyson and his contemporaries held on longer, and let go harder – albeit more ceremoniously – than we do.

---

* I write with Max Beerbohm's caricature vividly in mind: 'Mr. Tennyson, Reading *In Memoriam* to his Sovereign.' Dressed all in black, the shaggy, seated bard, arms outstretched, declaims from a manuscript to his diminutive Queen, also in black, a seated ball of concentrated attention. The room is bare of all but the two living figures, two empty chairs pressed up against the rear wall, and a portrait of Prince Albert centered above the mantle, the apex of a mourner's triangle. Perhaps aware of the importance of the outstretched hand to the symbolic design of *In Memoriam*, Max elongates and enlarges Tennyson's upraised left hand so that, without a trace of apparent disproportion, the hand almost equals in length the entire arm that upholds it and that points like an arrow to the portrait of Albert. Tennyson's booming Lincolnshire dialect seems to reverberate off the bare walls and travel in concentrated waves, repeated in the lines of the carpet, to his all but featureless Sovereign.

Figure 2: Max Beerbohm, *Mr. Tennyson, reading 'In Memoriam' to His Sovereign*, 1904.

The conflicting impulse to bury the dead, or to be buried with them, is enacted in Section 18, in which Hallam is finally laid to rest in English earth:

> 'Tis well; 'tis something; we may stand
>   Where he in English earth is laid,
>   And from his ashes may be made
> The violet of his native land.
> ......................................
> Come then, pure hands, and bear the head
>   That sleeps or wears the mask of sleep,
>   And come, whatever loves to weep,
> And hear the ritual of the dead. (ll. 1–4, 9–12)

That we might take pleasure in mourning ('love to weep') suggests more than graveside sentimentality. The pleasures of ritual and their attendant repetitions run deep and are as innate as rhythm to poetry or breathing to life. Ritual holds the hope of renewal, precisely what death denies; it applies the balm of continuity to the void of absence. It can say, 'Yet once more, O ye Laurels, and once more,' when the terrible fact is that there is no more, for Lycidas died ere his prime. 'The ritual of the dead' steers an exquisitely delicate course between the refreshing of grief through recollection and the dulling of pain through habituation. For the 'unquiet heart,' as Tennyson tells us in Section 5,

> A use in measured language lies;
>   The sad mechanic exercise,
> Like dull narcotics, numbing pain. (ll. 6–8)

This is more than the poet's mock modesty, or his justified modesty, perhaps even embarrassment, over those perfunctory sections of In Memoriam which we might prefer to forget or suppress, like yawns in a funeral parlor. 'Measured language,' 'metered' language, calms and lulls us, restores regularity to breathing that is wracked and broken by sobs. Verlaine's famous put-down of In Memoriam is misconceived: 'Tennyson was too noble, too *Anglais*, and when he should have been broken-hearted, had many reminiscences.'[21] Hearts truly broken can only gasp out in irregular spasms of pain. Mourning converts sobs into song, a wailing wall into the Kaddish, the great Hebrew prayer of mourning. In an especially tormented section of In Memoriam, Tennyson asks,

> but what am I?
> An infant crying in the night:
> An infant crying for the light:
> And with no language but a cry. (54.17–20)

That is as close as 'measured language' can get in suggesting the pre-lingual,[22] aboriginal terror of loss, the panic an infant feels when its mother disappears into the dark, or that Tennyson voiced on Arthur Hallam's death.

Anniversaries in In Memoriam perform the same function as ritual: they structure loss, just as their recurrence helps to structure the larger poem. This is the function of the three Christmas poems of In Memoriam, each commemorating a little less piercingly the grief over Hallam's absence, until the poet's

> regret
> Becomes an April violet,
> And buds and blossoms like the rest. (115.18–20)

But this is to reduce a great and greatly uneven poem to a formula. Despite the classic status of In Memoriam, much of its power resides in its power to shock. Thus in Section 18, in which the poet lays Hallam to rest in language that recalls the stately simplicity of the Anglican service for the dead, he also throws himself upon Hallam's body in a veiled but unmistakable image of a kiss. The pertinent lines immediately follow those in which the poet invites all who love to weep to 'hear the ritual of the dead':

> Ah yet, ev'n yet, if this might be,
> I, falling on his faithful heart,
> Would breathing thro' his lips impart
> The life that almost dies in me. (18.13–16)

The turn from the measured language of ritual to that of passion, the sudden reversal from letting go to holding on, is marked by the poet's anguished 'Ah yet, even yet,' as if he were struggling to thwart his own surge of feeling even as it rises in his throat. This burial poem marks the end of the 'Fair Ship' sequence of lyrics, with their imagery of drowning, and the context leads us to see in the lines an image of mouth-to-mouth resuscitation. We see, too, that Tennyson is alluding to the love than which there is none greater – to lay down one's life for one's friend. That he is also lying down *upon* his friend, lips pressed to lips, we also see, but not to the exclusion of the Biblical miracle from which the lines directly derive: Elisha 'went up, and lay upon the child, and put his mouth upon his mouth...and the flesh of the child waxed warm.'[23]

The nature of Tennyson's sexuality in *In Memoriam* has been in question ever since the publication of the poem. In venturing out upon these vexed waters, I would argue two apparently contradictory propositions: *In Memoriam* is one of the great love poems in English, about the love of one male for another, but it is not a homosexual poem. That the poet is living and his friend is dead alters our response to the love expressed, but does not preclude its being homosexual, as Hart Crane's 'Praise for an Urn – In Memoriam: Ernest Nelson' beautifully demonstrates. However, *In Memoriam* is also not homosexual in the rapturous, unknowing way of Gerard Manley Hopkins over the 'bellbright bodies' of bathing boys in 'Epithalamion'; nor in the knowing, rapturous way of Walt Whitman in the 'Calamus' poems. All three portray the unmistakably erotic attraction of a male poet to males, as unmistakably erotic, say, as the post-coital heterosexual rapture expressed in Dante Gabriel Rossetti's 'Nuptial Sleep.' The remarkable, defining quality of Tennyson's sexuality is not, as Robert B. Martin mistakenly argues, its weakness,[24] but its all-pervasiveness, a sexuality so primal and all-encompassing that it lacks gender specificity or constancy. The emotion Tennyson communicates in his greatest poetry is deeply sexual but not erotic, a distinction perhaps harder for men to grasp than for women but, perhaps, not unknown to the mother with an infant at her breast. On this primal level the all-pervasive 'hand' in *In Memoriam* (it appears in forty-two places) may also be a metonym for the breast. Tennyson's sexuality, in short, is polymorphous *unperverse*, and the more pertinent critical distinction for us in reading *In Memoriam* is not between the homosexual and the heterosexual, but between the sexual (or pre-sexual) and the erotic.

What persuades me of the truth of Tennyson's pervasive, freely gendered sexuality is a curious emendation Queen Victoria made in her copy of *In Memoriam*. In February 1862, shortly after Prince Albert's death, she found solace in Section 13, and, pencil in hand, altered in her own copy the words 'widower' to 'widow' and 'his' to 'her':[25]

> Tears of the widower, when he sees
>   A late-lost form that sleep reveals,
>   And moves his doubtful arms, and feels
> Her place is empty, fall like these. (ll. 1–4)

Both the passage and Victoria's emendation speak volumes about the poem and its audience. It is remarkable that Tennyson felt free enough to compare his grief over Hallam to that of a widower in his marriage bed, weeping over the void where his wife once lay. It is equally remarkable that the Queen with such ease could imagine herself in the place of the sex-changed widower. Yet Victoria has not so much altered Tennyson's intention as enriched or realized it: the first line is metrically irregular in the poet's version (it contains an extra syllable), requiring the reader to rush over 'wid-ow-er,' but metrically correct in the Queen's version. The meter and sense of the lines, our stereotypical expectations of weeping widows, all lead us, subliminally at least, to pick up Victoria's pencil. Tennyson, of course, is aware of the loose gendering of the quatrain and counterweights its covert femininity by paying homage in its second line to the most celebrated elegy in English to a deceased spouse, Milton's emphatically male 'Methought I saw my *late* espousèd Saint.'[26] With the tact that characterizes his art, Tennyson works to elide distinctions, including distinctions between male and female. Hence in the course of *In Memoriam*, the poet's love is compared to that of mother, father, fiancée; wife and husband; friend, brother, mate, comrade, widow, and widower; a ghost seeking a ghost; a poor girl in a great man's house; a dog that loves its master; a father giving away a bride. Assuming a multitude of roles yet always recognizably himself, Tennyson has chosen so many objects of love that it is as if he has not chosen any; or, to turn it around, as if in choosing the godlike Hallam, he has chosen all. Tennyson's sexuality is strong but remarkably mobile, the sexuality of an immensely sophisticated infant who knows pleasure but not yet choice.

This mobility in the playing of roles led Tennyson's admirers into a notorious misreading of *In Memoriam*. The first-composed 'Fair Ship' section ends in tender address to

> My Arthur, whom I shall not see
>   Till all my widowed race be run;
>   Dear as the mother to the son,
> More than my brothers are to me. (9.17–20)

'These touching lines,' wrote an early reviewer of *In Memoriam*, 'evidently come from the full heart of the widow of a military man.'[27] Hallam Tennyson, zealous in guarding his father's reputation against any imputation of doctrinal or sexual irregularity, appears unamused by the review, which he finds 'not on the whole sympathetic.' Humorless as Hallam Tennyson, and unlike modern critics of *In Memoriam*, I do not find the comment especially funny. I do, however, find it deeply sympathetic, a keen if unconscious tribute to Tennyson's success in voicing his most intimate emotions in ways that touch great chords of public feeling.

The recent discovery that *In Memoriam* is really a veiled tribute to homoerotic love marks, as I see it, a new parochialism, a kind of inverted prudery that finds it hard to recognize the legitimacy of any interests other than its own.[28] Here a certain historical awareness may prove liberating. The letters of Geraldine Jewsbury to Jane Carlyle, if written today, would, in the intensity of their endearments, be mistaken for the letters of a lesbian lover. We are at a loss in judging – or misjudging – the correspondence of Tennyson and Hallam, for all the letters of Alfred to Arthur were destroyed by Arthur's father, and most of Arthur's letters to Alfred were destroyed by Tennyson's son, Hallam.[29] The modern reader, smelling smoke, assumes homosexual fires, but it is exactly in our Freudian knowingness and historical ignorance that we are likely to go astray. Hallam Tennyson compiled his hagiographic *Memoir* (1897) of his father at the time of Oscar Wilde's trials, a period of rabid British homophobia that, combined with his own prudery, led him to suppress – and therefore to quicken unnaturally our own sensitivity to – all possible evidence of homosexuality in the relationship between his father and his own namesake. Over the many decades of Victoria's reign the cultural and sexual climate changed quite radically, and kept changing. If the early Victorians tended to be more centripetal and less troubled in their sexuality, the late Victorians tended to be more uptight or far-out – like Hallam Tennyson on the one hand, or caught, like poor Simeon Solomon on the other hand, soliciting sex in a public urinal. Christopher Ricks gets it exactly right when he observes that Hallam Tennyson 'made the great mistake of censoring just exactly those things in Tennyson which are triumphantly straight.' And he goes on to cite a censored letter in which Tennyson without a trace of self-consciousness jokes openly and easily with a mutual friend about sharing a roof but not the same bed with his friend Arthur.[30]

Still, we would be naïve to assume that there were no worms in the pre-Freudian garden, or that the Victorians failed to spot them. An early reviewer – the aptly named Manley Hopkins, father of Gerard – complained in *The Times* of Tennyson's display of 'amatory tenderness' toward an 'Amaryllis of the Chancery Bar.' (Hallam was studying law at the time of his death.) 'Very sweet and plaintive these verses are; but who would not give them a feminine application.'[31] The imputation of effeteness – or worse – is evident, and one has only to recall the frequency of 'manly' as a term of praise among the Victorians to recognize how hard and low a blow the reviewer has struck. To be 'manly' was to be brave, forthright and British; to be unmanly was to be effete, French, of dubious patriotism and irregular sexuality. Tennyson was hypersensitive to criticism of all kinds, and the charge of 'tenderness' – of unmanliness – struck home. I believe it motivated a number of textual changes in *In Memoriam*, although, for better or worse, there is no evidence that Hallam and Tennyson ever touched one another sexually or were other than heterosexual in their predilections and practices. But Tennyson's worry over the misconstruction of their relationship explodes in the defensiveness (naïve rather than unwittingly incriminating) of his reply to criticism of the line, 'So, dearest, now thy brows are cold' (74.5): 'If any body thinks I ever called him "dearest" in his life they are much mistaken, for I never even called him dear.'[32] To Tennyson's credit, the 'dearests' of *In Memoriam* survived the critics' jibes and his own discomfort. But the hand so poignantly awaited in Section 7 was originally 'his' hand, then became 'the' hand, and finally 'a hand, / A hand that can be clasped no more' (ll. 4–5). The loss of specificity brings a gain in subtlety: Hallam's initials are now inscribed at the end of the first stanza and the start of the second, surely no accident in a poem entitled *In Memoriam A. H. H.* The best-known revision reveals Tennyson's genuine anxiety and comes at the climax of his spiritual marriage to Hallam in Section 95:

> And all at once it seemed at last
>   *The* living soul was flash'd on mine,
> And mine in *this* was wound. (ll. 35–37; my italics)

I have always felt personally cheated by Tennyson's shying away from the original '*His* living soul... / And mine in *his* was wound.' If 'the' living soul is not Hallam's soul, entwined in Tennyson's, then whose is it? 'Perchance the Deity,' Tennyson replied to James Knowles; 'but my conscience was troubled by "his".'[33] The first phrase is as feckless as the second is forthright. True, Tennyson has progressively depersonalized and divinized Hallam, so there is a rarefied sense in which Hallam – 'Known and unknown, human, divine' (129.5) – has indeed become the Deity, in whom Tennyson is momentarily enwound. But as a mortal reader who has not yet shed the flesh or been whirled about in 'empyreal heights of thought,' I cling to something more substantial, to the weight and humanity of Tennyson's loss, and I feel betrayed by the obliteration of Hallam's person and gender. Hallam Tennyson gives another version of his father's comment to Knowles: '[My father] preferred, however, for fear of giving a wrong impression, the vaguer and more abstract later reading.'[34] The son is concerned with appearances, above all, with avoiding the appearance of homosexuality; the father is concerned not with propriety but conscience, possibly with guilt over his unorthodox divinization of his friend.

In the most impassioned lines of *In Memoriam*, the poet cries out to Hallam's ghost:

> Descend, and touch, and enter; hear
>   The wish too strong for words to name;
>   That in this blindness of the frame
> My Ghost may feel that thine is near. (93.13–16)

What a can of worms for the unwary exegete! Dare we name the wish too strong for words to name? The task would be easier were it not for a kind of back-wash from the famous line that ends Lord Alfred Douglas's 'Two Loves': "'Have thy will / I am the love that dare not speak its name'". The modern reader cannot read the words 'Descend, and touch, and enter' without sensing a plea for sexual penetration. Quite possibly Tennyson's fear of a homoerotic misconstruction now leads his reader to just such a surmise. His first thought for the line was 'Stoop soul & touch me: wed me: hear.'[35] 'Wed me' must have awakened second thoughts, leading Tennyson to substitute, unintentionally, the more sexually charged 'enter,' a charge all the greater after his excision of the sanitizing 'soul' in the manuscript version of line one. The Post-Freudian reader, believing that reality wells up from within us, from the unconscious, feels the sexual force of the line and is struck by its explicitness. Tennyson's contemporaries, in touch with a more ancient tradition, and used to looking up rather than down or within for the sources of the real, would have been more aware of the Christian iconographic, than the phallic, allusion: the impregnating power of the Holy Ghost descending as a ray of light into the ear of the attendant Virgin; or of the still more ancient tradition, classical and Hebraic, of the inspiring force of the Muse or the Godhead entering the soul or mouth of his prophet-poet. But Tennyson was writing at the end of a long tradition, and he saw continuity where we see contraries: neither reading of the line – the sexual or the sacred – excludes the other. In an essay that 'strongly affected' Tennyson, his young friend Hallam had written that 'erotic feeling is of origin peculiarly divine, and raises the soul to heights of existence, which no other passion is permitted to attain.'[36]

### 3

'Descend, and touch, and enter' follows a series of lyrics of rising hope of renewed contact with Hallam and prepares the way for the climactic vision of Section 95. Early in In Memoriam, when grief was keenest, Tennyson craved Hallam's corporeal hand. The desire for bodily touch was stronger when most weighted with the sense of impossibility, hands tossing with tangle and shell. Later in In Memoriam Tennyson moves from the modest but thwarted union of clasped hands to the union of married souls. Again, we are likely to see only repression or sublimation when Tennyson means more, or less, or other than we do. The ghost of Hallam that Tennyson implores to enter his own is more than a metaphor and other than a male body. It represents what used to be meant by a mystery, and a mystery, as Gerard Manley Hopkins once remarked, is not an interesting uncertainty but an incomprehensible certainty. Tennyson believed in ghosts and most of us do not, but the ghosts that Tennyson believed in are not the same as those whose existence we deny – spooks, or billboards that glow with mysterious light. After he and Victoria had been mourning, between them, for over eighty years, he wrote to her that the dead 'may be more living than the living' and 'while we are lamenting that they are not at our side, may still be with us.'[37] He would surely have been a Druid, had the Druids promised him the personal immortality of Arthur Hallam; Christianity held out the hope of immortal life, and hence of his ultimate reunion with Arthur Hallam. And so Tennyson, however beset by doubt, was a Christian. 'The cardinal point about Christianity,' he remarked to a bishop of his acquaintance, 'is the Life after Death.'[38] *In Memoriam* is a love poem addressed to a ghost whose 'vivid absence'[39] is felt in every line.

Hallam's absence is felt with special keenness in the panic of Section 50. Through some eighty separate lyrics (Sections 40–47) Tennyson obsessively pursues the question of Hallam's personal immortality, concluding with the triumphant assertion, 'And I shall know him when we meet' (47.8). But the work of mourning collapses just when it seemed all but over:

> Be near me when my light is low,
>     When the blood creeps, and the nerves prick
>     And tingle; and the heart is sick,
> And all the wheels of Being slow.
>
> Be near me when the sensuous frame
>     Is rack'd with pangs that conquer trust;
>     And Time, a maniac scattering dust,
> And Life, a Fury slinging flame.
>
> Be near me when my faith is dry,
>     And men the flies of latter spring,
>     That lay their eggs, and sting and sing
> And weave their petty cells and die.
>
> Be near me when I fade away,
>     To point the term of human strife,
>     And on the low dark verge of life
> The twilight of eternal day. (50.1–16)

An anxiety attack is not the most promising material for great poetry, but here, as in Section 54 ('an infant crying for the light'), Tennyson regresses to the terror of an infant abandoned in the dark. For it is not merely or simply the metaphorical 'light of life' that burns low. The fear of darkness here expressed is a palpable, physiological fear, and the being the poet calls upon for comfort is not an absent mother but a dead friend. The uncanny power of the passage resides in its inversion of expectation: the abandoned child is terrified not by the presence of a ghost but by its absence.

The poem opens on a highly personal note of panic but soon carries its private fears into the wider arena of public discourse: the long, frightening vistas of geological Time with their threat of ultimate extinction ('dust'); the drying up of religious faith; mankind not at the center of creation but a petty, ephemeral organism, a mean link in a doomed chain. One gender-centered detail – Life as a Fury – prepares us for the famous shriek of the malevolent goddess Nature in Section 56. The Furies, both as protectresses and, more familiarly, as avengers, are unmistakably female. Despite their archaic Greek dress, they appear here as recognizable Victorian images of the nature of nurture gone awry; they are Mother Nature ('Life') devouring her own brood, anglicized femmes fatales.[40]

Perhaps the greatest mystery in *In Memoriam* is that it manages to articulate so fully both the private obsessions of its author and the public concerns of its audience. Six words from Section 56 have become a kind of shorthand for a century of intellectual history, the revolution in perception that saw the benevolent Nature of the Romantics become the 'Nature red in tooth and claw' of Darwin, whose *Origin* appeared nearly a decade after *In Memoriam*. The chronology is less surprising once we realize that Tennyson's grim view of nature derived at least as much from the shock of Hallam's death as from his wide reading in science, particularly the science of geology, in the 1830s and 40s. Hallam was 'nature's best,' yet the same nature turns into the dark-handed felon who strikes him down in the great lyric that commemorates the anniversary of his death (Section 72). The panic of a child alone in the dark, implicit in Section 50 ('Be near me...'), becomes explicit at the end of Section 54, as the poet compares himself to 'an infant crying in the night' with 'no language but a cry.' Sections 55 and 56 have been staled by overquotation. But we may detect a more dramatic and personal aspect in these highly public poems. The piercing cry of the abandoned infant in Section 54 is answered by the rejecting shriek of its mother – Nature – in Section 56. In this carefully plotted mini-drama, Nature has overheard the poet's remark in Section 55 that she seems 'so careful of the type' but 'careless of the single life.' Her retort to the poet has the laconic malevolence and ferocity of the Fury of Section 50. And it is directed equally to her abandoned infant, to the despairing poet, and to his troubled audience wracked by the assault of science upon their faith:

> 'So careful of the type?' but no.
>   From scarped cliff and quarried stone
>   She cries, 'A thousand types are gone:
>   I care for nothing, all shall go.' (56.1–4)

No other major English poem stands in a more central relation to its culture or to the life of its author. Published in the midyear of the century and the midpoint of Tennyson's career, it sold some sixty thousand copies within months of publication and went through thirty separate editions during his lifetime. Something of its centrality is suggested by the prominence of the speaker and the juxtaposition of texts in the celebrated comment, 'Next to the Bible, In Memoriam is my comfort.'[41] Queen Victoria was, of course, speaking as a private citizen, but it is useful to recall that she reigned as head of the established religion as well as of the nation. By far the best-known poem of its age, In Memoriam was published anonymously, and Tennyson kept his name off the title page of subsequent editions (Martin, p. 341); but no one doubted for an instant who wrote it, except that discerning early reader who mistook Tennyson for a broken-hearted widow. The genius and the commonness of In Memoriam are entwined in ways that make us at moments distrust our conviction that it is a great and not merely 'representative' poem. Here I return to the question of Tennyson's banality and to those vignettes of the human family in grief that immediately precede the great 'Dark House' lyric. Does the confession of banality make the banality any less trite?

> That loss is common would not make
> My own less bitter, rather more:
> Too common! Never morning wore
> To evening, but some heart did break. (6.5–8)

I cite the quatrain because it is so patently 'Victorian'; its facile style accounts in good measure for the popularity of the poem and Victoria's enthusiasm. The sententious close cries out for petit point above a cluttered Victorian mantle, alongside the too-familiar and twice-repeated:

> 'Tis better to have loved and lost
> Than never to have loved at all. (27.15–16; 85.3–4)

But even as I quote the lines I recall Tennyson's comment that he is expressing sorrow in many voices, and one of them is the common 'voice of the human race' in grief. The Modernist critics of Tennyson could not stomach his common style, and they mistook this one note for his whole range. His mastery of the vernacular of the race in sorrow in part accounts for his eclipse among the hieratic moderns, who wrote for a more rarefied, private and alienated audience. Yet the privacy of Tennyson's grief never gets in the way of its public expression. The last two lines of the cited quatrain are, on a closer look, less commonplace than an elegant variation on verses by Lucretius[42] which Tennyson borrowed, polished and gave back to the British public. The first two lines seem all but calculated to offend a Modernist.[43] But Tennyson is rendering 'the different moods of sorrow as in drama,' in this instance a well-known drama filled with commonplaces: 'Thou know'st 'tis common; all that lives must die' (*Hamlet*, I.2.72).

Love poem, ghost story, tissue of commonplaces – In Memoriam is all of these, exquisitely attuned to its own cultural moment and also to the whole history of poetry, classical and English. Its commonplaces are the commonplaces of genius, the willed rests of a poet who chooses to lower his pitch, not the banality of failed originality. I recall seeing years ago over the bar of a Grantchester pub once frequented by Rupert Brooke the line from Tennyson's well-known New Year's anthem, 'Ring out, wild bells, to the wild sky' (Section 106). This is not Hallmark verse but Horowitz playing Sousa's 'Stars and Stripes Forever.'

Section 56, with Nature shrieking out against man's hope of immortality, marks the nadir of despair in In Memoriam. The calamity of individual loss so personally expressed earlier in the poem is now generalized and impersonalized in the evolutionary sections into fear of extinction of the entire race. Now at midpoint in his poem, the poet is furthest from God and from his godlike friend in the progress of his Victorian Divina Commedia.[44] The only possible movement is upward. And so Section 57 serves as a kind of hinge on which the poem turns toward hope and homecoming:

> Peace; come away: the song of woe
>   Is after all an earthly song:
>   Peace; come away: we do him wrong
> To sing so wildly: let us go.
>
> Come; let us go: your cheeks are pale;
>   But half my life I leave behind. (ll. 1–6)

The poet still has a long way to go but the lines mark a dramatic pause in the procession of his mourning. Their slow, muted cadence suggest a second burial of Hallam reminiscent of the first, long ago:

> 'Tis well; 'tis something; we may stand
>   Where he in English earth is laid…(18.1–2)

Our sense of an ending is confirmed by manuscript evidence suggesting that Tennyson originally intended Section 57 to close In Memoriam.[45] He was in fact in the middle of the journey of his life when the poem was published, and in leaving 'half my life…behind' he marks both the midpoint in his mourning and in his life. But he is standing beside an imaginary grave, and he very quietly tells us that in leaving Hallam below, he is leaving half of his own life – the better half, he believed – in the grave.

The closing lines of the lyric reenact in miniature the entire process of mourning, a turning toward and away from the dead:

> I hear it now, and o'er and o'er,
>   Eternal greetings to the dead;
>   And 'Ave, Ave, Ave,' said,
> 'Adieu, adieu,' for evermore. (ll. 13–16)

The poet greets and bids farewell to Hallam in the same breath, lingering even as he leaves. For to say 'adieu for evermore' is never to say adieu by saying it always. Tennyson said goodbye for seventeen years, from Hallam's death until the publication of *In Memoriam* on 1 June 1850. But even then he could not let go – if not of his friend's body, then of the text that so richly enshrines him and that he laboured over in successive editions for another thirty-four years.

In *Memoriam* is, of course, autobiographical, but its author's life is so engrafted upon the poem, the poem upon the life, that the two cannot viably be separated. In the year 1850 the rain-chilled, guilty ghost of Section 7 came in out of the cold, got married, and became Victoria's Laureate. Tennyson's allusion to the disquieted, wandering shade of Hamlet's father in Section 7 is also an allusion to Tennyson himself, to his own 'psychic homelessness' during the years of the composition of the poem.[46] Robert B. Martin describes the 'desperately long period of discontent and restlessness' that began with Tennyson's father's death in 1831 and intensified with Hallam's in 1833, when he became 'almost homeless, wandering from friend to friend, settling briefly with his family, then pulling up stakes and going off unexpectedly. ... He was almost a nomad.'[47] In the long course of his vagabondage he carried, along with his not-quite-clean linen, the manuscript of *In Memoriam* wherever he went, adding and revising, reading bits aloud here and there, shuffling sections around as he changed addresses. Once, he left the manuscript behind in a London cupboard and came very close to losing it.[48] His emotional life, if not his art, was almost in tatters. At least four of his brothers were confined for various periods in lunatic asylums, and all of the sons of the Reverend George Tennyson, including Alfred, had reason to fear that their father's violence and melancholia would be visited upon them.[49] In weaving his separate 'Elegies' into a coherent fabric, Tennyson was achieving an order that the narrative of his daily life conspicuously lacked. He had indeed found 'a use in measured language,' but his poetry during this tumultuous period served more than the narcotic function of numbing a mourner's pain: it held his life together, expressing and ordering his inmost being.

It is as if Tennyson himself were living, in the London digs of his friends, or in Lincolnshire, or wherever else he briefly decamped, the lives of the celebrated aliens and homeless voyagers he was making famous in his verse, or as if they had borrowed his life – no matter, the one is the shadow of the other. Tennyson wrote 'Ulysses' with more of 'the feeling of [Hallam's] loss upon me than many poems in *In Memoriam*.... There is more about myself in Ulysses.'[50] I cannot read Tennyson's comment on 'Ulysses' without hearing the word 'mourn' among the many voices that 'moan' throughout the slowest line and a half of English literature:

> The long day wanes: the slow moon climbs: the deep
> Moans round with many voices. (ll. 55–6)

Like *In Memoriam*, 'Ulysses' was begun immediately after Hallam's death. The poem is as much about the will to die, now that 'the great Achilles, *whom we knew*' (l. 64; my italics),[51] is dead, as it is about the conviction that 'life must be fought out to the end.'[52] Despite the ringing close, Tennyson subverts Ulysses's will to strive and to seek by his will to die – to abandon home, wife, son, scepter, and life itself in the quest 'to sail beyond the sunset' (l. 60) and 'see the great Achilles,' who can be embraced only in the company of the dead.

An alien at home, Ulysses wants to 'push off,' enacting a kind of reverse homecoming; his shipmates the Lotos-Eaters have sailed beyond the sunset and imagine their homecoming as a second death. The mortal Ulysses's quest to transcend the limits of mortality is answered by the withered but immortal Tithonus's plea to die, the classic wanderer and the classic survivor, the one displaced at home, the other wrenched from the normal course of life and pleading for a home beneath the earth. At the end of his other great Arthur poem, *Idylls of the King*, Tennyson epitomizes in three lines the alienation and bereavement that underlie *In Memoriam*:

> And I, the last, go forth companionless,
> And the days darken round me, and the years,
> Among new men, strange faces, other minds.
>
> ('The Passing of Arthur,' ll. 404–6)

Bedivere, the last survivor of the deserted Round Table, speaks as the dying Arthur embarks for Avilion. These germinative lines of *Idylls of the King* were written in the same notebook alongside the first sections of *In Memoriam*, which opens with the 'Fair Ship' bearing the remains of Arthur Hallam to England. 'Break, Break, Break' and 'Tithonus' were also composed soon after Hallam's death, as was the remarkably intimate and passionate love-lyric, 'Oh that 'twere possible.' Tennyson thought this Hallam-linked lyric the most touching he ever wrote and it served as the 'germ' of *Maud*.[53]

I know of no other personal catastrophe in the long history of English poetry that bore such rich or immediate fruit. By far the greatest portion of Tennyson's greatest poetry was inspired by, and drafted shortly after, Hallam's death. In this context, Tennyson's creeping away like a guilty thing from Hallam's empty house suggests more than the guilt of a survivor or the alienation of those who mourn too long or too loudly. The poet Apollo mistakenly slew his beloved friend Hyacinth, and from his blood in spring uprose from the ground sheets of hyacinth. Tennyson grew poetry from Hallam's corpse, turning regret into April violets, plaiting grief into a laureate's crown.

Yet in stressing Hallam's importance to Tennyson, I am perplexed by my inability to see Hallam with any real clarity. Why is he so shadowy a figure throughout *In Memoriam* – so vivid an absence but so pallid a mortal presence? The answer in part is that *In Memoriam* is not about Hallam but about

Tennyson's response to his death and to the effect of that death upon his beliefs and his poetry. Beyond that, I believe that Tennyson was more moved by the Hallam he lost than the Hallam he had actually known – the gifted undergraduate who dazzled his friends, loved Dante, fell in love with Emily Tennyson, and died of apoplexy in Vienna. The actual Hallam is remarkably fuzzy in *In Memoriam*, an awkward or offputting presence of 'seraphic intellect' and bland smile. 'I cannot see the features right,' Tennyson says all too truly, 'the hues are faint' (70.1, 3). Tennyson means that Hallam is too far exalted above him to be clearly depicted, like a receding star. But the words have a literal force we are likely to overlook. Tennyson's extreme near-sightedness was such that he never saw the precise play of human features unless they were pressed up against his own. His best portraiture, as distinct from his natural descriptions, is always internal. These psychological landscapes are of great precision, although the alert reader, like the careful robin in *Enoch Arden*, may occasionally catch a painterly physical detail; Queen Victoria noted that Hallam's eyes were blue, as were her Albert's. But Tennyson's obvious failure to persuade his reader of the physical reality and individuality of Hallam involves more than the physiology of the poet's vision. When Henry Hallam solicited contributions from his son's friends for a volume of Arthur's *Remains*, Tennyson demurred in words of quite clinical coldness: 'I find the object is yet too near to me to permit of any very accurate delineation.'[54] In time, of course, Tennyson came through handsomely, with *In Memoriam*. But his reason for the delay was oddly inappropriate for one who could not see an object *unless* it was nearby. In this instance, the object was not only too close emotionally to be delineated, it was in large measure inside Tennyson. For Tennyson may be said to have known this other, internalized Arthur Hallam from birth and to have met him in the flesh at Trinity College in April 1829. Only through such bending of chronology and logic can I make sense of Tennyson's having written 'The Two Voices,' the prototype of *In Memoriam*, at least three months *before* Hallam's death. Hallam Tennyson was so evidently struck by the verbal and thematic similarities between *In Memoriam* and 'The Two Voices' (originally entitled 'Thoughts of a Suicide') that he wrongly asserted that this dialogue of a divided self 'was begun under a cloud of his [Tennyson's] overwhelming sorrow after the death of Arthur Hallam.'[55] Yet the first two thirds of the poem, in which the suicidal voice is clearly triumphant, predates Hallam's death, and the unconvincing close was written soon after it. The little domestic idyll at the end is remarkably premonitory of the end of *In Memoriam* – and remarkably trite: the poet is awakened by the ringing of church bells on the Sabbath morn and gazes down upon a prudent husband, faithful wife, and 'little maiden...demure' as they enter church. Tennyson had found the skeletal setting (the poet apart in his tower, the ceremonies of life transpiring below) but not the language for the sublime close of *In Memoriam*.

Hallam's presence is central to Tennyson's poetry but works in mysterious ways. One has only to read the astonishing 'The Kraken,' written in the poet's adolescence, to realize that most of his themes and much of his language were in place years before he met the Arthur Hallam he so quickly loved and lost. It was a case of 'friendship at first sight'[56] on both sides, though the phrase, like its elder sibling, 'love at first sight,' is a misnomer. For while the phenomenon strikes us with the force and freshness of revelation, in reality it occurs not on first but on ten-thousandth sight and hence has the uncanny familiarity of déjà vu, of forgotten sights and parting touches whose impress has long faded. Love at first sight is the meeting of an antecedent disposition with its ideal object – in this instance, of Alfred Tennyson and Arthur Hallam, an 'object yet too near to me to permit of any very accurate delineation.'

If Tennyson anticipated Hallam before meeting him, he deferred their final parting until long after Hallam's death. He was not present at the funeral for the same reason he absented himself from the volume of Hallam's *Remains*. Robert B. Martin notes that at the time of the funeral Tennyson was entertaining an old college friend at Somersby.[57] I see no hypocrisy here nor even incongruity but evidence of Tennyson's ability to inhabit more than one world at one time. He was timidly fearful of criticism yet highly idiosyncratic, conventional and unconventional, at times defying propriety as he transcended the barriers of time and space in his self-induced moments of 'trance.'[58] He avoided the public ceremony in Hallam's ancestral church, preferring his own, much later memorial to A. H. H. Within two weeks of the publication of *In Memoriam A. H. H.*, Tennyson figured at another ceremonial occasion, his own long-deferred marriage to Emily Sellwood. It was as if the prior union had to be broken before the later union could be consummated. Indeed, his second marriage was 'consecrated' – the word is Emily's – over the body of his first.[59] Tennyson had never before seen Hallam's tomb. The wedding visit to Clevedon Church was an act of exorcism; or rather, in the more gracious spirit of the participants, an incorporation of the dead friend into the living union.

From the tomb of Arthur the friend at Clevedon the Tennysons travelled to the tomb of Arthur the King at Glastonbury. The second station on their wedded pilgrimage seems in retrospect preternaturally apt. For it revived Tennyson's boyhood memories of Malory, his Hallam-linked associations with his own 'Morte d'Arthur,' and strengthened his still inchoate resolve to dedicate the second half of his creative life to his other great Arthur poem, *Idylls of the King*. *In Memoriam* begins with a funeral and ends with a marriage; the *Idylls* begins with a marriage and ends with a funeral; the one is about an incarnate spirit who assumes the form of a man; the other is about the friend who becomes a divine ghost.

The language of grief in *In Memoriam* still speaks to us directly and movingly, but the language of hope – particularly the hope of personal immortality – is for most of us the remotest of whispers. There are, of course, historical reasons why the more hopeful, religious portions of *In Memoriam* are less accessible to us than they were to the earlier readers of the poem. Our own obsessions have become secularized, and the tolerance that comes with increased distance has made it easier for us to appreciate the importance of the ghost in *Hamlet* than the ghost in *In Memoriam*. We are at the end of a transitional moment in our relation to the Victorians, largely free of the generational, self-serving hostilities of the Modernists but still too close to 'permit of very accurate delineation.' They are like us and unlike us, and at this point we may come closer to them by stressing difference.

Imagine an aged, intelligent poet talking to his Queen, also quite intelligent and aged. Both are seated, an unusual courtesy extended by the Queen to her Laureate in deference to his gout. The poet frets over the question of personal immortality, exactly as he had fretted some four decades ago in *In Memoriam*, and he is aggrieved to think that in some future state old friends might not recognize one another. The Queen comforts him (the date is 7 August 1883, the place is Prince Albert's unchanged room) by quoting his own lines,

> Eternal form shall still divide
> The eternal soul from all beside;
> And I shall know him when we meet. (47.6–8)

This time there is no need for her to alter pronouns, for 'him' perfectly suits the separate objects of their love. Tennyson tells her a true-life story, as the one I am now recounting is true. He tells the Queen that

> he had been bathing and had taken his dog with him, and that when he came naked from the water his dog did not know him; this suggested to him that recognition might be difficult if not impossible in heaven.[60]

All the scholarship in the world can take us no closer to *In Memoriam* than this literal-minded parable of the perplexed dog and the naked man. The dog is to the man in the parable as the mortal poet is to his progressively divinized friend in the poem. The second half of *In Memoriam* is about how the two will know each other when they meet.

Hallam makes his last mortal appearance in *In Memoriam* on the lawn of Somersby in Section 89. Somersby was the scene of the poet's earliest associations and had been hallowed by later visits from Hallam. Tennyson never fully possessed persons or places until he had lost them, his 'passion of the past' being his strongest emotion. But in Section 89 that passion uncharacteristically manifests itself not in regret but in the perfect fulfillment of an 'all-golden afternoon' (l. 25). One of the finest lyrics in *In Memoriam*, it is also one of the least-known, overshadowed by its companion lyric, Section 95, to which it is closely linked in subject and setting. But this is a sun-drenched poem, 'the landscape winking through the heat' (l. 16) of the 'livelong summer day' (l. 31). Section 95 opens in darkness on the Somersby lawn and transpires at night, except for its visionary center. Section 89 is rooted in the poetry of earth and its secular contentments:

> Witch-elms that counterchange the floor
>   Of this flat lawn with dusk and bright;
>   And thou, with all thy breadth and height
> Of foliage, towering sycamore;
>
> How often, hither wandering down,
>   My Arthur found your shadows fair,
>   And shook to all the liberal air
> The dust and din and steam of town:
>
> He brought an eye for all he saw;
>   He mixt in all our simple sports;
>   They pleased him, fresh from brawling courts
> And dusty purlieus of the law.
>
> O joy to him in this retreat,
>   Inmantled in ambrosial dark,
>   To drink the cooler air, and mark
> The landscape winking thro' the heat:
>
> O sound to rout the brood of cares,
>   The sweep of scythe in morning dew,
>   The gust that round the garden flew,
> And tumbled half the mellowing pears!
>
> O bliss, when all in circle drawn
>   About him, heart and ear were fed
>   To hear him, as he lay and read
> The Tuscan poets on the lawn:
>
> Or in the all-golden afternoon
>   A guest, or happy sister, sung,
>   Or here she brought the harp and flung
> A ballad to the brightening moon. (ll. 1–28)

Fresh from the dusty Inns of Court (one recalls Manley Hopkins's Amaryllis of the Bar), reading Dante and Petrarch in the Lincolnshire countryside, Hallam figures as a sort of proto Scholar-Gipsy, a half-mythic guest in a very real social setting. In the center of this richly realized pastoral, he takes on a borrowed substantiality and is more nearly realized as a human presence than anywhere else in *In Memoriam*. Foreshadowings of Arnold shade into reminiscences of

Keats (*Hyperion*, 3.35) in the lush closing stanzas, as the poet and his friend walk through meadows 'ankle deep with flowers.' Hallam is still anchored to the Somersby setting but has merged with the landscape, as mythic and enigmatic as the figure with soft hair who sits careless on Keats' granary floor. The last stanza is pure impressionism:

> We talk'd: the stream beneath us ran,
> The wine-flask lying couch'd in moss,
>
> Or cool'd within the glooming wave;
>     And last, returning from afar,
>     Before the crimson-circled star
> Had fall'n into her father's grave,
>
> And brushing ankle-deep in flowers,
>     We heard behind the woodbine veil
>     The milk that bubbled in the pail,
> And buzzings of the honied hours. (ll. 43–52)

The secular contentment of Section 89 gives way to the rising expectation of Section 93 ('Descend, and touch, and enter'), a prayer that is answered in Section 95 by Hallam's return from the dead. The poem opens at night, but the darkness is equivocal, impregnated with the 'silvery haze' of midsummer nights, the white-nights of the north. The lesser lights of the familial grouping on the lawn – the unwavering candles, the filmy moths, the glimmering flanks of the cattle couched in the middle distance – prepare us for the supernatural flash in the center of the poem. But mostly it is the 'dark arms' of the trees, laid in an embrace around the field, that herald the crossing over from the natural to the supernatural:

> By night we linger'd on the lawn,
>     For underfoot the herb was dry;
>     And genial warmth; and o'er the sky
> The silvery haze of summer drawn;
>
> And calm that let the tapers burn
>     Unwavering: not a cricket chirr'd:
>     The brook alone far-off was heard,
> And on the board the fluttering urn:
>
> And bats went round in fragrant skies,
>     And wheel'd or lit the filmy shapes
>     That haunt the dusk, with ermine capes
> And woolly breasts and beaded eyes;

> While now we sang old songs that peal'd
>     From knoll to knoll, where, couch'd at ease,
>     The white kine glimmer'd, and the trees
> Laid their dark arms about the field. (ll. 1–16)

The reader expects dark *branches*, not *arms*, but that would not do metrically. *Limbs* works well in point of metre and sense but ruins the poem. For *arms* explicitly crosses the border separating the animal from the vegetable worlds, and the touch implicit in the encircling arms prepares us for the greater transgression of line 34 ('The dead man touch'd me from the past'). The cattle 'couch'd at ease' on the hills, like quasi-human guests around a pastoral table, work to the same effect as the enfolding arms of the trees.[61]

The family group withdraws, leaving the poet in darkness and in the company of Hallam's letters – 'fall'n leaves which kept their green' (l. 23). Hallam's 'silent-speaking words' touch the poet from the past and lead to the mystical moment at the center of the poem. The vision opens with a strangely insistent literalism ('word by word, and line by line') that gives an almost palpable chill to the touch of the dead man. But the center of this central poem of *In Memoriam* is hollow; Tennyson's language falters in abstraction as he tries too hard and too frontally to express the inexpressible:

> So word by word, and line by line,
>     The dead man touch'd me from the past,
>     And all at once it seem'd at last
> The living soul was flash'd on mine,
>
> And mine in this was wound, and whirl'd
>     About empyreal heights of thought,
>     And came on that which is, and caught
> The deep pulsations of the world,
>
> Aeonian music measuring out
>     The steps of Time—the shocks of Chance—
>     The blows of Death. At length my trance
> Was cancell'd, stricken thro' with doubt.
>
> Vague words! (ll. 33–45)

Time, Chance and Death are the very stuff of literature, but they can be rendered only through the power of their effects, not by printing them in capitals on the page. Tennyson knows this, and his failure surprises us only in its magnitude and in the candor of its confession ('Vague words!'). He calls the climax of his poem not a vision but a doubtful trance, which half-redeems his failure. And he follows the hollow center with lines of natural description as fluent and powerful as those that open the poem. Indeed, the supernatural center holds at all only by virtue of the conviction it borrows from the beginning and the end. The white kine glimmering, the dark arms of the trees, even the old songs that peal from knoll to knoll haunt our memories after the 'Aeonian music' of the trance has faded into the limbo of failed poetry. The inimitable end repeats the beginning, and thus elides the empty center:

> Till now the doubtful dusk reveal'd
> > The knolls once more where, couch'd at ease,
> > The white kine glimmer'd, and the trees
> Laid their dark arms about the field:
>
> And suck'd from out the distant gloom
> > A breeze began to tremble o'er
> > The large leaves of the sycamore,
> And fluctuate all the still perfume,
>
> And gathering freshlier overhead,
> > Rock'd the full-foliaged elms, and swung
> > The heavy-folded rose, and flung
> The lilies to and fro, and said
>
> 'The dawn, the dawn,' and died away;
> > And East and West, without a breath,
> > Mixt their dim lights, like life and death,
> To broaden into boundless day. (ll. 49–64)

The half-light of the dawn seems at first blush indistinguishable from the half-light of the dusk at the start. But there has been a change both within Section 95 and in the movement of the larger poem, which this section mirrors in miniature. The tomb-like, deserted house of Section 7 is now a house of light and life; and the blank day that ends the earlier lyric has broadened into the boundless day that ends Section 95. Tennyson often symbolizes the work of mourning in *In Memoriam* as a faltering progress from darkness to light. This lyric that epitomizes *In Memoriam* opens on the word 'night' and ends with 'day.'

## 4

It is an easy leap from the mystical marriage of Section 95 to the earthly marriage that closes *In Memoriam*. Too easy a leap, alas, for while the divinization of Hallam proceeds apace, the later sections are more successful thematically than poetically, apart from the great spring lyric in which the poet's hopes and his creative powers reawaken, his regret blossoming into an April violet (Section 115).

The Epilogue contains some of Tennyson's very best and worst poetry and has always been something of a stumbling-block even for his keenest readers. A great deal rides on the wedding of Edmund Lushington to Tennyson's youngest sister, Cecilia, the poet himself giving away the bride on a bright Victorian forenoon. Much of the verse is mannered and trite, the 'wilt thou' asked and answered, the bridesmaids pelting the wedded pair with flowers, the guests toasting them too periphrastically with 'the foaming grape of eastern France' (l. 80). The reader nods, yet even the tritest wedding has elements of drama, if only for the valor of the risks undertaken. This particular wedding, however, has an additional element of drama that is barely hidden out of sight, for it is consecrated over a corpse, or rather over a congregation of corpses: as the bride stands before the altar, her feet rest 'on the dead; / Their pensive tablets round her head' (ll. 50–1). Tennyson's society-page account of the wedding is printed uncomfortably close to the obituaries. The memorial tablets surrounding the bride and groom are of course not 'pensive,' but we who contemplate them are. For there are other ghosts in addition to the underlying dead who are present at the wedding, and in this shadowier scene, it is the dead themselves who are pensive onlookers, above all the ghost of Arthur Hallam, himself once engaged to marry Tennyson's sister Emily as Tennyson himself, who serves as both reporter and father of the bride ('noon is near / And I must give away the bride' [ll. 41–2]), was engaged to another Emily at the time he wrote the Epilogue. Though we rarely laugh at funerals, we often cry at weddings, for the rituals of joining and parting, like all rituals, have much in common, as if all human ceremony descended from a common ancestral language. From this longer perspective, the funereal start and marital close of In Memoriam look surprisingly alike. The feet of 'Immortal Love,' who opened the poem and who created life in man, are 'on the skull which [He] hast made' (l. 8), just as the bride, who is about to procreate in the marriage bed, stands on the dead. As Peter Sacks points out, the marriage 'is described as though it were somehow a funeral.'[62] The newly wedded couple sign their names in the wedding register

> ...which shall be read,
> Mute symbols of a joyful morn,
> By village eyes as yet unborn...(ll. 57–9)

The poet-reporter has no need to say outright what needs no saying: the same register will be read when the newlyweds have become pensive tablets embedded in the aisles. But he says it anyway, through the indirection of a pun ('joyful morn'), a rare device in Tennyson, but fitting in a poem which invites the attendance of whatever 'loves to weep, / And hear the ritual of the dead'

(18.11–12). In a stanza of Emily Dickinsonian abruptness, the wedded couple set out from church on their new life, drawn by white horses:

> But they must go, the time draws on,
>   And those white-favour'd horses wait:
>   They rise, but linger; it is late;
> Farewell, we kiss, and they are gone. (ll. 89–92)

Gone where? Change the white horses to black, and they head 'toward Eternity.'

Years ago, before I realized that Death rode alongside the carriage with the Edmund Lushingtons, I was impatient with Tennyson for abandoning the greater griefs of *In Memoriam* for the lesser 'cheer' of its wedded close. I still regret the style but am freshly astonished by the cunning of a poet who invites so many ghosts to his sister's wedding. Tennyson himself is a highly enigmatic presence at the ceremony, in attendance retrospectively and prospectively as well as in the flesh on October 10, 1842. The marriage of his Cambridge friend and former Apostle to his sister Cecilia is of course a kind of stand-in for the marriage that never took place between the Apostle Hallam and Tennyson's sister Emily. Both widowhoods – Emily Tennyson's and Alfred's – undergo a symbolic annulment with Tennyson giving away his other sister to a surrogate Hallam, Edmund Lushington, whose character in the Epilogue strikingly resembles earlier characterizations of Hallam.[63] Nor can the Epilogue be dissociated from Tennyson's own marriage, celebrated immediately after the publication of *In Memoriam*, also to an Emily, who brought Tennyson 'the peace of God' and gave him the title of his poem.[64]

But the marriage that overrides all others and is both the origin and end of *In Memoriam* is the marriage of Alfred Tennyson to Arthur Hallam. This union, the true Epithalamion of *In Memoriam*, is consummated in the last third of the Epilogue and takes place in heaven where, strictly speaking, 'they neither marry, nor are given in marriage, but are as the angels of God' (Matthew 22:30). To the lesser marriage of the Lushingtons, Tennyson gives his lesser style; for his own marriage in heaven he reserves his greatest poetry – the single long rolling period that begins with the poet's retiring in line 105 and toward which everything in *In Memoriam* moves. The abrupt shift in style marks the shift in worlds:

> Again the feast, the speech, the glee,
>   The shade of passing thought, the wealth
>   Of words and wit, the double health,
> The crowning cup, the three-times-three,
>
> And last the dance; —till I retire: (l. 105)
>   Dumb is that tower which spake so loud,

And high in heaven the streaming cloud,
And on the downs a rising fire:

And rise, O moon, from yonder down,
　　Till over down and over dale
　　All night the shining vapour sail
And pass the silent-lighted town,

The white-faced halls, the glancing rills,
　　And catch at every mountain head,
　　And o'er the friths that branch and spread
Their sleeping silver thro' the hills;

And touch with shade the bridal doors,
　　With tender gloom the roof, the wall;
　　And breaking let the splendour fall
To spangle all the happy shores

By which they rest, and ocean sounds,
　　And, star and system rolling past,
　　A soul shall draw from out the vast
And strike his being into bounds. (ll. 101–24)

The earthly marriage, apart from its ghostly details, recalls the Victorian versifier who wrote the commonplace ending of 'The Two Voices.' The heavenly marriage, Tennyson believed, put him in league with Dante: '[In Memoriam] begins with a funeral and ends with a marriage – begins with death and ends in promise of a new life – a sort of divine comedy – cheerful at the close.'[65] Tennyson's comments on his own poetry are often offputting and more than a little odd. I am appalled by the notion of Dante's 'cheer,' and a provincial wedding that might barely make it into the society pages does not merit comparison with The Divine Comedy. Yet, however strange, Tennyson's remark is deeply revealing in a hauntingly garbled way, like the ancient Edison recording of his own voice. The marriage that puts Tennyson in mind of Dante is not the Lushingtons' but his own to Arthur Hallam. A shared love of Dante was one of the strongest bonds between them. Hallam had taught Italian to his fiancée Emily, and he spoke and wrote it elegantly. Dante was 'the master-mover' of his spirit,[66] and Tennyson much admired his translation of the sonnets from the Vita Nuova.[67] The 'promise of a new life' that ends In Memoriam refers not only to the conception taking place within the moonlit bridal chamber but to the vita nuova that Dante's poetry gave to his beloved Beatrice, as Tennyson's poem gives new life to Arthur Hallam. If Dante was a little crazy to enthrone Beatrice next to God, transforming her into a type of Christ, Tennyson was no more so in enthroning his Arthur. The whole world, Dante believed, was 'widowed' by her death, nor could he see her again until his own widowed race had been won.[68]

'Cheerful' at the close: on second glance the word is no more inappropriate to the end of In Memoriam than is the word Commedia in Dante's title. Tennyson was perfectly aware of the generic meaning of comedy as a story that ends happily with the reintegration of the hero into society. Although Hallam is the object of Tennyson's quest in In Memoriam, the poet himself is the hero. The Lushington wedding marks his coming in out of the cold to link hands in a comedic finale. 'I will not shut me from my kind' (Section 108.1), he writes shortly before the Epilogue, marking a little too explicitly his progress from the rain-soaked ghost of Section 7 to father of the bride. Nowhere else in In Memoriam do we feel closer to the actuality of the Victorian moment, to all its cluttered accoutrements and grandparently associations, than at the Lushington wedding. Yet nowhere else does Tennyson incorporate so many motifs from a classical genre, the epithalamion.[69] The earthly comedy ends on a sunlit noon, as it always does, with music, with feasting, with marriage – 'And last the dance.'

The poet then retires from the social group, as he had retired prior to the entranced moment in Section 95. But this time he rises above the festivities, above the now-silent church tower, above the earth itself and its oceans. This is his celestial marriage, the *divine* comedy at the very end of the poem. The father of the bride now clasps hands with his heavenly friend – 'That friend of mine who lives in God' (l. 140) – and in so doing weds the cosmos. The love-offering is now complete, and the immense procession that is In Memoriam comes to rest on the word *moves*.

# 4

# TENNYSON AND THE PASSING OF ARTHUR*

Every great poem springs from some generative moment that gives rise to all the rest. The generative moment of *Idylls of the King* comes at the very end of the poem as we now read it, although the lines are among the first that Tennyson drafted in his elegy to the fallen Arthur. We all recall the scene – if not from Tennyson, then from Malory – as the three Queens receive the wounded king into the barge and Bedivere, bereft of his lord, cries aloud,

> Ah! my Lord Arthur, whither shall I go?
> Where shall I hide my forehead and my eyes?
> For now I see the true old times are dead,
>
> . . . . . . . . . . . . . . . . . . . . . . . . . . . . . . . . . . . . . . . . . . . . . . . . . . . . . .
>
> Such times have been not since the light that led
> The holy Elders with the gift of myrrh.
> But now the whole Round Table is dissolved
> Which was an image of the mighty world,
> And I, the last, go forth companionless,
> And the days darken round me, and the years,
> Among new men, strange faces, other minds. (PA, ll. 396–406)[1]

I sometimes believe that the great world of Arthurian myth came into being solely to memorialize this primal scene of loss, the loss of a once-perfect fellowship in a once-perfect world. Bedivere's last three lines are a remarkable recreation in miniature of the great Anglo-Saxon elegy 'The Wanderer.' A millennium of traditional English elegy, together with keenest personal loss over the death of Arthur Hallam, flows in equal measure into *Idylls of the King*.

---

* An earlier version of this essay was read at the Conference on The Passing of Arthur at Barnard College on November 15, 1986. I have let stand a few remarks directly addressed to my audience.

Malory tells us that Merlin 'made the *Round Table* in token of the roundness of the world.'[2] Circles are made in order to be broken. In the springtime of Arthur's realm, Tennyson's Vivien, seductress of Merlin and the femme fatale of the *Idylls*, prophesies that her ancient sun-worship 'will rise again, / And beat the cross to earth, and break the King / And all his Table' (BB, ll. 451–3). Much later, in the bleak winterscape of Arthur's passing, her prophecy is fulfilled. Bedivere carries the King's shattered body to the water's edge, beside a ruined chapel topped with a broken cross (PA, ll. 174–7).[*] In this landscape of apocalyptic desolation – 'A land of old upheaven from the abyss / By fire, to sink into the abyss again' (PA, ll. 82–3) – the three Queens arrive for Arthur's uncertain embarkation to Avalon. There, the 'flower of kings' may perhaps find a land of eternal spring, a heaven-haven 'Where falls not hail, or rain, or any snow, / Nor ever wind blows loudly' (PA, ll. 428–9).[3] There, healed of his grievous wound, Arthur may perhaps re-embark for his second coming to Camelot.

'*Flos Regum Arthurus*': Tennyson took the epigraph for the *Idylls* from Joseph of Exeter. But if Arthur is the very Flower and Epitome of Kings, the bright epithet conceals a dark underside, for flowers, like all flesh, wither and die. From the first line of his Coming to the last line of his Passing, it remains a great open question whether Tennyson's Flower of Kings is an annual or a perennial.

More equivocal even than the question of Arthur's return is the question of whether he ever really walked among us in the first place. I raise here more than the vexed issue of Arthur's historicity, about which Tennyson read everything in print. I mean to suggest that the *idea* of Arthur as Tennyson envisioned him carries with it a strong supposition of nonbeing, of a ghostly presence made all the more vivid by virtue of its very absence. For the grand peculiarity of Tennyson's Arthur, in both *Idylls of the King* and *In Memoriam*, is that the shadow he casts is more real than his substance. In so penumbrating his hero, Tennyson remained true to that most memorable of epitaphs, carved on King Arthur's purported tomb at Glastonbury: HIC JACET ARTHURUS,

---

[*] The passage begins with the strong alliterative beat of Anglo–Saxon verse (the 'bare black cliffs clang'd'). But with the last two lines, after Arthur and Bedivere have exited the echoing chasm, the language, now pure Tennyson, softens and opens out into the long vowels and liquid *l*s of the level lake:

> Dry clash'd his harness in the icy caves
> And barren chasms, and all to left and right
> The bare black cliff clang'd round him, as he based
> His feet on juts of slippery crag that rang
> Sharp-smitten with the dint of armèd heels—
> And on a sudden, lo! the level lake,
> And the long glories of the winter moon. (PA, ll. 354–60)

REX QUONDAM, REXQUE FUTURUS – *The Once and Future King*. The phrase haunts us less for what it says than for what it leaves out, its total elision of an Arthurian present. The quick iambic trimeter – 'the once and future King' – propels us from Arthur's remote past directly to his return in an unspecified future; it is tight-lipped about Arthur here and now.

So, too, is Tennyson. At once the central and most elusive figure in the *Idylls*, Arthur exists in time and transcends time; he exists in time because we who imagine him live, move, and have our being in time; and he transcends time by virtue of inhabiting a perpetual past and an eternally promised future. Malory's Arthur is born after the normal nine-month term at an unspecified season. Tennyson's King, both a Christ figure and a solar deity, is born 'all before his time' (CA, l. 210) – preternaturally – on the night of the New Year, in the season of Epiphany. His Coming is a kind of Incarnation; his Passing evokes the Passion: a shadow in a field of skulls, the mortally wounded Arthur exclaims, 'My God, thou has forgotten me in my death: / Nay – God my Christ – I pass but shall not die' (PA, ll. 27–8). Malory's Arthur is killed in early summer, eight weeks and a day after Easter Sunday. Tennyson's Arthur passes as he comes, in mid-winter, when 'the great light of heaven / Burned at his lowest in the rolling year' (PA, ll. 90–1).

His birth, like his death, is shrouded in mystery. That mystery is deepened, not dispelled, by the genealogical riddling of Merlin: 'From the great deep to the great deep he goes' (CA, l. 410). According to one account in 'The Coming,' Arthur's purported parents are the dark-haired, dark-eyed Uther and Ygerne; but Arthur, as befits a sun-king and the Son of God, 'is fair / Beyond the race of Britons and of men' (CA, ll. 329–30). Of uncertain pedigree, he is also without progeny. Arthur, that is, exists outside genealogy; outside history; perhaps also outside humanity – 'Beyond the race...of men.'[4]

Tennyson more than once hints that Arthur is illusory, conjured into being by magicians like himself, just as Merlin, Arthur's architect and wizard, conjures Camelot into being. We first see Camelot through the dazzled eyes of Gareth, the spires of the dim rich city appearing and disappearing in the shifting mists. Gareth rides through city-gates that depict

> New things and old co-twisted, as if Time
> Were nothing, so inveterately, that men
> Were giddy gazing there. (GL, ll. 222–4)

A great peal of music stops Gareth dead in his tracks, and Merlin's mystifications compound his confusion:

> For an ye heard a music [says Merlin], like enow
> They are building still, seeing the city is built
> To music, therefore never built at all,
> And therefore built forever. (GL, ll. 271–4)

Tennyson here draws on the myth, old as cities themselves, of the city as a sacred center, an *axis mundi* where heaven and hell intersect. Camelot is supernatural in origin, supertemporal in duration. Like Troy, which rose to the music of Apollo's lyre, Camelot is 'built to music.' But since, as Saint Paul warns, we can have 'no continuing city' here on earth (Hebrews 13.14), Camelot is never finally built. Yet the ideal that animates it predates its founding and will survive its fall, and hence the city is 'built forever.' Camelot embodies in stone the same paradox that Arthur embodies in flesh. A Byzantium of the artist-sage's imagination, Camelot, like its king, triumphs over time by never having entered time; its fall is as purely illusory as its founding.

Arthur is the point of focus at which the idealisms of all other characters in the *Idylls* converge; as their belief in Arthur's authority and reality breaks down, the king and his fair city vanish into the mists from which they first emerged. Bedivere, the last believer, companionless on the desolate verge of the world, watches Arthur dwindle to a mere speck on an empty horizon, his death-pale, death-cold King departing for a paradise that can never be, in the faint hope of returning to a kingdom that never was.

Bedivere's lament, like much else in Tennyson's 'The Passing of Arthur,' finds its source in the final book of Malory's *Morte d'Arthur*. But Bedivere's last three lines, spoken as he goes forth companionless, have no source in Malory; nor could they have, for they arise from direct personal experience – the poet's own – of overwhelming loss at the death not of the mythical king, but of Arthur the flesh-and-blood friend of Alfred Tennyson – Arthur Henry Hallam, to whom Tennyson dedicated his other great Arthur poem: *In Memoriam [To:] A. H. H.*

Arthur Hallam's death was the single most important event in Alfred Tennyson's life. In Section VII of *In Memoriam* –

> Dark house, by which once more I stand
>   Here in the long unlovely street,
>   Doors, where my heart was used to beat,
> So quickly, waiting for a hand,
>
> A hand that can be clasp'd no more

– Tennyson pictures himself as a ghost, guiltily haunting Hallam's empty, tomblike house, until the blank day breaks on the bald London street. At the end of *Idylls of the King*, Tennyson again stands alone and Arthurless, this time on the desolate verge of the world, the sole survivor of the last dim weird battle of the West, an alien compelled to

>      go forth companionless,
>   And the days darken round me, and the years,
>   Among new men, strange faces, other minds (PA, ll. 404–6)

– lines that strike a persistent chord throughout Tennyson and Victorian elegy, and to which I find myself unable not to return. Tennyson's profoundly personal quest for reunion with Hallam in *In Memoriam* becomes, in *Idylls of the King*, a profoundly impersonal despair for the passing not only of a hero, but of civilization itself.

In a moment, a word about why Arthurian myth exerted so powerful a hold on Tennyson's imagination and on Victorian culture at large, but I still cannot quite let go of Bedivere. Holding on, after all, is what Arthur's story is all about. Perhaps we are all Bediveres in our need to preserve some relic of an idealized past, be it the sour shards of our infant blanket or the bejeweled hilt of Excalibur. The special pathos of Bedivere's Peter-like betrayal of his lord's command – to return the sword to the great deep – is that Arthur mistakes Bedivere's heroic loyalty to his memory for vulgar theft. The literal-minded Bedivere cannot see that the words of poets, not the hilts of swords, memorialize the past. To Bedivere is left the burden of perpetuating the King's story after all living witness to his presence is gone. In the 'white winter' of his old age, Bedivere narrates 'The Passing of Arthur,' serving as both actor and chronicler in the idyll in which he figures. As the idyll draws to a close, its various narrators themselves seem to age, like the poet himself, who began the poem in his early twenties and made the last of his myriad additions and revisions fifty-eight years later, within months of his death. In the later idylls, the legend of Arthur becomes self-perpetuating and cannot be confined to any single teller, be it Bedivere or that nameless Bard – 'he that tells the Tale,' Tennyson calls him – who is at times Malory, at times Tennyson himself, at times the great chain of Arthurian chroniclers and poets who came before him.

Self-reflexive in virtually every line, the *Idylls* not only recounts Arthur's story but also recreates the process by which myths are made. We see the process at work in scenes that recall the former splendor of the Round Table even as it goes up in flames. Thus Arthur, alone with the repentant Guinevere at Almesbury Convent, recalls the glorious world he believes her sin has wrecked:

> ...that fair Order of my Table Round,
> A glorious company, the flower of men,
> To serve as model for the mighty world,
> And be the fair beginning of a time. (G, ll. 460–3)

In the idyll that immediately follows 'Guinevere' – 'The Passing of Arthur' – Bedivere, as if he had overheard Arthur at Almesbury, incorporates Arthur's description of the Round Table into his own lament. You recall the words – the ones I cannot let go –

> But now the whole Round Table is dissolved
> Which was an image of the mighty world,
> And I, the last, go forth companionless... (PA, ll. 402–4)

Arthur's very words – the Round Table as image of the mighty world – have now become canonical, a part of his own story, transmitted whole, like verbal relics, from character to character and place to place. Bedivere suffers a kind of anxiety of posterity, for if he discards Excalibur,

> What record, or what relic of my lord
> Should be to aftertime, but empty breath
> And rumours of a doubt? (PA, ll. 266–8)

The dying Arthur is himself preoccupied in arranging, like the folds of a shroud, his own afterhistory. He commands Bedivere to fling Excalibur into the mere; then shapes through prophecy the legend of which he is himself the subject: 'And, wheresoever I am sung or told / In aftertime, this also shall be known' (PA, ll. 202–3).

Characters within the larger fiction of the *Idylls* generate lesser fictions within it – mirrors within mirrors that reflect the whole. The result is that as the realm sinks ever deeper into the abyss, it reemerges in retrospective glory. Tennyson's most daring use of retrospect for this purpose occurs in 'Guinevere,' the idyll least indebted to any source. Before Arthur arrives at the Convent, cruelly to denounce, then to forgive, Guinevere, a naïve young novice keeps vigil with the contrite Queen. Unaware of Guinevere's identity, the novice prattles about magical signs and wonders that, years ago, accompanied the founding of the Round Table 'before the coming of the sinful Queen' (G, l. 268). The novice's father, now dead, had served as one of Arthur's first knights, and her account of his recollections, although dating back only one generation, takes on the aura of a garbled legend barely recoverable from the past. The mystery of the King's birth, invested with the highest powers of Tennyson's imagination in 'The Coming of Arthur,' is here lowered in key to a folktale. Divinity lapses into popular superstition; and for an instant the city built to music threatens to become a Victorian Disneyland with fairy palaces and magical spigots gushing wine. The novice's fantastical, vulgarized account of the wonders of Arthur's coming serves, by contrast, to authenticate the 'original' wonders, themselves of course no less fictional than the novice's. So too her morally simplistic indictment of the 'sinful Queen' and of Lancelot enlarges our sympathy for the adulterous lovers, who are 'marred…and marked' (LE, l. 246) by their sin but, uncannily, grow in grace because of it. The ruins of Camelot recall the city arising in its initial splendor, just as Arthur's passing contains the possibility of his return. The reciprocal movements of rise and fall are held in perfect poise by the seasonal cycle to which all twelve idylls are linked: the founding of the Round Table in earliest spring, its flourishing to the point of rankness in the long, hot summer idylls, its falling into the sere and yellow leaf in the autumnal 'Last Tournament,' its ruin in the chill mid-winter of 'The Passing,' with a distant hope of renewal to come. Incorporating this cycle into its narrative structure, *Idylls of the King* is itself a kind of literary second coming of Arthur, a resurrection in Victorian England of the long sequence of Arthuriads extending back centuries before Malory and forward through Spenser, Dryden, Scott, and Tennyson. The poem takes on the quality of a self-fulfilling prophecy and validates itself, like Scripture, by foretelling in one idyll what it fulfills in the next, until at the end the nameless narrator foretells the survival of his own poem, a prophecy that our gathered presence here today triumphantly confirms.

Tennyson drafted his 'Morte d'Arthur' late in 1833, under the first terrible shock of Arthur Hallam's death, at age twenty-two, of a cerebral hemorrhage. They had met four years earlier, as undergraduates at Trinity College, Cambridge, and at the time of his death Hallam was engaged to Tennyson's sister Emily. Dead too young to have shaped a life in public, the gifted Hallam lived on posthumously as a prince of friends, a king of intellects, among his remarkable circle of acquaintance. The draft of 'Morte d'Arthur,' which Tennyson incorporated verbatim into the completed *Idylls* as 'The Passing of Arthur,' appears in the same notebook that contains the earlier sections of *In Memoriam*. The first-composed but last-in-sequence of the *Idylls* is sandwiched between Section XXX of *In Memoriam*, which commemorates the Tennyson family's first desolate Christmas at Somersby without Hallam, and Section XXXI, which depicts Lazarus rising from the dead. The physical placement of the 'Morte' between the anniversary of a death and of a resurrection graphically expresses the poet's longing.[5] At the end of his life, in the autobiographical 'Merlin and the Gleam,' Tennyson wrote:

> Clouds and darkness
> Closed upon Camelot;
> Arthur had vanished
> I knew not wither,
> The king who loved me,
> And cannot die. (ll. 75 80)

The 'king who loved me' is the friend who died on 15 September, 1833, and whose passing left the young Tennyson stranded 'among new men, strange faces, other minds.'

Poets, I believe, are impelled to write the same poem over and over again, in myriad different guises, just as Dante Gabriel Rossetti painted the same face again and again. At first glance, *In Memoriam* and *Idylls of the King* could not appear more unlike: the one is a deeply personal elegy, about the death of an actual friend, set in the contemporary moment and concerned with contemporary issues like the conflict between evolutionary science and religious faith; the other is a consciously archaic recreation of mythical figures from a world that never was. But at bottom elegy and idylls are, if not the same poem, variations on the same theme – Tennyson's single overriding theme – the theme of loss; or, as he phrased to himself in early boyhood, the 'Passion of the Past.'[6] This passion makes of Tennyson the archetypal English elegist, a belated Virgil[7] reincarnate in Victorian England. 'Tears, Idle Tears,' Tennyson's most Virgilian lyric, mourns with a wild regret 'the days that are no more.' The 'far-off world' often seemed to him 'nearer than the present' (Memoir, 1:171–2), the unseen more tangible than the seen.

That absence was more vivid to Tennyson's senses than presence is a singularity of his nature: 'it is the distance that charms me in the landscape, the picture and the past, and not the immediate to-day in which I move.'[8] If poets are born, not made, then Tennyson was a born Arthurian. His eldest son, Hallam Tennyson, namesake of Arthur Hallam, writes in the Memoir, 'What he called "the greatest of all poetical subjects" perpetually haunted him' (2:125). Tennyson himself tells us that 'the vision of Arthur as I have drawn him...had come upon me when, little more than a boy, I first lighted upon Malory' (Memoir, 2:128). Malory's Morte d'Arthur assuredly 'influenced' the Idylls, just as Arthur Hallam's sudden death assuredly 'inspired' Tennyson to write In Memoriam. But causality in the psyche is quite unlike causality in external nature. What ultimately determines what we do and become are those external accidents that are in accord with our inner nature. Malory matters less than the antecedent disposition that drew Tennyson so early and powerfully to the myth of Arthur; Hallam matters less than the antecedent disposition that caused Tennyson to mourn so obsessively and so long for his absent friend, until poetry sprouted from his grave.

In Memoriam begins with a funeral and ends with a marriage-feast; the Idylls opens with a marriage – Arthur's to Guinevere – and ends with a funeral. Elegy and idyll are bound by a deep inner complementarity. Hallam Tennyson was the first to point out the curious sandwiching of the 'Morte d'Arthur' between two of the earliest sections of the elegy to Arthur Hallam. Mourning, at which Tennyson was something of a professional, is the ritual by which we learn both to hold on and let go, to clasp the dead and to live without them. In Memoriam and Idylls of the King, each written over a period of decades and then revised for decades more after their publication, are the most exquisitely protracted holdings-on and lettings-go in our literature. Late in In Memoriam Tennyson compresses a lifelong trauma into a phrase:

> ...and my regret
> Becomes an April violet,
> And buds and blossoms like the rest.

(Section 115, ll. 18–20)

Tennyson learned to fashion his greatest poetry out of the corpse of his friend, a process that quickened his guilt and preserved his sanity. Within months of

Hallam's death in Vienna – the bad tidings reached Tennyson early in October 1833 – he had begun *In Memoriam*; drafted 'Morte d'Arthur'; composed the originating lyric of *Maud* –

> Oh! that 'twere possible,
>   After long grief and pain,
> To find the arms of my true love
>   Round me once again![9]

– written 'Break, Break, Break'; and drafted his two greatest dramatic monologues, 'Ulysses' and 'Tithonus,' all centering on the experience of loss.

In the same year that Tennyson wrote his 'Morte d'Arthur,' Coleridge opined, 'As to Arthur, you could not by any means make a poem national to Englishmen. What have *we* to do with him?'[10] With a simplicity surprising in this subtlest of English critics, Coleridge took the common position – as common in 1833 as it is today – that Arthurian literature is escapist, irrelevant to the real concerns of the modern world. To this day the prejudice persists that Tennyson's doom-laden prophecy of the fall of the West is a Victorian-Gothic fairy-tale. The majority of Tennyson's contemporaries believed that the modern poet's proper business is to portray modern life, a position whose logic would have debarred Shakespeare from dramatizing the plight of King Arthur's ancient British neighbor and colleague, King Lear, or prevented Homer from depicting a war 'far on the plains of windy Troy' that had ended centuries before Homer was born. Tennyson was urged to write an epic not about knights in armor but about Work or Sanitation. He had to create the audience by which his poem came to be appreciated. And that is precisely what he did in the long intervals between drafting the 'Morte' in 1833–4, prefacing it with the embarrassingly apologetic frame-poem of 1842, and waiting another seventeen years before publishing in 1859 the next four *Idylls of the King*. Of course, the audience was latently present – Arthurians have always been among us – but they took a while to come out of the Victorian-Gothic closet. Arthur underwent a revival in the nineteenth century, particularly during the reign of Victoria, because England had become so quickly and radically *un*-Arthurian. Saint Augustine wrote *The City of God* as the barbarians were storming the gates of the earthly city; so, too, Camelot rose again as the railroads tore out the heart of ancient cities, the streets of Coketown shook with machines and the misery of exploited labor, the skies darkened with factory smoke, rivers ran foul with industrial wastes, and God most alarmingly disappeared from England's once green and pleasant land. The medieval revival, of which Arthurianism was a part, was not so much an attempt to escape the hard new world of industrial capitalism as a radical attempt to reform it. Tennyson's *Idylls*, Pugin's advocacy of Gothic architecture in *Contrasts*, Carlyle's *Past and Present*, Ruskin's 'Nature of Gothic' – all recreate the medieval past in order to remake the English present. The Victorian medievalizers are not idle dreamers but social critics, zealots, prophets. Reading Malory's *Morte d'Arthur* or *The Mabinogion* helps us understand Tennyson's *Idylls*, but so too does Lyell's *Principles of Geology* or Carlyle's *On Heroes*. Perhaps the surest road to Tennyson's Camelot is via another great Victorian epic that appeared in the bookshops alongside the *Idylls* in 1859, Darwin's *Origin of Species*. Evolution is an idea with two faces. One is smiling and beckons us onward and upward to ever higher forms; the other face is a death's head, bones encased in stone, a struggle ending in entropic extinction. Tennyson's two Arthur poems, in addition to their deeply personal content, are profound meditations on the leading idea of his century: evolution. In *In Memoriam*, Hallam figures as 'The herald of a higher race,' a 'noble type' of the perfected humanity into which we will ultimately evolve (CXVIII.14; Epilogue.138). In *Idylls of the King*, evolution undergoes a catastrophic reversal; mankind, in Arthur's anguished words, 'Reel[s] back into the beast' (LT, l. 125). Evolution has been tinged by Apocalypse. That three of the more notable long poems of the later nineteenth century – 'The Wreck of the Deutschland,' *The City of Dreadful Night*, and *Idylls of the King* – are apocalyptic in design and imagery is no more coincidental than that Yeats, who came to maturity at this time, is the great modern poet of Apocalypse. The fin-de-siècle became a type of the fin-du-monde. 'The blood-dimmed tide is loosed' might serve as epigraph for *Idylls of the King*, and the Rough Beast slouching toward Bethlehem in 'The Second Coming' is the perfect heraldic emblem for Arthur's last battle, which Tennyson himself eerily glossed as 'a presentment of human death' – of human *extinction* (Memoir, 2:132). The battle is fought in a landscape literally as old as the hills but as imminent as nuclear winter:

> A land of old upheaven from the abyss
> By fire, to sink into the abyss again;
> Where fragments of forgotten peoples dwelt,
> And the long mountains ended in a coast
> Of ever-shifting sand, and far away
> The phantom circle of a moaning sea.
>
> ............................................................
>
> Nor ever yet had Arthur fought a fight
> Like this last, dim, weird battle of the west.
> A deathwhite mist slept over sand and sea:
> Whereof the chill, to him who breathed it, drew
> Down with his blood, till all his heart was cold
> With formless fear.              (PA, ll. 82–98)

The Apocalypse is an ancient idea; evolution, when Tennyson wrote, a new one. The marriage of the two he entitled *Idylls of the King*.

# RUSKIN'S BENEDICTION: A READING OF
# *FORS CLAVIGERA*

The August 1872 issue of *Fors Clavigera* opens with a beautifully crisp frontispiece captioned, all in one long line, 'Part of the Chapel of St. Mary of the Thorn, PISA, as it was 27 years ago.' Centered directly below the line and completing the caption in almost pained brevity stand the words: 'Now in Ruins.' Drawing and caption are emblems of what is to come in the body of 'Benediction,' the most remarkable of the ninety-six public letters that comprise *Fors Clavigera*.

Ruskin's drawing of the chapel, done in his mid-twenties, depicts a Gothic idyll in stone, a delicate filigree of pinnacles and sculptured arcades, rose-windows and shaded gables all bathed in brilliant morning light. Frontispiece, caption, and ensuing text trace a continuous arc from felicity to enraged despair, the letter ending as Ruskin stares in incredulous horror while a Pisan stonemason sets to work demolishing the chapel. 'Now in Ruins' is Ruskin's summary judgment upon the fall of a Gothic paradise and the rise in its stead of the aggressively secular, industrialized Europe he detested. But the caption also carries a more private significance. For the long course of years between Ruskin's first drawing the chapel and witnessing its destruction[1] also saw the wreckage of his own hopes of ever gaining mastery over his disordered life. His books were becoming increasingly fragmentary and idiosyncratic. To the distress of his friends he had begun to write in *Fors* of the ominous 'storm-cloud of the nineteenth century' that was polluting the clear skies he had known in his childhood. The English public, he believed, had ignored or rejected his 'message,' and Rose La Touche, whom he had loved obsessively for over a decade, had refused his offer of marriage and was daily drifting further into unreason. The ruin of which Ruskin writes so movingly in Letter 20 is of himself as well as of 'St. Mary of the Thorn.'

The letter opens casually, with Ruskin drawing his reader into the attentive circle of 'My friends' and picking up, as friends will, the threads of interrupted

conversation. He had been spending the summer of 1872 in Venice, his rooms
at the Hotel Danieli only a moment's walk from the quay of the Ducal Palace
and almost in earshot of Mass at San Marco. In *Fors* of the previous month he
had complained angrily of the 'accursed whistling' (27:328) of a Lido steamer
boarding passengers at the quay. Now, resuming where he had left off and
seeking to reassure his readers of his equanimity, indeed of his sanity, he justifies
his calling the steamer 'accursed.' Ruskin's struggle to keep hold of himself
and in touch with his readers forms the inner drama of *Fors*, the writing of
which served both to focus and release his 'chronic fury.'[2] The measured pace
of his opening phrases –

> I never wrote more considerately [than in the last *Fors*]; using the
> longer and weaker word 'accursed' instead of the simple and proper
> one, 'cursed,' to take away, as far as I could, the appearance of unseemly
> haste—[3]

contrasts starkly with the cry of pain and rage soon to come. From its title
onwards 'Benediction' is about, and itself dramatically enacts, the contrary
states of accursedness and blessedness that Ruskin sets out to define. In form
it combines sermon and personal letter into a uniquely Ruskinian 'Epistle.' As
archaic in origin as the verses from the Epistle of James on blessing and cursing
that Ruskin takes as his main text, 'Benediction' is also as contemporary and
intimate as 'the beating of one's heart in a nightmare.'[4] The biblical allusions
threaded throughout the letter remind us that Ruskin's mother 'devoted him
to God' before he was born and that his first recorded words, preached from
an improvised pulpit of sofa pillows, were 'People, be good' (35:24–6). The
homiletic child was father of the socially conscious adult who, one year after
his inauguration at Oxford as Slade Professor of Fine Art in 1870, began writing
*Fors Clavigera* 'to quiet my conscience' (28:485) and founded the St. George's
Guild. The Guild's achievements were modest compared to Ruskin's ambitious
plans for slaying, almost single-handedly, the dragon of industrial capitalism
and converting England into pastoral communities of disciples, 'none wretched
but the sick; none idle but the dead.'[5] Many of the letters directly address the
affairs of this small band of followers, giving the series a distinct if unnoticed
kinship to the 'pastoral' Epistles of the New Testament. Traveling widely over
western Europe and the Mediterranean, proselytizing for the Guild in the pages
of *Fors* and preaching his message of co-operation and compassion, addressing
the members as their 'Master' and expounding on virtually every verse in the
Bible, Ruskin writes like a quixotic St. Paul who stayed in all the best hotels.
Often the letters reach beyond the small community of St. George's Guild to
a diaspora of kindred spirits spread over the English-speaking world. It is this
wider, invisible congregation that Ruskin summons through the monthly

readership of *Fors* and greets, at the start of 'Benediction,' with the salutation 'My Friends.'

The voice that speaks to us so easily and personally in the first few words of 'Benediction' quickly takes on a more formal, Episcopal air. Within a dozen lines our picture of Ruskin in his elegant Venetian rooms fades and we begin to hear a graver voice, Ruskin the exegete of Scripture intoning as if from an unseen pulpit these verses from the Epistle of James on the unruliness of our tongues: 'Therewith bless we God, and therewith curse we men; out of the same mouth proceedeth blessing and cursing. My brethren, these things ought not so to be.'

Overtly and covertly this text controls the letter and shapes even its seemingly wildest digressions, which in reality are not digressions at all but vivid exempla of Ruskin's sermon on the 'accursedness' of modern civilization and its assault upon his own sanity. That assault first manifests itself in the return of the Lido steamer as it abruptly invades Ruskin's main text and disrupts his exegesis of James. Like Ruskin, we are wrenched without transition from the measured commentary on blessing and cursing to the pulsating din outside his hotel window:

> Now, there is a little screw steamer just passing...; she is not twelve yards long, yet the beating of her screw has been so loud across the lagoon for the last five minutes, that I...left my work to go and look.

There follows a passage of such startling immediacy that Ruskin seems to step through the frame of his own narrative and enter the quayside scene he had been observing from his window the instant before. His Biblical commentary, first displaced by the screw steamer, further recedes as he recounts an incident set grammatically in the past but charged with the psychological urgency of the immediate present:

> Before I had finished writing that last sentence, the cry of a boy selling something black out of a basket on the quay became so sharply distinguished above the voices of the always debating gondoliers, that I must needs stop again, and go down to the quay to see what he had got to sell. They were half-rotten figs, shaken down, untimely, by the mid-summer storms: his cry of 'Fighiaie' scarcely ceased, being delivered, as I observed, just as clearly between his legs, when he was stooping to find an eatable portion of the black mess to serve a customer with, as when he was standing up. His face brought the tears into my eyes, so open, and sweet, and capable it was; and so sad. I gave him three very small halfpence, but took no figs, to his surprise: he little thought how cheap the sight of him and his basket was to me, at the money; nor what this fruit 'that could not be eaten, it was so evil,' sold cheap before

the palace of the Dukes of Venice, meant, to any one who could read
signs, either in earth, or her heaven and sea.

The reader is caught up in the urgency of the narrative, with its absolute fidelity
to perceived detail,[6] yet is detained and puzzled by a suggestion of significance
far in excess of any explicit statement. The boy, the Palace, the rotten fruit,
the well-dressed Englishman in tears – these are signs of the times that Ruskin
entreats us to read. They form part of the parable-like 'autobiographical myth'[7]
that parallels and illuminates the biblical commentary on the letter's surface.

Twenty years earlier, in *The Stones of Venice*, Ruskin had written of the Ducal
Palace as the center of the most sacred complex of civic and ecclesiastical
architecture in the world (9.38). He had especially praised the carving, on the
southwest corner of the Palace, of Adam and Eve gathering fruit beneath a
fig-tree (10:359). And in one of the letters of *Fors* he transcribed the verse
from Micah carved on the cornerstone of the Palace, as if in promise of earthly
plenty for all who live in the city: 'Every man shall dwell under his vine and
under his fig-tree' (29:34). Ruskin had educated a whole generation of readers
in biblical typology and in the iconography of Christian art, especially the art
and architecture of Venice. 'Benediction' is part of this larger exegetical
enterprise, and if we now falter over Ruskin's many scriptural allusions, his
contemporaries could virtually read them as they ran. The sad-faced boy bent
over his blighted figs, in front of the deserted Palace and beneath a statue of
Adam and Eve, themselves gathering figs, is an animate image of the Fall. The
latent obscenity of the cry shouted from between the boy's legs[8] clashes with
the open innocence of his features. Rising and stooping, half-fallen and half-
risen, he is scarcely redeemed by Ruskin's 'three very small halfpence.' Yet the
boy is seen through compassionate eyes: Ruskin's gesture of bestowing the
pennies but taking nothing in return suggests a furtive blessing. Like the city
whose corrupt splendor surrounds him, the boy retains a kind of faded sanctity,
marked on his face by its mixture of sadness and sweetness. He is a doomed
angel who has fallen into an accursed world where, even on the steps of its
grandest palace, the fruit 'could not be eaten, it was so evil.'[9]


## 2

Ruskin wrote 'Benediction' during odd intervals on three successive days. The
dates of 3$^{rd}$, 4$^{th}$, and 5$^{th}$ *July* at the head of each of the sections suggest the
spontaneity of a journal or diary, a spontaneity shared by all the letters despite
their being addressed to a general audience on a wide range of issues. No
quality of *Fors* is more remarkable than its disregard of the conventional
boundaries separating the public from the private. The first section moves
from biblical exegesis to the seeming digression of the figs. The second section

also opens with exegesis but ends – or rather, abruptly aborts itself – in a nightmare of private pain.

Accuracy of language, like clarity of sight, was for Ruskin at bottom a moral faculty, and in opening the second section of 'Benediction' by drawing a precise distinction between swearing and cursing he returns to the larger labor or exegesis which opened the letter and which lies at the heart of all his writings. But his extreme exactitude of articulation suggests an element of stress, like the hyper-enunciation of a parent trying to control his anger at a child. In a sharply pointed contrast Ruskin observes that swearing is 'invoking the witness of a Spirit to an assertion you wish to make,' whereas cursing is

> invoking the assistance of a Spirit, in a mischief you wish to inflict. When ill-educated and ill-tempered people clamorously confuse the two invocations, they are not, in reality, either cursing or swearing; but merely vomiting empty words indecently.

In the final phrase Ruskin manages to refine raw anger into wit. When still in control, the invective in *Fors* must have given Ruskin as much pleasure to write as it gives us to read, as in his comparison of the expanding British Empire to a 'slimy polype, multiplying by involuntary vivisection, and dropping half-putrid pieces of itself wherever it crawls or contracts' (27:451). Elsewhere, as in the great Christmas Letter of 1874, Ruskin's release of invective pales before our sense of his increasing isolation and pain, standing alone

> in the midst of this yelping, carnivorous crowd, mad for money and lust, tearing each other to pieces, and starving each other to death, and leaving heaps of their dung and ponds of their spittle on every palace floor and altar stone.[10]

In passages such as these, Ruskin's invective is itself a form of curse. The second section of 'Benediction' culminates in a curse upon modern civilization and assaults the reader like a shriek of pain.

Ruskin prepares for that assault by examining the two principal forms of malediction in English: the curse upon the spirit – 'God damn your soul' – and the curse upon the bodily members – 'God damn your eyes and limbs!' (The words still startle, despite all our liberties in print and film.) What do we in fact mean when we call down upon someone the blinding of an eye or the crippling of a limb? In the final third of the letter Ruskin will portray a living illustration of his text, two spiritually blind and palsied girls riding beside him in a closed railway carriage. But here he is intent upon understanding the malediction on the eyes and limbs, and in order to do so he contrasts the act of cursing with its scriptural opposite, blessing, as in Christ's 'Blessed are the eyes which see the things that ye see,' or Isaiah's promise that in Zion the lame man shall 'leap as an hart, and the tongue of the dumb sing.'[11] At this point we come upon a violently disjointed paragraph that itself embodies the contrary states of blessedness and cursedness that have all along been Ruskin's central subject. The paragraph can no more be abbreviated than a scream can be aborted in midcourse:

> Again, with regard to the limbs, or general powers of the body. Do you suppose that when it is promised that 'the lame man shall leap as an hart, and the tongue of the dumb sing'—(Steam-whistle interrupts me from the *Capo d'Istria*, which is lying in front of my window with her black nose pointed at the red nose of another steamer at the next pier. There are nine large ones at this instant,—half-past six, morning, 4th July,—lying between the Church of the Redeemer and the Canal of the Arsenal; one of them is ironclad, five smoking fiercely, and the biggest,— English and half a quarter of a mile long,—blowing steam from all manner of pipes in her sides, and with such a roar through her funnel— whistle number two from *Capo d'Istria*—that I could not make any one hear me speak in this room of benediction without an effort), do you suppose, I say, that such a form of benediction is just the same as saying that the lame man shall leap as a lion, and the tongue of the dumb mourn? Not so, but a special manner or action of the members is meant in both cases: (whistle number three from *Capo d'Istria*; I am writing on, steadily, so that you will be able to form an accurate idea, from this page, of the intervals of time in modern music. The roaring from the English boat goes on all the while, for bass to the *Capo d'Istria*'s treble, and a tenth steamer comes in sight round the Armenian Monastery)— a particular kind of activity is meant, I repeat, in both cases. The lame man is to leap, (whistle fourth from *Capo d'Istria*, this time at high pressure, going through my head like a knife) as an innocent and joyful creature leaps, and the lips of the dumb to move melodiously: they are to be blest, so; may not be unblest even in silence; but are the absolute contrary of blest, in evil utterance. (Fifth whistle, a double one, from *Capo d'Istria*, and it is seven o'clock, nearly; and here's my coffee, and I must stop writing. Sixth whistle—the *Capo d'Istria* is off, with her crew of morning bathers. Seventh,—from I don't know which of the boats outside—and I count no more.)

The verse from James that opened the letter – 'out of the same mouth proceedeth blessing and cursing' – here comes to life as two antiphonal voices issuing simultaneously *out of Ruskin's own mouth*. With absolute spontaneity yet absolute mastery, he composes a poetry of controlled cacophony, 'scoring' the paragraph as a duet of divided consciousness: the lips of his 'blessed,' episcopal self 'move melodiously' outside the parentheses while his 'accursed' self rages discordantly within them, outshouting the steam-whistles that mark, as he bitterly says, 'the intervals of time in modern music.'

The paragraph is intentionally unintelligible if we read it line-by-line down the page. For its 'meaning' is precisely the violent fragmentation of meaning in the modern world, a fragmentation Ruskin directly induces in his reader. Throughout *Fors* he portrays not only the passing scene outside his window but the inmost movements of his own mind as it is shaped – and threatened – by that scene. As vital as the act of seeing always was for Ruskin – 'To see clearly is poetry, prophecy, and religion, – all in one' (5:333) – his ultimate subject in *Fors* is not sight but insight, his own distraught consciousness as it engages the world. Through lightning transitions, allusions, backtrackings, shifts in tone, tense, and voice he obliterates the gap between self and scene, near and distant, present and past. The *Capo d'Istria* paragraph aggressively amplifies all these effects. The movement in and out of the parentheses locates us in two worlds, two times, two states of consciousness at once; the result is a dizzying immediacy akin to 'zooming' in photography. Earlier in the letter Ruskin had achieved a similar effect by telescoping the time between his observing and recording the same event: 'Before I had finished writing that last sentence...I must needs stop again, and go down to the quay.' Here words so closely trail the things they describe they seem to overtake the depicted actuality.

The reader feels an uncanny closeness to the events described in *Fors*, a proximity that in 'Benediction' becomes progressively menacing. In the opening section the threatened intrusion appeared in the form of the little screw steamer first heard at some distance crossing the lagoon. In the *Capo d'Istria* paragraph the intrusion intensifies into assault. Outside the parentheses the quiet cadences of the biblical exegesis serve as a neutral ground intensifying the infernal treble of the steam-whistles within the parentheses. We follow the melodious tones of the main text with the dozing half-attention we give to a voice from a distant pulpit; the phrases are long, the content familiar and intentionally untaxing, the elegant episcopal voice poised in the middle of a question and intoning the word *sing* when the first whistle cuts the text in two. In the inferno inside the parentheses, where the blessed do not sing but the damned shriek, the nine ships are spread out – like symbolic markers charting the distance dividing salvation from destruction, *blessing* from *cursing* – between the Church of the Redeemer and the Canal of the Arsenal. The significance of the location is obscured by the headlong rush of the paragraph and, for the modern reader, is likely to register only subliminally, if at all. But Ruskin had made his readers into *Dantisti*; only a few weeks earlier in *Fors Clavigera* he had translated Canto XXI of the *Inferno*, with its hideously graphic depiction of sinners plunged into a lake of pitch that boils 'as, in the Venetian Arsenal, the pitch boils in the winter time.'[12] Here, as always, Ruskin is topographically exact. Seen from the angle of his hotel window the ships were stationed exactly as described. Yet Ruskin could have oriented the reader in a thousand other ways, choosing instead the most symbolically resonant landmarks available to his purpose in all of Venice.

The speed with which Ruskin wrote *Fors Clavigera*, the seemingly anarchic spontaneity of most of the letters and the extreme stress of some, especially of 'Benediction,' may make my assertion of their underlying order appear unconvincing indeed. Yet their unity is not illusory, their spontaneity not affected. *Fors* is the inspired metamorphosis of chance into design. The first word of the title means *chance* or *accident*, but the full title, drawn primarily from Horace's *Odes* and suggesting 'implacable fate, the nail-bearer,' is heavy with the sense of fatality underlying all chance. Sheer chance, perhaps, determined that the *Capo d'Istria* should blast off in the middle of Ruskin's exegesis of Isaiah, but only the synthesizing genius of his imagination could so contrive a sentence that the first cacophonous blast falls on the word *sing*. So too the blessed lame man, as if cued into motion by the word *leap*, himself leaps in a perfect arc over the third parenthesis – the steam-whistle meanwhile slicing through Ruskin's head like a knife – and lands in innocent joy on the far side of Ruskin's agony.

Time-keeping in the paragraph begins at 'half-past six, morning, 4th July' and ends at 'seven o'clock, nearly; and here's my coffee, and I must stop writing.' The modulations in tone have been extraordinary – from Isaiah's vision of the blessed, to the *Inferno*, to the Prufrockian end ('and here's my coffee') in only a few lines. Like the sounding of the seven trumpets in Revelation, the count of the steam-whistles stops with the seventh blast, and by the final sentence the biblical exegesis has been wholly displaced by the parenthetical intrusion, from which there is no return to the main body of the letter. As if enclosed within his own parenthesis, Ruskin ends on a perfect ambiguity: he has ceased to enumerate the whistles and, in the midst of the annihilating din, he has ceased to matter: '– and I count no more.)'

### 3

A wide margin of white space follows 'these broken sentences,' and after a day's interruption Ruskin resumes the letter as if awakened from a bad dream. He steps back from the excruciating scene at his window and describes instead, in minute and loving detail, the painting of a sleeping princess he had first seen in Venice three years earlier. Carpaccio's *Dream of St. Ursula* figures in 'Benediction' as Ruskin's ideal pictorial representation of blessedness. His description is charged with an intensity and felicity that seem to arise from his deepest experience. For Ruskin had begun to see in the legend of St. Ursula, which he retold at length in *Fors,* parallels with the life of Rose La Touche. Ursula had been courted by a heathen prince. The young Rose, much troubled by Ruskin's growing 'heathenism,' had deferred his marriage proposal for three years, as Ursula had deferred the proposal of her prince. In the deathlike repose of the dreaming princess, whose hair and eyes and lips he drew in countless studies while closeted with the painting in a private room in the Galleria dell' Academia, he saw a prefiguration of Rose's death. A few months before Rose died, emaciated and insane at the age of twenty-five, Ruskin sketched her in delicate profile, her head down-tilted, eyes half-closed, as if in sleep, perhaps in death.[*]

Even before he had first met Rose as a child of ten, their meeting had been prefigured thirteen years earlier, in 1845, in the Church of San Martino in Lucca. There he saw, and never forgot, Jacopo della Quercia's exquisitely sculpted effigy of the young bride Ilaria di Caretto. In his close-up study of her head, drawn in the same year as his profile of the dying Rose, he renders della Quercia's delicate chiseling of a lock of her hair as if it were still moist from the fever flush of death. And he transposes the fillet that rings Ilaria's forehead

Figure 3: John Ruskin, *Portrait of Miss Rose La Touche,* 1874.

---

[*] Her shoulders are bare; no trace of clothing is visible; nor is there any hint of her breasts. Tim Hilton suggests, rightly, I believe, that Rose was anorexic, a suggestion reinforced by her years of fasting as a spiritual penance. Anorexia has yet to be linked as a cause or effect

Figure 4: John Ruskin, copy of Carpaccio's *The Dream of Saint Ursula*, 1876.

into the lace-like coronet that encircles Rose's hair. Carpaccio's dreaming princess, della Quercia's effigy of the young Ilaria, and the dying Rose: three sister-images compose the elegiac triptych underlying the most powerfully felt paragraphs of Ruskin's 'Benediction.'[13]

Ruskin's description of Ursula's sunlit bedroom, her clothing, her features, is literally a labor of love, a protracted exegetical ecstasy in which not a tuft of fabric or tone of flesh escapes his attention. In the rigid, unbending line of Ursula's body and bedclothes he foresaw Ursula's grave and Rose's death. Carpaccio in fact foretells the impending death of Ursula: a diminutive Angel of Death stands in her bedroom doorway bearing a palm leaf in his right hand and in his left, a shroud. Her feet lie stiffly beneath her bedclothes. Ruskin takes Carpaccio's hint:

> The young girl lies straight, bending neither at waist nor knee, the sheet
> rising and falling over her in a narrow unbroken wave, like the shape of
> the coverlid of the last sleep, when the turf scarcely rises. (27:344)

The sentence undulates, evoking the breath of life even as it foreshadows death. The turf *rises*, as if from a breath beneath.

---

of psychosis. However, it frequently has consequences in addition to emaciation: the suppression of menstruation and underdevelopment of the breasts. With cruel irony Ruskin's deepest wish had been granted: Rose died half-woman, half child. (See Hilton, *John Ruskin: The Later Years* [New Haven and London: Yale University Press, 2000], p. 26.)

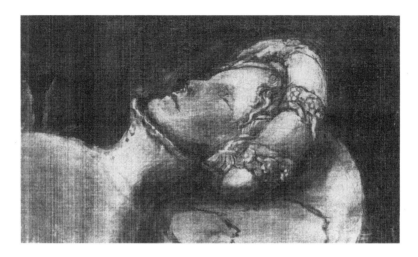

Figure 5: John Ruskin, *Study of the Head of Ilaria di Caretto*, from the effigy by Jacopo della Quercia, 1874.

The Angel of Death, as Ruskin describes him, enters Ursula's bedchamber without haste, his small body casting a shadow, as if he were mortal. Ursula has dreamed him into being, foreseeing as she sleeps her own martyrdom and marriage to Christ, who is to be her only spouse. A month after writing 'Benediction' Ruskin saw Rose on the estate of mutual friends. 'His last words to me were a blessing,' she wrote:

> I felt too dumb with pain to answer him.... When we see 'face to face' in that Kingdom where love will be perfected and yet there will be no marrying or giving in marriage we shall understand one another. Meantime God cannot have meant nothing but pain to grow out of the strange link of love that still unites us.[14]

Among its many public and private meanings, 'Benediction' is a veiled tribute to Rose, a tribute darkened by forebodings of her death. Soon after she died Ruskin wrote in *Fors* that Carpaccio's 'lesson' in the St Ursula series is that no bridegroom on earth rejoices over his bride 'as they rejoice who marry not, nor are given in marriage, but are as the angels of God, in Heaven' (28:746). Ruskin here alludes to the same verse in Matthew that Rose had echoed in refusing him.[15] And the very last letter of *Fors* is a thinly disguised requiem for Rose, opening and closing with her name.

Ruskin's image of the sleeping Rose-Ursula comes at the mid-point of 'Benediction,' the still center of the letter where the princess 'dreams...with blessed eyes that need no earthly dawn.' Her bedroom is portrayed as a tomb, a marriage-chamber, a shrine.

Sermons contain *exempli*: Ruskin's emblem of Life-in-Death in 'Benediction' is the sleeping St. Ursula; his emblem of 'accursedness' comes in the next paragraph, in an enclosed railway carriage which Ruskin uncomfortably shares in stony silence with two miserable American girls en route to Verona. In Ruskin's eyes, the girls are parodic incarnations of Death-in-Life, adolescent Medusas who writhe like serpents in an indolent dance of death. Travelling with all the comforts of the modern world, passing through an exquisite landscape of vine-clad hills, they embody the biblical texts that underlie the letter: 'accursed' limbs once whole but now palsied and lame, unblessed eyes blind to the sights outside their carriage window, tongues grown sullen and dumb. The stigma of their mortality clings to them as do the twice-repeated 'flies and dust,' and like the novels they tear apart page by page, they seem themselves to be in some slow, self-tormenting process of decomposition:

> By infinite self-indulgence, they had reduced themselves simply to two pieces of white putty that could feel pain. The flies and the dust stuck to them as to clay, and they perceived, between Venice and Verona, nothing but the flies and the dust. They pulled down the blinds the moment they entered the carriage, and then sprawled, and writhed, and tossed among the cushions of it, in vain contest, during the whole fifty miles, with every miserable sensation of bodily affliction that could make time intolerable. They were dressed in thin white frocks, coming vaguely open at the backs as they stretched or wriggled; they had French novels, lemons, and lumps of sugar, to beguile their state with; the novels hanging together by the ends of string that had once stitched them, or adhering at the corners in densely bruised dog's-ears, out of which the girls, wetting their fingers, occasionally extricated a gluey leaf. From time to time they cut a lemon open, ground a lump of sugar backwards and forwards over it till every fibre was in a treacly pulp; then sucked the pulp, and gnawed the white skin into leathery strings for the sake of its bitter. Only one sentence was exchanged in the fifty miles, on the subject of things outside the carriage (the Alps being once visible from a station where they had drawn up the blinds).
>
> 'Don't those snow-caps make you cool?'
> 'No—I wish they did.'
> And so they went their way, with sealed eyes and tormented limbs, their numbered miles of pain.
> There are the two states for you, in clearest opposition; Blessed, and Accursed.

One final image of accursedness remains – the smashing of the marble cross atop Santa Maria della Spina – and with that annihilating act Ruskin closes

'Benediction.' For over six centuries, he writes, the chapel had stood on the banks of the Arno, housing a relic from the crown of thorns and receiving the prayers of sailors as they headed for the open sea. Ruskin was drawing the cross for his Slade lectures at Oxford when he saw 'the workman's ashamed face, as he struck the old marble cross to pieces. Stolidly and languidly he dealt the blows,—down-looking.' The face of the fig-boy was sad but 'open and sweet' – half-fallen and half-graced – but the stonemason's face is wholly unredeemed, except for its mark of shame, and the consequences of his work are wholly irremediable.

The dehumanizing effect of work in the modern world is one of Ruskin's great themes in *Fors*, and two of his chief aims in founding the St. George's Guild were to end industry's assault upon the environment, natural and urban, and to make work fulfilling rather than crippling for the individual laborer. The pain Ruskin conveys at the destruction of the chapel is not an antiquarian's regret over the loss of a landmark but outrage at the misdirection of modern labor that, under the guise of public works, is intrinsically brutalizing and destructive of the human past. The many strands of 'Benediction' all draw together in these closing sentences: the startling curse upon the eyes and limbs in the previous section has now been twice embodied in the action of the letter, first in 'the sealed eyes and tormented limbs' of the writhing girls and finally in the downcast eyes of the guilty stonemason, his 'pair of human arms out of employ' because 'now in 1872' the world rows by steam (a reference back to the *Capo d'Istria*), digs by steam and worships steam.

Like Paul concluding his Epistles, Ruskin ends Letter 20 with a benediction. The complimentary close – 'Believe me, faithfully yours' – is at once conventionally valedictory and distinctly liturgical in tone. We can take the redoubled close as elegant variations on *sincerely yours*; or we can find ourselves compelled by the force of the immediately preceding words – 'the God of their Fathers' – to hear the Pauline plea for belief in *believe me* and for faith in *faithfully yours*. Of Ruskin's many voices in 'Benediction' – preacher, social critic, elegist, exegete, art critic, diarist, tourist, Master of St. George's Guild – none carries more authority than the voice that blesses us at the very end. The child who began his ministry with 'People, be good' here speaks in the name of his heavenly Father; and it is the mark of Ruskin's greatness that he *can* so speak and still strike us as triumphantly sane:

A costly kind of stone-breaking, this, for Italian parishes to set paupers on! Are there not rocks enough of Apennine, think you, they could break down instead? For truly, the God of their Fathers, and of their land, would rather see them mar his own work, than his children's.

Believe me, faithfully yours,

JOHN RUSKIN

# 6

# WATER INTO WINE: THE MIRACLE OF RUSKIN'S *PRAETERITA*[1]

Forty years ago, at an exhibition of Ruskin memorabilia, I was drawn to a large cardboard sheet covered with irregular pencil lines. Seen up close, the halting hand, once exquisitely controlled in drawing the spring of a Gothic arch or a wayside thistle, struggled to form two proper names: the lowest and the last of Ruskin's attempted signatures dropped off the edge of the page.

'Dear me! I seem to have forgotten how to write my own name,' Ruskin apologized to an autograph collector who had travelled to Brantwood, his Lake District home in his later years (35:xxxix).[2] Just before lapsing into his last, largely mute decade, in country hallowed by the great English poet of memory, Ruskin had completed the triumphant close of *Praeterita*, the last words he ever wrote for publication. He had struggled to complete twenty-eight of an originally projected thirty-six chapters of his autobiography, issued irregularly between 1885 and 1889, in lucid intervals between ever more frequent and incapacitating attacks of madness. The most devastating occurred soon after he drew a black line at the bottom of the last page and wrote, '*End* / Brantwood. / 19th June, 1889.' Thereafter, until his death on January 20, 1900, he lived an essentially posthumous existence under the benign custody of his Scottish cousin, Joan Agnew Severn, who appears as a young girl in the final chapter of *Praeterita*. The chapter is digressive and fragmentary, as is much of *Praeterita* itself. But 'Joanna's Care' is a remarkable fragment, for its closing paragraphs contain a double miracle – a depiction of Christ turning water into wine at Cana, and Ruskin's private miracle in transforming incoherence and panic into a dazzling display of his own genius. All that was most vital in Ruskin's life, all that is most central and luminous in *Praeterita*, returns and is transfigured in his last words.

These are large claims. To validate them I must step back from Ruskin's last words, indeed from *Praeterita* itself, and ask what it meant to write an autobiography after Wordsworth had radically altered the nature and direction of autobiographical narrative with the publication of *The Prelude* in 1850. After Wordsworth, the overriding object of the autobiographer's quest is not God but the discovery of his own aboriginal self; he journeys not forward and upward to the moment of conversion, but backward and inward to rediscover the child who has fathered the writer that he has become. The post-Romantic autobiographer abandons linear narrative and finds his end in his beginning,[3] just as Wordsworth had discovered the true source of his genius in the infant who dreams to the blended murmurs of the River Derwent and his nurse's song. Half a century after Wordsworth awakened to consciousness, Ruskin's first memory crystallized on the shores of Derwent Water. His nurse led him up to Friar's Crag, where the child gazed across the lake whose waters he could not then have known coursed past Wordsworth's infant home. Like Wordsworth, a lover of still and moving waters, Ruskin begins his autobiographical quest, as he foreshadows its end, with the child who stares into the springs of Wandel and the waters of the River Tay. My own circuitous journey through *Praeterita* reflects Ruskin's own deliberate a-chronicity. But however often we circle back in order to move forward, we will never wander far from the self-chosen emblem of Ruskin's genius, the Edenic river that flows through his opening pages and resurfaces in the closing paragraphs.

The classic spiritual autobiographies before Wordsworth – Augustine's, say, or Bunyan's – hinge on a single climactic turn, swift or slow. Conversion means a *turning around*, an ending that signals a new beginning. The turn may be sudden, like Paul's lightning conversion at Damascus, or slow, like Augustine's halting journey from the fleshpots of Carthage to his epiphany in the garden, the still-sinful Augustine clasping his knees in fetal position, as if to signify his imminent rebirth.

A generation after Wordsworth and before Ruskin, in the most important conversion narrative in nineteenth-century England, Newman succeeded in combining the older Christian narrative of conversion with the Wordsworthian, non-linear exploration of the seamless continuities of the self. The result is a brilliant hybrid. In the opening lines of the *Apologia Pro Vita Sua* (1864–5), Newman describes a child who dreams that he might be an angel and crosses himself upon entering a darkened room. The child has in a sense *already* converted, or is at least fully recognizable as the father of Father Newman, the convert to Roman Catholicism some forty years into the future. No lines in the *Apologia* are more important than the opening lines, and none are more profoundly Wordsworthian. In the course of the *Apologia*, Newman does not discover a new self, for he has no need to be reborn. Rather, in converting from Anglicanism to Roman Catholicism, he finds a more amenable home, a religion more doctrinally congruous with the self that had been in place from the very beginning.

Writing his autobiography nearly a quarter-century after Newman's, Ruskin employs a traditional Christian narrative of conversion only to subvert it through a kind of muted parody that he calls his 'unconversion.' His turning away from the Evangelicalism of his childhood occurs in a dimly-lit chapel in Turin in the summer of 1858. Distressed by the ugliness of the setting and by what is being said, he walks out of a grim Waldensian service, where a harsh-voiced cleric is preaching against the wickedness of the fallen world outside the chapel walls. He crosses a sunlit square filled with music, enters the Royal Gallery, and, standing before Veronese's *Solomon and the Queen of Sheba*, quietly abandons the Evangelicalism his dour mother had instilled in him from earliest childhood (35: 495–6). Margaret Ruskin's efforts at indoctrination in fact began *before* her son's birth: 'My mother had…solemnly devoted me to God before I was born, in imitation of Hannah. Very good women are remarkably apt to make away with their children prematurely in this manner' (35:24). Ruskin's revelation-in-reverse occurs not in a garden but in an art gallery; the music in whose perfect cadences he finds true discipline and devotion is not sacred but secular; and the painting on which he gazes in the golden afternoon light celebrates in lushest color and fleshly form a royal exchange of this world's riches and beauty.

Yet the words of the Old and New Testament were of inestimable importance to Ruskin, in essence his beginning and end as a writer and as a moral being. And his lifelong practice of Biblical exegesis, especially his habit of interpreting persons and events typologically – as divine foreshadowings or fulfillments of prior or subsequent persons or events – is profoundly embedded in all of his writings.[4] But to read *Praeterita* as a conversion narrative is to try to wrench it into a form that it at times mimics but finally refuses to fit. The hero of *Praeterita*, like the hero of *The Prelude*, seeks – and finds – himself. 'A Traveller I am,' Wordsworth writes, borrowing the cloak of a secular pilgrim to describe his backward journey into time, 'And all my Tale is of myself' (*The Prelude* III, 196–7).[5] The writing of *Praeterita*, Ruskin says, has 'the effect on my own mind of meeting myself, by turning back, face to face' (35:279). Both works in their moments of greatest imaginative power are elegiac and retrospective, even as they move forward chronologically through their subjects' lives. They are not a 'setting aside,' but a reverential recapturing, of 'childish things.' And it is not their Creator but themselves whom Wordsworth and Ruskin see 'face to face' in the glass of memory. If the Christian autobiographer is twice born, Ruskin and Wordsworth are already in place at birth. Their task as autobiographers is to journey back to the very shores of their being, to the selves that predate the mundane events that seem to shape them.

At the end of Volume I of *Praeterita*, in a paragraph of retrospection, Ruskin looks back over fifty years to the brook shore of his youth and finds himself essentially unchanged. No empty vessel, his 'little pitcher' already contains whole 'vialsful' of Wordsworth's reverence, Shelley's sensitivity, Turner's accuracy. In a striking phrase, he describes his tadpole self as 'chemically inalterable':

> But so stubborn and chemically inalterable the laws of prescription were, that now, looking back from 1886 to that brook shore of 1837, whence I could see the whole of my youth, I find myself in nothing whatsoever *changed*. Some of me is dead, more of me stronger. I have learned a few things, forgotten many; in the total of me, I am but the same youth, disappointed and rheumatic. (35:220)

Ruskin becomes what he already was. He does not enter the world as a little *tabula rasa*, as did John Stuart Mill, whose autobiographical task was to create a viable self beyond the shadow of his all-controlling father; he does not set out mired in Original Sin, like the suckling infant at the start of Augustine's *Confessions*. Nor does he lose his life in order to find it but rediscovers that life, over and over.[6] One day in June of 1841, after months of severe depression and coughing up of blood, he returns to the Alps in the company of his parents: 'I had found my life again,' he writes, placing the emphasis on *again*:

> What good of religion, love, admiration, or hope, had ever been taught me, or felt by my best nature, rekindled at once; and my line of work...determined for me. I went down thankfully to my father and mother.... (35:297)[7]

Like *The Prelude*, *Praeterita* portrays successive encounters between an antecedent disposition and certain external accidents made memorable by virtue of their consonance with its author's inner nature. Ruskin neatly illustrates this interaction with a present he received on his thirteenth birthday, a copy of Samuel Rogers's *Italy*, illustrated by Turner. The thoughtless biographer, Ruskin writes, might attribute to the gift the future direction of his life's work, beginning with *Modern Painters* – the work in which Ruskin, in the course of defending Turner's genius, established his own. But the thoughtless biographer, Ruskin tells us, has gotten it backwards: what really matters is that the adolescent Ruskin was prepared to perceive Turner's originality and power.

Despite their difference in genre, the true begetter of *Praeterita* is *The Prelude*, as the true child of *Praeterita* is Proust's *In Search of Time Past*.[8] The external accidents that first brought Wordsworth in touch with the source of his genius were the hills and roaring cataracts of the Lake District; for Ruskin it was the springs of the River Wandel in the once-unspoiled suburbs of London; for

Proust it was a mother's kiss and a taste recollected in the tranquility of a cork-lined room. All three are poets of the past on a reverse pilgrimage back to the world of primary sensations and colors of earliest childhood, recalled as if by a blind man suddenly gifted with sight.

Autobiography in any genre is inconceivable without narrative, but the great autobiographies take us back in time in order to transcend time. Conversion narratives achieve this transcendence in a single, climactic moment: once we have seen God's face, we seek no further travel. The peculiarity of *The Prelude* and *Praeterita* is that their 'epiphanies' are multiple, their pilgrimages circular. Instead of recounting a life that leads them providentially to a final moment of revelation, Wordsworth and Ruskin construct a narrative punctuated by recurrent visionary moments, linked and luminous episodes of self-consecration, often felt in the presence of mountains or moving waters. During these privileged moments, they do not shed their old selves but come into quickened contact with their own pre-existent genius and, like self-anointed priests, consecrate themselves to their life's work. Emperors of autobiography, they crown themselves:

> ...to the open fields I told
> A prophecy: poetic numbers came
> Spontaneously, and clothed in priestly robe
> My spirit, thus singled out, as it might seem,
> For holy services: great hopes were mine;
> My own voice cheared me...[9]

The comparable moment in *Praeterita* occurs in a mountain pass in the Jura, where, on a preternaturally clear day, Ruskin sees the distant Alps strung out along one hundred miles of horizon. Like an adolescent Moses glimpsing the Promised Land, he beholds

> in distinct vision the Holy Land of my future work and true home in this world. My eyes had been opened, and my heart with them, to see and to possess royally such a kingdom! (35:167)

Two years earlier, in the summer of 1833, when he was fourteen, Ruskin saw the Alps for the first time. They are too sacred to name:

> ... – suddenly – behold – beyond!
> There was no thought in any of us for a moment of their being clouds. They were clear as crystal, sharp on the pure horizon sky, and already tinged with rose by the sinking sun. Infinitely beyond all that we had ever thought or dreamed, —the seen walls of lost Eden could not have

been more beautiful to us; not more awful, round heaven, the walls of sacred Death. (35:115)

A work of repeated returns, of remembered raptures and anguished losses, *Praeterita* in one of its earliest scenes describes the walled, Edenic garden at Herne Hill, Ruskin's childhood home. But his paradise, as he calls it, had no companionable beasts, even though his mother, an unlikely Eve in her middle forties, stood beside him, pruning the apple and pear trees whose first fruits he was forbidden to eat. Sixty-two years after his father first brought Margaret Ruskin and their son to Herne Hill, Ruskin returned to his old nursery on the top storey, and on the one hundredth anniversary of his father's birth, he wrote the preface to *Praeterita*, a thank-offering that he places on the grave of his parents. During all the intervening decades, Ruskin felt as if he had lived in a kind of exile, travelling 'even in my own land' as a 'Spectator' (35:119).

When John James Ruskin purchased an even grander home at Denmark Hill, Ruskin, who had just come of age, took the move as a kind of expulsion. From the garret windows of Herne Hill he could glimpse the distant glitter of the Thames and Effra. But Denmark Hill, unlike Eden, was not even near a stream and the Ruskins never again felt 'at home' (35:318). After leaving the enclosed garden of childhood, whatever glimpses of Paradise Ruskin caught were from the outside, looking in at an Eden that had already been lost. For him, the Fall was not into sin but out of childhood. His most intense pleasure lay not in anticipation but retrospection, his keenest emotion not in the rapture of possession but in the pangs of remembered loss. The Alps that he first beholds from the garden-terrace of Schaffhausen are compared to the seen walls of a *lost* Eden, glimpsed from a great distance, across the chasm of 'sacred Death.' Only in the closing paragraph of *Praeterita*, in his last lucid moment as a writer, does Ruskin re-enter Paradise through the golden, welcoming gates of Siena.

## 2

In the opening paragraphs of *Praeterita*, Ruskin recalls an early childhood visit to his Aunt Jessie's riverside home at Perth. A fruit-garden sloped down to the River Tay, and a door opened onto

the water, which ran past it, clear-brown over the pebbles three or four feet deep; swift-eddying, —an infinite thing for a child to look down into. (35:15)

An open door, a garden, a child staring into swift-flowing water – surely this is the primal scene of all autobiography. I always imagine the very young Ruskin perched awkwardly on his haunches – an immemorial child-posture, exactly as Ruskin's sentence squats, with deliberate awkwardness, on its own prepositional end: '—an infinite thing … to look down *into*.' The child stares into the source of its own life, life figured as a river, ever-changing and ever itself, a mystery whose source and end are out of sight, carrying the child further from, and deeper into, himself.

The title of Ruskin's first chapter is 'The Springs of Wandel,' by which he means the source of the river that flowed near the home of his Aunt Bridget. But he also means the earliest sources of his own being in the springtime of his life. The last sentence of the chapter, a kind of rippling, metrical dance, depicts the 'cress-set rivulets in which the sand danced and minnows darted above the Springs of Wandel' (35:33). Assonance and internal rhyme play through *cress…set…lets*; the word 'and' appears once in its own right and three times in disguise, darting in and out of *sand…danced…and…Wandel*. The last four words of the chapter – 'the Springs of Wandel' – repeat the chapter title, as if to underscore the fertile circularities of the larger work of which it is a part.

This interplay of part and whole marks all of Ruskin's most vital writing, so that despite the dizzying multiplicity of subjects within his collected *Works*, a single sensibility animates them all. Hence the remarkable thematic continuity between his very first composition, written in his seventh year, and reprinted in facsimile in *Praeterita*, and the thirty-nine volumes that follow. The hero of

HARRY AND LUCY…
PRINTED and composed by a little boy
and also drawn

shares his author's lifelong love of skies, mountains and water. A precocious hydromaniac, Harry constructs little locks and sluices that remained purely fictive until his creator, four decades later, constructed actual falls and sluices for his own and Rose La Touche's delight in the once streamless garden of Denmark Hill.[10] At the very end of *Praeterita*, young Harry's waterworks resurface, transfigured into the paradisiacal stream paved with crystal that closes Ruskin's career as a writer.

Mountains are the high altar of *Praeterita* but moving water is its very life. In a passage of rare irritation at Wordsworth, Ruskin quarrels with a line from 'Tintern Abbey' that slights this near-worship of water: 'The sounding cataract / Haunted me like a passion.' Ruskin is offended, for the pure instinctual love of landscape and ocean 'is not *like*, but *is*, a passion' (35:219). He believes that he is like other children in all respects, except for this one overriding passion. He cannot recall his first sight of the sea, for he 'grew into the sense of ocean,' as he grew into his own nature (35:105–6).

A mere literary tracing of 'water imagery' in *Praeterita* misses the deeper, stranger truth that generates the imagery in the first place and that runs like an underground current through all of his writing. Fastidious, Victorian, Christian, Ruskin was also in some older part of his being an ancient Greek for whom nature was not 'landscape' but *divinity*, inhabited by gods in human form. With a prose of pure animism he describes the earth and all its myriad inhabitants, seen and unseen, as holy – 'the living inhabitation of the world—the grazing and nesting in it,—the spiritual power of the air, the rocks, the waters...' (35:166). The celebrated descriptions in *Modern Painters* of skies and clouds, mountains and seas, have as their ostensible object the demonstration of Turner's superiority to all other painters in depicting the features of nature. But the passages are far in excess of any stated purpose; they border on mania and go beyond Ruskin's adolescent, exhibitionistic desire to outrival Turner with his own many thousands of words. Prose-hymns of adoration to the holiness and potency of nature, they resurface in *Praeterita* in the Alpine passage of self-consecration and in the description of the Rhone as it flows out of Geneva. The same pre-Christian aspect of his mind animates *The Queen of the Air* (1869), subtitled 'A Study of the Greek Myths of Cloud and Storm,' but in its most magical depths a prayer to the Virgin Goddess Athena. These two interwoven strands of Ruskin's thought – Evangelical Christian and ancient Greek – come together in one of the most highly-charged passages in *Praeterita*, already cited, in which Ruskin recalls the day in 1835 when, at the Col de la Faucille and in sight of the Alps, he discovers the Holy Land of his future work. Ruskin's idiom then shifts from the dying Moses' vision of Zion to an animistic panorama of the mountains and valleys and rivers stretched out before him:

> My eyes had been opened, and my heart with them, to see and to possess royally such a kingdom! Far as the eye could reach—that land and its moving or pausing waters; Arve, and his gates of Cluse, and his glacier fountains; Rhone, and the infinitude of his sapphire lake,—his peace beneath the narcissus meads of Vevay—his cruelties beneath the promontories of Sierre. And all that rose against and melted into the sky, of mountain and mountain snow; and all that living plain, burning with human gladness—studded with white homes,—a milky way of star-dwellings cast across its sunlit blue. (35:167–8)

The panoramic expansiveness of the close of 'The Col de la Faucille' recalls the cosmic pastoral at the close of Book VIII of the *Iliad*, with its circle of a thousand campfires, pensive horses and restive men, mirrored above by the circling stars. The River Arve and *his* gates, like the Rhone and *his* sapphire lake, looks at first glance like overwriting – fanciful personifications almost a century after Wordsworth, in his Preface to the *Lyrical Ballads*, had attacked the 'poetic diction' of his Augustan predecessors. But Wordsworth's real quarrel with the Augustans, like Ruskin's with the artificiality of 'cold-hearted Pope'

in 'The Pathetic Fallacy' (5:216), is not that the language of the Augustan
poets is old-fashioned but that it is not ancient enough. The peculiarity of
Ruskin's language in the Arve passage is that the imagination underlying it is
contemporary with Hesiod and Homer. *Praeterita* does not soar again in the
same way until, in the most celebrated of his descriptive passages, he divinizes
the Rhone.

Like divinity, beauty in an extreme degree inspires an awe akin to fear in
the eye of the beholder. From earliest childhood Ruskin's fascination with water
was tinged with fear. The child Ruskin is a kind of hothouse Wordsworth, and
both the overprotected Ruskin and the early-orphaned Wordsworth 'grew up /
Fostered alike by beauty and by fear' (*The Prelude*, I: 305–6). At his Aunt
Jessie's house, by the banks of the River Tay, Ruskin passed his days in 'perpetual
watching of all the ways of running water,' but where the river ran deep, and
pooled into swirls of smooth blackness, he felt fear: 'where Tay gathered herself
like Medusa [into twisted ropes of current], I never passed without awe'
(35:67).[11] 'The river of the water of life' in Revelation, the child intuited, also
carries us toward death. One of Ruskin's very early memories was of water, but
even here a barely perceptible undercurrent of fear tugs against the visual
rapture. From the house of his birth in Brunswick Square, he could look out at

> A marvellous iron post, out of which the water-carts were filled through
> beautiful trap doors, by pipes like boa-constrictors; and I was never
> weary of contemplating that mystery, and the delicious dripping
> consequent.... (35:15–16)

Trap doors are dangerous, and boa-constrictors can make away with little boys
very quickly.

It is an ironic, not a sentimentalized, Eden that Ruskin inhabits in *Praeterita*,
and therein lies both the charm and the power of his story. He is content with
'*occasional* glimpses of the rivers of Paradise' (35:20; italics added) because he
is allowed no more, and more than one paradisiacal stream in *Praeterita* is
paved over by city streets or befouled with industrial and human waste.
*Praeterita* bears witness to a doubly painful story – the turning of England's
once green and pleasant land into a wasteland, and the devastation of Ruskin's
inner world by solitude and loss. An elegy in the guise of autobiography,
*Praeterita* tells a painful story engagingly; it is about a childhood at once
overprotected and solitary, lived within a walled Eden. Ruskin takes an old
man's pleasure in lingering over whatever gives him pleasure to recall, and he
takes an old man's license in suppressing, in so far as it lies within his power to
suppress, whatever gives him pain to recall. But he does not lie. He was
emotionally damaged by his parents, and he tells us so in the most devastating
sentence in *Praeterita*. Not a sentence, in fact, but a fragment that goes far

towards explaining why Ruskin grew up in emotional fragments. He has just enumerated the very real blessings of his childhood (peace, fixed habits of attention, etc.). Then he turns to the 'equally dominant calamities.' The calamity of calamities comes first, seven words that constitute an entire paragraph, naked in the brevity of its understatement:

> First, that I had nothing to love.
> My parents were – in a sort – visible powers of nature to me, no more loved than the sun and the moon: only I should have been annoyed and puzzled if either of them had gone out; (how much, now, when both are darkened!).... (35:44–5)

The adult Ruskin recaptures the child's accepting sense of the unbending aloofness of his parents. They appear to him as omnipotent powers – distant, untouching bodies in an altogether different orbit; he senses neither warmth nor love from paternal sun or maternal moon. Some fatal lack of true proximity, some refusal of reciprocal touch or feeling, has turned these parents into metaphors, suns or satellites that might go cold and lose their light, leaving their child-beholder not in grief but in perplexity. A chilling play on words lurks within the metaphor: the parental planets might 'go out,' like *real* parents from a real nursery, leaving their child in darkness. Finally, the adult Ruskin, speaking from inside the parenthesis, mourns the father and mother who have been eclipsed ('darkened') by death.

Yet Ruskin's metaphor of distant sun and moon requires correcting. True, he was emotionally damaged by his childhood, but less through a deficiency of love than by a misdirected excess. For he was enveloped by a parental love so innocently and anxiously all-encompassing that it left him no room to love back in return.[12] But he was also blessed by a self-enclosed quiet uniquely suited to foster his visual and verbal genius. Had he perceived only the calamities or only the blessings, rage would have blinded him in one direction, sentimentality and denial in the other. He perfects instead a beautifully modulated ease that conveys pain with grace, yet without concealment, like a crystalline stream in whose swift currents one might nonetheless drown. The opening chapters of *Praeterita* are filled with such clear but dangerous waters, like those that run through his once widely read fairy-tale, *The King of the Golden River*, which Ruskin wrote to please the little girl who later became the wife that he notoriously failed to please.

To the dominant calamity of 'nothing to love,' Ruskin attributes not selfishness or lack of feeling, but his adult incapacity to control the torrent of emotion when it later came with a 'violence utterly rampant and unmanageable' (35:45). This strikes me as astute self-analysis and goes far towards helping Ruskin's reader understand why Effie Gray appears in *Praeterita* only as the little girl for whom he wrote a fairy-tale, and not at all as the sexually attractive, justifiably angry woman who annulled their marriage in the seventh year of its non-consummation. It suggests, too, why Rose La Touche appears in *Praeterita* only as a child thirty years his junior but not at all as the young woman whom he desperately wanted to marry but who refused him. Rose's refusal and death are too catastrophic for Ruskin to record. She speaks to us only as a young girl in the present tense, first in the penultimate chapter, in a long, loving, precociously Ruskinian travelogue of a letter to her new drawing master. She speaks to us again, also in the present tense, in the closing paragraphs of *Praeterita* in a phrase that, as we might guess, has to do with moving water. She calls, shockingly, the paradisiacal stream that Ruskin has constructed for her 'The Gutter.'

But it is places, not persons, that ultimately matter in *Praeterita* – not even Rose, or Ruskin's parents, who appear so close and yet so distant, enclosed within their well-appointed carriage as the great landscapes of Western Europe passed before them. Landscapes, or images in paint or stone, received and returned in full measure the passion that Ruskin offered. Sight rather than touch was his preferred medium of exchange. A distancing irony almost always lies on or just below the surface of his portraits of persons in *Praeterita*, creating a space where connection had been too painful or too close.

No irony at all undercuts Ruskin's portraits of the places he loved. One region in particular – the Jura mountains – elicits from him an affection more commonly reserved for persons or pets. The Jura are seen close-up, clambered over, portrayed as gently rounded gateways opening on the distant majesty of the Alps. Separating France from Switzerland, their highest peaks rising scarcely above five thousand feet, they awaken Ruskin's fondness for things modest in scale and hallowed by early association. When touring the Jura – or anywhere on the Continent – the Ruskins carried their house on their backs. The family of three, self-enclosed and self-engrossed, travelled in a style unique to themselves: frill-less first class. Preceded in their custom-fitted carriage by their courier, Salvador, they stayed always in the same clean rooms in the same fine old inns, always near a stream or river – La Cloche at Dijon, L'Hotel de la Poste at Champagnole (their 'home' in the Jura), the Trois Couronnes at Vevay, L'Hotel du Mont Blanc at St. Martins. The names themselves are as enticing as a leisurely lunch in the provinces.

The singular magic of Ruskin's pages on the Jura inheres in their virtual stillness, his quiet lovemaking to the landscape:

> But no whisper, nor murmur, nor patter, nor song, of streamlet disturbs the enchanted silence of open Jura. The rain-cloud clasps her cliffs and floats along her fields; it passes, and in an hour the rocks are dry, and only beads of dew left in the Alchemilla leaves—but of rivulet, or

brook,— no vestige yesterday, or to-day, or to-morrow. Through unseen
fissures and filmy crannies the waters of cliff and plain have alike vanished,
only far down in the depths of the main valley glides the strong river,
unconscious of change. (35:161)

Ruskin writes not of 'the Jura *mountains*,' not even of '*the* Jura,' but simply of
*Jura*, as if he were in the presence of an enchanting, silent, innocently exposed
('open') girl of that name, '*her* cliffs' clasped or embraced by the rain-cloud,
who floats over her and showers down droplets of dew, like Zeus descending in
a shower of gold upon Danae. The impregnation by the rain ends as mysteriously
as it began, passing unseen through Jura's fissures and crevices, vanishing only
to reappear below in the valley, miles away, feeding 'the strong river.' The
river, as male in its strong glide as the rain-cloud that clasps Jura's cliffs, is
'unconscious' of the source that feeds it. In ascribing unconsciousness to the
river, Ruskin slyly suggests a *capacity* for consciousness – for river-consciousness,
that is. He had written in *The Queen of the Air* that the links between 'dead
matter and animation drift everywhere unseen' (19:362). The Jura passage is
a living tissue of such linkages.

But in the year 1886 Ruskin could not write of a mountain range as an
enchanting young woman without first modifying, in some important way, his
reader's normal assumptions about literary genres and the kinds of feeling
appropriate to each. A treatise on geology is one thing; a love-poem to a young
woman another; autobiography, a third. How to write all three at once, and
do so sanely, informatively and beautifully? Ruskin does so by introducing Jura
with a brief poem in perfect anapests of which we are almost certainly unaware:

Bŭt nŏ whispĕr, nŏr ḿ urmŭr, nŏr pá ttĕr, nŏr soń g… [13]

This is poetry, but poetry of great particularity and precision. Ruskin specifies
precisely those sounds – whispers, murmurs, patters – normally heard by an
auditor near any mountain stream *other than* in the Jura. The repeated *nos* and
*nors* stress the defining geological oddity of the region: the apparent absence
of its streams and rivers due to the porosity of the ground. Ruskin had written
in the previous paragraphs on technical geological matters; here he is less
concerned with shales and limestones than with the effect of the landscape on
the humans who inhabit it, including himself. And his language accordingly
shifts from the language of knowing to the language of loving. But for Ruskin,
knowing and loving were correlatives, the lover not chilled by science, the
science not distorted by feeling. Absolute clarity of vision, he argued, was the
defining quality of the best science as of the best poetry. Had Homer or Hesiod
ever seen the 'enchanted' Jura, I believe they would have portrayed her in
words quite like Ruskin's. Admittedly, Ruskin's love-poem to Jura's elusive

streams is a little odd, but no more so in its way than King Solomon's lush love-song to his sister and spouse, who is a 'spring shut up, a fountain sealed…a fountain of gardens, a well of living waters and streams' (Song of Solomon 4:12–15).

The vanishing rivers of the Jura rise again in glory in Ruskin's description of the Rhone as it courses out of Geneva – 'fifteen feet thick, of not flowing, but flying water' (35:326). I read the passage as a veiled celebration of the miraculous survival of Ruskin's own genius. Had he been able to complete *Praeterita*, the passage would have appeared almost exactly in the center of the work, in the chapter entitled 'The Simplon.'[14] As is, somewhat decentered, it was composed less than a year after a particularly crippling attack of madness and only a few weeks before the onset of another.[15] Ruskin's *Diaries* of the period – the middle 1880s – are a cornucopia of symptoms and obsessions, including the malevolent 'Storm-Cloud of the Nineteenth Century' about which he lectured in London immediately before beginning *Praeterita*. That Ruskin could have written such a passage under such conditions is a fact so improbable that both Kenneth Clark and Joan Evans, astute critics of Ruskin, backdate it by over four decades to 1844, when the Ruskins were in Geneva on the occasion their son much later writes about with total recall – walking with his parents from Mr. Bautte's jewelry shop down to the Rhone – forty-two years later, on 22 May 1886.[16] But the ultimate source of the passage is earlier still – the Springs of Wandel and the Banks of Tay, now swollen into the 'one mighty wave' of the Rhone. The scene changes; the child is changeless.

The Geneva that Ruskin so lovingly depicts in 'The Simplon' is an urban Eden, the Rhone a 'river of Paradise.' Each of the repeated familial returns to Geneva magnifies 'the well-remembered joys' of his prior visits (35:320). As Ruskin moves back in time, he adopts a child's perspective, so that Geneva figures as a diminutive paradise, a 'bird's nest of a place,' yet 'the centre of religious and social thought…to all living Europe' (35:321). This miniaturized Geneva is virtually a model city built of well-cut wooden blocks, like those that delighted Ruskin in his nursery: 'a little town, composed of a cluster of water-mills, a street of penthouses, two wooden bridges, two dozen of stone houses on a little hill' (35:321). Secure as a nest, the town is encircled by an equally diminutive landscape of orchards and trees that in the distance look like 'dots, and the farmsteads, minikin as if they were the fairy-finest of models made to be packed in a box' (35:324). Expansive lake and torrential river are at first seen only in glimpses beyond Geneva's garden gates and ramparts, as Ruskin rejoices in the return not only to Geneva but to remembered rhythms and regularities within the gates of Herne Hill, where he sat recessed at his little table, unperturbed 'as an Idol in a niche' (35:39). His idyllic picture of life in the Swiss canton – 'hay-time and fruit-time, school-time and play, for generation after generation' (35:323) – falls into an instinctually Ruskinian prose-metre, an undersong that marks his most felicitous recollections, whether of Herne Hill or Geneva, the Wandel or the Rhone.

These moments are marked by a systole and diastole, a pulsating contraction and expansion, of visual field and of feeling. The diminutive city contracts itself even further in the mysterious shop of Mr. Bautte, the master jeweller, then expands into the infinitude of the Rhone. (Mr. Bautte, not M. Bautte, for the Ruskins carried their language on their backs as well as their house, Anglicizing wherever they went). One approaches Mr. Bautte with awe, for he is a supreme artificer and can be reached only after penetrating a labyrinth of dim recesses and climbing a winding stair. A Genevan jeweler but also a figure of myth, he works only the purest gold that can be shaped into 'a certain Bauttesque subtlety of linked and wreathed design, which the experienced eye recognized when worn in Paris and Geneva' (35:326).[17] An odd mix of the mythical and the mundane plays over Ruskin's encounter with Mr. Bautte: money discreetly changes hands, precious packages are wrapped, but it is not clear if we have dealt directly with the 'Ruling power' of the shop or a mere clerk. A bourgeois Hephaestus without the limp, Mr. Bautte is our link to the even greater, eternal artificer we meet outside his shop. We descend the stairs, enter the light, walk twenty paces, and suddenly see the Rhone through Ruskin's 'river-of-paradise blue' eyes:

> For all other rivers there is a surface, and an underneath, and a vaguely displeasing idea of the bottom. But the Rhone flows like one lambent jewel; its surface is nowhere, its ethereal self is everywhere, the iridescent rush and translucent strength of it blue to the shore and radiant to the depth.
>
> Fifteen feet thick, of not flowing, but flying water; not water, neither,—melted glacier, rather, one should call it; the force of the ice is with it, and the wreathing of the clouds, the gladness of the sky, and the continuance of Time.
>
> Waves of clear sea are, indeed, lovely to watch, but they are always coming or gone, never in any taken shape to be seen for a second. But here was one mighty wave that was always itself, and every fluted swirl of it, constant as the wreathing of a shell. No wasting away of the fallen foam, no pause for gathering of power, no helpless ebb of discouraged recoil; but alike through bright day and lulling night, the never-pausing plunge, and never-fading flash, and never-hushing whisper, and, while the sun was up, the ever-answering glow of unearthly aquamarine, ultramarine, violet-blue, gentian-blue, peacock-blue, river-of-paradise

blue, glass of a painted window melted in the sun, and the witch of the
Alps flinging the spun tresses of it for ever from her snow. (35:326–7)

Witches haunt those who track them, and the Witch of the Alps, trailing her
bands of iridescent droplets, appears to have flitted onto the pages of *Praeterita*
from HARRY AND LUCY, whose six-year old author saw her apparition rising
from the mist of a rainbow.[18] A vaporized Mr. Bautte, the Witch of the Alps is
an artist who magically weaves the iridescence of a rainbow, or perhaps she is
woven into being by the rainbow – it is difficult to tell the weaver from the
web in this paragraph about a natural artistry of fluting and spinning and
'wreathing' that surpasses even Mr. Bautte's 'subtlety of linked and wreathed
design.' In such an ideal city, art and nature mirror one another. Ripples and
currents of the river 'twist the light' into 'Bauttesque' 'golden braids' and inlay
the threads with 'turquoise enamel' (35:326–7). The Rhone itself flows like
'one lambent jewel' ringed by the mini-paradise of Geneva, the city itself a
larger jewel in the glittering setting of the Alps. Ever-changing yet ever itself,
the Rhone is a potent, protean river-god in touch with eternity. The river is in
time and transcends time, 'one mighty wave' flowing in an eternal present.
Through a kind of sublime mimesis, Ruskin sustains an energy of articulation
akin to the Rhone's inexhaustible rush. All the fountains of the English
language play in sunlight over these pages in an apotheosis of his own genius.

    Underlying the passage I sense a deeper bond between the object described
and the mind that beholds it. For both Ruskin and river there is 'no wasting
away…no pause for gathering of power, no helpless ebb of discouraged recoil.'
One sentence in particular, in a paragraph too long to cite, strikes me as
especially self-reflexive. The Rhone, after it plunges into Lake Geneva, grows
slack and seems to enter a 'lake-sleep.' But at its point of exit, where Ruskin
locates himself in memory as he writes, the Rhone again comes to life:

> It seemed as if the mountain stream was in mere bliss at recovering itself
> again out of the lake-sleep, and raced because it rejoiced in racing.…
> There were pieces of wave that danced all day as if Perdita were looking
> on to learn.[19] (35:327)

The Rhone passage races because it reflects Ruskin's rejoicing at the recovery
of his own powers after a long sleep. Its rapture is for a happily remembered
past amidst a tormented present. Ruskin had seen Satan leap out at him from
behind a mirror one night in February of 1878; all that night he lay naked and
wrestled with his demon, and for many days and nights thereafter. It seems
reasonable that he should express joy and gratitude when he later felt sane
and limber and could again flex his intellect.[20]

## 3

Perhaps all autobiography should begin in the womb and end in the sixth or seventh year, at the HARRY AND LUCY stage. For the magic of the genre, like the magic of a mirror, is strongest in the earliest encounters. With maturity the autobiographer becomes as estranged from his aboriginal self as we become estranged from the companions of our childhood. The mirror grows dim, and the autobiographer writes of himself in his later years as if he were a mere biographer of himself. Turning back, he can no longer meet himself 'face to face' (35:279).

*Praeterita* is unusual in that Ruskin's powers of recall remain unclouded. But he intermittently loses control of his narrative under the pressure of severe mental illness. At the end of Volume II and in much of the final volume his subject – himself – threatens to break into fragments. Yet the path to closure is by no means steadily downhill. The great chapters on Geneva ('The Simplon') and on Ruskin's unconversion ('The Grand Chartreuse') are oases in a growing narrative desert. More often present pain occludes Ruskin's vision of the past: 'I cannot go on in this chapter...being disturbed by instant troubles which take away my powers of tranquil thought, whether of the Dead or living...' (35:465, fn. 3).[21] The most striking disparities between narrative control and collapse occur in the final chapter, 'Joanna's Care.' Much of the chapter is an ill-sorted anthology of self-quotations from old diaries, passages from books read or overheard in early childhood, sudden outbursts of ill-temper – all vanishing in the uncanny serenity and lucidity of the closing paragraphs.

'Joanna's Care' opens in 1864, the year of John James Ruskin's sudden death, the last event that time and the spectre of recurrent madness permitted Ruskin to record. But it is a hurried notation, chilling in its brevity. Ruskin voices no grief for his father's death, not because he felt too little but because he felt too much: to rehearse their long, loving but embittered dialogue might again imperil his sanity and fracture the placid surface of *Praeterita*. And so, after scant mention of his death, John James figures only as a ghostly presence from Ruskin's childhood, a disembodied voice, an 'absolutely beautiful reader' of Sir Walter Scott's novels in Scott's own faultless Edinburgh accent (35:61, 543). Scott had first appeared in *Praeterita* in the opening sentence, alongside John James and Homer: 'I am, and my father was before me, a violent Tory of the old school; – Walter Scott's school, that is to say, and Homer's.' Fittingly, Scott reappears at the end, first in footnotes, then rises into the text. The landscape and firths of his novels threaten to usurp Ruskin's own narrative. But on a deeper level Scott marks not a digression but the closing of a circle that enables Ruskin to end *Praeterita*. For the lengthy paragraphs from and about Scott early in the chapter serve Ruskin as a kind of unvoiced mourning for the death of his father, just as the dense cluster of Biblical texts at its end is an unspoken tribute to his mother, whose daily readings of Scripture with her son constituted the 'one *essential* part' of his education (35:43). The old man who disjointedly recalls whole scenes from Scott and recreates the early landscapes of his parents' Scotland has again become the child to whom John James had read the novels aloud while Mrs. Ruskin knitted and their son sipped milk 'in a little recess, wholly sacred to me; and in which I remained in the evenings as an Idol in a niche...' (35:39).

The preface to *Praeterita* had been written in Ruskin's old Herne Hill nursery, just above his father's bedroom, where the child was allowed to stand in motionless witness of his father's shaving (35:38). Over the dressing table hung a most engaging, schoolboy watercolor by John James of Conway Castle and its tidal firth. Around the figures in the watercolor the father wove a Scott-like tapestry of stories to the delight of his son. After the death of his parents and the purchase of Brantwood, Ruskin hung 'Conway Castle' in his own bedroom, to which he was confined during bouts of madness by 'little Joanie' of 'Joanna's Care.' The picture still hangs next to the bed in which he died. Preface and final chapter frame the story of Ruskin's life.

All his life Ruskin was digressive: 'I roll on like a ball...[with] no friction to contend with,' he apologized in a boyhood letter to his father (36:4). But along with the labyrinthine branchings of his thought went an almost magical gift of connection – a phrase, an image, even a single word at chapter's end that binds all the disparate strands together. Intellectually hyperactive from earliest childhood, Ruskin understandably most loved what was most predictable and familiar, those rhythms of recurrence he first experienced in his nursery and later recreated through rituals of return he practised as a kind of private religion: the return to certain well-lit rooms in certain inns, to particular landscapes, to anniversaries of his parents' birth and death, above all to the day on which he had hoped to marry Rose La Touche, and the day of her death. Early in *Praeterita* he writes of the 'monastic severities' of his childhood not as grounds for grievance but sources of joy, his days as fixed as 'the sunrise and sunset to a nestling.' He remembers with most pleasure the times that were 'most regular and most solitary' (35:131). The raptures of his Continental tours paled before the quieter, assured pleasures of the family homecoming, his mother to her knitting or pruning in the garden, his father reading aloud.

*Nostalgia* is too soft and sentimentalized a word to express Ruskin's mourning over the lost places of his childhood. Childhood itself holds for him all the palpability and mystery of place, and he mourns for lost or despoiled places more grievously than for lost persons, except perhaps for Rose. The word *nostalgia* contains the word for pain, *algia*, our pain over the mortal irreversibility of time, the futility of returning to a place we no longer inhabit in search of a self that no longer resides there. Two or three times near the end of *Praeterita*,

Ruskin's nostalgia collapses into regression; instead of recapturing the past, he comes close to losing language altogether. A chilling childishness of diction and emotion creeps into the text: '...my little Joanie sang me yesterday, 13$^{th}$ May, 1889, "Farewell Manchester," and "Golden Slumbers"' (35:553). (On that date, Mrs. Severn, an ample matron and mother of five children, was in her forty-eighth year.) Like a very young child, Ruskin throws a temper tantrum immediately after describing a dance of little Joanie's and just before he concludes *Praeterita*. A kind of sexual panic obtrudes into the text as he harangues against the lasciviousness of modern dancing – English maidenhood bedecked with stuffed birds, strutting and hoofing to the tune of Mendelssohn's Wedding March. Then, with no transition whatsoever, comes the quiet rapture of the penultimate paragraph:

> I draw back to my own home, twenty years ago, permitted to thank heaven once more for the peace, and hope, and loveliness of it, and the Elysian walks with Joanie, and Paradisiacal with Rosie, under the peach-blossom branches by the little glittering stream which I had paved with crystal for them. I had built behind the highest cluster of laurels a reservoir, from which, on sunny afternoons, I could let a quite rippling film of water run for a couple of hours down behind the hayfield, where the grass in spring still grew fresh and deep. There used to be always a corncrake or two in it. Twilight after twilight I have hunted that bird, and never once got glimpse of it: the voice was always at the other side of the field, or in the inscrutable air or earth. And the little stream had its falls, and pools, and imaginary lakes. Here and there it laid for itself lines of graceful sand; there and here it lost itself under beads of chalcedony. It wasn't the Liffey, nor the Nith, nor the Wandel; but the two girls were surely a little cruel to call it 'The Gutter!' Happiest times, for all of us, that ever were to be; not but that Joanie and her Arthur are giddy enough, both of them yet, with their five little ones, but they have been sorely anxious about me, and I have been sorrowful enough for myself, ever since I lost sight of that peach-blossom avenue. 'Eden-land' Rosie calls it sometimes in her letters. Whether its tiny river were of the waters of Abana, or Euphrates, or Thamesis, I know not, but they were sweeter to my thirst than the fountains of Trevi or Branda. (35:560–1)

Ruskin draws back in time to Rose's girlhood and Joan's youth, Joan then living with Ruskin's widowed mother and himself at Denmark Hill, where Rose was a frequent visitor. But he also draws back in the sense of taking himself out of combat and, at least for the duration of the closing paragraphs, avoiding the 'daily maddening rage' in which he lived (37:113). In the Preface, he had described *Praeterita* as an old man's gathering of 'visionary flowers.'

Chief of the visionary flowers he now gathers is Rose, herself gathered by 'gloomy Dis' fourteen years earlier, but now transformed back into a child.

But dates and places at this culminating moment in Ruskin's narrative no longer matter, for he has left the world of time and entered the world of myth. He avoids naming his own home of twenty years earlier – Denmark Hill – because he is writing about all of his homes, including the home and garden of Herne Hill and the primal garden in Genesis. A lover of the small and the enclosed, Ruskin was never more at home than as an idol in a niche indoors or at play in the walled garden outside. Avrom Fleischman traces the topos of the enclosed garden (*hortus conclusus*) back to the Song of Songs: 'A garden inclosed is my sister, my spouse; a spring shut up, a fountain sealed.'[22] At a depth that scholarship cannot fathom but imagination cannot deny, Ruskin's Edenic walks with Rose at *Praeterita*'s end are his spousal song to a child-bride who later refused him for her groom in heaven, where, as she wrote in words intended for Ruskin, 'there will be no marrying or giving in marriage.'[23]

From the moment that Ruskin could read until he matriculated at Oxford, he embarked on an annual reading of the Bible, beginning with the first verse of Genesis and, reading aloud under the stern tutelage of his mother, ending with the last verse of the Apocalypse, then beginning again with Genesis the next day. Heather Henderson makes the fine point that the cycle of mother and son recapitulates the larger cycle of the Bible itself, merging opening and end, like Revelation: 'I am Alpha and Omega, the beginning and the end' (Rev. 21:6). *Praeterita* ends by returning to its own beginning, to Ruskin's childhood garden of 'Eden land.'

But the garden that opens and closes *Praeterita* is an *ironic* Eden, for it is planted in a south London suburb and tended by a mother whose chief pleasure was in her plants. Ruskin hints at the irony even as he writes of paradisiacal walks under peach blossom branches. At first the irony is as elusive as the corncrake, then it bursts loose in Rose's derisive, 'The Gutter.' Had Ruskin written of a nightingale and not a corncrake in his Eden, the passage would be the effusion of a failed poet. But (except in delirium) he always sees clearly and says clearly what is before his eyes, absolute clarity of vision and expression being the alpha and omega of his teaching. And so it assuredly was a corncrake, inhabitant of marshes and tall grasses, whose voice he hears calling from a wet, reedy corner of his seven-acre garden. The nightingale is the pre-eminent songbird of English poetry, followed closely by the high-flying lark. No Bird of Paradise, the ungainly corncrake is an endearing parody of a bird – reluctant to fly, dragging its legs, looking like a big-footed chicken and sounding like a noisemaker that is winding down. (Its Latin name, *crex crex*, I take to be onomatopoetic.) Ruskin pursues it to no avail because it is a shy bird, of secretive habits, heard more often than seen. The corncrake vanishes in the half-light of twilight, disappearing in 'the inscrutable air or earth.' This is the same mysterious, unfathomable light that illuminates Siena in the closing paragraph. But there the twilight holds intimations of immortality; here it leads us into a ditch. For this paragraph is about paradise lost, and the closing paragraph is about Ruskin's ascent to paradise regained.

In the lost paradise of the penultimate paragraph, the 'little glittering stream' Ruskin builds for Rose disappears from sight, like the corncrake or the vanishing streams of Jura. But Ruskin's mini-river of Eden vanishes only momentarily, 'under beads of chalcedony,' which Ruskin used as a bed for his crystal stream. Chalcedony also appears in Revelation (21:19), as the third of the precious stones inlaid into the foundation of the Heavenly City through which flows the 'pure river of water of life, clear as crystal' (22:1). This is the same water that Christ, in a prefiguration of marriage to His Church, turns into wine at Cana and that Rose refused to drink with Ruskin in the sacrament of Holy Matrimony.

The reverse of the miracle at Cana is the turning of the pure water of life into the foul waters of a trough or gutter. It may well be, as Tim Peltason suggests, that the 'little cruelty of The Gutter' stands in discreetly for Rose's devastating refusal to enter Paradise with Ruskin (668). At this moment of confluence of so much in his life, Ruskin brings into a single sentence the paradisiacal stream he built for Rose, her inversion of Paradise into a Gutter, his memory of the first of his Edenic rivers – the Springs of Wandel – and still another Edenic river, the Liffey in County Kildare. There the La Touches had their principal residence, and when Rose was a child Ruskin returned her visits to Denmark Hill by taking her for outings along the banks of the Liffey and on its emerald waters. A letter of Ruskin's from Ireland soon after they met is strangely prophetic of Rose's death fourteen years later. He writes of her as if she were her own effigy, exactly as he sketched her, from life, her eyes half-closed as if in sleep, the year before she died, tormented and insane: '…but she had such queer little fits sometimes, like patience on a monument. She walked like a little white statue through the twilight woods, talking solemnly…'[24]

Rose's voice is heard twice in the penultimate paragraph, once in derision ('The Gutter') and once in praise: '"Eden-land," Rosie calls it sometimes in her letters.' *Calls* startles us, coming as it does from the long dead Rose. But this is not the helpless drift of the immediately preceding pages, where Ruskin meanders uncontrollably between past and present, rapture and rage. He is perfectly well-oriented in time and place. But he chooses the historical present because in her letters Rose is writing in the present, or rather, *speaking* in the present. Rose *calls* rather than *writes* because Ruskin has no need to read her written words: he knows them by heart and hears Rose speak them in his head. That Rose's words remain alive for Ruskin is a little unsettling, but no more so than that the letters of Tennyson's beloved Arthur Hallam, near the close of *In Memoriam*, speak to him in the present tense, dead leaves that have kept their green.

The paragraph ends in a rush of rivers and fountains: the crystal stream of Ruskin's invented Eden; the Euphrates that watered the Biblical Eden; the Thames, whose distant glitter Ruskin could see from the top storey of Herne Hill; the curative waters of the Abana, which healed a leper in 2 Kings 5; and finally the fountains of Trevi and Branda, which will see us through to the 'End / Brantwood. / 19 June 1889,' even as they recall the miraculous fountain that sprang up in front of the house of Ruskin's birth.

> How things bind and blend themselves together! The last time I saw the Fountain of Trevi, it was from Arthur's father's room – Joseph Severn's, where we both took Joanie to see him in 1872, and the old man made a sweet drawing of his pretty daughter-in-law, now in her schoolroom; he himself then eager infinishing his last picture of the Marriage in Cana, which he had caused to take place under a vine trellis, and delighted himself by painting the crystal and ruby glittering of the changing rivulet of water out of the Greek vase, glowing into wine. Fonte Branda I last saw with Charles Norton, under the same arches where Dante saw it. We drank of it together, and walked together that evening on the hills above, where the fireflies among the scented thickets shone fitfully in the still undarkened air. *How* they shone! moving like fine-broken starlight through the purple leaves. How they shone! through the sunset that faded into thunderous night as I entered Siena three days before, the white edges of the mountainous clouds still lighted from the west, and the openly golden sky still calm behind the Gate of Siena's heart, with its still golden words, 'Cor magis tibi Sena pandit,' and the fireflies everywhere in sky and cloud rising and falling, mixed with the lightning, and more intense than the stars. (35:561–2)

The opening sentence states what the two closing paragraphs enact: the bringing together of the persons, times, and places that shaped Ruskin's life. He momentarily steps back from the self who writes *Praeterita* and expresses wonderment over the fortuitous design of his life – and all of life. First he had exclaimed over how 'things bind themselves together,' then had a fuller second thought, adding *and blend*. *Bind* by itself is too merely mechanical, suggesting a linking or yoking with none of the suppleness or freedom of *blend*. (The fireflies do not *bind* with the stars but *mix* or *blend*.) The two monosyllables, so closely paired, are bound by strong alliterative links at beginning and end, like the bindings and blendings that comprise *Praeterita*.

Ruskin was working very rapidly, for he knew, according to a text that he virtually adopted as a motto, 'The night cometh when no man can work.' Writing against so imminent a deadline, could he possibly have intended all the connections I am about to suggest? The question is too simple, our distinction between 'conscious' and 'unconscious' much too crude to be of help. Ruskin had a bridging word – *Fors*[25] – meaning fortune, fate, or chance to designate that unfathomable coincidence of chance and fate, accident and design that, in combination with our own responsive will, weaves and unweaves the design of our lives and that, at any given moment, puts this or that in our minds or arms, or denies us this or that, even as we seek or flee them. He had close to total recall of all that he ever seen or read since early childhood and believed that the great imaginative artist is 'dream-gifted,' given a kind of *Fors* of the imagination that enables him to summon at precisely the right moment the exact image, tone, color, remembered syllable, reaching back to very earliest childhood, that most perfectly accords with his larger design.[26]

I do not believe it is possible to read a meaning into the words *see, sight, blind*, or *nothing, nought, never, no,* and *know* that Shakespeare did not intend in *King Lear*, though I cannot begin to understand how he could have intended all the connections he makes among each of them as he writes; so it is with Ruskin and a handful of other great imaginative writers in English.

Ruskin's associations, then, in these closing paragraphs are remarkably free but not at all random. While he violates chronology, he does so in favor of a compositional principle analogous to recurrent motifs in music. At one point he refers to his narrative as 'chance told' (35:128), explaining that *Praeterita* will be most complete if he writes it as related subjects occur to him. But 'chance told' is misleading, until one realizes that Ruskin means by the term the inspired design of the 'dream-gifted' artist.

Believing this, I glance for the last time at *bind* and *blend* and see the fortuitous (from the Latin: *fors*) *blind* and *bend* hidden within the words; identical letters reshuffled into near opposites. Ruskin feared that he was going blind, mistaking the harmless 'floaters' within his vitreous humor for 'swimming strings and eels' that appeared to cover the evening sky.[27] The *bend* in *blend* puts me in mind of a photograph of Ruskin taken not long after he had completed *Praeterita*: he appears so inert and stooped that he might have been poured into the wicker chair on his lawn at Brantwood. He sits, hand raised to his bearded mouth, as he listens – or appears to listen – to his old undergraduate friend, Dr. Henry Acland, who balances on both their laps an old folio volume, perhaps of photographs of Ruskin before he grew bent. Thirty years earlier, on the occasion of his father's sudden death, Ruskin wrote a letter to Acland that, alluding to *Lear*, captures the strange mix of embittered love and guilty self-reproach that marked his adult relations with his father. 'You have never had,' he wrote,

> nor with all your medical experience have you ever, probably, seen—the loss of a father who would have sacrificed his life for his son, and yet forced his son to sacrifice his life to him, and sacrifice it in vain. It is an exquisite piece of tragedy altogether—very much like Lear, in a ludicrous commercial way—Cordelia remaining unchanged and her friends writing to her afterwards—wasn't she sorry for the pain she had given her father by not speaking when she should? (36:471)

How things bind and blend themselves together!

### 4

In his final paragraph Ruskin gives only one date to hang on to, but it is profoundly significant: his visit in 1872 to the rooms of the painter Joseph Severn, then in his eightieth year. Severn was at work on a painting whose subject – 'The Marriage at Cana' – enables Ruskin to move in memory from the sick Rose, who refused his marriage proposal in the same year, to the Rose whom he enthrones in heaven in his closing words. Fifty-one years before the Ruskin party entered Severn's studio in Rome, the young Severn had nursed the dying Keats, sketching his feverish head so delicately that you can still feel the heat and dampness of Keats's hair. Keats's poems had lain on the child Ruskin's work-table, when his father read Scott aloud to his Idol in a Niche. 'Little Joanie,' a newly-wed in 1872, had married the painter's son, Arthur Severn, so there was a familial connection among all those in the room. The elder Severn died before completing his painting of the larger family gathering at Cana, leaving it unfinished in his studio, just as Ruskin left *Praeterita* incomplete. He describes the artist as 'eager in finishing his last picture'; Ruskin is himself within a few words of completing the final chapter of his last book. Last words about 'last things' by two old men: the painted miracle serves Ruskin as an emblem of his verbal miracle at the end of the book of his life.

But the Marriage at Cana – both Jesus's miracle and Severn's painting – held still deeper meanings for Ruskin. In the previous paragraph Rose mischievously called the crystal waters of Ruskin's paradise 'The Gutter.' In the final paragraph Severn delights in painting, and Ruskin in recalling, Jesus's miraculous transformation of the 'crystal' water at the wedding feast into wine. The rainbow arc of the water 'glowing' into wine mirrors the deep chiasmic structure of the two paragraphs: the descent from Ruskin's demi-paradise into the Gutter, and his ascent to the golden gate of Siena, which Ruskin depicts as a type of the New Jerusalem that 'I John saw…coming down from God out of heaven, prepared as a bride adorned for her husband' (Revelation

21:2).[28] Severn's painting, like Ruskin's paragraph, attempts to arrest time by depicting the eternal present of the miraculous marriage at Cana. Ruskin achieves the effect of Severn's unbroken rainbow arc of water-into-wine by abandoning past and future tenses for the never-ending action of the present participle: 'painting…glittering…changing…glowing into wine.'[29]

The water that becomes wine at Cana prefigures two sacraments, the blood of Christ at the Last Supper and the sacrament of marriage. Marriage is the most sacred human instance of binding, of spouse to spouse and of both to Christ, as marriage itself is a blending or union of two persons into 'one flesh.' This is the union that Rose did not so much refuse as eternally defer, and it is inconceivable that Ruskin would not have recalled her anguished renunciation of his proposal, either when he wrote of the visit in *Praeterita* in 1889, or when he stood in front of Severn's painting in 1872, the same year in which Rose wrote:

> I will not judge or condemn you. But I *must* turn away from you.…
> When I think of what you *might* have been, to Christ, to other human
> souls, to me! How the angels must have sorrowed over you!… All I can
> do is speak of you to Christ. At His feet we might meet; in His love our
> hearts might be drawn together again.[30]

In the same year (1872), Rose wrote to a mutual friend that Ruskin's last words to her were a blessing and that they would finally understand one another when, 'face to face,' they met in 'that Kingdom where love will be perfected – and yet there will be no marrying or giving in marriage.'[31] Rose alludes to a text from Matthew that Ruskin knew from earliest childhood: 'For in the resurrection they neither marry, nor are given in marriage, but are as the angels of God in heaven' (22:30). This was not at all the kind of marriage that Ruskin desperately sought with Rose, but in the moment of writing *Praeterita*, suspended between his recollections of Rose's childhood and intimations of his own death, it is the timelessly consummated marriage at Cana that came flooding into his mind.

Rose is of course important to the end of *Praeterita*, but Dante is perhaps even more so, though the two are closely linked in Ruskin's closing words. Dante had shown Ruskin the way by transforming his mourning for a young woman into a literary apotheosis. Like Rose, Dante's beloved Beatrice had died in her twenties; Dante enthrones her near the center of the mystical Rose at the close of the *Paradiso*. So, too, Ruskin places Rose at the center of *his* paradise at the close of *Praeterita*. And he signals his debt to Dante, both as writer and inspired mourner, by giving Dante the last word in *Praeterita*, stars, which is also the closing word (*stelle*) of each of the three parts of the *Commedia*. Ruskin had introduced Rose in the preceding chapter, entitled 'L'Esterelle,' a variant of *Estella* or *star*. Like Dante he mythologizes the young woman he loved. 'Last Friday noon my mistress looked at us and passed silently.' The words are not Dante's of Beatrice but Ruskin's of Rose, who denied his salutation on passing him in a London street (35:lxxiii).

Dante enters *Praeterita* through an association of Ruskin's with Charles Eliot Norton, a polymathic professor of fine arts and literature at Harvard and a mentor figure for Ruskin, although eight years his junior. Ruskin's 'first real tutor' (35:520), Norton was a Dante scholar and also one of his literary executors. That Norton and 'little Joanie' burned the love-letters of Rose and Ruskin soon after his death – his letters to Rose were 'perhaps the most beautiful things he ever wrote' – is a mischance of *Fors* that Ruskin could not have foreseen. Rose's first letter to Ruskin survives only because he chose to print it in 'L'Esterelle,' against all prudent advice (35:lxxvi, 529). All the others he placed, along with locks of Rose's hair, in a rosewood box, a kind of reliquary that he carried wherever he went. Wood, paper and hair all fed the pyre.

But here, at the end of the final chapter, in yet another ceremony of binding and blending, Ruskin and Norton drink the waters of Fonte Branda celebrated by Dante. They then climb 'the hills above,' Norton serving as a Virgilian guide to Ruskin on their pilgrimage to Dante's Siena.[32] From this point to the end, the last paragraph achieves the effect of a sustained ascent. For the eye-oriented Ruskin, scale, perspective, depth-of-field are always carefully inscribed into his most deeply-felt passages. All three are radically different from those in the preceding paragraph, as befits the contrast between a suburban London garden and the hilltops of Siena. Seen as 'little glittering stream' or as 'Gutter,' the garden of childhood is diminutive, a domestication of the sublime; grown women are perceived as little girls ('Joanie' and 'Rosie'); they walk beneath an avenue of peach blossoms, the eye glances down and into the miniature falls, as the child Ruskin once gazed down and into the swift-eddying Tay.[33]

The shift in scale and perspective from the seen walls of this lost Eden ('I have been sorrowful enough…ever since I lost sight of that peach-blossom avenue') to the hills of Siena is as sudden as the shift from Mr. Bautte's recessed little shop to the open, brilliant expanse of the Rhone, with its vast lake and the Alps rising in the distance. In the closing paragraph, the prospect is at once frightening and sublime – a golden city overshadowed by mountainous thunder-clouds, as befits a dying prophet in sight of a promised land.

Ruskin crosses some not-quite-earthly threshold as he drinks of Dante's fountain, then sees the line of fireflies as he walks 'on the hills above.' Above *what?* Siena is a city set on a hill. Within its massive ramparts nothing rises above the cool marble bands of the Duomo and the improbable elegance of the towering Palazzo Pubblico. William Arrowsmith suggests that Ruskin and Norton, after slaking their thirst, walked up to the hills of Casentino in search of the source of Fonte Branda,[34] as in early childhood he had sought the sources of the Wandel and the Tay (35:609). But the hills that Ruskin now seeks rise above no earthly city; they are the luminous, golden hills of the imagination, hills such as Dante sees in the Circle of the Blessed Souls in the Heaven of the Sun:

> And—look!—beyond the light already there,
> an added luster rose around those rings,
> even as a horizon brightening.
>     And even as, at the approach of evening,
> new lights begin to show along the sky,
> so that the sight seems and does not seem real....[35]

Siena glowing in the twilit sky is the supreme moment of binding and blending in *Praeterita* – of night and day, past and present, time and eternity. It is also a blending of heaven and hell. In 1870 Ruskin wrote a letter describing his arrival at Siena under conditions identical to those he describes in *Praeterita*. This is surely the biographical origin of the firefly passage in *Praeterita*, as Dante is Ruskin's literary source:

> Siena...has at this season a climate like the loveliest and purest English summer, with only the somewhat, to me, awful addition of fire-flies innumerable, which as soon as the sunset is fairly passed into twilight, light up the dark ilex groves with flitting torches, or at least, lights as large as candles, and in the sky, larger than the stars. We got to Siena in a heavy thunderstorm of sheet-lightning in a quiet evening, and the incessant flashes and showers of fire-flies between, made the whole scene look anything rather than *celestial*. (20:liv)

'Anything rather than *celestial*' is a circumlocution for *infernal*, and the *Inferno* also underlies the close of *Praeterita*, although its presence is more muted than that of the *Paradiso*. Dante's master-forger Adamo, parched and burnt beyond all bearing, yearns above all for the sweet waters of Fonte Branda, which Dante himself had seen half a millennium before Ruskin and Norton.[36] And a little higher in Hell, in Ulysses' circle, Dante uses a simile strongly suggestive of Ruskin's fireflies:

> As many as the fireflies the peasant
> (while resting on a hillside in the season
> when he who lights the world least hides his face),
>     just when the fly gives way to the mosquito,
> sees glimmering below, down in the valley,
> there where perhaps he gathers grapes and tills—
>     so many were the flames that glittered in
> the eighth abyss... (XXVI, 25–32)

For Dante's peasant, as for Ruskin and his guide, time, season and the angle of vision (high on a hill, looking through the line of fireflies) are identical.

E.T. Cook, Ruskin's disciple and editor, recalls Ruskin's saying that during episodes of madness his visions 'were mostly of [the] Inferno; but sometimes visions of Paradise, and one was almost recompensed.'[37] Here, at the end of *Praeterita*, the proportions are reversed, for Ruskin has finally emerged from the *selva oscura* earlier in 'Joanna's Care,' with its thicket of footnotes and digressions on obscene dancing and little girls lighting up large cigars.[38]

Uncannily, beginning with the heavily aspirated, twice repeated '*How* they shone!', Ruskin's sentences themselves begin to pulse and breathe. Time moves, then stops with the repetition of 'How they shone!', then moves again in syncopation with the undulating line of lights that punctuate the darkness. The effect is at once ecstatic and serene, the note of religious ecstasy, the long-held note of the *Paradiso*.

The fireflies shine in the *still* undarkened air, the clouds are *still* lighted in the west, the words on Siena's gate *still* glow in the golden light. Again, repetition serves as a pause between breaths, but it is an uneasy pause, more tremulous than calm. The repose of the word *still* plays against the menace of its opposite: a light that still glows is about to go out, the 'mountainous clouds' will soon blot out the sun, thunder will drown the stillness, the still undarkened air will soon be black as night or death. All is an equipoise of fluctuating opposites, like the 'fine-broken starlight' of the fireflies, the briefest pulsations of light and dark from an ephemeral creature whose short season is already passing into autumn. The leaves appear purple because of the lateness of the season or the lateness of the day, but late in either case. William Arrowsmith bottles the broken starlight in an inspired gloss: 'the idea is fragmented eternity.'[39]

We are high on a hill in a darkening wood ('thicket') that has lost most of its menace, for it is scented and still fitfully lit. But in a scarcely perceptible glide, Ruskin conflates two moments, the *now* of his hillside walk with Norton and his arrival in Siena three days *before*. Since Ruskin nowhere specifies the date of his arrival, *three days before* is a roadside sign without any reference point. But we know all that we need to know: Ruskin has quietly left his guide behind him and now, alone, negotiates his final passage.

The long final sentence has only one main verb that comes at the very beginning – 'How they shone! through the sunset....' Throughout the seventy words that follow, time is suspended within a verbless world of rising and falling and mixing of everything in motion and nothing coming to rest. Becoming is indistinguishable from pure being as landscape and cityscape appear to dissolve back into their primal elements of earth, air, fire and water. The fiery deluge of the thunderstorm impends but does not burst. Time rushes and time stops as in the moment just before the heavens break loose in Turner's late, great *Shade and Darkness: The Evening of the Deluge*.

Time allowed Ruskin only one last revision before the coming of the night. He knew in the first draft that he would end as Dante ended, with the stars. He began to write 'more *lustrous* than the stars,' then crossed it out for *lovely*. *Lustrous* is one of the weaker words in English for light, too diffuse for the moving points of light before his eyes. And *lovely* is a difficult word to use well, even for Ruskin, and it had come too easily. The fireflies are seen up close, within the scented thicket, and in such proximity cast a light that appears larger and brighter than the stars. So Ruskin cancels *lovely* for *intense*, contrasting the brilliance of the fireflies with the darkness of the fast-encroaching night.[40]

I read Ruskin's last, long sentence as a threshold poem that takes us from one world to another, from time to eternity. The crossing occurs at the Gate of Siena, with its still golden words, 'Cor magis tibi Sena pandit' – 'More than her gates, Siena opens her heart to you.'[41] Siena is a city set on a golden hill, for Ruskin the richest in beauty and order of all earthly cities, the ideal city of Ambrogio Lorenzetti's great 'Allegory of Good Government' that Ruskin had seen in the Palazzo Pubblico. It is also a type of that twelve-gated city in Revelation where death shall cease and the gates 'shall not be shut at all by day: for there shall be no night there' (21:25) and the Bride shall greet all who thirst, saying, 'Let him take the water of life freely' (22:17).

Gate upon gate opens in Ruskin's mind as he writes, leading back to the gate of Scripture that his mother first opened for him, the 'gate of heaven' that Jacob sees atop the ladder reaching from earth to angels, the gates of the Psalmist that lift up their heads to 'the King of glory,' the gate Isaiah sees that 'shall not be shut' day or night and that opens in Revelation, the gate of golden words that beckon Ruskin to enter through the ramparts of Siena. His perspective widens from the Gothic arches of Fonte Branda to embrace city and countryside, earth and sky, fireflies and stars. He is at the end of his life as a writer but also at its beginning, when, as a child, taking in his first sight of the Alps, he stood before the 'Gates' that opened for him 'a new life – to cease no more, except at the Gates of the Hills whence one returns not' (35:113).

# 7

# MR. DARWIN COLLECTS HIMSELF

Late in life, from the chilling perspective of a posthumous self, Charles Darwin wrote a brief account of his own origins. 'I have attempted to write the following account of myself, as if I were a dead man in another world looking back at my own life.'[1] Darwin pushes the act of self-objectification to its theoretical limits: he gazes into the autobiographer's mirror and sees, staring back, not Charles Darwin but an aged instance of the species *homo sapiens*. Writing of himself as a dead man is not at all difficult, he tells us, 'for life is nearly over with me.'[2] The central activity of his life had been the collecting and interpreting of natural phenomena. Now, believing himself to be at life's end, he collects himself, a specimen dispassionately impaled on the keen pin of his self-observation.

Darwin began his *Recollections of the Development of my Mind and Character*[3] late in May of 1876, when he was sixty-seven years old. He wrote quickly and casually and, except for some later additions, completed the work in ten weeks. Twice in the opening paragraph he refers to the *Recollections* as a 'sketch,' with all the rapidity and informality the word implies. In no sense a full-scale self-portrait, the *Recollections* constitute a discontinuous narrative, by turns anecdotal and reflective, that captures the features of an old man in search of his formative self and desirous of preserving his past for his progeny. He had spent a lifetime studying sexual propagation and heredity. In the month in which he began his *Recollections* he learned that he was to become a grandfather for the first time,[4] and in the opening paragraph he tells us that it would have greatly interested him to read an autobiographical sketch of his grandfather Erasmus. He is conscious of five generations of Darwins as he remarks, with habitual understatement, that the *Recollections* 'might possibly interest my children or their children.'[5] Not *my grandchildren*, the phrase we expect; in the more impersonal 'my children or their children' we detect the characteristic estrangement from conventional associations that enabled Darwin to be both detached and loving. He must have known that, as a world-renowned scientist, his *Recollections* would be widely read. Yet the work was written not for the world at large but as an exercise in self-exploration for himself and his immediate family. The perspective is at once intimate and objective, quite like that in 'A Biographical Sketch of an Infant,' a pioneering study in child development based on Darwin's observations of, and benign experiment upon, his first-born son, William Erasmus.[6]

One of the as-yet-unborn grandchildren for whom Darwin wrote his *Recollections*, Nora Darwin Barlow, edited in 1958 the first unexpurgated edition in English. But Lady Barlow gave to her otherwise invaluable edition the unfortunate title *The Autobiography of Charles Darwin*.[7] *Autobiography* arouses in the reader false generic expectations, for it suggests a more self-consciously shaped and 'literary' life than Darwin ever intended. The militantly prosaic opening, the disclaimer of any audience other than his family, the disavowal of any pretense to style, all make it clear that Darwin believed himself to be writing in spite of, rather than within, the quasi-novelistic conventions of English autobiography.

The most striking moment in the *Recollections* occurs on the willowy banks of the River Cam. Happier out of the classroom than in it, the young Darwin preferred the dank habitats of the local beetles, whom he hunted under the bark of the ancient willows that overhang the river between Cambridge and Grantchester. Sport, outdoor education and innate passion all in one, the pursuit of beetles aroused in the young Darwin an eagerness that other undergraduates gave to horses or, more rarely, to books. In proof of his 'zeal,' Darwin writes in the *Recollections*, he one day tore off some rotting bark, then

> saw two rare beetles and seized one in each hand; then I saw a third and new kind, which I could not bear to lose, so that I popped the one which I held in my right hand into my mouth. Alas it ejected some intensely acrid fluid, which burnt my tongue so that I was forced to spit the beetle out, which was lost, as well as the third one. (*Autobiography*, p. 62)

Darwin remembered virtually everything he ever saw or touched (his mother is an arresting exception), and the 'third and new' beetle remained fixed in his mind as an irksome absence for over fifty years. The pain, for Darwin, lay not in the burned tongue but in the lost treasure. No larger than a ladybug, with tiny jet-black head and jet-black cross emblazoned across its prickly orange back, *Panagaeus crux major* figures in Darwin's letters as *sacred*, his nightingale of insects, emblem of his lifelong pursuit of the elusive beauty of natural fact.[8]

The young Darwin felled birds with the same zeal that he hunted beetles. He awaited the start of the shooting season as the coming of 'bliss on earth,' and he placed his open hunting boots beside his bed at night, the better to reach the fields by sunrise.[9] In time the mockingbirds of the Galapagos Islands stirred within him intimations of transmutation, and the thought of inflicting gratuitous pain became so painful that he could not bear to bait a live worm. But before the voyage of the *Beagle*, before he had discovered his vocation, Darwin appeared in his pleasures to be something of an idler and barbarian. He behaved like what he indeed *was*, a genial, sports-loving youth of the provincial gentry. Only his slow-dawning genius set him apart from his peers, but it went unremarked by his teachers, by his family, and perhaps especially by himself. It remained the great bafflement of his later life, a bafflement recorded in the *Recollections* with a candor mistaken by his critics for mock-modesty, that the youth who chased beetles and downed whole flocks of birds – 'very bad shooting this season, the first day I killed 10 brace'[10] – evolved into the Charles Darwin who forever altered our understanding of nature and of our place within it.

2

The grand organizing metaphor of autobiography, sacred or secular, depicts life as a journey, a voyage of discovery in which the old self gives birth to the new.[11] Darwin had the strange fortune of enacting the autobiographer's metaphor. For 1,737 cramped days and nights he circumnavigated the globe as naturalist aboard the HMS *Beagle*. Upon his return, his father remarked to his sisters, 'Why, the shape of his head is quite altered.'[12] Dr. Robert Darwin, who, according to his son, had 'almost supernatural' powers of 'reading the characters, and even the thoughts' of others,[13] saw at once that the voyage of the *Beagle* had been for Charles a voyage of discovery. Forty years after his return, Darwin wrote in the *Recollections* that his five years aboard the *Beagle* constituted 'by far the most important event in my life and has determined my whole career.'[14] One wishes that he had written more of his own evolution, but introspection was not his particular gift, and from the subdued perspective of old age in his country retreat-cum-laboratory at Down House, his earlier, ecstatic realization of his life's work when exploring the tropical forests of Brazil and the frigid wastes of Tierra del Fuego must have seemed distant indeed. The mystery for Darwin's biographer is not the life-altering effect of his years aboard the *Beagle*. Rather it is that Charles Darwin, desultory student and medical-school dropout, was invited to serve as ship's naturalist on an important government mission of surveying and scientific research. Yet when the invitation reached him late in August of 1831, Darwin at age twenty-two was very likely the best-qualified young man for the job in England.

Even in his earliest days at school, Darwin tells us at the start of the *Recollections*, his enthusiasm for natural history, especially for collecting, was intense:

> I tried to make out the names of plants, and collected all sorts of things, shells, seals, franks, and minerals. The passion for collecting, which

leads a man to be a systematic naturalist, a virtuoso or a miser, was very strong in me, and was clearly innate, as none of my sisters or brothers ever had this taste. (*Autobiography*, pp. 22–23)

Misers not only hoard but love to count, and the passion for enumeration developed very early in Darwin, alongside the passion to hunt and to collect. After shooting his first snipe, his hands so trembled with excitement that he could scarcely reload his gun. Yet he paused long enough after each kill to keep an exact record of the scores of birds he felled each season. 'How I did enjoy shooting,' he writes of his idyllic days on the estate of his Uncle Josiah[15] at Maer, 'but I think that I must have been half-consciously ashamed of my zeal, for I tried to persuade myself that shooting was almost an intellectual employment...'[16] By 'intellectual employment' Darwin has in mind the discipline and energy of observation required of the hunter, the same discipline that later enabled him to collect in a mere two days, as he records in his *Diary of the Voyage of the H.M.S. Beagle*, 'all the animals, plants, insects & reptiles' on Charles Island, an outlying link of the Galapagos Archipelago some nine miles in breadth.[17] At Maer Hall he kept track of his kills by knotting a string tied to a buttonhole. On the cramped, strewn deck of the *Beagle*, and in his ten-by-eleven-foot cabin, which served him as bedroom, living-room, and laboratory, and which also housed the ship's charts and library and, by day, two other officers, he examined and classified each of his tens of thousands of specimens, ranging from minute *Cirripedia* to the huge fossil head of a *Megatherium*, all of which he crated and sent back to England by the shiploads, to the astonishment of those who viewed a rodent-like head 'the size of a Hippopotamus' and 'an Ant-Eater of the size of a horse!'[18]

The *Beagle* became Darwin's Ark. In nets dragged astern and on expeditions up the High Andes, he gathered two of every kind, male and female.[19] Twenty-eight years after setting sail, he published *The Origin of Species*, an epic 'deconstruction' of Genesis in which he retells the story of our beginnings and erases the Flood. Of the vast literature spawned by the *Beagle*, nothing is stranger than the 'Very Few Remarks with Reference to the Deluge' which Robert Fitz-Roy, Darwin's brilliant and melancholic Captain, appended to the 1839 *Narrative* of the voyage. Later a fanatical foe of Darwin's unorthodoxy and finally a suicide, Fitz-Roy in the 'Remarks' delivers a sermon to his young sailors, rebukes their feeble faith, imagines himself calming the stormy waters of Galilee as he conjures up a tremendous picture of Noah fronting the Flood and contends that the gigantic fossil species unearthed by his shipmate Darwin had failed to survive into modern times because they could not fit into the Ark.[20] Fellow researchers on the same voyage, the Captain and the ship's naturalist interpreted the same evidence in opposite ways. Fitz-Roy foundered, as it were, on the shoals of fundamentalism, while Darwin piloted the *Beagle* into the twenty-first century. From our own secular perspective, the two men appear to inhabit different universes. In fact they are antagonists by virtue of their very proximity, bound to each other as doubt is to faith, heresy to orthodoxy, science to myth. 'Science is the criticism of Myth,' Yeats wrote; 'There would be no Darwin had there been no Book of Genesis.'[21]

The child's compulsion to count, the miser's to hoard, the aboriginal urge to hunt, all drove the young Darwin in directions that he did not fully understand but that ultimately led to the publication of *The Origin of Species*. In the evolution of his own career he saw mimicked the larger evolution of the race, from the 'primeval instincts of the barbarian' to the higher pleasures of observation and reason.[22] 'I am become quite devoted to Nat. History,' he wrote to his sister Caroline after nine months at sea; 'you cannot imagine what a fine miserlike pleasure I enjoy, when examining an animal differing widely from any known genus. No schoolboy ever opened a box of plumcake so eagerly as I shall mine....'[23] Years later the same image of acquisition recurs in a letter to William Fox, his boyhood tutor in entomology and a fellow beetlemaniac: 'I am working very hard at my book [*The Origin of Species*]...[and] am like Croesus overwhelmed with my riches in facts...I shall not go to press at soonest for a couple of years.'[24] Four months later, in June of 1858, he received from Alfred Wallace the remarkable letter on the transmutation of species that jolted him into publishing *The Origin* in the following year. Darwin's legendary thoroughness, his need to proceed incrementally through massive accumulation of fact, his wish to win the race as the tortoise and not the hare of science, doubtless delayed the publication of *The Origin* for at least a decade. But I suspect another, complementary motive. A boy's pockets are a private place; and misers count their hoard in darkened rooms. The most frank and open-natured of men, at the center of a world-wide network of researchers in a multitude of fields, all touching antennae at local scientific societies or through the penny post, Darwin was also, and paradoxically, a recluse. Hoarding and disclosing are curiously entwined; Darwin was at once gregarious and secretive in his disclosure of nature's secrets.

Darwin's childhood eagerness to collect and to classify coincided with what Gillian Beer calls his 'passion for fabulation,'[25] a kind of natural magic of his own devising by which he sought to explain or control the world around him. At the Rev. Case's day-school at Shrewsbury, he told a classmate that he

> could produce variously coloured Polyanthuses and Primroses by watering them with certain coloured fluids, which was of course a monstrous fable, and had never been tried by me...[26] [As] a little boy I was much given to inventing deliberate falsehoods, and this was always done for the sake of causing excitement. For instance, I once gathered much valuable fruit from my Father's trees and hid them in the shrubbery,

and then ran in breathless haste to spread the news that I had discovered
a hoard of stolen fruit. (*Autobiography*, p. 23)

These scenes of childhood transgression are charged with a significance of
which Darwin appears innocent, or perhaps chooses not to disclose. Yet it is
difficult not to see in his theft of fruit from his Father's garden shades of the
primal transgression in Eden. The young Darwin, however, feels not guilt but
exaltation over the inventiveness of his deceits. A precocious and parodic
Satan of a boy, he surmounts his Father's high garden wall in the cool of the
evening, then plucks the fruit with a long stick rigged to a flower pot.[27] Like
the young Augustine compounding his crime by its sheer gratuitousness, Darwin
races off with the stolen apples only to give them away in a neighboring cottage.
Ancient archetypes are embedded just below the surface of Darwin's narrative,
as if in his own childhood he were naturalizing or secularizing our culture's
central myth of guilt, as he was later to naturalize the central myth of our
Beginnings in *The Origin*.

The most resonant of these early fictions touches on Darwin's mother and
is preserved not by Darwin himself but by his son Francis in the *Recollections*.
In a footnote William Leighton, the same schoolboy to whom Darwin told the
tale about coloring primroses, recalls how Darwin brought a flower to school
and said

> that his mother had taught him how by looking at the inside of the
> blossom the name of the plant could be discovered. Mr. Leighton goes
> on, 'This greatly roused my attention and curiosity, and I inquired of
> him how this could be done?'—but his lesson was naturally enough not
> transmissible.[28]

A haunting absence in Darwin's *Recollections* as in his life, Susannah Darwin
figures more as a forgotten fragrance than a nurturing presence. Her son
remembered her only by the bed in which she died, by the tears his father
shed, by her black velvet gown and her work table. Susannah's voice, body, or
touch is nowhere present in his writing. Yet from the same period of his life,
and with ironic inaptness that suggests displacement, Darwin recalled with
great clarity the burial of a total stranger, a brilliantly uniformed soldier at a
nearby church:

> ...it is surprising how clearly I can still see the horse with the man's
> empty boots and carbine suspended to the saddle, and the firing over
> the grave. (*Autobiography*, p. 24)

Years afterward Darwin appears to have distanced himself even further from
his mother's death by moving it back in time. 'My mother died during my

infancy and I can say hardly anything about her,' he wrote in his sixty-fifth year.[29] Charles was in fact eight years and five months old when Susannah Darwin died. Unusually old for childbearing when he was born – she was forty-four – she seemed unusually young to those who mourned her death at fifty-two.

Darwin appears alienated not only from her memory but also from all consciousness of grief. In his mid-thirties he wrote a moving letter of consolation to his cousin William Fox upon the death of his wife:

> I truly sympathise with you, though never in my life, having lost one near relation, I daresay I cannot imagine, how severe grief, such as yours, must be, and how little the longest expectation can resign one to the blow, when it falls.[30]

Only the clotted syntax, and the ambiguous comma after 'life,' which momentarily reverses Darwin's intended meaning, suggest his latent awareness of a truth beneath the truth he denied: his anger at an absent mother. Susannah Darwin is never named in the *Recollections* or in the 'Autobiographical Fragment' of 1838. Nothing is known of the cause of her death except that her illness was the kind known as 'lingering,' a condition calculated to vex a child in its combination of ungratifying presence and incomprehensible absence. Her poor health during Darwin's early years, and the fact that she was old enough to have been his grandmother at his birth,[31] in part account for her absence from his memory. Yet the causes seem inadequate to the effect: almost total obliteration.[32] She comes to life only in the footnote on peering into flowers, as a girl astride a horse in a family portrait, and in a phrase from one of her few surviving letters. At the center of a portrait of the Wedgwoods she is an arresting figure, stylish, pensive, shapely, the eldest of the seven children ranged under the watchful eye of their parents.[33] In the letter, written in her early forties with a 'prognosticating sigh,' she tells her brother Josiah, 'Every one seems young but me.'[34] The footnote on looking inside a flower to discover a plant's name is especially enigmatic, for in the context of Darwin's confession of monstrous fables, the reader cannot tell if Darwin made up the story he told Leighton, if his mother was in turn telling a fable, or if the child gave a magical interpretation to his mother's otherwise plausible words. Nearly seventy years after hearing the story from Darwin, Leighton, who became an eminent lichenologist, speculated that Susannah Darwin might have been trying to introduce Charles to the Linnaean system of classification.[35] The surmise is less improbable than it seems, given her known interest in flowers and in the breeding of pigeons, two areas of her son's research.[36] In the passage I have already cited on his miser-like passion for collecting, Darwin explains how as a very young child he 'tried to make out the names of plants,' an unusual locution in place of the more idiomatic 'learn the names.' Darwin's words seem to retain a vestigial memory of his mother's telling him to look inside the flower to discover a plant's name, as if the name were magically encoded within its corolla of petals and might by an act of Darwin's will be made to disclose itself. He did indeed spend much of his life studying plants, and in time they disclosed not only their names and natures but the remarkable ingenuities of their sexual adaptations. The result was a series of books on the contrivances by which orchids are fertilized, on the movements and habits of climbing plants, on cross-fertilization in the vegetable kingdom, together with a flood of articles on 'Primula, and on their Remarkable Sexual Relations,' 'On the Action of Sea-Water on the Germination of Seeds,' in addition to a host of other publications on botanical subjects, including forty-nine contributions to the *Gardener's Chronicle*.[37]

## 3

Darwin's apparent forgetting of his mother is the more remarkable in view of his virtually total recall of his father. 'His recollection of everything that was connected with him was peculiarly distinct,' Francis Darwin writes: 'It was astonishing how clearly he remembered his father's opinions.'[38] Of course, Dr. Darwin lived on well into his son's adulthood,[*] and, if only as a remarkable physical presence, he was impossible to forget. Enormous in build yet fine in feature, when Dr. Darwin last stepped onto a scale he weighed 336 pounds, after which he grew considerably heavier and wisely abandoned the habit of weighing himself. 'He was the largest man I ever saw,' Charles writes at the start of a fourteen-page verbal portrait of his father, a late addition to the *Recollections* that straddles, awkwardly and imposingly, the beginning of his own narrative.

---

[*] Charles was in his fortieth year when his father, 'who possessed an extraordinary memory, especially for dates' (*Autobiography*, p. 39), died at the age of eighty-two. In the *Recollections* he misstates the year of death as 1847 instead of 1848 (*Autobiography*, p. 117), but we should resist the temptation to overinterpret such slips. Darwin was generally poor at remembering dates and anniversaries, perhaps because their random nature made them inhospitable to the generation of theories. As a teenager he inquired of his sister Caroline, 'I want to know how old I shall be next Birthday. I believe 17…' (letter of 6 January 1826, *Correspondence*, I, 26). His favorite child Annie, over whose death at the age of ten he grieved for the rest of his life, died at midday on 23 April 1851. In the *Recollections* he misstates the date as 24th April, although the 23rd – the birthdays of St. George and Shakespeare – is difficult to dislodge from English memory. Within days of Annie's death Darwin wrote a prose elegy on her loss, possibly the most beautiful passage in all of his writings. He recalls with a remarkable exactitude, unblurred by grief, her buoyant joyousness as she pirouetted ahead of him on their walks, her whole form 'radiant with the pleasure of giving pleasure.' (See Francis Darwin, *Life and Letters*, I, 109–11.)

Easy to caricature, grossly misunderstood, Robert Waring Darwin figured as an ogre among Darwin's earlier biographers, a misconception based in part on an oft-quoted passage in the *Recollections*, in part on the compelling power of the Oedipal myth, perhaps also on the folklorish associations of fathers with giants and giants with tyranny. Early in the *Recollections* Darwin writes that he was considered by all of his schoolmasters and by his father

> as a very ordinary boy, rather below the common standard in intellect. To my deep mortification my father once said to me, 'You care for nothing but shooting, dogs, and rat-catching, and you will be a disgrace to yourself and all your family.' But my father, who was the kindest man I ever knew, and whose memory I love with all my heart, must have been angry and somewhat unjust when he used such words. (*Autobiography*, p. 28)

That Darwin retained his father's words with sufficient exactitude to put them in quotations after sixty years suggests something of the pain they inflicted. The timidity of the understated '*somewhat* unjust' preserves intact the child's fear of indicting a parent. The 'somewhat' also casts doubt on Darwin's assertion of his father's kindness, as though he were atoning for even so mild an accusation by the hyperbole of his praise. Yet to appreciate the full force of the passage, we must recognize the fact of the father's kindness, the son's love of his memory, but also his resentment of the indisputable cruelty and injustice of these particular words. They stand out so sharply in Charles's mind because they were so wrong in their prognostication and so *uncharacteristic* in their harshness and anger.

The misapprehension of Dr. Darwin as a domestic bully persists, despite its evident falseness. Psychoanalytic readings of Darwin's 'case' assume a violent but repressed hostility towards a tyrannical father, a repression which produced the assorted illnesses – nausea, vomiting, palpitations, flatulence, boils, dizziness, eczema – which did in fact plague Darwin through much of his adult life.[39] Dr. Rankine Good is the most articulate advocate of the Oedipal thesis. According to Good,

> a wealth of evidence…unmistakably points to…[Darwin's] symptoms as a distorted expression of the aggression, hate, and resentment felt, at an unconscious level, by Darwin towards his tyrannical father, although, at a conscious level, we find the reaction-formation of the reverence for his father which was boundless and most touching … For Darwin *did* revolt against his father. He did so in a typical obsessional way (and like most revolutionaries) by transposing the unconscious emotional conflict to a conscious intellectual one – concerning evolution. Thus, if Darwin did not slay his father in the flesh, then in his *The Origin of*

*Species, The Descent of Man,* &c., he certainly slew the Heavenly Father in the realm of natural history.[40]

Dr. Good assumes, erroneously, that Darwin's love of his father was a mere mask for the reality of his resentment; rather, the two emotions coexisted throughout his life, the one acknowledged, the other not. No reader of the Darwin family letters can fail to be struck by their extraordinary warmth and geniality, a familial high spirits irradiated by love. The letters to and from the Mount while Charles is aboard the *Beagle* comprise a kind of epistolary adventure story, with Charles providing the plot in the form of his daily discoveries, his sisters supplying the local news, and the whole presided over by the silent presence of 'Papa.' The aged scientist who opens his *Recollections* as if he were a dead man from another world seems light-years distant from the ebullient youth who describes his setting out from Plymouth harbor in a raging gale. 'Papa's eyes were full of tears,' Caroline writes on receiving Charles's account of his stormy embarkation, 'when he thought first of your miserable night and then of your good-natured Captain in all the confusion paying you a visit and arranging your hammock.'[41] Charles learned of his father's tears of concern in a letter from Caroline he opened in April 1832, when anchored off Rio de Janiero:

> The sun was bright & the view resplendent; our little ship was working like a fish; so I said to myself, I will only just look at the signatures: it would not do;... I rushed below; there to feast over the thrilling enjoyment of reading about you all: at first the contrast of home, vividly brought before ones eyes, makes the present more exciting; but the feeling is soon divided & then absorbed by the wish of seeing those who make all associations dear. –
>
> It is seldom that one individual has the power [of] giving to another such a sum of pleasure, as you this day have granted me. —I know not whether the conviction of being loved, be more delightful or the corresponding one of loving in return. —I ought for I have experienced them both in excess. — *(Correspondence,* I, 220)

I find no repressed hostility in these words, only a remarkable ease in the expression and receipt of love. Years later Charles's sister Catherine wrote him of their father's last days, and again I find evidence not of tyranny but of the persistence of bonds of affection exceptional in a motherless family:

> My father is perfectly collected, and placid...so uncomplaining, so full of everybody else, of all the servants, the servants' children, etc. He attempted to speak about you this morning, but was so excessively overcome he was utterly unable; we begged him not to speak...God

comfort you, my dearest Charles, you were so beloved by him. (Letter of 11 and 13 [?] November 1848, *Emma Darwin*, II, 119–20)

Yet Dr. Darwin's harsh words persisted in his son's memory, their power perhaps deriving from the fact that Charles seems to have shared his father's dim view of his prospects. So too did all of his schoolmasters, as he points out just before citing his father's words. The Headmaster of Shrewsbury School dragged him before his classmates, held him by the ear, and declared, 'This stupid fellow will attend to his gases and his rubbish, but not work at anything useful.' Such tales of intellectual rags-to-riches have a certain charm, for they give hope to us all, but this one is very likely rooted in fact[42] and shares an important element with Dr. Darwin's accusation of caring for nothing but shooting and rat-catching. In neither is Charles accused of doltish sloth but of engaging in what appears to his elders – and doubtless also to himself – to be unprofitable activity. The 'gases' for which the Rev. Butler chides the young Charles were very likely the products of his chemistry experiments with his brother Erasmus in a crude garden laboratory at the Mount, prototype of the rudimentary instrumentation and improvised equipment – saucers, tin biscuit boxes, bits of thread – of his laboratory at Down House. The shooting and rat-catching that enraged Dr. Darwin were his early self-education in natural history. 'I consider that all I have learnt of any value has been self-taught,' he remarked late in life. Asked if his formal education had been of any value, he replied with bitter brevity, 'None whatever.'[43] It is not surprising that Darwin underestimated what he had learned, especially at Cambridge, in the course of his almost exclusively classical education, for his teachers, with the decisive exception of his botany professor, the Rev. John Henslow, badly underestimated him. He similarly, and perhaps for the same reason, underestimated his father's contribution to his intellectual culture.[44] His mentors and his father were justified in accusing him of idleness had he been preparing to become, as his father first hoped, a physician like himself or, failing that, a clergyman. They were wrong if he was in training to become the author of *The Origin of Species*, an outcome as unlikely to the young Darwin as learning he had been 'elected King of England.'[45] An idle schoolboy, Darwin was anything but an idle child. 'Idleness' is a word he often uses but a state of mind he rarely experienced. He uses the word in the idiosyncratic sense not of 'inactivity' but of 'working fiercely at an activity that gives him pleasure,'[46] such as chasing beetles when he should be translating Virgil, or experiencing the coruscation of ideas on transmutation that poured into his head and notebooks in 1838 when he ought to have been revising his notes on *The Geology of the Voyage of the Beagle*. 'I have been sorely tempted to be idle,' he wrote to Charles Lyell,

that is as far as pure geology is concerned, by the delightful number of new views, which have been coming in, thickly and steadily, on the

classification and affinities and instincts of animals – bearing on the
question of species – note book, after note book has been filled, with
facts, which begin to group themselves *clearly* under sub-laws.
(*Correspondence*, II, 107)

In time, after accusations of childhood idleness lost some of their sting and
Darwin had found his true vocation, he could play on the paradox of his working
hard on research that the world at large considered idle. He apologizes to his
sister Caroline for being a poor correspondent, for it is difficult 'to write if one
does not write often, and to do that is very hard work for a very idle yet busy
man.'[47] By the time he had become the world-renowned author of *The Origin
of Species*, the word 'idleness' had lost much of its idiosyncratic flavor: 'I cannot
be idle, much as I wish it, and am never comfortable except when at work.
The word holiday is written in a dead language for me.'[48] Darwin had translated
his childhood play into his life's work.

With the illusory clarity of hindsight, it is difficult for us to appreciate the
mixture of uncertainty and apparent prescience that marks the slow unfolding
of Darwin's career. Because he so altered the intellectual world we inhabit,
including our conception of what a scientist is and does, we fail to appreciate
how uncharted a course he followed. A trivial instance: during his engagingly
prosaic courtship, filled with love-letters about pots and pans and the wages of
London parlor-maids, Emma Wedgwood asks him to correct any flaws of style
in her letters, for 'in the wife of a literary man' such faults 'would not do you
credit.'[49] Darwin had already drafted his book on the formation of coral reefs
and had twice been invited to read papers before the London Geological Society,
yet Emma thinks of him as a *man of letters*, not a scientist. She does so not
because of ignorance (she was a woman of keen judgment and intelligence)
but because at the time she wrote – November 1838 – the word *scientist* did
not exist in English. William Whewell, a philosopher of science and President
of the Geological Society which Darwin had addressed, wrote in 1840, 'We
need very much a name to describe a cultivator of science in general. I should
incline to call him a Scientist.'[50]

Much later in the century, to judge from a curious sentence in Francis
Darwin's *Life and Letters* (1887), the idea of science as an independent
profession was still not yet clearly established. Francis is unaware of the
contradiction that immediately strikes the modern reader on either side of the
colon following 'Fitz-Roy':

There is no evidence of any intention of entering a profession after his
return from the voyage, and early in 1840 he wrote to Fitz-Roy: 'I have
nothing to wish for, excepting stronger health to go on with the subjects
to which I have joyfully determined to devote my life.' (*Life and Letters*,
I, 243)

By 'profession' Francis has in mind the traditional callings of cleric, physician, lawyer, or teacher. The profession that Darwin so joyfully determined upon – that of 'cultivator of science in general' – he in considerable measure created. Had he not lost his faith in Christianity (there was no sudden spiritual crisis, only an imperceptibly gradual falling away of convictions never passionately held), he would almost certainly have combined, as did his fellow beetle-chasers and his Cambridge mentor John Henslow, the profession of clergyman with his interests as a naturalist. Important science had of course been practiced for centuries, but after Darwin had abandoned medicine and the clergy, there was no organized profession of science for him to enter: no graduate schools to attend, no Guggenheim or National Science Foundation fellowships, no Woods Holes or Brookhavens or Institutes for Advanced Study, no vast scientific bureaucracy – academic, governmental, and private – to support and direct research.

Darwin was essentially self-trained. He mastered dissection, for example, by cutting up some ten thousand barnacles that passed in and out of Down House, briny mementos of his *Beagle* days. He was an amateur of science, but an amateur of world class, and some of his notorious diffidence[51] doubtless stems from the self-doubt of the self-taught. Yet the same self-education gave him an extraordinary freedom from professionally conditioned presuppositions that enabled him to do major research in half a dozen specialities. Turning understatement into something of a fine art, he maintained so low a profile that in time he all but vanished behind his bushy beard, or beneath the hedges of Down House, which he elevated into a protective vegetable shield by lowering the lane that passed in front of the grounds. Once settled into middle age and the raising of a family, he preferred the quiet, local role of 'squarson' – a kind of squire-parson-farmer[52] – to the dreaded exposure brought on by his worldwide fame. Among the householders of the village of Downe in Bagshaw's *Directory* of 1847, Charles Darwin is listed as 'farmer,' a credible designation given the time he spent with pigs, horses, breeding, and manure. When his childhood pockets became too small, his father bought him a specimen cabinet, and when his curiosity outgrew the vast tribe of *cleoptera*, he hired others to gather specimens and to teach him. As a medical student at Edinburgh he found the lectures 'intolerably dull' and fled the operating room after seeing a child mangled in the days before anesthesia.[53] But he paid high wages to a former black slave who was resident in Edinburgh – 'a very pleasant and intelligent man' – to teach him the taxidermy of birds.[54] He also stole time from the medical curriculum to sail with the dredgermen and oyster-fishers of Newhaven. The fruits of his researches issued in two scientific papers read to an undergraduate society. In one of the papers, with a boyish braggadocio that contrasts starkly with his later self-effacement, he lays claim to a discovery that 'does not appear to have been hitherto observed either by Lamarck, Cuvier, Lamouroux, or any other author.'[55]

For all his shooting, bug-hunting and academic mediocrity at Edinburgh and Cambridge, Darwin also found time for reading. In the *Recollections* he mentions two books read at Cambridge that deeply influenced *The Voyage of the Beagle* and *The Origin of Species*. In the Rev. William Paley's *Natural Theology* (1802) he encountered the classic formulation of the 'argument from design' that he later stood on its head, through the inverted and heretical teleology of Natural Selection.[56] He read Alexander von Humboldt's *Personal Narrative of Travels to…the New Continent* (1799–1804) with such enraptured attention that he in effect *dreamed* the voyage of the *Beagle* before he ever embarked upon it.[57] Darwin's sensibility had been formed on the modest hills and quiet rivers of Shropshire. Humboldt's fusion of exotic sublimity and scientific exactitude, his descriptions of tropical forests and frozen volcanic peaks, fired Darwin's imagination. What began as enthusiasm blossomed into obsession. In his final weeks at Cambridge, four months before the *Beagle* invitation arrived, he wrote to Caroline Darwin:

> All the while I am writing now my head is running about the tropics: in the morning I go and gaze at Palm trees in the hot-house and come home and read Humboldt: my enthusiasm is so great that I cannot hardly sit still on my chair…Henslow promises to cram me in geology. –I never will be easy till I see the peak of Teneriffe and the great Dragon tree; sandy, dazzling, plains, and gloomy silent forest are alternately uppermost in my mind…I have written myself into a Tropical glow. (Letter of 28 April 1831, *Correspondence*, I, 122)

He taught himself Spanish, planned to book passage with some Cambridge friends to Tenerife, and, of inestimable importance to his later work, began the systematic study of geology. Just after hastening back from a geological tour in Wales for the start of the shooting season at Maer, he was handed the letter from Professor Henslow that determined the future course of his life:

> I have been asked…to recommend…a naturalist as companion to Capt Fitzroy employed by Government to survey the S. extremity of America – I have stated that I consider you to be the best qualified person I know of who is likely to undertake such a situation – I state this not on the supposition of your being a *finished* Naturalist, but as amply qualified for collecting, observing, & noting any thing worthy to be noted in Natural History…. The voyage is to last 2 years & if you take plenty of Books with you, any thing you please may be done –You will have ample opportunities at command – In short I suppose there was never a finer chance for a man of zeal & spirit. (Letter of 24 August 1831, *Correspondence*, I, 128–9)

The timing must have seemed providential, for Darwin at twenty-two was still a believing, if unzealous, Christian. Had the invitation come a year or two earlier, he would have been an unnoticed and unpromising undergraduate. A few years later he would quite probably have been married and ordained, with responsibilities that would have precluded his accepting the offer, as they prevented his naturalist friend and senior, the Rev. Leonard Jenyns, who refused the position before it was offered to Darwin. He was in a state of extraordinary intellectual receptivity and physical well-being that propelled him across seas and deserts and up the peaks of the High Andes, where he climbed above the frozen corpse of a horse of less endurance than he.[58] The timing in the larger intellectual world was equally fortuitous. Professor Henslow's parting present to his young protege was Volume I of Charles Lyell's just-published *Principles of Geology* (1830). Lyell's undermining of the Biblical account of Creation and of the Flood is implicit in his subtitle, if never stated in his text: *An Attempt to Explain the Former Changes of the Earth's Surface, by Reference to Causes Now in Operation*. Lyell made it possible for Darwin to interpret the significance of the geological evidence he found encoded high in the Cordillera or under the waters of the Keeling Islands. Perhaps more important, he alerted Darwin to physical processes that, over previously unimaginable aeons of time, account for great changes through gradual increments, processes that Darwin later extended from the province of geology to that of living things.

But Darwin's 'authoritarian and tyrannical father,'[59] as legend has it, adamantly opposed the voyage. The fact is a good deal stranger, as we learn from the *Recollections*:

> I was instantly eager to accept the offer, but my father strongly objected, adding the words fortunate for me, – 'If you can find any man of common sense, who advises you to go, I will give my consent.' (*Autobiography*, p. 71)

As if the strain of disappointed expectation might be too great to bear, Darwin at first declined Henslow's invitation in a letter whose scrupulousness is as evident as its pain.[60] On the same day (30 August, 1831), Dr. Darwin wrote to his brother-in-law Josiah that Charles had been invited to sail on

> a voyage of discovery for 2 years. –I strongly object to it on various grounds, but I will not detail my reasons that he may have your unbiassed opinion on the subject, & if you think differently from me I shall wish him to follow your advice. (*Correspondence*, I, 132)

In this exchange of domestic civilities on a heroic scale, Dr. Darwin asked Charles to argue his eight objections to the voyage before his uncle at Maer. Charles did so, fairly and vigorously, stressing the dangers of the voyage and its possible damage to his future character as a clergyman. Uncle Josiah responded to each of his brother-in-law's objections, the last point in his letter serving as a virtual prophecy of Charles's future:

> 8- The undertaking would be useless as regards his profession [as a clergyman], but looking upon him as a man of enlarged curiosity, it affords him such an opportunity of seeing men and things as happens to few. (Letter of 31 August, 1831, *Correspondence*, I, 134)

The flurry of letters between Mare Hall and the Mount ends with one of Dr. Darwin's few surviving letters (he disliked holding a pen, perhaps because of the girth of his fingers):

> Dear Wedgwood,
>     Charles is very grateful for your taking so much trouble and interest in his plans. I made up my mind to give up all objections, if you should not see it in the same view as I did. –
>     Charles has stated my objections quite fairly and fully –if he still continues in the same mind after further enquiry, I will give him all the assistance in my power.
> Many thanks for your kindness –yours / affectionly / R.W. Darwin
> (*Correspondence*, I, 135)

Dr. Darwin's promise of assistance was more than a gracious gesture. By virtue of his large medical practice and shrewd investments, he was a wealthy man. The post of naturalist aboard the *Beagle* was unpaid. Charles had no means of support other than his father's generosity, freely forthcoming even after he had abandoned Dr. Darwin's first preference of a profession and might well abandon his second. Assistance meant, in addition to moral support, paying for Charles's books, clothes, instruments, and food.

## 4

There followed what Stephen Jay Gould has called 'perhaps the greatest intellectual adventure ever experienced by one man.'[61] It is not my purpose to describe that adventure but to focus on the ageing scientist who recalled it forty years later in the tranquility of Down House, a more commodious and anchored *Beagle*, where he slowly settled into the posthumous self that authored the *Recollections*. In his granddaughter Nora's edition, that posthumous self gazes at the reader from a photograph taken within a year of his death. He leans against a veranda pillar covered with the climbing vines he described in *The Power of Movement in Plants*. One of the tendrils touches the rim of his black, round-rimmed hat; another appears to grope for the collar of his black, clerical-looking cape. The tangled tendrils of the vine appear to mimic the

Figure 6: Charles Darwin in his last years on the verandah of Down House, 1880.

bushy fringes of his beard. Darwin was an egalitarian across the whole spectrum of living things.* Something of a crawler himself, he had a special sympathy for 'lower,' slow-moving creatures – worms, barnacles, creeping plants. The peculiarity of his genius is its slowness, thought without apparent motion, a quality rendered by the repose of the photograph, the cocoon-like enclosure

---

* 'Animals whom we have made our slaves we do not like to consider our equals. –((Do not slave-holders wish to make the black man other kind)) animals with affections, imitation, fear of death, pain, sorrow for the dead – respect...' ('Transmutation Notebooks,' B 231, cited in *Metaphysics, Materialism*, p. 187). Darwin was singularly free of all *conditioned* repugnances – to a particular color of skin, to the odors of intimate organs, to the smell of feces. When courting his wife, he frequented the London Zoo and observed the sex-play of Orangutans. But first he remarks on a kind of mammalian fellowship between dogs and humans:

> A dog whines, & so does man. –dogs laugh for joy, so does dog bark (not shout) when opening his mouth in romps, he smiles.... We need not feel so much surprise at male animals smelling vagina of females. – when it is recollected that smell of one's own pud[enda] not disagree[able.] – Ourang outang at Zoology Gardens touched pud of young males & smells its fingers. Seeing a dog & horse & man yawn, makes me feel how <much> all animals <are> built on one structure. (*Metaphysics, Materialism*, p. 21)

The orangutan smells not its paws but its *fingers*; Darwin delights in our close kinship with other primates, a family connection that scandalized his contemporaries.

of the cloak. We so habitually associate genius with quickness – the 'Eureka!' of Archimedes or the acceleration of Newton's falling apple – that we cannot imagine a powerful mind that works slowly, but to stupendous effect. 'He used to say that he was not quick enough to hold an argument with anyone,' Francis Darwin writes; he then adds, without malice, 'and I think this was true.'[62] The eyes that look directly into the lens are kind but irremediably sad. The effect is haunting, a riddling portrait of a man, who, quite to his own surprise and regret, found himself at the center of the fiercest intellectual and religious quarrel of the nineteenth century. At first glance the aged figure might be mistaken for a country parson. But the broad, round-brimmed hat gives him the look of a *padre*, one of the village priests he had seen fifty years earlier in the villages of South America.

Of all Darwin's singularities, none was more consequential than his capacity to visualize the passage of time in slow-motion. He sensed and measured time not in hours or years but over aeons. He had what he called a *'glacial eye,'* by which he meant a Methuselahian capacity to track and hold in his mind's eye the incremental processes that gave rise to mountains, or the accretive building by millions of animalicules – 'myriads of tiny architects'[63] – that over time raised from the ocean floor the coral island of Cocos, a process that he mirrored in miniature in the long gestation of *The Origin* itself.*

In Darwin's world of elongated temporal vistas, elegy is a virtual impossibility, for we measure loss in human time. Even when he writes of his own ageing, Darwin remains essentially an outsider. All of his life Darwin had concentrated his intelligence on the observation of external nature. With respect to the world within his own mind he was neither especially interested nor informative. He returned Francis Galton's questionnaire on mental traits with a characteristically self-effacing note: 'I have answered the questions as well as I could, but they are miserably answered, for I have never tried to look into my own mind.'[64] The note is doubly surprising, for it was sent three years *after* he wrote his *Recollections*.

The great, formative autobiographies of Western literature – the *Confessions* of St. Augustine and of Rousseau, the *Prelude* of Wordsworth, come to mind – were written by men who were by nature self-obsessed. Darwin is unique as an

---

* Darwin dilates time; Carlyle, in contrast, foreshortens its passage. In his histories, events separated by centuries seem to occur simultaneously. Evolution accelerates into its opposite: metamorphosis. In *Past and Present* the walled Abbey of St. Edmundsbury appears alongside the Workhouse of St. Ives, contrasting communities of fellowship and alienation. In *The French Revolution*, as the walls of the Bastille fall to the roar of the crowd, we also see the fall of Troy and of Jericho, ancient prototypes of the modern event. Carlyle is a master of time-annihilating juxtapositions; Darwin, a meticulous chronicler of incremental change.

autobiographer in the degree to which he remained a stranger to himself. He was selfless in the double sense of exceptional generosity and exceptional elusiveness as a person, despite the openness and simplicity remarked upon by all who knew him. Highly idiosyncratic, eccentric to a degree unusual even for an Englishman, he possessed so transparent a self that he never obtruded upon his own field of vision.[65] Such freedom from the distractions of self-consciousness gave him extraordinary analytic cunning whenever he chose himself as the object of his own observation. Seated before a mirror, he engaged in an uncanny act of self-objectification that enabled him to watch himself laugh, to persist in the laughter and to hear that laughter with such detachment that it registered as *noise*:

> Looking at one's face whilst laughing in glass and then as one ceases, or stops the noise, the face clearly passes into smiles –laugh long prior to talking, hence one can help speaking, but laughing involuntary. – ('Transmutation Notebooks,' N 6, in *Metaphysics, Materialism*, p. 71)

The self-enchantment that underlies all autobiography, and that lends the genre a fascination akin to that of watching another person asleep, is here totally absent. Darwin turns the defining act of narcissism – gazing at one's own image – into an act of self-effacement.

There is a chilling element in such detachment, a coldness popularly associated with the objectivity of science. The *Recollections* reinforce the stereotype to the point of caricature: the scientist in so deep a freeze he has become 'a dead man.'[66] Darwin's metaphor is careless (dead men see nothing) and disconcerting, like the image at the end of the *Recollections* of his mind as an unfeeling 'machine for grinding general laws out of large collections of facts.'[67] From the perspective of his posthumous self, there had been an irrecoverable falling away from the youth who had once exclaimed, in anticipation of sailing on the *Beagle*, 'Gloria in excelsis is the most moderate beginning I can think of!'[68] Yet despite Darwin's own disclaimers, acuity of mind and intensity of feeling persisted to the end. Four years after completing the *Recollections*, he crowds the words 'astound[ing],' 'remarkable,' and 'marvellous' into a few excited lines to Joseph Hooker describing the sensitivity of plants to gravity and light. At the time of his death he was still puzzling over the significance of 'bloom,' the frost-white coating on certain leaves and fruits.[69]

# 8

# THE OXFORD ELEGISTS: NEWMAN, ARNOLD, HOPKINS

I cannot take my eyes from an old watercolor of Oxford, her many spires rising in the checkered sunlight above the lush verdure of meadows and hills. Pastoral landscape and ancient town are caught in perfect equipoise, the greens of the tree tops encircling the muted greys of the myriad towers and pinnacles of the University, 'green shouldering grey,' as Gerard Manley Hopkins phrased it.[1] John Wycliffe, the great early translator of the Bible, called Oxford 'the Vineyard of the Lord.'[2] For a millennium the town and the university which rose from its center have figured as a kind of urban Eden in the English imagination.

But by the mid-nineteenth century, Oxford had become an endangered Eden, increasingly blighted by industrialization and suburbanization, and fragmented as an ideal site where faith and reason, spirit and intellect, nature and architecture had once harmoniously joined in one spot. For successive generations Oxford had a way of profoundly and lastingly affecting her graduates, a disproportionate number of whom rose to high position in the Anglican Church and in government. In the world of literature, John Henry Newman, Matthew Arnold and Gerard Manley Hopkins all fell under Oxford's spell. 'Beautiful city!' Arnold apostrophized a quarter of a century after first seeing her spires:

> so venerable, so lovely, so unravaged by the fierce intellectual life of our century, so serene! ...And yet, steeped in sentiment as she lies, spreading her gardens to the moonlight, and whispering from her towers the last enchantment of the Middle Age, who will deny that Oxford, by her ineffable charm, keeps ever calling us nearer to the true goal of all of us, to the ideal, to perfection,—to beauty, in a word, which is only truth seen from another side? ...Adorable dreamer, whose heart has been so romantic! who hast given thyself so prodigally, given thyself to sides and to heroes not mine...home of lost causes, and forsaken

beliefs, and unpopular names, and impossible loyalties! (Preface, *Essays in Criticism*, 1865)

Arnold severely questions even as he praises his beloved city, implying, from his secular perspective, that Oxford is herself enchanted, an unravaged seductress enthralled to a medieval past and blind to the contentious present. Love, and a still-enraptured rejection of love, play themselves out in this best known of prose elegies to Oxford.

Yet even as Arnold roamed the Oxford countryside as an undergraduate in the early 1840s, himself a sort of adolescent 'Scholar-Gipsy,' the industrial midlands were turning themselves into Dickensian Coketowns of belching machines, miasmic fumes and rivers that had become open sewers. *Hard Times* (1854) appeared in the same decade that William Morris, Dante Gabriel Rossetti, and Edward Burne-Jones painted scenes from Malory's *Morte d'Arthur* on the walls of the new debating hall of the Oxford Union – quaint frescoes that began to fade almost before they had dried. Perched on their scaffolding, the Pre-Raphaelite brethren unintentionally enacted a scene from Tennyson's *Idylls of the King*, in which one of Arthur's knights pauses before the shimmering spires of Camelot, the city appearing and disappearing in the mists: 'Lord, there is no such city anywhere, / But all a vision....'[3] Like Camelot, Oxford has always inspired a certain quality of now-you-see-it, now-you-don't. Such a place of course awakens nostalgia, the food of dreams, but nostalgia easily liquefies into mere sentiment and rarely produces great literature. Yet Oxford *has* produced such literature, for Oxford is less a sentiment than an embodied idea, shaped equally by nature and by man, and articulated as powerfully yet delicately as the many-faceted spire of St. Mary the Virgin, the University Church, from whose pulpit Newman, Vicar from 1828 until his resignation in 1843, preached sermons that were greeted as epochs in the spiritual life of the nation.

By the 1830s Newman had become the voice of the Oxford Movement, which sought to reawaken among Anglicans the depth of doctrinal commitment and reverence for ritual of the ancient English Church, a kind of Romantic revival in religion after the long, dry sleep of the eighteenth century. He preached a 'middle way' – the Via Media – between the 'excesses' of Roman Catholicism on the one hand (the intrusion of papal authority, 'Mariolatry,' – all that set Protestant teeth on edge) and the 'deficiencies' of radical Protestantism on the other (the militant denial of all authority other than that of Scripture). Newman's church stood on a site consecrated in Anglo-Saxon times, and the city, once a walled town, grew up around it, along with the University. The three martyred Anglican bishops – Latimer, Ridley and Cranmer – were tried in the chancel of St. Mary's in 1554, then sentenced to be burned alive within earshot of the pulpit by the Catholic Queen Mary Tudor. John Wesley preached from the same pulpit in the eighteenth century. In 1827, the year before Newman began his ministry at St. Mary's, as if in providential anticipation of the size of his audiences, a new pulpit was installed and galleries erected in the nave, creating a kind of sacred national stage. Yet the effect of the interior space is neither theatrical nor massive but one of chaste beauty and aerial delicacy, as becomes a church consecrated to the Virgin. The eye is drawn down the graceful nave to the spiral stairs that rise to a wooden pulpit crowned by a halo-like baldaquin.

Town and gown flocked to hear Newman preach from that sacred mount, the gallery seating five to six hundred undergraduates plus members of the parish, the undergraduates silently intoning their faith: 'Credo in Newmanum.'[4] Newman preached on Sunday afternoons, the light fading from nave and gallery, an elegiac time of day and week. Because of an idiosyncrasy of gait – his tread was exceptionally light, quiet and rapid – Newman appeared to glide into the pulpit like an apparition. A frail, thin form framed by stained glass saints, he read from his text, rarely looking at his audience and scarcely ever gesticulating. The effect on his congregation seems all out of proportion to the cause, until we recall the absolute felicity and directness of Newman's words and the uncanny melodiousness of his articulation. He had a kind of perfect pitch of the *spoken* word – a 'silver' intonation delivered in a tenor register. I cannot begin to justify the logic of my associating Newman's voice with an anecdote Charles Darwin tells of his father, but the two always come together in my mind, like consonant bells: a devout old lady, hoping to convert Darwin's skeptical father, said to him, 'Doctor, I know that sugar is sweet in my mouth, and I know that my Redeemer liveth.'[5] Hearing Newman preach must have left that sweet taste in the mouth, a taste, apparently, that never faded. When only a handful of Newman's former Oxford congregants were still alive, a survivor recalled that voice from the past as a 'mysterious bond of union' which, after it was silenced by Newman's conversion to Catholicism, left an 'aching blank,' an 'awful pause, which fell on Oxford.'

Orchestrating scores of individual recollections of Newman into a single sustained note, Arnold in his finest prose elegy memorializes the voice that had risen from St. Mary's pulpit two generations earlier. Remarkably, he writes of the still-living Newman as if he were in fact a ghost – a long gone 'spiritual apparition.' Years earlier Arnold had eulogized Oxford as ineffably lovely but in thrall to lost causes and ancient enchantments. Now, the aged Newman has become for Arnold the incarnate *genius loci* of Oxford, and he feels toward both place and person the profoundest veneration, indeed love,[6] in tension with his own deep need to reject their allure as intellectually untenable:

> Forty years ago, when I was an undergraduate at Oxford, voices were in the air there which haunt my memory still. Happy the man who in that susceptible season of youth hears such voices! they are a possession to

him for ever. No such voices as those which we heard in our youth at
Oxford are sounding there now. Oxford has more criticism now, more
knowledge, more light; but such voices as those of our youth it has no
longer. The name of Cardinal Newman is a great name to the
imagination still; his genius and his style are still things of power. But
he is over eighty years of age; he is in the Oratory at Birmingham; he
has adopted, for the doubts and difficulties which beset men's minds
today, a solution which, to speak frankly, is impossible. Forty years ago
he was in the very prime of life; he was close at hand to us at Oxford; he
was preaching in St. Mary's pulpit every Sunday; he seemed about to
renew what was for us the most national and natural institution in the
world, the Church of England. Who could resist the charm of that
spiritual apparition, gliding in the dim afternoon light through the aisles
of St. Mary's, rising into the pulpit, and then, in the most entrancing of
voices, breaking the silence with words and thoughts which were a
religious music – subtle, sweet, mournful? ('Emerson,' 1883)

Arnold gives, and Arnold takes away: Newman enchants, but the enchantment
is half-created by smoke and mirrors, dim lights and apparitions. Newman
intones a 'religious music'; he does not articulate religious truth. For Newman's
solution to religious doubts and difficulties – conversion to Catholicism – was
for Arnold 'frankly impossible.'


## 2

Newman unfolds the story of that conversion in the *Apologia Pro Vita Sua*
(1864–5). He had been attacked in print by the Reverend Charles Kingsley
for being, in essence, a fool or a knave – a fool for believing in the dogmas and
miracles of the Roman Catholic Church, or a knave for pretending to believe
them. Kingsley, an espouser of 'muscular Christianity' and a celebrant of the
bliss of connubial sex, evidently had a visceral loathing of what he took to be
Newman's intellectual deviousness and effeminacy. He was also, as an English
gentleman, appalled by Newman's 'betrayal' of England by converting to Rome.
Nor was he alone in seeing that conversion as a national scandal. Indeed,
given Newman's prominence in the Anglican Church, his defection had the
shock-effect of Burgess and Maclean surfacing in Moscow at the height of the
Cold War. But perhaps the accusation that most pained Newman was tucked
into a parenthesis in Kingsley's pamphlet, 'What, Then, Does Dr. Newman
Mean?' (1864): proselytizing priests, 'like Dr. Newman, have turned round on
their mother-Church (I had almost said their mother-Country) with contumely
and slander.' Kingsley insinuates in his pamphlet a nefarious link between
Newman's betrayal of his church, his nation, and the God-given norms of

heterosexuality.[7] The potent word *pervert* was just coming into use to signify a deviant from the true faith; not until the 1890s, when Oscar Wilde was convicted for martyring himself by acting out in life what Walter Pater covertly espoused in his books, did *pervert* come to mean a lover of members of one's own sex. But Kingsley had repeatedly accused Newman of being 'unmanly,' the gendered equivalent of being un-English, a charge reinforced by Newman's intellectual fastidiousness, his celibacy and 'high severe' regard for virginity.[*] Newman himself may have felt disgust on imagining sexual intercourse, yet, as a Catholic priest he of course honored and celebrated the sacrament of marriage. From childhood on he believed that he was 'called' to celibacy, just as he was convinced that the world was mere shadows and imaginings – words he caused to be placed on his tombstone – and that all human ties, however tender, are the mere embrace of illusion. Such a temperament is inevitably elegiac, ego-centered, bordering on the solipsistic. 'God intended me to be lonely,' he wrote to his younger sister: 'He has so framed my mind that I am in a great measure beyond the sympathies of other people and thrown upon Himself.' And he took as a sort of motto the aggressively paradoxical apothegm, 'egotism is the true modesty.'[8]

Perhaps Newman became so passionately attached to places because he felt so keenly the transience of all other ties. The *Apologia* is a lonely book, populated less by persons – we learn nothing of his parents or siblings – than by the delineation of his religious beliefs. Yet in his daily life, as in his spiritual autobiography, he becomes deeply attached to certain persons, is much loved by them, and grieves over their loss. Indeed, Newman is a master of partings. His most moving sermon, 'The Parting of Friends,' his last utterance as an Anglican, was preached in a church overflowing with flowers and tears. And two of the great scenes in the *Apologia* portray his parting from his Anglican friends at Oxford and, at the very end, his farewell blessing to his fellow priests at the Birmingham Oratory, a small monastic community which he founded soon after his conversion and which remained his home until his death. Such scenes are implicit refutations of Kingsley's caricature of Newman as a devious, self-serving defector. But more fundamentally they are expressions of their poignant, Virgilian conviction that at best all we can embrace is shadows.

---

[*] An amusing, if startling, sentence from Newman's autobiographical novel *Loss and Gain: The Story of a Convert* (1848) comes to mind. Charles Reding, the hero, encounters a newly-married clergyman, arm-and-arm with his pretty bride: a 'faintish feeling' overcomes our hero, 'somewhat such as might beset a man hearing a call for pork-chops when he was sea-sick' (Part 2, ch. 2).

Accused of credulity, Newman boldly begins the *Apologia* by telling us not how reasonable he is but how credulous he was:

> I used to wish the Arabian Tales were true.... I thought life might be a dream, or I an Angel, and all this world a deception....

He ends by persuading us that Newman the child, is father of Father Newman the adult, who discovers that far more than the Arabian Nights is true, indeed that the only infallible repository of Truth is the Catholic Church. But antecedent to that discovery lay Newman's most fundamental conviction – that overriding the unreality of material phenomena lay 'two and two only absolute and luminously self evident beings, myself and my Creator.'[9] This is the most startling sentence in the *Apologia*. Man and God are facing mirrors, as they are in Genesis, God having created man in His own image. Yet Newman *precedes* God.

Seen in retrospect, all of Newman's life before Kingsley's assault upon him was lived in providential anticipation of his writing the *Apologia*. He completed the book in ten weekly instalments: 'Excuse my penmanship,' he apologized to his publisher; 'my fingers have been *walking* nearly 20 miles a day.'[10] But Newman's preparation had taken sixty-three years. A lifetime's collection of notes, letters, and journals lay at hand, along with a fully articulated psychology of belief and persuasion and an encyclopedic knowledge of the Christian Church, ancient and modern. He knew that he must provide a closely reasoned argument, historical and personal, for his conversion. But he had little regard for what he dismissed as 'paper logic.'* Above all, he knew that to answer Kingsley – 'He called me a *liar*'[11] – he required not a point-by-point refutation but a convincing and intimate self-portrait of 'that living intelligence, by which I write, and argue, and act.'[12] A quarter of a century before the *Apologia*, Newman had written of the true means by which our hearts are reached and

---

* The phrase is worth lingering over. 'For myself,' Newman writes,

> it was not logic that carried me on; as well might one say that the quicksilver in the barometer changes the weather. It is the concrete being that reasons; pass a number of years, and I find my mind in a new place; how? the whole man moves; paper logic is but the record of it. All the logic in the world would not have made me move faster towards Rome than I did. (*Apologia*, p. 136)

The mind is mere quicksilver – rapid, mercurial, subject (like the weather) to vagaries and influences beyond its own ken, a mere linear trace of those larger, mysterious, unpredictable, yet all-encompassing influences that lead the 'whole man' to believe this or that. 'Reason' is thus only a kind of *ex post facto* rationale for unconscious processes, a strikingly modern conception for a scholar of the ancient Church whose mind was as sharp as Occam's Razor.

our minds changed. The passage does double duty, for it is both a map of the strategy of the *Apologia* and of the innermost being of Newman the believer:

> The heart is commonly reached, not through the reason, but through the imagination, by means of direct impressions, by the testimony of facts and events, by history, by description. Persons influence us, voices melt us, looks subdue us, deeds inflame us. Many a man will live and die upon a dogma: no man will be a martyr for a conclusion.... After all, man is *not* a reasoning animal; he is a seeing, feeling, contemplating, acting animal.... Life is for action. ...to act you must assume, and that assumption is faith.[13]

In Victorian fiction the heart is commonly reached through deathbed scenes, which are legion, but – for obvious reasons – are a rarity in autobiography. The great deathbed scene in the *Apologia* (Chapter 4), a season 'when doors are closed and curtains drawn,' depicts Newman's last moments as an Anglican. Self-centered and God-centered, Newman also had a great gift for friendship. At the chapter's end, his Oxford friends come to pay their last respects to their former Anglican brother. Newman causes us to feel the breaking of those ties like the severing of chords within ourselves. His closing sentences are beautifully understated, the more moving because so sparse, so circumstantial, so chastely controlled – a valediction to a former self, to his Oxford home, to the friends who had given him warmth and light. Such is the efficacy of the passage that in reading it I always imagine Newman as recumbent, though he nowhere indicates this. The procession of those who bid their last farewells is no chill catalogue of names, for we have met them all only a few pages before. Newman had been profuse in expressing his affection and reverence *then* so he could be austere *now*: the Reverend John Keble, who had inaugurated the Oxford Movement with a sermon preached from the pulpit of St. Mary's – 'with what awe did I look at him!'[14] – an awe that had grown into love. Or the gentle Dr. Pusey, whom Newman lacked the heart to convince of their doctrinal differences, Pusey living in an 'affectionate dream' of accord that now had to be shattered. And lest we mistake the closing paragraphs for coldness, we have still freshly in mind a sentence from one of Newman's old letters that precedes it by only a few pages:

> And then, how much I am giving up in so many ways! and to me sacrifices irreparable, not only from my age, when people hate changing, but from my especial love of old associations and the pleasures of memory. (*Apologia*, p. 177)

To end on this note might strike us as excessive, perhaps self-pitying. Instead, we are left with a few flowers – a wall of snapdragon – emblems of Newman's shattered dream of perpetual residence at Oxford – and the reassuringly simple words: 'friends,' 'dear,' and 'kind':

> I left Oxford for good on Monday, February 23, 1846. On the Saturday and Sunday before, I was in my house at Littlemore simply by myself, as I had been for the first day or two when I had originally taken possession of it. I slept on Sunday night at my dear friend's, Mr. Johnson's, at the Observatory. Various friends came to see the last of me; Mr. Copeland, Mr. Church, Mr. Buckle, Mr. Pattison, and Mr. Lewis. Dr. Pusey too came up to take leave of me; and I called on Dr. Ogle, one of my very oldest friends, for he was my private Tutor, when I was an Undergraduate. In him I took leave of my first College, Trinity, which was so dear to me, and which held on its foundation so many who had been kind to me both when I was a boy, and all through my Oxford life. Trinity had never been unkind to me. There used to be much snap-dragon growing on the walls opposite my freshman's rooms there, and I had for years taken it as the emblem of my own perpetual residence even unto death in my University.
>
> On the morning of the 23rd I left the Observatory. I have never seen Oxford since, excepting its spires, as they are seen from the railway. (*Apologia*, pp. 182–3)

Newman had a special fondness for snapdragon, native to southern Europe and always something of an alien in England. It was not until February of 1878 that he ended his long, self-imposed exile from Oxford. *The Times* reported Newman's triumphal return to receive an honorary degree. He visited the aged Dr. Pusey and was fêted at Trinity high table. When he had first arrived at Trinity in 1816, his only real companion, he wrote, was the snapdragon on the wall separating his college from Balliol, visible from his undergraduate rooms. In 1880, after the Catholic Church all too belatedly made him a Cardinal, he revisited the same rooms and inquired if the snapdragon still grew on the wall between Trinity and Balliol. Despite his deep mistrust of 'the reality of material phenomena,' Newman had a passion for places, for the scent of flowers, and a profound need for the proximity of human faces.

The closing chapter of the *Apologia* contains some of Newman's grandest prose, and also his most personal and elegiac. He tells us that becoming a Catholic was like returning to port after a rough sea, that the Church is God's saving bulwark against the wild, tempestuous intellect of man in a fallen world. As he turns from his earlier self-defence to the defence of his Church, his writing rises above the personal and colloquial and assumes a sweep and grandeur not heard in English prose since the great divines of the first Elizabethan Age. But then, in the closing paragraphs, Newman strikes an altogether more personal note as he addresses the dwindling company of his brethren at the Birmingham Oratory. Newman had always loved the sound of church bells, perhaps especially the six majestic bells that rang from the tower of St. Mary's. On arriving at Oxford fresh out of school he wrote rhapsodically in his journal of 'Bells pealing. The pleasure of hearing them. It leads the mind to a longing after some thing I know not what. ...something dear to us and well known to us, very soothing. Such is my feeling at this minute, as I hear them.'[15] A muffled, scarcely perceptible bell sounds quietly through the closing paragraphs, each a single sentence, a death knell for the whole dwindling company soon to be dust, names that Newman intones liturgically, melodically, as if in requiem for them and for himself:

> I have closed this history of myself with St. Philip's name upon St. Philip's feast-day; and, having done so, to whom can I more suitably offer it, as a memorial of affection and gratitude, than to St. Philip's sons, my dearest brothers of this House, the Priests of the Birmingham Oratory, AMBROSE ST. JOHN, HENRY AUSTIN MILLS, HENRY BITTLESTON, EDWARD CASWALL, WILLIAM PAINE NEVILLE, and HENRY IGNATIUS DUDLEY RYDER? who have been so faithful to me; who have been so sensitive of my needs; who have been so indulgent to my failings... – with whom I have lived so long, with whom I hope to die.
>
> And to you especially, dear AMBROSE ST. JOHN; whom God gave me, when He took every one else away; who are the link between my old life and my new; who have now for twenty-one years been so devoted to me, so patient, so zealous, so tender; who have let me lean so hard upon you; who have watched me so narrowly; who have never thought of yourself, if I was in question.
>
> And in you I gather up and bear in memory those familiar affectionate companions and counsellors, who in Oxford were given to me, one after another, to be my daily solace and relief; and all those others, of great name and high example, who were my thorough friends, and showed me true attachment in times long past...
>
> And I earnestly pray for this whole company, with a hope against hope, that all of us who were once so united, and so happy in our union, may even now be brought at length, by the power of the Divine Will, into One Fold and under One Shepherd.

*May* 26, 1864.                                    In Festo Corp. Christ.

Ambrose St. John had served at Newman's side since their early days together at Oxford. God may have intended Newman 'to be lonely,' but he was buried beside his 'beloved disciple' in a single grave.

## 3

The 'spiritual apparition' that glided through the aisles of St. Mary's in the 1830s materialized in the flesh for Matthew Arnold in 1880 when, at a reception honoring Newman's belated elevation to the Cardinalate, Arnold bowed in deference and Newman took the Apostle of Culture's hand in his own. This laying on of hands is at first blush a little surprising. For the secular, intellectually liberal Arnold, advocate of the free play of the mind, had found Newman's embrace of the dogma of Roman Catholicism 'frankly impossible.' Yet Arnold never quite freed himself from Newman's spell, indeed never wholly wished himself free, just as he remained enraptured by the 'ineffable' charm of Newman's Oxford, the 'home of lost causes.' Here we confront the ambivalence underlying Arnold's poetry and prose – a nostalgia-haunted sensibility in a mind of startling modernity. Arnold writes in our own idiom: his prose would not seem out of place in a current issue of *The New York Review*. Beneath his Oxonian urbanity he writes with all of our own anxiety, self-consciousness, self-doubt; he leans forward with an almost audible sigh into our world, whose contentious intellectual landscape he anticipates at the close of 'Dover Beach':

> And we are here as on a darkling plain
> Swept with confused alarms of struggle and flight,
> Where ignorant armies clash by night.

Longed-for certainties in tension with confused alarms; the quest for intellectual balance in an 'iron time / Of doubts, disputes, distractions, fears';[16] a seeking after wholeness in the face of fragmentation: these are the tensions that animate Arnold's prose and that eventually silenced his poetry. His criticism is filled with seeming certainty – capital C Criticism and capital C Culture – that dissolves under closer scrutiny. His poetry traverses the same unstable ground. In 'Stanzas from the Grande Chartreuse' he finds himself in a high, chill monastery, an alien walking among hooded ghosts,

> Wandering between two worlds, one dead,
> The other powerless to be born... (ll. 85–6)

The once-living, coherent world of the Middle Ages is now fossilized within the sterile walls of the monastery. Newman had compared his conversion to Catholicism to coming home to port after a rough sea. For Arnold, the 'Sea of Faith' has receded, leaving in its wake only a 'melancholy, long, withdrawing roar' ('Dover Beach,' l. 25).

One isolated bay of that once-full sea still lapped at the walls and cloistered quadrangles of Victorian Oxford. Forty years after Arnold matriculated at Balliol, the fellows were still required to be celibate, and in Arnold's day almost all the heads of colleges were Anglican clergymen. Still medieval in aspect, Oxford preserved the even older dream of pastoral in its verdant byways and meadows; horses drank from the Cherwell only a few feet from the pinnacled spire of Magdalen tower, sheep and cattle grazed on Christ Church Meadow. The pastoral landscapes of Arnold's poetry look back at a vanishing world in an iron time of doubts and fears. Yet in an age in which the Great Western Railway roared ever closer to the very center of Oxford, pastoral had become an endangered species, threatening to collapse into potted Wordsworth or reheated Keats. Arnold largely skirts this peril, for he is too self-consciously intelligent to be unaware of the incongruity of writing pastoral in the new age of steam, an age which, in Carlyle's phrase, worshiped the Machine. Indeed, the very fragility of pastoral in mid-Victorian England is one of Arnold's major themes. His most moving poetry is, paradoxically, about failure – the failure of poetry to sustain itself in a post-Romantic world, and the failure of his own powers as a poet. The keynote of Arnold's poetry is its *vulnerability*: 'But fly our paths, our feverish contact fly!' he cries out to his alter ego, the Scholar-Gipsy, who is in danger of vanishing even as Arnold brings him to life.

The setting of 'The Scholar-Gipsy' and 'Thyrsis,' Arnold's best-known elegies, is the Oxford landscape of Hinksey, Fyfield, and the 'green-muffled Cumner hills,' from which the poet's eye travels down to the towers of Oxford, 'that sweet city with her dreaming spires.'[17] This is the magical country that Arthur Clough and Arnold haunted as undergraduates, a landscape of rolling hills and distant spires, of elms and oaks, chestnuts and cherries, primroses and pink convolvuluses. The very names of the hamlets and streams that Arnold invokes are idylls in themselves: Ilsley Downs and Bablock Hythe, Iffley and Wytham, the river Isis washing the ruined walls of Fair Rosamond's Godstow Nunnery. The Scholar-Gipsy figures as the elusive personification of this landscape, but he is also, as befits an elegy to a paradise lost, a figure out of an ancient book, Joseph Glanville's *Vanity of Dogmatizing* (1661). Arnold retells the legend of the impoverished scholar who quits Oxford for a freer, vagabond life among the Gipsies, a prototypic 'Beat' poet and emblem of the fugitive within Arnold himself, caught between two worlds of a vanished past and

> ...this strange disease of modern life,
> With its sick hurry, its divided aims.
> Its heads o'ertax'd, its palsied hearts. (ll. 203–5)

Arnold's most original poetry is about the near impossibility of writing poetry in mid-Victorian England; his finest prose, an elegy to his culture's lost wholeness.

*Culture and Anarchy* (1869) is Arnold's attempt to create a stabilizing antidote to the free-thinking, dissenting, protestantizing, democratizing England of the Second Reform Bill.[18] For Arnold sought in his espousal of Culture a kind of national and secular equivalent to the fixed authority Newman had found in the Catholic Church. Newman's presence, and hence Oxford's presence, is felt throughout *Culture and Anarchy*, most especially in the famous first chapter on 'Sweetness and Light,' which Arnold originally gave as his farewell lecture as Professor of Poetry. He invokes the 'beauty and sweetness' of Newman's Oxford as an ideal of human perfection, which he calls Culture, and he pays touching tribute to the Oxford Movement as the failed instrument of achieving that perfection. He reiterates the phrase 'sweetness and light' like a liturgical incantation, the words evoking the supple, secularized ideal of Culture, which he defines as 'the study of perfection,' a softened version of Jesus's startling 'Be ye therefore perfect.'[19] For *Culture and Anarchy* is, however equivocally, at bottom a religious work in its espousal of a utopian state comprised of our 'best selves' – a sort of Anglican *Republic* but with no creed. The twin graces that Culture espouses are sweetness (moral poise) and light (intellectual flexibility). Arnold attempts to capture for Culture the authority of Scripture while abjuring all dogma. Hence he defines Culture in cadences that evoke, even as they quietly attempt to supersede, St. Paul's definition of Charity:

> Charity suffereth long, and is kind; charity envieth not; charity vaunteth not itself, is not puffed up...seeketh not her own, is not easily provoked....

> Culture looks beyond machinery, culture hates hatred; culture has but one great passion, the passion for sweetness and light....[20]

T. S. Eliot, shortly before his conversion to Anglo-Catholicism, and with conspicuous lack of 'sweetness,' attacked Arnold for attempting to 'set up Culture in place of Religion, and to leave Religion to be laid waste by feeling.'[*] From his dogmatic and fundamentalist perspective, Eliot is right: the *effect* of Arnold's Culture is, inevitably, to weaken the authority of the Church. But, always edgy when writing of Arnold, Eliot grossly misperceives Arnold's motivation, accusing him of subverting what he in fact tried to salvage. Culture may be a leaky house built on a weak foundation – Newman certainly thought it was[21] – but it is not an insidious attempt to undermine that foundation.

---

[*] 'Arnold and Pater,' 1930, *Selected Essays* (1950), p. 436. Compare the even more vitriolic assault in Eliot's 'Arnold' of 1933: 'In philosophy and theology he was an undergraduate; in religion a Philistine.' Eliot turns Arnold's term for the crass middle class upon its coiner. But religious philistines write bestsellers on how God can make you rich, or they gather at prayer breakfasts at the White House. No religious Philistine could have written as conscientious and troubled a book as Arnold's *Literature and Dogma* (1873).

Arnold felt equally the powerful cohesive force of Christianity at its height and the skeptical, divisive pressures of a world that had toppled kings and priests and enthroned the majority. A brave book, *Culture and Anarchy* looks back to Newman's Oxford even as it attempts to negotiate the perilous passage into democracy. But the counsel of perfection is at bottom a counsel of despair. Arnold's proposed alternative to anarchy – a classless society composed of our collective 'best selves' is, to borrow his own phrase, 'frankly impossible.'

4

Gerard Manley Hopkins attended Matthew Arnold's lectures as Professor of Poetry, was tutored in the pale green rooms of Walter Pater, and received into the Catholic Church by Father Newman. On first arriving at Oxford in the spring of 1863, Hopkins and his Anglican father went to the Sunday service at the University Church of St. Mary's, still resonant with the fame of Newman's sermons. Like Newman, Hopkins chose to exile himself from the place he most loved on earth. 'Not to love my University,' he wrote near the end of his life, 'would undo the very buttons of my being....'[22]

In the first rapture of his residence – 'I am almost too happy,' he wrote to his mother[23] – Hopkins composed two love sonnets 'To Oxford,' his 'park' and his 'pleasaunce,' a city of musical towers and cloistered groves. With the flourish of an Elizabethan courtier, he portrays himself as a suitor bound in 'fealty' to his mistress-city: 'More sweet-familiar grows my love to thee.' Eleven years after leaving Oxford, Hopkins returned in 1878 as a hard-working parish priest, finding both himself and his beloved Oxford much changed. His poetry, too, had changed, now more intense, compacted, idiosyncratic. The opening quatrain of 'Duns Scotus's Oxford' gorgeously evokes the medieval university town, where the great philosopher-theologian had lectured in the first years of the fourteenth century:

> Towery city and branchy between towers;
> Cuckoo-echoing, bell-swarmèd, lark-charmèd,
>    rook-rackèd, river-rounded;
> The dapple-eared lily below thee; that country and town did
> Once encounter in, here coped and poisèd powers...

This is the medieval city that had survived miraculously into the mid-nineteenth century, a harmony of urban and pastoral, tree branches visible between college spires, the song of cuckoo and lark echoed in the music of bells. 'River-rounded' is especially felicitous, for Oxford is an inland-island, encircled on three sides by the rivers Isis and Cherwell,[24] just as the cloistered colleges are walled off from the city and the city itself is ringed or rounded by hills, 'country and town' set off against one another ('coped') in perfect equipoise ('poisèd powers').

But that ancient harmony had been broken by the 'graceless growth' of red-brick suburbs – the 'base and brickish skirt' that had sprouted up around Oxford since Hopkins's first idyllic residence:

> Thou hast a base and brickish skirt there, sours
> That neighbour-nature thy grey beauty is grounded
> Best in; graceless growth, thou hast confounded
> Rural rural keeping – folk, flocks, and flowers.
>
> Yet ah! this air I gather and I release
> He lived on; these weeds and waters, these walls are what
> He haunted who of all men most sways my spirits to peace;
> Of realty the rarest-veinèd unraveller; a not
> Rivalled insight, be rival Italy or Greece;
> Who fired France for Mary without spot.

Medieval Oxford, Duns Scotus's Oxford, had preserved that distinctive balance of gray stone ringed by green, where the alliteratively linked worlds of man and nature ('folk, flocks, and flowers') throve together but are now all confounded. So Hopkins turns back in his mind to the Oxford of the great Franciscan theologian – the 'rarest-veinèd unraveller' of reality, for he is no longer at home where he works or walks.

The Church of St. Aloysius, built close to the center of Oxford shortly before Hopkins arrived as a parish priest, was about as welcome in the historic Anglican university town as the new station of the Great Western Railway. Massive, banal, built of yellow brick with graceless windows and surmounted by a dwarfish tower more resembling a stunted turret than a church spire, St. Aloysius, with its working-class parishioners, embodied an English Catholic aesthetic with which the fastidious Hopkins felt least at ease. English Catholics felt especially alienated from the surrounding Anglican community. University-educated converts to Catholicism experienced the double estrangement of being despised by the church they abandoned and distrusted by the church they adopted. Not surprisingly, Hopkins often found himself 'in a black mood'[24] during what amounted to the internal exile of his second Oxford sojourn.

He maintained his undergraduate habit of long, solitary walks through the countryside, seeking a counterweight to the stresses and rigorous demands of his strict Jesuit order. One spot in particular had always drawn him: the tiny, all-but-enisled hamlet of Binsey, with its row of aspens alongside the Thames, the bells of the University still in clear hearing, and the diminutive twelfth-century church of St. Margaret's only half a mile north-west, with its holy well sacred to the memory of St. Frideswide, patron saint of Oxford, Hopkins having long been enamored of holy wells and shrines to virgin saints. Deep in the frigid winter of 1879 he began a letter to his friend the Reverend Richard Dixon with an account of the Oxford countryside as 'but its own skeleton in winter-time,' the landscape already 'abridged and soured.'[26] By 'abridged' Hopkins means curtailed by ugly development, but he may also have intended a pun on the new Iron Bridge, as harsh as its name, erected in 1865, to the west of which lay the streams and poplars of Binsey. The long letter to Dixon that opens with forebodings for the Oxford countryside ends with a postscript dated 13 March, 1879, announcing the felling of the great double row of poplars that had lined the towpath: 'the aspens that lined the river are everyone felled.' Not *all* felled, but *everyone* felled, every single living one lopped of its irreplaceable individuality. He wrote the elegy on the day the poplars were felled:

Binsey Poplars
*felled* 1879

My aspens dear, whose airy cages quelled,
Quelled or quenched in leaves the leaping sun,
All felled, felled, are all felled;
  Of a fresh and following folded rank
    Not spared, not one
    That dandled a sandalled
   Shadow that swam or sank
On meadow and river and wind-wandering
  weed-winding bank.

 O if we but knew what we do
    When we delve or hew –
   Hack and rack the growing green!
    Since country is so tender
   To touch, her being só slender,
   That, like this sleek and seeing ball
   But a prick will make no eye at all,
  Where we, even where we mean
    To mend her we end her,
   When we hew or delve:
After-comers cannot guess the beauty been.
  Ten or twelve, only ten or twelve
   Strokes of havoc uń selve
    The sweet especial scene,
   Rural scene, a rural scene,
   Sweet especial rural scene.[27]

The quiet, thrice repeated diminuendo of the end is a song heard inwardly, as if with eyes shut, like a nursery rhyme a child repeats to fix in memory. A few years before composing 'Binsey Poplars,' Hopkins looked out of the seminary garden at Stoneyhurst and saw an ash being cut down: 'looking out and seeing it maimed there came at the moment a great pang and I wished to die and not see the inscapes of the world destroyed any more.'[28] The word 'maimed' suggests the mutilation of a limb or an organ, like the pricked eyeball in the center of the poem.* Humans and trees share limbs, a usage so common we ignore its animism; we also share mortality with trees – the poplars are downed like soldiers in a row, falling with a dull, repeated, stressed thud: 'All felled, felled, are all felled.' But Hopkins' grief over the felled trees is more than an ecologist's or aesthete's regret over the loss of airy branches that once drank the sun: it is an inconsolable grief over a sacrilege, a violation of nature figured as a 'tender…slender' girl who is brutally raped: a 'hacking' and 'pricking' transferred to his own body, his organ of sight, as if it were savaged like his 'aspens dear.'

Like Ruskin, his visual mentor, Hopkins was eye-driven, virtually photo-erotic, and much of their finest writing delineates the act of seeing.[29] Both men shared a sacramental view of nature as God's Second Book, inscribed in the features of the earth. Hence Hopkins would rather die than see the inscapes of the world destroyed. Inscape is 'individually-distinctive beauty,'[30] the unique patterning that each created thing displays as the mark of its Creator – from kingfishers to stars and trees and the features of human faces, the Creation itself figuring as a kind of second Incarnation:

> …For Christ plays in ten thousand places,
> Lovely in limbs, and lovely in eyes not his
> To the Father through the features of men's faces.
> ('As Kingfishers Catch Fire')

---

* Hopkins was fascinated by extremities of pain, from the 'crack'd flesh' of St. Lawrence 'hissing on the grate' in his prize school poem, 'The Escorial,' to the pressing to death by heavy stones of the pregnant 'Margaret Clitheroe' (now saint), a late elegiac fragment of singular beauty. Of particular pertinence here is his description, in a letter to Bridges (September 1888), of a young medical student who gouged out his own eyes, 'which was nevertheless barbarously done with a stick and some wire. The eyes were found among nettles in a field.' The gratuitous detail of the pierced eyeball found next to nettles recalls 'Binsey Poplars': 'But a prick will make no eye at all' (l. 15).

As a schoolboy, Hopkins fasted, depriving himself of water until his tongue turned black. And as a Jesuit, he practiced extreme, self-inflicted penances in a community in which close proximity to others was unavoidable but all physical contact prohibited. The eros of denial and the eros of surrender are closely intertwined, as Hopkins's covert entries over masturbation in his *Journals* suggest.

But I believe that an even older sense of sacredness underlies Hopkins's response to the desecration of the poplars, a presence that haunted the olive groves of ancient Greece, that made of the poplar the sacred tree of Apollo, and that still haunts the precincts of St. Margaret's well.[31] All gifted graduates of Oxford were students of ancient Greece and Rome. Ruskin's analysis of Homer's landscapes in *Modern Painters*, Pater's evocation at the start of *Marius the Epicurean* of the old Roman religion of *numa*, with its familial rites and immemorial oaks, and even the devoutly Roman Catholic Hopkins, in his raptures over bluebells and ancient sites, pre-Christian in origin –*Binsey* itself derives from the Anglo-Saxon for 'Bynna's river island'[32] – all reveal an ecumenical imagination equally at home in pagan Arcadia or Bethlehem. The leaves of the poplar, sacred to Apollo, are also said to quiver (*populus tremuloides*) in horror at having their limbs cut off to form the cross at Calvary. Of all the Victorians, dogmatic Father Hopkins, with his contempt for 'pagan' religion, seems furthest from the beliefs of Greece and Rome. But a strong sense of the sacred poetry of the earth survives into Christian times and is a defining note of all of our elegists.

Hopkins's grief over a desecrated landscape does not alone account for the changed temper of his poetry between his earlier sonnets of rapture of the late 1870s and the Sonnets of Desolation of the mid-1880s. 'The Wreck of the Deutschland,' Hopkins's ode occasioned by the drowning of five Franciscan nuns in the mouth of the Thames, is his great, liberating experiment, the quarry for all his later poetry, whether ecstatic or despairing. The rejection of Hopkins's most ambitious and original creation by the leading Catholic journal, *The Month*, surely compounded his sense of estrangement. Yet from the first dawning of consciousness he was aware of his own singularity. On a retreat in 1880, while meditating on *The Spiritual Exercises of St. Ignatius Loyola*, he tries to define his own utter uniqueness:

> When I consider my selfbeing, my consciousness and feeling of myself, of *I* and *me* above and in all things, which is more distinctive than the taste of ale or alum, more distinctive than the smell of walnutleaf or camphor.... Nothing else in nature comes near this unspeakable stress of pitch...this selfbeing of my own.... But to me there is no resemblance: searching nature I taste *self* but at one tankard, that of my own being.[33]

Absolute singularity is the defining mark of Hopkins's person and poetry. An 1878 photograph of Father Hopkins with his Catholic colleague on the portico of St. Aloysius's nicely illustrates his sense of apartness.[34] He stands stiffly aloof at the edge of the group, among them but not of them, looking not at the camera but upwards, with a fixed gaze of mild, enigmatic discontent.

Figure 7: Gerard Manley Hopkins (far left) with the Catholic Club at St. Aloysius's. Oxford, 1879.

In 'To Seem the Stranger Lies my Lot,' the most direct and austere of the Sonnets of Desolation, Hopkins is estranged not only from others but from himself:

> To seem the stranger lies my lot, my life
> Among strangers. Father and mother dear,
> Brothers and sisters are in Christ not near
> And he my peace / my parting, sword and strife.
>
> England, whose honour O all my heart woos, wife
> To my creating thought, would neither hear
> Me, were I pleading, plead nor do I: I wear-
> y of idle a being but by where wars are rife.
>
> I am in Ireland now; now I am at a thírd
> Remove. Not but in all removes I can
> Kind love both give and get. Only what word
>
> Wisest my heart breeds dark heaven's baffling ban
> Bars or hell's spell thwarts. This to hoard unheard,
> Heard unheeded, leaves me a lonely began.

Hopkins's self has all but occluded the world: 'I,' 'my' and 'me' recur fifteen times in fourteen lines, back-to-back in the sonnet's seventh line. Hopkins is thrice removed – from his family,[*] from his native church, and from England. His words go unheeded. Not a soul other than Robert Bridges read the sonnet during his lifetime. The clotted syntax at the end of the poem bespeaks his own 'thwarted' state as the unreciprocated lover of 'rare-dear Britain,' whose conversion he prays for in the ecstatic end of 'The Wreck of the Deutschland.' Norman White compares reading the sonnet to coming upon an epitaph on one's own tombstone. But the last line of the epitaph is wrenched into obscurity, the verb *begin* forced to do the work of an aborted, non-existent noun: Hopkins is 'a lonely *began*,' for the words for which he lived and labored have gone 'unheard…unheeded.'

The Sonnets of Desolation are also about Hopkins's estrangement from God, whose existence and power he never for a moment doubts, but of whose love he feels utterly unworthy. Perhaps even worse, he begins to fear during his profound and protracted depression in the middle 1880s that he might be going mad.[35] The sonnets came to him 'like inspirations unbidden and against my will,'[36] unwanted in-breathings, inspirations shrouded in terror, but inspirations nonetheless, in which he now 'inscapes' not the divinely individuated beauties of nature but the horrific landscape of his own mind:

> O the mind, mind has mountains; cliffs of fall
> Frightful, sheer, no-man-fathomed.
>
> ('No Worst, There Is None,' ll. 9–10)

His years in Ireland (1884–9), the years of the Sonnets of Desolation, were 'hard wearying…wasted years' in which he lived in a 'coffin of weakness and dejection…,' his writings so many 'ruins and wrecks.'[37] Like Ruskin, who late in life was intermittently insane, Hopkins heroically created great art out of the most intense personal pathology.

Yet fear of the ultimate solitude of madness was only an extreme form of the estrangement that Hopkins felt all of his life. His strong homosexual orientation (a desire whose expression he wholly suppressed) in a homophobic

---

[*] At the time of his conversion, Hopkins wrote to Newman that his parents' replies to his letters 'were terrible. I cannot read them twice.' But Hopkins's letters to them are deliberately provocative: 'You are so kind as not to forbid me your house, to which I have no claim, on condition, if I understand it, that I promise not to try to convert my brothers and sisters.' His letters are full of 'hard sayings,' to which his father replied, after a reasonable plea that his son defer his decision, 'O Gerard my darling boy are you indeed gone from me?' (White, p. 142) Despite great pain on both sides, their estrangement was never total. Near the end of Gerard's life, in 1887, Manley Hopkins published *The Cardinal Numbers*, to which his son had substantially contributed. The father's acknowledgment must be the strangest on record. He expresses thanks 'to my near relative the Rev. G. M. Hopkins, of University College, Dublin.' The *distance* in 'near relative' is as pained as it is chilling. (See White, p. 6.)

culture,[*] his Oxonian upper-class speech as a priest ministering to the working-class Irish, his slight frail body and faintly effeminate aestheticism, his naïve English patriotism among Irish nationalists, all accentuated an oddity of which Hopkins was only imperfectly aware. He confesses in a letter to his friend and former Oxford classmate Robert Bridges to suffering much – indeed being 'ruined for life' – because of his 'alleged singularities.'[38] The singularities, however, were not alleged but real. W.H. Gardner subtitled his pioneering study of Hopkins 'A Study of Poetic Idiosyncracy,' but Hopkins's idiosyncracy extended beyond his coined words, odd syntax, and sprung rhythm. He was, as R.B. Martin subtitles his biography of Hopkins, 'A Very Private Soul.' He fractured language in order to keep and communicate himself whole. Like Newman, but figuratively, he walked with a very light step; a student at University College, Dublin, reported after Hopkins's death that he was 'practically unknown to us,' although it was said that he had written some verses.[39] Gifted with almost preternatural powers of sight and articulation, he was tone-deaf to the responses of others, especially their responses to himself. In 1877, at St. Beuno's College in Wales during the year of his ordination, he preached a sermon to his fellow Jesuits, who, according to his own account, 'laughed at it prodigiously, I saw some of them roll in their chairs with laughter.'[40] One can only guess the response of a fashionable London congregation to his sermon comparing the seven sacraments to a full-uddered cow through whose teats grace flows. The simile works beautifully and endearingly from Hopkins's perspective, the physical nourishment freely given by the lactating cow symbolizing the sustenance of the Mother Church, but he is blind to its comedy.

---

[*] Hopkins decided against a possible career as an artist because of his strong erotic response to drawing the male figure. Only to the 'beauty and perfection of [Christ's] body' could he respond guiltlessly. A daring literalism animates his description of Christ's body in a sermon preached to his working-class parishioners in Liverpool:

> In his body he was most beautiful...his hair inclining to auburn, parted in the midst, curling and clustering about the ears and neck.... I leave it to you, brethren, then to picture him, in whom the fullness of godhead dwelt bodily, in his bearing how majestic, how strong and yet how lovely and lissome in his limbs.... In his Passion all this strength was spent, this lissomness crippled, this beauty wrecked, this majesty beaten down. But...for myself I make no secret I look forward with eager desire to seeing the matchless beauty of Christ's body in the heavenly light. (White, p. 317)

See R.B. Martin, *Gerard Manley Hopkins* (New York: Putnam, 1991), chap. 3, for Hopkins's powerful attraction to his classmate Digby Dolben.

Hopkins's perspective is not the world's, which baffles and estranges but does not silence him.*

For a devout Christian, adversity, even catastrophe, pales in significance against the hope of eternal life. At the heart of the Christian story lies a tortured son and a grieving mother, but overriding their griefs is the miracle of the resurrection. Perhaps that is why Hopkins, at last rejoined by his parents, is reported to have said, on his deathbed, 'I am so happy, I am so happy.'[42] Elegy, for the Christian, is a prelude to rejoicing. Hopkins's voice of hope sounds only once, but suddenly and dramatically, in the very late 'That Nature Is a Heraclitean Fire and of the Comfort of the Resurrection' (1888). This protracted sonnet with three codas opens on a celebratory note reminiscent of the much earlier 'Hurrahing in Harvest':

> Cloud-puffball, torn tufts, tossed pillows / flaunt forth,
>     then chevy on an air-
> built thoroughfare: heaven-roysterers, in gay-gangs / they
>     throng; they glitter in marches.

But the dazzling Heraclitean display of the elements soon burns itself out in entropy, man himself mired and consumed in the 'Million-fueled' bonfire of nature. Then in mid-line, as if at the burst of the Last Trumpet, the poet exclaims,

> ...Enough! The Resurrection...

Though our flesh has fallen to the 'residuary worm,' our imperishable soul remains, through Christ's sacrifice, an 'immortal diamond.'

---

* Like Newman, Hopkins remained something of an exile within his adopted Church. Both are elegists, if only by virtue of their alienation. Whenever Newman's genius seemed poised to lift him to eminence within the Church, he was thwarted, often cruelly. In 1852 he was made rector-elect of the prospective Catholic University in Dublin, where Hopkins, forty years later, drudged at grading examinations during his last dreary years. But Newman's labors were rendered fruitless and he resigned in 1856, his appointment having never been confirmed. Two months after he became editor of the liberal Catholic magazine the *Rambler*, he was again compelled to resign. He did not become a Cardinal until his seventy-ninth year, when further deferment would have created a scandal. By the time Hopkins was stationed at University College, Newman's idea of a great Catholic University had dwindled into a ramshackle institution with third-rate students and dead rats housed in its drains, from which Hopkins very likely caught the typhoid fever that killed him.[41] The offering that Hopkins had hoped to lay at the altar of his Church – 'The Wreck of the Deutschland' – went unread and unpublished until the end of the First World War.

At the end of his career as an unheard, unheeded poet, Hopkins rises, as it were, from the sweat-drenched bed of 'Carrion Comfort' and composes 'Thou art indeed just, Lord.' He speaks in a tone at once firm and tender, reverent and bold, as he pleads his case, Job-like, before his Lord.

> *Justus quidem tu es, Domine, si disputem tecum; verumtamen*
> *Justa loquar ad te: Quare via impiorum prosperatur? &c.*[43]

> Thou art indeed just, Lord, if I contend
> With thee; but, sir, so what I plead is just.
> Why do sinners' ways prosper? and why must
> Disappointment all I endeavour end?
>
> Wert thou my enemy, O thou my friend,
> How wouldst thou worse, I wonder, than thou dost
> Defeat, thwart me? Oh, the sots and thralls of lust
> Do in spare hours more thrive than I that spend,
>
> Sir, life upon thy cause. See, banks and brakes
> Now leavèd how thick! lacèd they are again
> With fretty chervil, look, and fresh wind shakes
>
> Them; birds build—but not I build; no, but strain,
> Time's eunuch, and not breed one work that wakes.
> Mine, O thou lord of life, send my roots rain.

The epigraph is from Jeremiah, himself a poet in exile. But Hopkins moves quickly from literal paraphrase to an anguished complaint of his own sterility in the season of nature's rebirth. 'Thou' and 'thee' are counterpoised with 'I' at opposite ends of each of the first two lines, like judge and defendant before the bar. By the end of the first quatrain Hopkins speaks in his own distinctive idiom. He rearranges the normal word order – Why must all that I endeavor end in disappointment? – terminating the line emphatically with the end-stopped end, which is heard twice previously in the same line in the *ent* of 'disappointment' and in the *end* of 'endeavour'.

Yet even as Hopkins's questioning of God's justice grows more insistent, his tone becomes more tender: 'Lord' and 'sir' of the first quatrain is now the daring 'thou my friend' at the start of the second. God the devouring torturer of 'Carrion Comfort,' rude wringer of the world under His right foot, is here a gentleman ('sir') seemingly acquainted with the poet. And though there can be no true equality between master and servant, there appears to be a bond of mutual respect between them, even as the poet's accusations rise in intensity. Still, he allows himself the little flourish in the seventh line: 'Oh, the sots and thralls of lust' fare better than he, the Lord's servant. For an instant Hopkins dons Elizabethan garb and declaims a Hamlet-like mini-soliloquy.

The pivotal word of the sonnet – 'spend' – comes at the turn from octave to sestet at the end of line 8:

> ...Oh, the sots and thralls of lust
> Do in spare hours more thrive than I that spend,
> Sir, life upon thy cause...

One can spend time or energy on fruitless causes, or spend oneself into bankruptcy; but *to spend* had a more overtly sexual meaning for the Victorians – *to ejaculate* – a meaning of which Hopkins was surely aware. This sexually charged subtext suffuses the sestet, where the poet transports us from an imagined courtroom to a burgeoning and fertile woodland in spring. His subject, too, changes, from the unjust thwarting of his chances in life to his impotence as a begetter of poems. Nature's fecundity mocks his sterility, for he has become 'Time's eunuch.' Hopkins borrowed this striking phrase from his own earlier letter to Bridges; 'It kills me to be time's eunuch and never to beget.' And again to Bridges, in 1888: 'All impulse fails me... Nothing comes: I am a eunuch – but it is for the kingdom of heaven's sake.'[44] The waning of his creativity compounded his depression, which in turn sapped at his creativity. Shortly before composing 'Thou art indeed just,' Hopkins complained that 'All my undertakings miscarry: I am like a straining eunuch.'[45] Here Hopkins figures as both a castrated male and an infertile woman whose conceptions miscarry. But at the end of his last letter to Dixon, he again finds himself fertile and writes of his relief at having 'conceived a sonnet.'[46] It deeply pained Hopkins that he was to remain a barren branch on the human tree, a fate he appears to have foreknown. As an undergraduate, before taking vows of celibacy, he wrote:

> Trees by their yield
> Are known; but I –
> My sap is sealed,
> My root is dry.[47]

The earlier poem is prophetic of the later, in which the poet 'spend[s]' but does 'not breed one work that wakes.' To *awaken* is to *arouse*, and all of nature awakens gorgeously in the closing lines. The fresh breeze shakes the wild parsley ('fretty chervil'). The birds build nests for their young, but Hopkins lies dry and fallow in a fertile season. The poem that opened in court ends in prayer: 'Mine, O thou lord of life, send my roots rain.' 'Mine' does double duty, modifying both 'lord' and 'roots,' but calling especially and imperatively for the impregnating rain of the Lord. Hopkins's prayer was answered, the rains came, and he conceived this exquisite sonnet.

Although Hopkins was in the bleak midwinter of his Dublin years, the poem was written in early spring. Perhaps that is why he could return in the closing lines to the same pastoral landscapes beloved by Newman and Arnold. Before the felling of the Binsey poplars, in the early raptures of his Oxford residence, Hopkins had written of the myriad towers and pinnacles of the city rising above meadows and hills. There, on a solitary spring walk to Binsey, he had seen fields 'pinned' with daisies, the banks and brakes yellow with buttercups. And in the rapid stenographic notation of his journal, he hears 'the cuckoo singing [on] one side, on the other from the ground and unseen the woodlark.'[48] This same landscape, seen for one last time through weary and estranged eyes, closes 'Thou art indeed just, Lord.'

# 9

# SWINBURNE AND THE RAVAGES
# OF TIME

Swinburne is a poet not of natural objects but of natural energies – of winds and surging waters. His scale is macrocosmic, his focus less upon the small celandine than upon the spines of mountains, less upon things seen than upon forces felt. At times he is nearly a blind poet, all tongue and ear and touch. His poetry moves away from the art of painting and, in Pater's phrase, aspires to the condition of music; after reading Swinburne one retains not an image but a tonality and a rhythm.

Traditionally, the English poet has prided himself on particularity, which the New Critics exalted as the clearest sign of genius. Donne's 'bracelet of bright haire about the bone' has dazzled readers for nearly a century. Our very conception of poetry has been shaped by the practices of the metaphysical poets and by Keats's dictum that the poet must have 'distinctness for his luxury.' We are at a loss in reading a poet who, like Swinburne, is diffuse not by default but by design.

From the perspective of Keats's principles, Gerard Manley Hopkins is in the mainstream of nineteenth-century verse and Swinburne is the eccentric. For Hopkins's attempt to etch in words the dappled individuality of things was as much a cultural as a personal preoccupation. Hopkins was simply an extreme exponent of the impulse to render with absolute accuracy the distinct profusion of nature itself. One recognizes the same impulse in the splendid exactitude of Tennyson's verse and Ruskin's prose, in the bright, crowded, microscopically accurate foliage of the Pre-Raphaelites, in Browning's eft, queer, creeping things, or even, for that matter, in the solid clutter of any Victorian mantelpiece.

Memory betrays us into believing Swinburne to be far more ornate than he is. Dismissed as over-lush and decadent, he is in point of diction the most *austere* of the greatly gifted English poets of his century. Early in his career he evokes the heady, Pre-Raphaelite scent of oversweet violets, but in his greatest poetry Swinburne is more starkly monosyllabic than Wordsworth.[1] The knight doomed to a sexually joyless service, in 'Laus Veneris,' craves death in a stanza containing thirty-seven sparse words, all but four of them monosyllables:

> Ah yet would God this flesh of mine might be
>    Where air might wash and long leaves cover me,
> Where tides of grass break into foam of flowers,
>    Or where the wind's feet shine along the sea. (ll. 53–7)

Edmund Wilson condemns Swinburne for his 'generalizing visageless monosyllables'; I would praise him as the supreme master in English of the bleak beauty of little words.

Wilson has argued that Swinburne the poet is a nullity and that his true gifts lay with the novel, in which he escapes the monotonous vocabulary of his verse: 'He can never surprise or delight by a colloquial turn of phrase, a sharply observed detail, a magical touch of color.'[2] This might be helpful if it were true, which it is not, or if it were reasonable to condemn Swinburne for not succeeding in what he did not attempt to do. If there are few sudden glories in his verse, they are suppressed in the interests of a more sustained harmony. Great art, he believed, does not vex or fret the beholder with 'mere brilliance of point and sharpness of stroke, and such intemperate excellence as gives astonishment the precedence of admiration: such beauties as strike you and startle and go out.'[3] Hopkins pushes language as far as it can go toward pointedness and sharpness of stroke; Swinburne moves it with equal daring in the opposite direction, diffusing where Hopkins concentrates, generalizing where Hopkins specifies. Together, they are the linguistic bravos of Victorian verse.

By diffuseness, however, I mean something very different from vagueness. The vague poet cannot see or speak clearly – in short, is not a poet. Swinburne is often called vague, but no one who has read his best poetry closely could ever accuse him of imprecision or carelessness with words. T.S. Eliot did not look closely enough at a famous chorus of Swinburne and charged him with laxity:

> Before the beginning of years
>    There came to the making of man
> Time, with a gift of tears;
>    Grief, with a glass that ran; (ll. 314–7)

The verses appear to make a 'tremendous statement, like statements made in our dreams,' Eliot writes of this chorus from *Atalanta in Calydon*; 'when we wake up we find that the glass that ran would do better for time than for grief, and that the gift of tears would be as appropriately bestowed by grief as by time.'[4]

The reversed verses that Eliot prefers – time with an hour-glass, grief with tears – are trite, and Swinburne wisely avoided them. But he had more positive reasons for overturning our expectation, as immediately becomes clear if we complete Eliot's truncated quotation:

> Grief, with a glass that ran;
> Pleasure, with pain for leaven;
> Summer, with flowers that fell;
> Remembrance fallen from heaven,
> And madness risen from hell... (ll. 317–21)

The chorus, like the play it mirrors, is about the terrible ambiguity of the gods' gifts to men. We are given the bitter-sweet gift of time, but time passes even as it is given, and hence our tears; yet the pangs of grief also fade with the hours, like the summer blossom. As we read the lines, we are half aware of the conventional imagery underlying them, our mind reacting as does our ear to a departure from regular rhythm, half hearing the normal beat and half hearing the eccentric.

Swinburne constantly breaks down our habitual word associations, but the rupture is so light that we scarcely notice it. The kind of gentle dislocation that Eliot condemned in the chorus from *Atalanta* gives to Swinburne's poetry the quality of a prolonged, mildly mixed metaphor, a quality which Eliot himself brilliantly exploited in his own poetry. This sense of disorientation, together with Swinburne's insistent, mesmeric metres, induces a surrealist heightening of consciousness that we associate with dreaming and that Swinburne realized with beautiful daring in 'The Leper,' a ballad about a necrophiliac monk who makes love to the remnants of his lady. Grotesquely explicit, the poem is also inexplicably lovely, like the disintegrating lady, 'sweeter than all sweet.' The word *sweet* floats like a perfume throughout 'The Leper.' It recurs most often at those moments when the sense of the poem is most repugnant, sweet sound and fetid sense miraculously counterpoised through thirty-five stanzas.

I first read this strangest of elegies to a lost love as an erotic parody of a seventeenth-century religious lyric. But parody mocks what it imitates. Instead, Swinburne pays tribute to a long tradition of religious poetry but loads his religio-lyrical ballad with shockingly sensational content. The key to this most repugnant – and perhaps exquisite – of his poems may be found in his 1862 essay in praise of *Les Fleurs du Mal* (Swinburne was one of Baudelaire's first English admirers), which he wrote at the same time that he radically revised the original poem, adding the subject of necrophilia: 'Even of the loathsomest bodily putrescence and decay he can make some noble use; pluck out its meaning and secret, even its beauty, in a certain way, from actual carrion.'[5] In the first of the poem's many strategic surprises, we learn that the narrator of this ballad-cum-dramatic monologue[6] is a cleric in holy orders (Swinburne uses clerk in its archaic sense). In an ascending order of monstrousness, the narrator of this black *In Memoriam* recounts his deeds in the most naïve of voices (imagine a reading by Peter Laurie in monk's habit):

> Nothing is better, I well think,
>     Than love; the hidden well-water
> Is not so delicate to drink:
>     This was well seen of me and her.
>
> I served her in a royal house;
>     I served her wine and curious meat.
> For will to kiss between her brows
>     I had no heart to sleep or eat.
>
> Mere scorn God knows she had of me,
>     A poor scribe, nowise great or fair,
> Who plucked his clerk's hood back to see
>     Her curled-up lips and amorous hair.
>
> I vex my head with thinking this.
>     Yea, though God always hated me,
> And hates me now that I can kiss
>     Her eyes, plait up her hair to see
>
> How she thin wore it on the brows,
>     Yet am I glad to have her dead
> Here in this wretched wattled house
>     Where I can kiss her eyes and head.
>
> Nothing is better, I well know,
>     Than love; no amber in cold sea
> Or gathered berries under snow:
>     That is well seen of her and me. (ll. 1–24)

We soon learn that the lady had died of leprosy, the 'sweet fault' for which her former lover, a knight, had spurned her. The monk had been their pander, then the voyeur of their lovemaking:

> Yea, he inside whose grasp all night
>     Her fervent body leapt or lay,
> Stained with sharp kisses red and white,
>     Found her a plague to spurn away. (ll. 65–8)

With perfect tact of tone Swinburne skirts around the shoals of the pornographic but never founders. Through a kind of verbal pointillism, he plays on the word *sweet* as both noun ('my sweet') and adjective in each of the following stanzas, simultaneously evoking the language of erotic endearment and the sickly sweet stench of death:

> (Cold rushes for such little feet –
>     Both feet could lie into my hand.
> A marvel was it of my sweet
>     Her upright body could so stand.)
>
> 'Sweet friend, God give you thank and grace;
>     Now am I clean and whole of shame,
> Nor men shall burn me in the face
>     For my sweet fault that scandals them.'
>
> I tell you over word by word.
>     She, sitting edgewise on her bed,
> Holding her feet, said thus. The third,
>     A sweeter thing than these, I said.
>
> God, that makes time and ruins it,
>     And alters not, abiding God,
> Changed with disease her body sweet,
>     The body of love wherein she abode. (ll. 33–48)

The last stanza is a miracle of economy – God, time, love, mutability and death – a litany of all the great themes of literature in four short lines.

The final, quiet shocker comes in the twenty-fourth stanza, when we learn that the lady has in fact been dead for six months, her lover embracing the remnants of her cold feet:

> Six months, and I sit still and hold
>     In two cold palms her cold two feet.
> Her hair, half grey half ruined gold,
>     Thrills me and burns me in kissing it.
>
> Love bites and stings me through, to see
>     Her keen face made of sunken bones.
> Her worn-off eyelids madden me,
>     That were shot through with purple once. (ll. 101–8)

The lover seems almost to pant, although quietly, as he praises through aspirated *h*s her bare ruined tresses: '*h*er *h*air, *h*alf grey and *h*alf ruined gold.' Only in the last three lines does the lady's skull peep through, and the delicate poise between beauty and 'the loathsomest bodily putrescence' threatens to collapse into the purely grotesque.[*]

But Swinburne mutes all such suggestion with the naïve beauty and simplicity of the monk's closing lines. He has by now contracted the lady's leprosy, grown blind from it, the page on which he inscribes his story 'writ awry and blurred':

> It may be all my love went wrong –
> 　A scribe's work writ awry and blurred,
> Scrawled after the blind evensong –
> 　Spoilt music with no perfect word.
>
> But surely I would fain have done
> 　All things the best I could. Perchance
> Because I failed, came short of one,
> 　She kept at heart that other man's.
>
> I am grown blind with all these things:
> 　It may be now she hath in sight
> Some better knowledge; still there clings
> 　The old question. Will not God do right? (ll. 129–40)

In his final, prayer-like lines, the monk alludes to the words of St. Paul: 'For now we see through a glass, darkly; but then face to face: now I know in part; but then shall I know even as I am known.' In his furthest reach of daring, the lunatic monk suggests that his lady may now in death be blessed and sighted, while he gropes in darkness and ignorance with the last stages of his disease, purged by the fires of passion and mortal illness. Now vaguely aware that he may have transgressed – 'It may be all my love went wrong' – he takes upon himself as much guilt as his pathology will allow, a guilt that he has all along half-voiced through self-abasement and self-loathing. The true audacity of 'The Leper' inheres not in its monstrous subject matter but in Swinburne's making, through the transfiguring power of language, the morally loathsome aesthetically beautiful. For his degenerate monk sings a singularly chaste love-death music – simple, ballad-like, mostly monosyllabic. Subject matter never taints style, style never euphemizes subject. Not until the early years of the twentieth century, when Richard Strauss's Salome kisses the mouth of the beheaded John the Baptist, does decadence again achieve such a sublime apotheosis.

---

[*] With the slide or glide of the half-rhyme – bones/once, z gliding into s – Swinburne subliminally suggests ooze.

## 2

Swinburne's adjectives, as with 'sweet' in 'The Leper,' have a way of detaching themselves from the nouns they adjoin and modifying instead whole lines or stanzas. He deliberately suppresses the specifying, limiting function of the adjective in order to discharge its meaning through the total poem. The search for *le mot juste* is, in the young Swinburne at least, the search for *le ton juste*, for the word which will not stick like a burr in the consciousness but serve unnoticed as a supporting note in a chord of color. Hence the intentional blandness of his diction, and his over-fondness for generalizing modifiers like 'bright,' 'sad,' 'light,' 'glad' and 'sweet.' Swinburne's earlier, Pre-Raphaelite imitations are especially rich in such diction and should be read as *etudes* in verbal coloration. The opening lines of 'A Ballad of Life,' the first of the *Poems and Ballads* of 1866, offer the reader a conditioning exercise in those lightly limiting adjectives and bland plural nouns[7] that enable Swinburne to arrange words as if they were pigments, or notes in a scale. Pairs of 'glad's, 'sweet's, and 'sad's resolve themselves into a single neutral chord, as muted as a flame rained upon:

> I found in dreams a place of wind and flowers,
>> Full of *sweet* trees and colour of *glad* grass,
>> In midst whereof there was
> A lady clothed like summer with *sweet* hours.
> Her beauty, fervent as a fiery moon,
>> Made my blood burn and swoon
>> Like a flame rained upon.
> Sorrow had filled her shaken eyelids' blue,
> And her mouth's *sad* red heavy rose all through
>> Seemed *sad* with *glad* things gone.

In these flawless minor lyrics – 'A Ballad of Life,' 'Hermaphroditus,' 'A Match,' 'Before the Mirror,' 'The Roundel' – language takes on a life independent of any ostensible subject. Words, severed from the soil of things, send out aerial roots of their own. One seems to be overhearing an exquisitely beautiful voice singing at a distance; the melody carries, but the words come muffled, as if in a foreign tongue:

> If love were what the rose is,
>> And I were like the leaf,
> Our lives would grow together
> In sad or singing weather,
> Blown fields or flowerful closes,
>> Green pasture or gray grief;
> If love were what the rose is,
>> And I were like the leaf....

> If you were queen of pleasure,
>     And I were king of pain,
> We'd hunt down love together,
> Pluck out his flying-feather,
> And teach his feet a measure,
>     And find his mouth a rein;
> If you were queen of pleasure,
>     And I were king of pain. ('A Match')

Self-engendered, self-contained, the poem is inspired not by the emotion of love but by the emotion of poetry itself.

All that Swinburne learned in composing these exercises in verbal color he put to use in the much later and more ambitious *Tristram of Lyonesse* (1882). The 'Prelude' to *Tristram* usually makes its way into the anthologies, but the rest of the poem is virtually unread, although it is one of the great erotic elegies in English. *Tristram* is undervalued largely because the wrong demands have been made upon it. As narrative or as a drama of action the poem inevitably disappoints, in precisely the ways that Wagner's *Tristan und Isolde* disappoints. In both of these essentially *lyrical* re-creations of the legend, action and characterization are wholly subordinate to the all-absorbing theme of love. Just as there are no independent arias in *Tristan*, so there are no striking images in *Tristram* that are not repeated as leitmotifs and thus reabsorbed into the enveloping texture of the verse. The Londoner who read Swinburne's poem upon its publication in 1882 and then, just one month later, heard the English premier of Wagner's music drama might well have felt a certain *déjà entendu*.[8]

From its opening lines to its close, *Tristram of Lyonesse* is about four lips that 'become one burning mouth.' As so often in Swinburne, the 'image' is more tactile than visual. It first appears when Tristram and Iseult drink the potion; it recurs in a series of variants, most notably in Tristram's praise of 'the mute clear music of her amorous mouth,' a line whose enunciation moves the mouth into the position of a kiss. The image closes the poem as Iseult bows her head over the dead Tristram, 'And their four lips became one silent mouth.'

Although love is doomed, bleak, sick and sterile in almost all of Swinburne's poetry, in *Tristram* one senses his unique exultation in portraying sex that is fulfilled, however fated. Perhaps *because* the lovers are so clearly foredoomed he could write so richly of their fulfillment. In this central legend symbolizing the lovesickness of the Western world, Swinburne creates by far his healthiest poetry:

> Only with stress of soft fierce hands she prest
> Between the throbbing blossoms of her breast
> His ardent face, and through his hair her breath
> Went quivering as when life is hard on death;
> And with strong trembling fingers she strained fast

His head into her bosom; till at last,
Satiate with sweetness of that burning bed,
His eyes afire with tears, he raised his head
And laughed into her lips; and all his heart
Filled hers; then face from face fell, and apart
Each hung on each with panting lips, and felt
Sense into sense and spirit in spirit melt. (ll. 1443–1454)

These lines occur in Canto II, 'The Queen's Pleasance,' the poem's great *liebesnacht* in which rest at last gains mastery 'in the lovely fight of love and sleep.' All of nature is absorbed into the passion of love, until the perfumed air seems an extension of the lovers' breath, the soft grass an extension of their bodies. Swinburne concluded *Tristram of Lyonesse* with a final verse paragraph that, to my knowledge, has no precedent in any other version of the legend. King Mark builds the lovers a stone chapel at the sea's edge, and in their death the lovers undergo a second doom. For the waves shatter the chapel and the sea closes over their uncoffined bones. Fulfilled love in Swinburne pays the penalty of double death.

The association of love with death is the underlying theme of almost all Swinburne's major poetry. He is of course best known for a variant on that theme – the pain implicit in all pleasure. Virtually incapable of using the word *pleasure* without its alliterative opposite, Swinburne *is* undeniably sado-masochistic, but this lurid aspect of his lyricism has obscured his true achievement. His greatest love poetry is addressed not to those literary ladies with sharp teeth – Dolores, Faustine and the rest – but to his bitter, salt mother the sea, and to those bleakly beautiful, ravaged margins of earth that yield their substance to her.

Swinburne is the laureate of barrenness in all its forms. I find myself further from the essential matter of his poetry when I learn, as his critics stress of late, that he was fond of being whipped, than when I read his nobly sad letter congratulating Edmund Gosse on his marriage: 'I suppose it must be the best thing that can befall a man to win and keep the woman that he loves while yet young; at any rate I can congratulate my friend on his good hap without any too jealous afterthought of the reverse experience which left my own young manhood a barren stock.'[9] Virtually all of Swinburne's most powerful poetry is an elegy to the evanescence of love.

The signs of Swinburne's 'reverse experience' are everywhere in his poetry. In the autobiographical 'Thalassius,' for example, Swinburne tells of his painful encounter with the young god of Love. Terrifyingly transformed, Love 'waxes immeasurable' and from his erected height says to the poet:

O fool, my name is sorrow;
Thou fool, my name is death. (ll. 302–3)

Of course, Swinburne's trauma in love would not have so scarred him were it not for an antecedent disposition toward being bruised. His peculiar vulnerability and ambivalence to pain express themselves in the figure of the *femme fatale* who dominates all of his early writing.\* Although she is a familiar type in nineteenth-century literature, this 'fair fearful Venus made of deadly foam' (*Chastelard*, V, ii) objectifies Swinburne's personal sense of the deathliness of desire and the desirability of death. The hero of *Chastelard* (1865), for example, commits the curiously passive indiscretion of watching Mary Stuart disrobe, in order to compel her to behead him. In an ecstasy of self-prostration, Chastelard says to his Queen:

> Stretch your throat that I may kiss all round
> Where mine shall be cut through; suppose my mouth
> The axe-edge to bite so sweet a throat in twain
> With bitter iron, should not it turn soft
> As lip is soft to lip? (V, ii)

*Chastelard* is too specialized in theme and derivative in style to engage the general reader, although as an exercise in unrelenting eroticism, this mid-Victorian Salome retains the power to shock. In *Atalanta* Swinburne steps outside the torrid circle of his obsessions and creates a world as bright, virginal, and swift as *Chastelard* is sick with too many roses. Yet he still manages to use the myth of the virgin huntress as a vehicle for his private sensibility. Atalanta is a *frigid* Venus who destroys her lover Meleager as mercilessly as Aphrodite destroys Hippolytus.[10]

No tact is fine enough to discriminate among all the various shades in Swinburne's portrait of love. At times he takes a schoolboy's hot delight simply in handling the theme. At times he writes like a patrician revolutionary attacking sexual prudery as John Stuart Mill attacked intellectual conformity. Occasionally love serves him as an excuse for embroidering rhymes in which birds or flowers would do as well. But the theme can get gravely out of hand, as in 'Anactoria,' in which he writes with morbid power of the pleasures of inflicting pain:

> I would find grievous ways to have thee slain,
> Intense device, and superflux of pain;

---

\* Swinburne's biographers have made too much of his reading of Sade's *Justine* in 1862 as the 'source' of the algolagnia in *Poems and Ballads*, First Series. Over a decade earlier, as a schoolboy freshly arrived at Eton, Swinburne wrote a pseudo-Elizabethan drama describing, in part, the tortures of the Christian martyrs in imperial Rome:

Sulpitius – What music will the creaking of the rack
       Make to his heart.

Vex thee with amorous agonies, and shake
Life at thy lips, and leave it there to ache;
Strain out thy soul with pangs too soft to kill,
Intolerable interludes, and infinite ill;
Relapse and reluctation of the breath,
Dumb tunes and shuddering semitones of death....

Ah that my lips were tuneless lips, but pressed
To the bruised blossom of thy scourged white breast!
Ah that my mouth for Muses' milk were fed
On the sweet blood thy sweet small wounds had bled!
That with my tongue I felt them, and could taste
The faint flakes from thy bosom to the waist!
That I could drink thy veins as wine, and eat
Thy breasts like honey! that from face to feet
Thy body were abolished and consumed,
And in my flesh thy very flesh entombed!...

Would I not plague thee dying overmuch?
Would I not hurt thee perfectly? not touch
Thy pores of sense with torture, and make bright
Thine eyes with bloodlike tears and grievous light?
Strike pang from pang as note is struck from note,
Catch the sob's middle music in thy throat,
Take thy limbs living, and new-mould with these
A lyre of many faultless agonies? (ll. 27–34, 105–14, 133–40)

The horror of the last couplet is heightened by its exquisite verbal wit, as faultless as Marvell's green thought in a green shade.

———————————————

Pamphilius – My soul shall welcome it
    As the sweet strain that ushers me to bliss....
        Fetch more irons
Hotter than these that tear me; pour fresh oils
On the flames that consume my flesh; away!
Can you not force one shriek? what are your gods
That cannot torture? (La Jeunesse de Swinburne, II, 119)

Despite the sadistic content of such poetry, one can never be certain if Swinburne intends merely to shock the reader, or if he is expressing his profoundest impulses. Nor can we draw a clear line between his 'literary' and his 'actual' experience. A book read could be more real to him than a face seen. Swinburne's grief over the marriage of his cousin Mary Gordon was, I am sure, one of the most intense experiences of his life; as intense, that is, as his love of the sea, or of the works of Sade and Victor Hugo.

The passion in 'Anactoria' goes well beyond Swinburne's desire throughout *Poems and Ballads* to *épater le bourgeois*. Only in two or three prose passages of *Lesbia Brandon* does one sense the same overwhelming pressure toward personal release, the same breathing closeness of the author to his text. Elsewhere in *Poems and Ballads* Swinburne handles similar themes in cooler tones. Poems whose explicit sadism and antitheism aroused or shocked generations of readers seem today to veer away from blasphemy toward burlesque. Yet Swinburne's death occasioned a sermon by the aptly titled Vice Dean of Canterbury Cathedral on the need of Christ's blood itself to wash away 'the pollution which Swinburne's poetry introduced into English literature.'[11]

Instead of pollution, I find a certain innocence in Swinburne's perversity. As in his letters, with their Etonian slang and naughty allusions to the Divine Marquis, his eroticism is often more infantile than immoral. Perhaps critical judgment is so unsettled over Swinburne because he is at once a great poet of the futility of love and a precocious schoolboy making off-color rhymes. Nor does it simplify matters that he is possibly the most gifted parodist and mimic in English. Swinburne in jest often appears most in earnest, and his apparent earnestness is often a jest, as in his hymn to Notre Dame des Sept Douleurs:

> Could you hurt me, sweet lips, though I hurt you?
>   Men touch them, and change in a trice
> The lilies and languors of virtue
>   For the raptures and roses of vice;
> Those lie where thy foot on the floor is,
>   These crown and caress thee and chain,
> O splendid and sterile Dolores,
>   Our Lady of Pain....
>
> Thou wert fair in the fearless old fashion,
>   And thy limbs are as melodies yet,
> And move to the music of passion,
>   With lithe and lascivious regret.
> What ailed us, O gods, to desert you
>   For creeds that refuse and restrain?
> Come down and redeem us from virtue,
>   Our Lady of Pain. ('Dolores,' ll. 65–72, 273–80)

In this litany of a sado-masochist's lust, Dolores presides over the marriage of Pleasure and Pain in a ceremony that mimics a black mass. Beneath the deftly controlled surface, one recognizes several of the major themes of *Poems and Ballads*: the intricate connection of pleasure and pain; the dual desire to experience and inflict suffering; a will to fall prey to the destructive sexual force of woman, and the fear of so falling; a need for total self-abasement and a counter-impulse to rebel; a deeply religious reverence before a mystery, and as profound a desire to blaspheme. The devout Christina Rossetti blotted out the words 'The supreme evil God' from her copy of *Atalanta in Calydon*.

God is the supreme sadist in *Poems and Ballads*. Swinburne defies Him eloquently and delightedly: 'Him would I reach, him smite, him desecrate,' he writes in 'Anactoria' of the God who grinds men in order to feed the mute, melancholy lust of heaven. At times Swinburne's poetry of pure defiance achieves a Job-like integrity; at times it suggests a schoolboy's provoking his headmaster to lay on the rod. This antitheist verse never succeeds as great poetry, although it is often great rhetoric, as in the 'Hymn to Proserpine,' with its lament for the conquest of the pagan world by the pale Galilean.

Swinburne's rebellion against the tyrant God finds its complement in his worship of man. One recalls that this blasphemer of the pieties of his age once arrived at a dinner party bearing a footstool, so that he could pay proper homage to Robert Browning. In his verse as in his life, Swinburne was both rigidly defiant and pliantly responsive, self-exultant and self-abasing, a rebel and a mimic. His long sequence of poems of praise begins with tributes to Landor and Hugo in *Poems and Ballads* and ends, some fifty years later, with his humble effusions to the babies of Wimbledon Common.[12]

Swinburne's second volume of poems, *Songs Before Sunrise* (1871), is in all apparent respects the opposite of *Poems and Ballads*. Erotic verses give way to marching songs in praise of Italian liberation. We leave the sultry atmosphere of the boudoir and breathe instead the bracing air of the *Risorgimento*; our Lady of Liberty displaces our Lady of Pain. Yet the two ladies inspire in Swinburne similar emotions of self-prostration and worship. In 'The Oblation,' for example, he addresses Liberty as a dominatrix under whose feet he craves to be trodden:

> All things were nothing to give
> Once to have sense of you more,
> Touch you and taste of you sweet,
> Think you and breathe you and live,
> Swept of your wings as they soar,
> Trodden by chance of your feet. (ll. 7–12)

The sincerity of Swinburne's attachment to the goddess of Liberty is unassailable, although he composed many of his odes to her while walking to a brothel where he paid to be flogged.[13]

The fault with *Songs before Sunrise* and its companion volume, *Songs of Two Nations* (1875), is not their covert pathology but their dullness. Dolores and Faustine at least could bite, but Lady Liberty merely bores. The abstract diction, the manic, trumpet-blast tone, the rhetorical straining – 'O soul, O God,

O glory of liberty' ('The Eve of Revolution,' stanza eleven) – soon exhaust the reader's capacity to respond. With startling self-knowledge, Swinburne anticipated the cause of his failure in *Songs before Sunrise*.[14] 'There is I think room for a book of songs of the European revolution,' he wrote to William Michael Rossetti on beginning the volume, 'and if sung as thoroughly as Hugo or as Whitman would sing them, they ought to ring for some time to some distance of echo. The only fear is that one may be disabled by one's desire – made impotent by excess of strain'.[15] The love of liberty was one of the most abiding and intense emotions that Swinburne knew. His rhetorical excess in *Songs before Sunrise* marks his ineffectual effort to translate great conviction into great art.

3

All that is forced or febrile in *Songs before Sunrise* achieves quiet fulfillment in the *Poems and Ballads* of 1878. In the *First Series* of *Poems and Ballads*, one felt the exuberance of genius discovering itself; in the second series the voice has achieved self-mastery and sings in chaste magnificence. The volume appeared during the grimmest period of Swinburne's life, when he lived alone in London in suicidal dissipation. One senses the solitude, but none of the squalor. In the best of his elegies to dead poets interspersed through *Poems and Ballads*, Swinburne seems to lay his own youth to rest and prepare to retire from the exercise of his highest powers. One year after the volume was published, his friend Theodore Watts-Dunton found him in an alcoholic stupor and took him to live at Putney. For thirty years their home at 'No. 2, The Pines,' served Swinburne as a kind of suburban sanitorium. 'The Pines' became the tomb of a great poet and the birthplace of a distinguished man of letters who wrote on Shakespeare and Blake, Victor Hugo, Marlowe and Mary Queen of Scots. One of the finest lyrics in *Poems and Ballads* is entitled 'A Vision of Spring in Winter'; the volume itself is a prevision of Swinburne's long winter, seen from the last moment of his spring.

The leitmotif of *Poems and Ballads* is the triumph of time over love, over life, and over the generative power of earth and man. These are Swinburne's essential themes, and *Poems and Ballads*, 1878, is remarkable only in that it plays upon them so persistently and with his subtlest music. The sado-masochist verses of *Poems and Ballads*, First Series, are less the heart of Swinburne's poetic matter than a variation on this larger theme of the forces in nature that divide and destroy us. 'Laus Veneris,' 'Les Noyades,' 'The Leper,' and 'Anactoria' are extreme cases of the classic Swinburne situation in which lovers are, so to speak, disjointed.[16] Once in the *First Series* – in 'The Triumph of Time' – and once in the *Second Series* – in 'A Forsaken Garden' – all of these elements meet in perfect balance. They are Swinburne's archetypical lyrics, adjacent stanzas of a single, larger poem.

In both poems one feels the full force of loss, and the counterforce of its acceptance. This stoicism of the heart, which falls short of bitterness on the one hand, and the sentimentality of unresisted regret on the other, is the defining note of Swinburne's love poetry. It is struck in the opening stanza of 'The Triumph of Time,' in which the propulsive rush of the metre paces time's triumph over the lovers, changing all things except the fact of their inevitable separation:

> Before our lives divide for ever,
>     While time is with us and hands are free,
> (Time, swift to fasten and swift to sever
>     Hand from hand, as we stand by the sea)
> I will say no word that a man might say
>     Whose whole life's love goes down in a day;
> For this could never have been; and never
>     Though the gods and the years relent, shall be. (ll. 1–8)

I mentioned the lovers in 'The Triumph of Time,' but, remarkably, there are scarcely any lovers in Swinburne's poetry. There is much passion but little conjunction; emotion is felt but not communicated and not returned. Swinburne has mistakenly acquired the reputation of an erotic poet; he is rather the elegist of love's impossibility. Perhaps that is why, even in his most sensual verses, one feels a peculiar innocence, just as in his most moving love poetry one feels a profound barrenness:

> It will grow not again, this fruit of my heart,
>     Smitten with sunbeams, ruined with rain.
> The singing seasons divide and depart,
>     Winter and summer depart in twain.
> It will grow not again, it is ruined at root,
>     The bloodlike blossom, the dull red fruit;
> Though the heart yet sickens, the lips yet smart,
>     With sullen savour of poisonous pain. (ll. 17–24)

All of Swinburne's finer love poetry is set by the sea – the cold, clean, 'mother-maid' who is more palpable than the ever-shadowy beloved who refuses, or is unaware of, the poet's love. The return to the sea in 'The Triumph of Time' occurs near the end of the poem, in three stanzas more strange than Swinburne's critics have yet acknowledged:

> I will go back to the great sweet mother,
>     Mother and lover of men, the sea.
> I will go down to her, I and none other,

Close with her, kiss her and mix her with me;
Cling to her, strive with her, hold her fast:
O fair white mother, in days long past
Born without sister, born without brother,
    Set free my soul as thy soul is free.

O fair green-girdled mother of mine,
    Sea, that art clothed with the sun and the rain,
Thy sweet hard kisses are strong like wine,
    Thy large embraces are keen like pain.
Save me and hide me with all thy waves,
Find me one grave of thy thousand graves,
Those pure cold populous graves of thine
    Wrought without hand in a world without stain.

I shall sleep, and move with the moving ships,
    Change as the winds change, veer in the tide;
My lips will feast on the foam of thy lips,
    I shall rise with thy rising, with thee subside;
Sleep, and not know if she be, if she were,
Filled full with life to the eyes and hair,
As a rose is fulfilled to the roseleaf tips
    With splendid summer and perfume and pride. (ll. 257–64)

The lines are at once infantile – 'save me and hide me' – and overwhelming.
One recalls that Swinburne's earliest memory was of shrieking with delight as
his father tossed him headfirst into the waves. Fifty years later he wrote to his
sister of the ecstasy he felt in swimming off the Sussex Downs:

> I ran like a boy, tore off my clothes, and hurled myself into the water.
> And it was but for a few minutes – but I was in Heaven! The whole sea
> was literally golden as well as green – it was liquid and living sunlight in
> which one lived and moved and had one's being. And to feel that in
> deep water is to feel – as long as one is swimming out, if only a minute
> or two – as if one was in another world of life, and one far more glorious
> than even Dante ever dreamed of in his Paradise.[17]

That paradise held many pleasures, among them the pleasure of death – that
primordial return to 'the great sweet mother,' whose rocking rhythms Swinburne
captures in lines that, like some fluid lullaby, mix the image of lovemaking
with the image of drowning: 'My lips will feast on the foam of thy lips, / I shall
rise with thy rising, with thee subside.' The passage is animistic in its
primitiveness of emotion. The decadent, verbally sophisticated Swinburne was
in another part of his being pre-civilized, a wind-worshipper and a sea-
worshipper whose poetry springs from sources more antique than words.

In 'A Forsaken Garden,' as in 'The Triumph of Time,' this fusion of the artificial with the aboriginal achieves a fragile power. The setting is an eighteenth-century garden gone to seed and thorn. A faint, salt-sprayed scent of faded flowers and ghostly lovers hovers over the opening stanzas. It is springtime, but neither leaves nor loves will bloom again in this rocky wasteland poised over the sea. The actual garden that inspired the imagined garden of the poem was on the Isle of Wight, where Swinburne spent the springs of his childhood in a setting of near-tropical luxuriance. In late summer the Swinburnes went north to the family seat at Capheaton, Northumberland, where the bare moors, gray seas, and autumnal summits must have seemed to the young Swinburne like winter suddenly overlaid upon spring. The two seasons became forever fixed in his mind in their sudden proximity and sharpness of contrast, so that he could scarcely feel the one without its opposite. The sea that rolls through the great closing stanzas of 'A Forsaken Garden' is a chill, northern sea, a blast of death bringing a second ruin, as in *Tristram of Lyonesse*,[18] to a rich but ravaged landscape. Swinburne's ghostly elegy for long-dead lovers gives way to a prevision of the burial of the earth itself:

> All are at one now, roses and lovers,
>     Not known of the cliffs or the fields or the sea;
> Not a breath of the time that has been hovers
>     In the air now soft with a summer to be.
> Not a breath shall sweeten the seasons hereafter
>     Of flowers or of lovers that laugh now or weep,
> When as they who are free now of weeping and laughter
>     We shall sleep.
>
> Here death may deal not again for ever;
>     Here change may come not till all change end.
> From the graves they have made they shall rise up never,
>     Who have left nought living to ravage and rend.
> Earth, stones and thorns of the wild ground growing,
>     While the sun and the rain live, these shall be;
> Till a last wind's breath upon all these blowing
>     Roll the sea.
>
> Till the slow sea rise and the sheer cliff crumble,
>     Till terrace and meadow the deep gulfs drink,
> Till the strength of the waves of the high tides humble
>     The fields that lessen, the rocks that shrink;
> Here now in his triumph where all things falter,
>     Stretched out on the spoils that his own hand spread,
> Like a god self-slain on his own strange altar,
>     Death lies dead. (ll. 57–80)

As in much of his most moving poetry, Swinburne writes here not of time present, but of a time immemorially before time, or of the eternity that follows time. The steady pulse of the monosyllables, the starkness of the diction, the open generalized barrenness of the setting – 'earth, stones, and thorns' – evoke some primordial drama of the elements, as though nature has suddenly shed the coloration of millennia and resolved back into earth, water, fire, and wind. The lifeless landscape is charged with hidden life, only to make its final ravagement the more complete: the wind breathes, the rocks shrink, the sea rises, the gulfs drink, the fields are humbled. The wreck is so total that Death itself, with nothing mutable left to prey upon, lies dead. The personification ought to ring hollow – a poetical flourish in an elemental landscape. But this touch of artifice makes more awesome the larger, cosmic death that Swinburne heard blowing through nature like a low, bone-shaking rumble and that he here evokes in the form of the wind's last breath rolling sea over earth in the final Deluge.

One hears the same elemental music in 'At a Month's End,' another elegy to doomed love in *Poems and Ballads*, Second Series. The lovers, no longer in love, stand by night at the sea's edge and watch the serried spears of the waves storm toward the shore:

> Hardly we saw the high moon hanging,
>   Heard hardly through the windy night
> Far waters ringing, low reefs clanging,
>   Under wan skies and waste white light.
>
> With chafe and change of surges chiming,
>   The clashing channels rocked and rang
> Large music, wave to wild wave timing,
>   And all the choral water sang. (ll. 9–16)

The lapsed love plays itself out against a background of alliterative choiring of the elements. Drifting clouds, waves, gulls, wind, the earth's margins, these are the phenomena on which Swinburne's senses instinctually fixed, the background of earth against which his people stand, dwarfed and apart:

> Across, aslant, a scudding sea mew
>   Swam, dipped, and dropped, and grazed the sea;
> And one with me I could not dream you:
>   And one with you I could not be.
>
> As the white wing the white wave's fringes
>   Touched and slid over and flashed past –
> As a pale cloud a pale flame tinges
>   From the moon's lowest light and last –

As a star feels the sun and falters,
  Touched to death by diviner eyes –
As on the old gods' untended altars
  The old fire of withered worship dies –

         …

So once with fiery breath and flying
  Your winged heart touched mine and went,
And the swift spirits kissed, and sighing,
  Sundered and smiled and were content. (ll. 37–48, 53–6)

The lovers in 'At a Month's End'* seem not only lost to each other but eclipsed by the larger motions of nature around them. Always in Swinburne the pure, fluid power of wind and sea sweeps everything before it, just as the cataclysmic rush of avalanche and inundation obliterates the paltry human figures in J.M.W. Turner's *Val d'Aosta*. Like Turner, too, Swinburne finds in the vast undifferentiated sea the visible emblem of his genius, with its exaltation of energy over form, infinite nuance over discrete detail. One stanza from 'At a Month's End' might have come from Turner's own catalogue descriptions of his seascapes:

Faint lights fell this way, that way floated,
  Quick sparks of sea fire keen like eyes
From the rolled surf that flashed, and noted
  Shores and faint cliffs and bays and skies. (ll. 17–20)

---

* Swinburne may have drawn the closing stanzas directly from personal experience. For over a month during the winter of 1867–8, in the most caricaturable of the many caricaturable incidents of his life, the diminutive Swinburne was encouraged by Dante Gabriel Rossetti to have an affair with Adah Isaacs Menken, a full-bodied international charmer, circus-rider and poet. The two became most companionable, but not proper lovers, Miss Menken finally remarking to Rossetti, 'I can't make him understand that biting's no use!' (*Letters*, VI, 246). It seems likely that she loomed in Swinburne's mind as the ample panther in the following lines, which are so strikingly different in tone from the earlier stanzas quoted above;

But I, who leave my queen of panthers,
  As a tired honey heavy bee
Gilt with sweet dust from gold grained anthers
  Leaves the rose chalice, what for me?

From the ardours of the chaliced centre,
  From the amorous anther's golden grime,
That scorch and smutch all wings that enter,
  I fly forth hot from honey-time. (ll. 117–21)

One recognizes in both artists the same technical virtuosity, alongside an enormous responsiveness to the aboriginal forces of nature. Swinburne's landscapes, like Turner's, abstract all the sharp, divisible aspects of nature into an essential luminosity, such as God might have beheld on completing the Creation:

> ...one clear hueless haze of glimmering hues
> The sea's line and the land's line and the sky's.
>
> ('Thalassius,' ll. 100–1)

'Indistinctness is my forte,' Turner retorted to a patron who chided him for vagueness, a fault which modern critics still impute to Turner's early admirer, Swinburne.[19] Both men practice a highly structured art that has freed itself from the canons of conventional representation. No single word in a Swinburne poem quite corresponds to a given thing, just as no single dab of paint on a Turner canvas corresponds to a natural object; the correspondence is always between the total configuration of the poem or painting and the total configuration of nature. The adjective floating freely away from its substantive in a Swinburne poem is like the blob of pigment that is neither sea nor foam nor sky, but all of these, in a Turner painting. Such an art prizes color over outline, light over form, music over meaning. Its concern, as Swinburne wrote of poetry, but might as well have written of Impressionism in general, 'is rather to render the effect of a thing than the thing itself.'[20]

Swinburne's love of mixed effects gives to his descriptive verse much of its Turnerian quality. His poetry is charged with the tension of delicately poised opposites: shadows thinned by light, lights broken by shade, sunset passing into moonrise, sea merging with sky. He is obsessed by the moment when one thing shades off into its opposite, or when contraries fuse, as in 'Hermaphroditus,' one of his earliest and finest poems. Yet apart from his profound aesthetic affinity with Turner, we are left with the unique idiosyncrasy of Swinburne himself, who was equipped with superb senses, each of which must have transmitted a peculiar counterpoint. This basic, polarizing rhythm runs through his being and manifests itself in his compulsive use of alliterating antitheses in prose and verse. Much in Swinburne that has been criticized as mere mannerism – paradox, alliteration, elaborate antithesis – strikes me as deriving from his deepest impulses, although the question of 'sincerity' is always vexing in his verse. In a sense, Swinburne *perceived* in paradoxes, and his recurrent synesthetic images express perfectly that passing of pain into pleasure, bitter into sweet, loathing into desire, which lay at the root of his profoundest experiences. He loves nature best in her moments of transition, as if drawn to dusk and dawn as the day's hermaphrodisms:

> Over two shadowless waters, adrift as a pinnace in peril,
>     Hangs as in heavy suspense, charged with irresolute light,

> Softly the soul of the sunset upholden awhile on the sterile
> Waves and wastes of the land, half repossessed by the night.
>                          ('Evening on the Broads,' ll. 1–4)

His imagery of these times of change is most mixed and rich when, as in 'Evening on the Broads,' he fuses touch, sound and sight to describe twilight at sea as 'a molten music of colour'; and in a line from 'Laus Veneris' that it is wisest not to gloss at all, the knight is maddened by erotic fumes rising from 'the sea's panting mouth of *dry* desire.'

At times Swinburne will elaborate a single antithesis into an entire poem. 'A Vision of Spring in Winter' is a beautifully poised evocation of life arising from dormancy as the poet himself declines from spring toward winter; the counter-movements of rebirth and loss are as delicately juxtaposed as the snowdrop set in the vanishing snow at the poem's opening. But in two of Swinburne's finest poems, both elegies – 'The Garden of Proserpine' and 'Ave Atque Vale' – there is no counter-movement, only a quiet celebration of the absolute finality of death. The idea of renewal, or of rebirth into immortality, lies at the heart of classical and Christian elegy. Proserpine's annual rising from the underworld reawakens life each spring, Lycidas will move on to pastures new, Shelley's Adonais 'is not dead,' and Tennyson in *In Memoriam*, after 'one far-off divine event,' will once again clasp the hand of his beloved Arthur Hallam. But Swinburne's Proserpine inhabits an eternal underworld where no flowers bloom, only

> Dead dreams of days forsaken,
> Blind buds that snows have shaken,
> Wild leaves that winds have taken,
>       Red strays of ruined springs. (ll. 69–72)

So, too, the flowers that Swinburne strews upon the corpse of his brother poet, Baudelaire, have a wintry smell and are chill to the touch. Both poems negate the implicit promise of elegy – that the mourner's regret will in time blossom into 'an April violet' (*In Memoriam*, Section 115), the dead rising again or living forever in the memory of the living. Swinburne's Proserpine, however, is a virginal reaper, herself forever confined to the underworld, a gatherer of

> …all things mortal,
> with cold immortal hands. (ll. 51–2)

At the poem's end, when the reader anticipates a return to renewed life, Swinburne offers instead a hymn of gratitude that no sleeper need ever again awaken, for Proserpine's shadowy underground garden is, in fact, a mausoleum:

> From too much love of living,
> From hope and fear set free,

We thank with brief thanksgiving
  Whatever gods may be
That no life lives for ever;
That dead men rise up never;
That even the weariest river
  Winds somewhere safe to sea.

Then star nor sun shall waken,
  Nor any change of light:
Nor sound of waters shaken,
  Nor any sound or sight:
Nor wintry leaves nor vernal,
Nor days nor things diurnal;
  Only the sleep eternal
In an eternal night. (ll. 81–96)

'Ave Atque Vale,' the greatest of Swinburne's elegies, opens with an uncanny evocation of the mixed, sweetly acrid scent of *Les Fleurs du Mal*.* The convention of strewing flowers takes on a sudden, palpable reality as we seem to *smell* the very leaves of Baudelaire's book:

Shall I strew on thee rose or rue or laurel,
  Brother, on this that was the veil of thee?
  Or quiet sea-flower moulded by the sea,
Or simplest growth of meadow-sweet or sorrel,
  Such as the summer-sleepy Dryads weave,
  Waked up by snow-soft sudden rains at eve?
Or wilt thou rather, as on earth before,
  Half-faded fiery blossoms, pale with heat
  And full of bitter summer, but more sweet
To thee than gleanings of a northern shore
  Trod by no tropic feet? (ll. 1–11)

However evocative of the earth, the flowers Swinburne strews are of course highly artificial, as befits the elaborate intricacy of his rhymes, rhythms, and assonance – all paying Baudelaire the high tribute of perfect imitation. In

---

* Cf. Swinburne's parallel attempt to suggest the flavor of Villon's life and verse in 'A Ballad of François Villon.' This tribute to a poet who created beauty out of a life of depravity illustrates Swinburne's most extreme use of balanced antithetical adjectives. The line 'Villon, our *sad bad glad mad* brother's name' recurs four times in four stanzas. The refrain frames a poem whose diction recalls Swinburne's tonal use of adjective in 'A Ballad of Life.' The title 'Ave Atque Vale' – Hail and Farewell – alludes to Catullus' elegy to his brother: *Frater ave atque vale.*

'Thyrsis,' Matthew Arnold's elegy to Arthur Clough, the poet seems half embarrassed to employ classical conventions – 'shepherd-pipes' and the rest – amidst the 'sick hurry' of modern life. Swinburne celebrates the old conventions, going back to Catullus, and before Catullus. Yet 'Ave Atque Vale' is as modern as Baudelaire's poetry – and as ancient and hieratic in its tropes and gestures as the first forlorn notes of the first elegist's flute.[21] Near the close of the elegy, Apollo, father of poets and himself a singer, mourns this most recently dead of his many children; he bends down over the body

> And hallows with strange tears and alien sighs
> Thine unmelodious mouth and sunless eyes, (ll. 151–2)

– eyes forever shut and mouth, Swinburne ever so delicately suggests, perhaps filled with sod. At the elegy's end, we turn from the bitter-sweet scent of *Les Fleurs du Mal* to the chill smell of the earth that receives the poet's body. Swinburne offers his fallen brother not Apollo's laurel crown but a thin-leafed, wintry garland – the poem 'Ave Atque Vale' itself – a hushed tribute of one great poet placed on the grave of another:

> For thee, O now a silent soul, my brother,
>      Take at my hands this garland, and farewell.
>      Thin is the leaf, and chill the wintry smell,
> And chill the solemn earth, a fatal mother,
>      With sadder than the Niobean womb,
>      And in the hollow of her breasts a tomb.
> Content thee, howsoe'er, whose days are done;
>      There lies not any troublous thing before,
>      Nor sight nor sound to war against thee more,
> For whom all winds are quiet as the sun,
>      All waters as the shore. (ll. 188–98)

Only once again, in *Tristram of Lyonesse*, did Swinburne achieve the sustained excellence of 'Ave Atque Vale.' He continued to publish volumes of verse into the twentieth century, but for the most part the later poetry is a peculiarly vacant sort of versage that exists stillborn in a world of its own. One thinks of Swinburne's increasing deafness at Putney, and somehow the poetry suggests a muted soliloquy. The saddest lines in all of Swinburne appear in 'A Midsummer Holiday' (1884), dedicated to Watts-Dunton. The setting is indistinguishable from those great, bleak earlier lyrics of the sea's encroachments on the land; here, however, the sea has shrunk to a suburban pond reflecting the ghost of a dead poet:

> Friend, the lonely land is bright for you and me
> All its wild ways through: but this methinks is best,

Here to watch how kindly time and change agree
Where the small town smiles, a warm still sea-side nest.

Yet there are moments of astonishing strength in late Swinburne. Much of 'By the North Sea,' more of the little known 'Evening on the Broads,' all of 'A Nympholept'[22] defeat one's impulse to impose a curve of growth, flowering, and decline upon the actual pattern of his creativity. Swinburne always wrote a good deal of dead and silly verse, rather more of both toward the end of his career. That his most lifeless poetry is in all outward respects – metre, diction and subject – virtually indistinguishable from his greatest poetry is one of the mysteries of his art. His genius is extraordinary above all for its *intermittency*; the verse-making engine spins constantly for half a century, but the surges of engaged power are sudden and unpredictable. Tennyson called him 'a reed through which all things blow into music.' Sometimes the melody carries; often it does not. Swinburne had a curious passion for monotony, which was undoubtedly linked to his love of bleak, monochromatic effects. Out of this love came his most powerful poetry; out of it also came whole poems too like his own description of the Dunwich coast:

Miles, and miles, and miles of desolation!
Leagues on leagues on leagues without a change!

('By the North Sea')

My final reservation toward Swinburne concerns a certain arrested development. Wordsworth's genius flowers, then endlessly wanes: 'Tintern Abbey' unfolds an organic evolution of growths, losses, and gains. Neither Swinburne nor his verse seems to undergo much change; a single note is struck early and held obsessively long. The reader wants a richer range of subject, more nuance of idea. But Swinburne composes by compounding, not synthesizing. Too often, his method is merely quantitative: 'I have added yet four more jets of boiling and gushing infamy to the perennial and poisonous fountain of Dolores.'[23] One wishes that his eccentric genius could have retained all its power while ridding itself of rigidity and repetitiveness. It did not, and the death of development in Swinburne may have been as large a loss to English poetry as the physical death of Keats.

# 10

# WALTER PATER AND THE ART OF EVANESCENCE

A lover of beauty in all of its forms, but especially of the male figure, Walter Pater suffered the misfortune of being incarnate in an ungainly body surmounted by a large, unlovely head. His contemporaries were invariably struck by the disparity between Pater's unprepossessing person and his finely wrought prose, in which he celebrates a beauty which no mirror could ever return. Pater ends the most artful of his *Imaginary Portraits* – of Watteau, the 'Prince of Court Painters' – with a sentence that might serve as his own epitaph: 'He was always a seeker after something in the world that is there in no satisfying measure, or not at all.'[1]

Such a temperament is intrinsically elegiac, fixated on the fleeting – the heady scent of roses the moment before they fade or on the handsome faces of the freshly dead. These 'still lifes' are artfully planted throughout Pater's writings, perhaps most memorably at the end of *Emerald Uthwart*, the most self-illuminating of his imaginary portraits. Two schoolboy companions, their friendship patterned on the 'Greek' model, enlist in the army, serve heroically, but are court-martialed for an unspecified crime. The elder is shot before a firing squad, the younger discharged in disgrace. Emerald returns to his birthplace, where he dies of an old gunshot wound and is buried amidst a riot of richly scented roses. But first a surgeon performs an autopsy on this 'golden-haired Apollo,' his youthful features crowned by an abundance of fair hair, his flesh composed in death and as yet without a trace of dissolution. The surgeon-narrator gazes longingly and guiltily – 'I felt like a criminal'[2] – into the open coffin. This second narrator appears suddenly, a *deus ex machina* in an awkwardly appended 'Postscript, from the Diary of a Surgeon.' In the guise of the surgeon, the reticent Pater could allow himself to express what he could not put into a first-person narrative. The surgeon touches the exposed breast of the dead youth, removes a musket-ball, and the flowers are hastily returned to the coffin, presumably to mask the incision and any scent of decay. Emerald's hands and finely chiseled nose remain visible among the roses:

> I was struck by the great beauty of the organic developments...the wind ruffled the hair a little; the lips were still red. I shall not forget it. (Buckler, p. 372)

The tremulous hair, Pater quietly intimates, will continue to grow after the coffin has been sealed.

Pater's works are a gallery of these not-quite still lifes of beautiful youths, the more fortunate of whom die young. The exception is Marius the Epicurean, who survives into early middle age, but Marius is embalmed in a narrative so intentionally devoid of action or motion that we remember him as a perpetually youthful seeker of what the world offers in no satisfying measure, or not at all.

George Moore contrasts the grace and beauty of Marius with his creator's halting gait and ungainly appearance, 'an uncouth figure like a figure moulded out of lead.'[3] In middle life Pater grew a huge 'mudguard' of a moustache, as if to hide his uncomely mouth behind a hedge. He shared with his adored spinster sisters[4] the 'Pater poke' – a slight humping of the back.[5] He walked down Oxford's High Street with a straight-ahead stare that disinvited all greeting. A host of his contemporaries – Arthur Symons, Frank Harris, Edmund Gosse, George Moore, and, most famously, Henry James – all compared Pater's face to a mask: 'He is the mask without a face,' James wrote shortly after Pater's death.[6] William Rothenstein sketched the elderly Pater quite flatteringly; on seeing the full-face drawing, Pater exclaimed, 'Do I look like a Barbary ape?'[7] Never at ease in his own body, Pater compared himself to one of Aristophanes's frogs, and when asked at a luncheon party what form he would choose in a second life, he answered, 'a carp' swimming immemorially 'in the green waters of some royal chateau.'[8] Protected by a moat, half-hidden in the green water, seeing but scarcely seen, Pater's imaginary alter-ego swims in sight of the royalty whose ceremonies and rich plumage always captivated him. His chosen reincarnation is singularly apt: the carp is blunt-headed, thick-bodied, broad lipped, flamboyantly colored – a bewhiskered dandy of a fish. In mid-life Pater in fact began to dress like an understated dandy – impeccably groomed, sporting a black tailcoat, top hat, gold-tipped umbrella and a brilliant, apple green silk tie – a preparer of the way for his more daringly dressed disciple Oscar Wilde.

But Pater the dandy was at the same time severely austere in manner, suggesting to some of his contemporaries a monk-like counter-image, to others the disciplined, stiffly erect bearing of a 'retired major in the rifle brigade.'[9] His appearance and his prose reflect a complex dialectic of self-display and self-denial. Pater's rooms at Brasenose College (they overlooked Newman's St. Mary the Virgin) suggest the same duality. They were sparsely furnished, severely simple in style, but paneled in the pale green favored by the aesthetes of the day and set off by a few choice *objets*. A dwarf orange tree and a bowl of dried rose leaves barely hinted at the world outside Pater's cloistered rooms. Pater wrought into his outside appearance and his immediate surroundings the same seeming contradictions everywhere embodied in his prose style – the provocative constraint of the ascetic in tension with the aesthetic, the one heightened by its proximity to the other. Carry the asceticism of the saint and the aesthete's love of beauty a little further, Pater writes in *Marius the Epicurean*, and their positions might actually 'touch.'[10]

Richard Ellmann characterized *The Renaissance* as an exercise in the seduction of young men by the wiles of culture.[11] But the seduction is achieved more through a teasing restraint than by overt display. In the 'Conclusion' to *The Renaissance*, Pater famously enjoins his readers to seek not the fruit of experience but experience itself, 'To burn always with this hard, gem-like flame.' But the hard, phallic flame must inevitably falter, and it excites less through its heat than its gem-like coolness. Despite its powerful erotic undercurrents, Pater's prose is highly disciplined, indeed austere in its controlled effects. Oscar Wilde held that 'asceticism is the keynote of Mr. Pater's prose.'[12] The austere eroticism of Pater's prose suggests an indefinitely deferred climax in which the flame of beauty always burns alongside the chill of death, life's shortness lending a 'new seduction' to the bloom of the world. In an early version of the 'Conclusion,' Pater writes that a passion in which 'the outlets are sealed begets a tension of nerve, in which the sensible world comes to one with a reinforced brilliance and relief – all redness is turned into blood, all waters into tears.' The sense of death and the desire for beauty 'are intertwined,' the desire for beauty 'quickened by the sense of death.'[13] By 'quickened' Pater means both *intensified* and *brought to life* – the quick and the dead in closest proximity, so that the lover of beauty is perforce a lover of death. Beauty and death, passion and its denial, pain and pleasure, male and female all undergo strange transfigurations in Pater's writings, which are at once elegiac, coldly marmoreal and persistently erotic. Max Beerbohm captures the first two qualities but altogether misses the third in accusing Pater of treating

> English as a dead language…that sedulous ritual wherewith he laid out every sentence as in a shroud – hanging, like a widower, long over its marmoreal beauty or ever he could lay it at length in his book, its sepulchre.[14]

Beerbohm wittily parodies the studied perfection of Pater's prose but ignores its suppressed sexual fervor. I am reminded that at the end of *Emerald Uthwart* the surgeon-narrator, Pater's narcissus-like surrogate, all but leaps with his eyes into the open coffin of his adored creation.

At times Pater's writing seems wrenched into the service of private obsessions – homoerotic, sado-masochistic, necrophiliac. I have in mind his late, quite dotty 'Age of Athletic Prizemen' (1894), or the brutal, blow-by-blow execution of a minor character in his historical fiction *Gaston de Latour*, a scene suppressed for over a century until its publication in 1995.[15] In the 'Prizemen' essay Pater gazes longingly at the delicate muscularity of young Greek athletes – his *Korai* – on display in the British Museum. In a startling parenthesis, he invites the reader to gaze into the mouth of Myron's Discobolus: '(look into, look at the curves of, the blossomlike cavity of the opened mouth.)'[16] Apart from this unguarded rapture, the essay is a sentimental elegy for the fading of male beauty on the playing fields of Oxford and its preservation in the statuary of ancient Attica.

The same yielding to private preoccupations obtrudes into the 'Anteros' chapter in *Gaston de Latour*. Here Pater explores the 'recondite relationship of what we may call erotic humility to erotic pride.'[17] The result is a brilliant anatomy of the sexual politics of sado-masochism as embodied in the disdainful, aristocratic Jasmin and his low-born, servile adorer, Raoul. Like twins 'cut in two but still alive,' Pater compares them to Aristophanes' myth in the *Symposium* of an aboriginally complete sexual being, split in two by Zeus, each half 'now seeking to be one again with its fellow, itself.'[18] Aristophanes depicts a comic version, Pater a tragic, of sexual pursuit. He transposes the stereotypic paradigm of the aggressive male and passive female into a single gender – male master and male slave, for 'female souls are not necessarily lodged in women's bosoms.'[19] And so the young Jasmin, Raoul's *homme fatal*, preens himself at the royal court, bedecked in jewels and gold – an image fit to keep a drowsy emperor awake – while the handsome but plebian Raoul languishes below. It is as if Pater, born in a London slum and described by one of his schoolmates as their resident gargoyle, has fantasized himself into both the gorgeous Jasmin and the adoring Raoul, a carp reincarnated as a pauper-prince.

But this fairy tale romance between alter egos takes a gratuitously brutal turn after Raoul commits a crime on Jasmin's behalf and is hideously broken on the wheel, to the 'passing regret' of Jasmin. First Raoul is passed, half-naked, through the crowd that witnesses the execution, handling and turning him 'this way and that, as passively as a dead child.'[20] Then each bone in his body is separately broken as Raoul, in an ecstasy of stoical masochism, lays down his life for his friend, an utterly silent victim before a transfixed and silent mob. Raoul achieves in death an erotic apotheosis of Paterian passivity.*

---

* Freud's essay on 'The Sexual Aberrations' reads like an abstract of the Jasmin/Raoul twinned relationship. Freud describes the male desire to subjugate or to derive satisfaction 'conditional upon suffering...at the hands of the sexual object.' Masochism is an extension of sadism, its active [Jasmin] and passive [Raoul] manifestations 'turned round upon the subject's own self.' Both forms 'are habitually found to occur together in the same individual.... A sadist is always at the same time a masochist....' *Three Essays on the Theory of Sexuality* (New York: Basic Books, 1962), pp. 23–5.

But with the wrecking of his body, the narrative, too, is left in ruins as Pater abruptly resumes the pallid and faltering narrative of his shadowy hero, Gaston de Latour.

The problem with 'The Age of Athletic Prizemen,' as I have suggested, is not its homoeroticism, but that it is flaccid and ill-written; the problem with Raoul's torture-execution is not that it is ill-written – I confess to finding it morbidly compelling – but that it altogether overpowers the story of Gaston. Yet no subject is of itself beyond the pale of great literature or art, as Goya's pop-eyed and appalling 'Saturn Devouring His Son' makes clear. So, too, the most beautiful of Boccaccio's hundred tales describes Isabella's none too neat exhumation of the head of her murdered lover, which she plants in a pot of basil and waters with her tears. The ultimate enigma of Pater is that the same obsessive, at times ghoulish, themes that propel his writing at its worst also energize his writing at its best – writing in which he quietly yet radically subverts all of the restrictive sexual, aesthetic, and moral norms of Victorian culture.

Queer studies, understandably, has focused on one aspect of Pater's antinomianism, his homoerotic subtext. But the door to Pater's closet has been pretty transparent since his first signed publication, 'Notes on Leonardo da Vinci' (1864), and the closet itself contains much more of interest than the bodies of beautiful youths. That is why Pater could exert so profound (if underappreciated) an influence on modern literature. Denis Donoghue puts it best:

> It is not a question of influence but of presence. Pater is a shade or trace in virtually every writer of any significance from Hopkins and Wilde to Ashbery.... Pater is as evident in Eliot's poems as in Joyce's fictions. It was Pater...who set modern literature upon its antithetical – he would say its antinomian – course. In practice this means he made modern English literature European....[21]

Pater the reluctant revolutionary – that is his great, overriding enterprise, and that is what makes him important today. His assault on the culture of Victorian England is most powerfully embodied in the three works to which I now turn: the autobiographical 'Child in the House,' *The Renaissance*, and *Marius the Epicurean*.

## 2

On a scrap of paper found among his manuscripts Pater wrote of 'The Child in the House': 'Voila, the germinating, original, source, specimen of all my *imaginative* work.'[22] And so it is, in a scant eighteen pages. The story opens with Florian Deleal, a boy of twelve, encountering by the wayside a burdened old man, a sort of Bunyanesque pilgrim, or perhaps a venerable Wordsworthian derelict who has strayed south from the Lake District. But the allegorical opening takes a sharp Paterian turn into the hyper-vivid world of childhood impressions 'which are tossed and fall and lie about us, so, or so' in our earliest years, then enter the 'house-room' of memory and become a kind of 'material shrine or sanctuary of sentiment,' a system of 'visible symbolism [that] interweaves itself through all our thoughts and passions.'[23] Pater is less interested in 'soul-making' than in the accretive process of what he calls 'brain-building,'[24] a kind of concretizing of consciousness through the flooding in of myriad atoms of sensation, the osmotic interpenetration of internal and external, so that the house both forms and reflects the spirit of the child and the child becomes the living reliquary of the house.

The Paterian child is father of the man but his consciousness materializes not amidst the mountains and sounding cataracts of the Lake District, but in a house the better loved because it is 'inclosed' and 'sealed.' Wordsworth's half-wild Boy of Winander hoots at owls who hoot back at him in return. Pater's child comes to self-awareness seated silently beside his mother in an open window overlooking a suburban garden on a June afternoon till time comes to a stop. In these lines composed, as it were, a few miles north of the Victoria and Albert Museum, Pater domesticates the Wordsworthian sublime.[25] If I seem condescending, I do not intend to be, any more than I think that Wordsworth's majestic seas of mist on Mount Snowden are a fitter subject for poetry than T. S. Eliot's London fog. Pater is not a hothouse Wordsworth but the midwife of modernism. I cannot read the following sentence from Virginia Woolf's 'Modern Fiction' without sensing the strong presence of her 'absent father,' Walter Pater:

> Let us record the atoms as they fall upon the mind in the order in which they fall, let us trace the pattern, however disconnected and incoherent in appearance, which each sight or incident scores upon the consciousness.[26]

The great tutors that nourish Wordsworth's early sensibility in the *Prelude* are beauty and fear.[27] Florian's tutors, floating in through an open window, or in the form of a beloved, disease-wasted Angora, a mere relic of itself, are 'beauty and pain,' an overpowering sense of loveliness rendered all the keener by the presence of death. The child seeks another pet and finds it close at hand in a starling that he snares. The episode occurs in a paragraph that in itself might constitute the subject of this essay:

> So he wanted another pet; and as there were starlings about the place, which could be taught to speak, one of them was caught, and he meant to treat it kindly; but in the night its young ones could be heard crying

after it, and the responsive cry of the mother-bird towards them; and at last, with the first light, though not till after some debate with himself, he went down and opened the cage, and saw a sharp bound of the prisoner up to her nestlings; and therewith came the sense of remorse, – that he too has become an accomplice in moving, to the limit of his small power, the springs and handles of that great machine in things, constructed so ingeniously to play pain-fugues on the delicate nerve-work of living creatures. (Brzenk, pp. 24–5)

The captive bird has migrated from Book I of the *Prelude* onto Pater's pages, two passages in which kinship and disparity could not be more pronounced. Both passages portray the snaring of a 'Mother Bird' and a child's guilt over denuding her nest. But the boy Wordsworth *becomes* the thing he hunts, predator of a predator as he hangs, bird-like, suspended in the wind; Wordsworth humanizes the bird – she builds a *lodge*, not a nest – and naturalizes himself: he becomes a 'plunderer'

> In the high places, on the lonesome peaks,
> Where'er among the mountains and the winds
> The mother-bird had built her lodge. Though mean
> My object and inglorious, yet the end
> Was not ignoble. Oh, when I have hung
> Above the raven's nest, by knots of grass
> And half-inch fissures in the slippery rock
> But ill sustained, and almost, as it seemed,
> Suspended by the blast which blew amain,
> Shouldering the naked crag, oh, at that time
> While on the perilous ridge I hung alone,
> With what strange utterance did the loud dry wind
> Blow through my ears; the sky seemed not a sky
> Of earth, and with what motion moved the clouds![28]
>
> (Book I, ll. 337–50, 1805 version)

Pater's humanized starling (a prisoner who can be taught 'to speak') cries to its young ones in answer to their cries, heard within the still, enclosed setting of the house. And from those cries the child learns the deathly lesson that nature ingeniously plays 'pain fugues' upon the living tissue of her creatures, just as Swinburne's Sappho had made of the tortured body of her beloved Anactoria 'a lyre of many faultless agonies.' Pater's persistent aestheticizing of pain is the most shocking of his inversions of normative values; beauty, even if wrought into being by pain, always trumps all else, including the good and the true. Perhaps the supreme instance occurs in *Gaston de Latour*, where the broken and bloodied body of Raoul, bound upon a wheel, figures as 'a rose upon a trellis.'[29] This is deeply disturbing, of course, in some sense monstrous, but Pater is a specialist in what might be termed the moral oxymoron, a yoking together of antithetical values. In a lower key he writes in *The Renaissance* of the 'comely decadence' of the later Middle Ages.[30] Street life in Leonardo's Milan is filled with 'brilliant sins and exquisite amusements':[31] the sins of the Milanese are to be ranked on a scale not from venal to mortal but from dull to dazzling. In one of his earliest and most radical essays, he characterizes the religion of the Middle Ages as 'a *beautiful disease* or disorder of the senses.'[32] In a later essay on Leonardo he writes of 'a whole octave of fantastic crime' committed in Perugia, as if crimes might be arranged like notes on a scale, lifting a leaf from De Quincey, who had aestheticized crime in his proto-decadent 'On Murder Considered as One of the Fine Arts' (1827).

Death surfaces in Pater in two guises, eroticized and sacralized, the two often conflated. Both are depicted in 'The Child in the House.' Death as sacred is laden for Pater with ancestral associations of home and of the earth, our final home. Womb and tomb, birthplace and grave, are near neighbors on Pater's pages. Emerald Uthwart returns to be planted among ancestral graves. Florian Deleal's 'peculiarly strong sense of home'[33] and love of mother earth reminds us that the young Walter Pater, like the young Wordsworth, was early orphaned of both parents. And so Florian takes solace in revisiting his 'home churchyard,' where the family dead lie buried 'cheek to cheek, and with the rain soaking in upon one from above.'[34] Strangely, the scene is not macabre, not Poe-like, but reverential in its ancestor worship. Like all boundaries in Pater, the boundary between the living and the dead is permeable, the rain soaking alike the living and the dead. The highly cultivated Florian is brother to Wordsworth's rustic girl in 'We Are Seven' who refuses to distinguish between her living siblings and her dead brothers, buried under the grass only a few paces from her home in graves over which she plays and sings. Wordsworth wished his days might be bound 'each to each by natural piety.'[35] Both Wordsworth and Pater, so unlike in almost all else, are bound each to each by a natural piety, by a reverence for places or persons more ancient than Greece, older even than Demeter, places hallowed into poetry by long vanished sounds and faces, by powers no less real for being unseen. This shared sense of the unbroken community of the living and the dead, this aboriginal reverence for the poetry of earth, makes Pater an especially perceptive critic of the poet who made a study of graveyard epitaphs. Hence in his essay on Wordsworth, Pater praises the poet's unique power as an elegist of

> local sanctities…connecting the stones and trees of a particular spot of
> earth with the great events of life, till the low walls, the green mounds,
> the half-obliterated epitaphs seem full of voices, and a sort of natural
> oracles, the very religion of these people of the dales appeared but as

another link between them and the earth, and was literally a religion of nature. (Buckler, p. 421)

For Pater, all religions originate in a 'universal pagan sentiment' that predates civilization and lingers 'far onwards into the Christian world, ineradicable, like some vegetable growth.'[36] Pater perhaps had in mind those early Christian sarcophagi, with traces of soil still clinging to their sides, the frieze of diminutive figures resembling ancient Romans, which of course they were. Thoughts of death come to us not merely with dread but with 'a rush of home-sickness' – the same anguish that overcomes the Child in the House as he prepares to leave it, or that compels Emerald Uthwart to return to his birthplace to die among his entombed ancestors. These rituals of return and rebirth, rooted 'in the earth of man's nature,' are the 'anodyne' of all religions, administered like an 'opiate' and retaining the taste of earth and of wine.[37]

Pater is less known for his earth-rooted elegies than for his more sensational depictions of death, one of which all but halts the narrative of 'The Child in the House.' The scene is doubly arresting, for it could not have been witnessed by the child Flavian but only by the adult Pater, in fact or in fantasy. The young Flavian has become a worshiper of beauty:

[And] with this desire of physical beauty mingled itself early the fear of death – the fear of death intensified by the desire of beauty. Hitherto he had never gazed upon dead faces, as sometimes, afterwards, at the *Morgue* in Paris, or in that fair cemetery at Munich, where all the dead must go and lie in state before burial, behind glass windows, among the flowers and incense and holy candles – the aged clergy with their sacred ornaments, the young men in their dancing-shoes and spotless white linen – after which visits, those waxen, resistless faces would always live with him for many days, making the broadest sunshine sickly. (Brzenk, pp. 28–9)

The transparent glass both invites and restrains any closer scrutiny of the dead.* Like the panes of glass, the flowers (Florian's name itself means *flower*) mask the smell of corruption. In his essay on 'Leonardo' Pater writes of the 'fascination of corruption'[38] that permeates every pore of the Uffizi *Medusa*,[39] a fascination evident in both Leonardo and in himself. Disgust and attraction, conventional

---

* Lytton Strachey puts it more bluntly: the Victorians 'were enclosed in glass...it's damned difficult to copulate through a glass case.' Letter to Maynard Kaynes, quoted in Michael Holroyd, *Lytton Strachey: A Biography* (London: Heinemann, 1970), p. 312.

opposites, are for Pater entwined like incestuous twins cleaving together. 'The way to perfection,' he writes of the evolution of Leonardo's style, 'is through a series of disgusts.'[40] Pater conflates the English sense of *revulsion* and the French of *savor*. The scene in the Munich morgue is a series of keenly savored disgusts.

The freshly dead youths are displayed in a quasi-religious crypt, where incense does double duty as a sweet sanctifier of the dead and as a fumigant. However briefly, the spotless dancers have become perfect works of art, frozen into immobility. Their faces are 'waxen,' suggesting the ghastly pallor of wax and its smoothened, death-like, textureless surface. Their 'resistless' faces reflect the expressionless passivity of death, a passivity always erotically charged for Pater. But 'resistless,' through a cunning transposition, also means *irresistible*. The Munich youths are a gallery of spotless Raouls, before Raoul's disfiguration.

Frank Kermode makes a striking connection between Pater's aestheticized image of the Munich dancers and the later life-in-death, death-in-life imagery of Yeats: the dead face that paradoxically stands for what is 'most "vital" in art.'[41] Pater's youths are expressionless less because they are dead than because in death they have achieved the perfection of pure being. To borrow a phrase from Pater's essay on Winckelmann, they embody the 'supreme artistic view of life.'[42] Or as Yeats puts it in 'Among School Children,' they are no longer 'swayed to music,' for they have, as it were, *become* music. '*All art*,' Pater wrote in his essay on Giorgione, '*constantly aspires towards the condition of music*,'[43] in which the subject cannot be distinguished from its expression, the matter from the form. In Yeats's famous variation on Pater's theme, 'How can we know the dancer from the dance?'*

Pater's preoccupation with death was widely shared by his contemporaries, including the Queen and her Poet Laureate. A great artist such as Pater finds points of contact between his most compelling obsessions and the preoccupations of his age, converting his quirks into art. A kiss that the child De Quincey furtively planted on the corpse of an adored sister became the creative trauma that inspired the finest passage in his autobiography.[44] Dickens sought out the Paris Morgue 'with a dreadful insatiability' and recorded his pleasure in 'Looking at something that could not return a look.' The morgues of the great European capitals offered the public a kind of black theatre,

---

* Yeats wrote in 'The Tragic Generation' that 'we looked consciously to Pater for our philosophy.' [*Autobiography*, II (New York: Macmillan, 1965), p. 201]. A tribute to Pater, the chapter is also a requiem for the *fin de siecle* poets – Ernest Dowson, Francis Thompson, Arthur Symons, and Oscar Wilde – whose lives, Yeats believed, were ruined in the wake of their reading *The Renaissance* and *Marius the Epicurean*. Yeats describes *Marius* as seeming to him 'the only great prose in modern English....' (*Autobiography*, 201).

particularly in Paris, where the mutilated body of a boy of ten, embalmed, well-chilled, and lightly rouged, was on display for six weeks, 'a longer run than many plays.'[45] Mme. Tussaud's Waxworks opened to large crowds in 1835, offering the public a kind of heated morgue in which the effigies were perpendicular rather than prone. Contrary to popular belief, the fascination of the waxen figures lay not in how lifelike they looked but how deathlike, while seemingly still alive – meticulously molded *revenants* posing as celebrated murderers hovering over their cowering victims. Pater's waxen, resistless youths are, by comparison, Elgin marbles of utter composure, placid reflections of the Victorian vogue of death.

The final death-scene in 'The Child in the House' is that of the house itself, whose bare rooms, now 'denuded and white,' Florian leaves for the last time with a 'wild pity of regret.' But first he must return to retrieve a forgotten pet bird, emblem, perhaps of his own soul, which would perish in the closed rooms that lie 'so pale, with a look of meekness in their denudation,' as if the house itself were in mourning for the departing child. The child then leaves the house, as, in time, his soul must depart from his body. His rite of passage into the larger world is tinged with the passionate longing that Pater feels for all things enclosed, sealed and at rest.

## 3

The 'Conclusion' to *The Renaissance* so scandalized contemporary readers that Pater, ever bold in thought but timid in action, excised it from the second edition.[46] But he added to the title page the head of a magnificently coiffured youth 'of doubtful sex'[47] who dominates the title page and appears to gaze, unperturbed, into the treacherous text that follows. And he interpolated into the first chapter a quaintly told, once immensely popular, thirteenth century hagiographic tale of two homosexual knights – 'Amis and Amile' – one of whom bathes the body of his leprous lover in the blood of his own decapitated sons. As in Swinburne's 'Leper,' in Pater's verbatim translation a sweetly decorous style consorts with scandalous subject matter. At the tale's end, the lovers, buried apart, are miraculously reunited in one grave, for like Saul and Jonathan, or Newman and his beloved Ambrose St. John, 'in their death they were not divided.'[48]

These two perturbations that Pater inserted into the text of the second edition (1877) – the androgynous head and the tale of 'Amis and Amile' – come immediately before and after the brief 'Preface.' Less famous than the 'Conclusion,' the 'Preface' is at least as radical, for in it Pater succeeds in eroticizing and personalizing the perception of beauty. Beauty is not an absolute quality inhering in objects, but is wholly 'relative' and proportional to the pleasure it evokes in the perceiver.[49] Further, Pater destabilizes the distinctions between male and female, just as he blurs the boundaries between life and art. He writes of poets and artists as if they were themselves works of art, and of works of art (the 'Mona Lisa' is the supreme instance) as if they had lives of their own: 'What is this song or picture, this engaging personality presented in life or in a book, to *me*?'[50]

Finally, Pater calls into question the clear demarcation between historical 'periods,' such as between the Middle Ages and the Renaissance. Hence he coins the term 'medieval renaissance'[51] to designate that liberating rebirth of spirit within the twelfth and thirteenth centuries that later flowers in the Italian Renaissance. And the Renaissance lingers on in Pater's pages until 1768, with the murder of the great historian of Hellenic art, Winckelmann, in Trieste, garroted while awaiting the arrival of the young Goethe, by a pock-marked, pigtailed thief ironically named Arcangeli.

Pater's revisionism in *The Renaissance* is directed primarily against his contemporaries Arnold and Ruskin, the first seemingly praised and the second never named but ever present. Ruskin was the first Slade Professor of Art at Oxford, a position to which Pater later aspired but was denied because of the odour of scandal attached to his writing and shadowing his life. Ruskin had argued in *Modern Painters* that the greatest painting conveys to the spectator 'the greatest number of the greatest ideas.'[52] But Pater insists, in direct opposition to Ruskin's moral aesthetic, that a painting must first delight the senses by its essential pictorial qualities and that 'a great picture has no more definite message for us than an accidental play of sunlight and shadow' on a wall or floor, indeed is itself 'such a space of fallen light' caught more exquisitely by the artist than by nature herself.[53] Ruskin's cardinal aesthetic principle in *Modern Painters* – truth to nature – becomes in Pater the exaltation of abstract form, freed from the tyranny of subject matter and entirely apart from any representational qualities.

Ruskin's *Stones of Venice* fares no better in Pater's pages than *Modern Painters*. No two views of the Renaissance could be more unlike than Pater's and Ruskin's. For Pater, the Renaissance was a 'complex and many-sided' rebirth of the 'worship of the body,' a liberation of the European mind from the asceticism of an earlier Christianity. In the 'Preface' he calls such a movement an 'outbreak of the human spirit,' as in a breaking out from prison. But an outbreak can also connote a disease, and in *The Stones of Venice* Renaissance architecture figures as a 'foul torrent' fatal to the beauty and vitality of the earlier Byzantine and Gothic periods. The icon of Pater's Renaissance is Botticelli's 'Birth of Venus.' For Ruskin, the Renaissance is not a cradle but a grave – the sarcophagus of a latter-day Whore of Babylon, still gorgeously clothed but desolate and 'drunk with the wine of her fornication.'[54]

Pater does an end run around Ruskin; he subverts Arnold by seeming to praise him. The key that unlocks his anti-Arnoldian intentions immediately follows a quotation from Arnold's 'Function of Criticism':

'To see the object as in itself it really is,' has justly been said to be the aim of all true criticism whatever, and in aesthetic criticism the first step towards seeing one's object as it really is, is to know one's own impression as it really is, to discriminate it, to realize it distinctly. (*The Renaissance*, p. 19)

Pater's *and* ('and...the first step') should of course be a *but*. This muffled denotation of a non-sequitur turns Arnold's effort to establish objective criteria of critical judgment upside down. Less than a generation later, in 'The Critic as Artist,' Oscar Wilde makes outrageously explicit what Pater chose merely to imply:

The highest criticism, then, is more creative than creation, and the primary aim of the critic is to see the object as in itself it really is not...

The central chapters of *The Renaissance* focus on artists of the first rank – Botticelli, Giorgione, and Leonardo – but Pater has a special affinity for the not-quite-great, for artists like Luca della Robbia, whose histories are largely lost and from whose lives 'all tumult of sound and colour have passed away.'[55] This same affinity for the unspectacular shows itself in Pater's preference for the quiet landscapes and flat expanses of the rivers of France – the painterly topography of transient effects favored by the French Impressionists – over the sublimities of the Alps. In the same way he is drawn to the local and the provincial over the metropolitan, or to the byways of literature rather than to the main events. Two of his finest essays are on English writers a little to the side of the mainstream – Sir Thomas Browne and Charles Lamb.

Art seeks to arrest the evanescent, and Pater is supremely the artist of the evanescent. Hence he is captivated by the ephemerality that the Tuscan sculptor della Robbia captures in clay: 'the passing of a smile over the face of a child, the ripple of air on a still day over the curtain of a window ajar.'[56] A faint breeze seems to ripple through the cadences following the comma after 'child,' the sentence ending not as our ear anticipates on the noun 'window,' but held open, like the window itself, by the trailing adjective 'ajar.' Made of clay and pigments mixed from the earth, della Robbia's earthenware Madonnas and rounded fruits seem still to partake of the earth (*terra cotta* means *baked earth*).

Pater is always at his best when evoking particular places, as in this nearly perfect sentence in which the blues and milky whites of the Tuscan sky seem to have alighted upon one of della Robbia's bas-reliefs ensconced in the recesses of a local church:

> I suppose nothing brings the real air of a Tuscan town so vividly to mind as those pieces of pale blue and white earthenware, by which he is best known, like fragments of the milky sky itself, fallen into the cool streets, and breaking into the darkened churches. (*The Renaissance*, pp. 49–50)

The visual becomes virtually tactile, cool to the touch. Pater seems to be savoring a freshly decanted Tuscan wine that doesn't travel well but must be drunk in its native province.

The brief chapters on lesser known artists and poets are especially rich in the poetry of place, for they portray not the commanding personalities of a Leonardo or Michaelangelo but artists who were nourished by their places of origin and of whose works Pater writes as if they were virtual outcroppings of their native *paysage*. The chapter on Joachim du Bellay is as much about the sands of the Loire, or about La Bauce, the granary of France, 'where the vast rolling fields seem to anticipate the great western sea itself,'[57] as it is about du Bellay or the poetry of the *Pleiad* of the mid-sixteenth century. Their poetry is as ephemeral as dew, composed of sudden lights that transfigure

> some trivial thing, a weather-vane, a windmill, a winnowing fan, the dust in the barn door. A moment – and the thing has vanished, because it was pure effect; but it leaves a relish behind it, a longing that the accident may happen again. (*The Renaissance*, p. 140)

The first sentence is about objects in transient motion – the wind, or dust suspended in the light of a barn door. The second is pure impressionism, sensation without a single concrete noun. Pater especially loves such effects for their suggestive sorrow, their power to evoke 'the final regret of all human creatures for the familiar earth and limited sky.'[58] He would have loved flowers less if they lasted longer.

'The School of Giorgione' is the most purely Paterian of the chapters in *The Renaissance*. An elegy to the art of evanescence, the chapter itself is a kind of vanishing act. By its end we are left not with a painter but with his 'school' and a half-dozen paintings of uncertain attribution; one, a fresco on a Venetian wall, has all but faded into a crimson shadow. The result is an indelible impression of deliquescence, as if Giorgione himself were but a space of 'fallen light.'[59] Page by page the 'six or eight' famous Giorgiones at Dresden, Florence and the Louvre dwindle to but one, *The Concert* in the Pitti Palace, 'undoubtedly Giorgione's.'[60] (But time the ironist has taken even that away, for Pater's sources were probably wrong, and *The Concert* is now thought to be by Titian.) We are left, as it were, with the Platonic *idea* of Giorgione – a note, a color, a tone, a musical idea without a material subject. And this is exactly what Pater evokes in a magical paragraph based on a composite portrait, derived primarily from *The Concert*, of what survives of Giorgione and his school, a kind of theme and variations on this most elusively 'musical' of artists:

> In sketch or finished picture, in various collections, we may follow [the motif of music] through many intricate variations – men fainting at music; music at the pool-side while people fish, or mingled with the sound of the pitcher in the well, or heard across running water, or among the flocks; the tuning of instruments; people with intent faces, as if listening, like those described by Plato in an ingenious passage of the Republic, to detect the smallest interval of musical sound, the smallest undulation in the air, or feeling for music in thought on a stringless instrument, ear and finger refining themselves infinitely, in the appetite for sweet sound; a momentary touch of an instrument in the twilight, as one passes through some unfamiliar room, in a chance company. (*The Renaissance*, p. 119)

Pater here realizes his own aphorism: fusing form and matter, he achieves in prose '*the condition of music*.'[61]

Freud's highly 'imaginary portrait' of Leonardo da Vinci – a portrait based, unfortunately, on a mistranslation[*] – pays respectful tribute to the Leonardo of Pater, who pioneers what has later become known as the art of psychobiography. Pater traces the defining mark of Leonardo's genius back to two early childhood fixations – 'the smiling of women and the motion of great waters.'[62] The smile most famously appears on the lips of Mona Lisa but first enters Pater's essay in the form of the beckoning, smiling, androgynous figure known as 'St. John the Baptist' in the Louvre, a figure whose treacherous smile, 'delicate brown flesh and woman's hair,' Pater wryly remarks, 'no one would go out into the wilderness to seek.'[63] The courtesan-like St. John bears a faint, reed-like staff or cross in one hand, and with the other points a remarkably phallic finger upward in an ambiguous gesture that could signify either his role

---

[*] A mistranslation of the Italian for *vulture* as *kite*. See *Leonardo da Vinci and a Memory of His Childhood*, trans. Alan Tyson (New York: W. W. Norton, 1964), p. 9. Freud also assumes, without evidence, that Mona Lisa bears the smile of Leonardo's mother. See also George Boas's most informative essay, 'The Mona Lisa in the History of Taste,' *Journal of the History of Ideas* (1940), vol. I, no. 2, pp. 207–24. For Freud's indebtedness to Pater, see Tyson, pp. 18, 60, 61, 65.

as preparer of the way for One greater than he or, equally, a common obscenity. Pater notes the strange likeness of the so-called St. John to a Bacchus hanging near it, a resemblance that puts him in mind of Heine's notion that the old pagan gods, now out of work, found employment in the new religion.[64]

This idea of a pagan residue in Leonardo's work resurfaces in Pater's description of 'The Last Supper' and of 'Mona Lisa.' But to range more broadly for a moment, the tracing of this nexus of cultural affinities lies at the heart of much of Pater's writing. For Pater attempts to do for culture what Darwin had done for nature – to trace, not in rocks or among species, but among cultures, that wide web of affinities that link Demeter to the Virgin Mother or, more to our purpose, that makes Plato's banquet of Love in the *Symposium* a prototype of the Christian God of Love's 'Last Supper' in Leonardo's half-ruined fresco.

Here again I turn to Pater's early essay on William Morris, the quarry for so much of his subsequent writing, including *The Renaissance*. Indeed, *The Renaissance* is but a fleshing out of these few sentences:

> The composite experience of all the ages is part of each one of us: to deduct from that experience, to obliterate any part of it, to come face to face with a people of a past age, as if the Middle Age, the Renaissance, the eighteenth century had not been, is as impossible as to become a little child, or to enter again into the womb and be born.... [It] is not possible to repress a single phase of that humanity...because we live and move and have our being in the life of humanity...[65]

Pater portrays the 'Mona Lisa' as just such an icon of 'the composite experience of all the ages,' the 'deposit, little cell by cell,' of Pagan and Christian, male and female, ancient and modern – a kind of evolved sum of human experience, from the ancient 'rocks among which she sits' to the present moment. In the passage from 'Aesthetic Poetry' Pater puts old wine into new bottles. The God of Acts 17:28, in whom 'we live, and move, and have our being' has become the 'composite experience' into which we are all born and have our being. Jesus had said, 'Except a man be born again, he cannot see the kingdom of God...can he enter a second time into his mother's womb?' (John 3:3–4). Pater asserts that we have no second life, apart from the collective experience encoded and preserved in culture.

This central passage from Pater's first published essay finds its completing counterpart in *Plato and Platonism* (1893), the last book he published in his lifetime:

> For in truth we come into the world, each one of us, 'not in nakedness' but by the natural course of organic development clothed far more completely than even Pythagoras supposed in a vesture of the past, nay, fatally shrouded, it might seem, in those laws or tricks of heredity which

we mistake for our volition; in the language which is more than one half of our thoughts; in the moral and mental habits, the customs, the literature, the very houses, which we did not make for ourselves; in the vesture of a past, which is (so science would assure us) not ours, but of the race, the species...[66]

Much of contemporary literary theory can be extracted from these lines ('language' writes books, not authors, and so forth) but their true importance resides less in their postmodernity than in their hard-nosed historical and biological determinism, the power of the past encoded in our culture and in our very genes.[67]

Pater's stress on the survival of Paganism into Christianity underlies his description of *The Last Supper*, which Leonardo completed in 1497 but which has flaked and faded ever since.[68] With a delicate indirection he suggests that underlying this most hallowed moment in the life of Christ, like a kind of *pentimento* or underpainting, is the ghostly shadow of another banquet, the parting of guests in Plato's *Symposium*. Pater's suggestion is a bit shocking, given the special sanctity of the subject. But Leonardo, like Pater, was no Fra Angelico. At the start of his essay Pater cites Vasari's remark that Leonardo 'was a bold speculator, holding lightly by other men's beliefs, setting *philosophy* above *religion*.'[69] Pater sets Philosophy not above but alongside Religion, as if a saddened Socrates underlay the tragic visage of Christ. He effects this doubling through a play on the word *Host*:

Here was another effort to lift a given subject out of the range of its traditional associations. Strange, after all the mystic developments of the middle age, was the effort to see the Eucharist, not as the pale Host of the altar, but as one taking leave of his friends. Five years afterwards the young Raphael, at Florence, painted it with sweet and solemn effect in the refectory of Saint Onofrio; but still with all the mystical unreality of the school of Perugino. Vasari pretends that the central head was never finished. But finished or unfinished, or owing part of its effect to a mellowing decay, the head of Jesus does but consummate the sentiment of the whole company – ghosts through which you see the wall, faint as the shadows of the leaves upon the wall on autumn afternoons. This figure is but the faintest, the most spectral of them all. It is the image of what the history it symbolises has been more and more ever since, paler and paler as it recedes from us. Criticism came with its appeal from mystical unrealities to originals, and restored no life-like reality but these transparent shadows – spirits which have not flesh and bones. (*The Renaissance*, p. 95)

'Symposium' and 'Last Supper': the one banquet takes Love for its subject, with Socrates crowned at the end; the other places the God of Love in isolation at its center, soon to wear a Crown of Thorns, but here seated and solitary, with no visible halo, foreseeing his own martyrdom, as Socrates courted his martyrdom before the Athenian jury. Leonardo's haloless Apostles are disputatious guests at a none-too-tranquil parting of friends. Guests and Host on the walls of Sta. Maria della Grazie fade before our eyes – ghosts through whom you can see the refectory wall, attenuated by time and the fading of belief. Leonardo, who 'fixed the outward type of Christ for succeeding centuries,'[70] here depicts His slow dissolution. The 'Host' is transfigured into a ghost in the company of ghosts ('transparent shadows') in the closing sentence. Jesus's last words in the Gospel of St. John – Consummatum est; 'it is finished' – echo through Pater's word consummate, but that consummation has now grown 'faint as the shadows of the leaves upon the wall of autumn afternoons,' a fourfold desubstantiation into mere shadows of dying leaves in a dying season at the end of the day.[71]

Pater secularizes the Jesus of The Last Supper; he all but divinizes the quite plain, early middle-aged Mona Lisa. It is a pity that Pater chose not to write on her younger, fairer, hauntingly beautiful counterpart, 'Ginevra de' Benci.' A portrait from life, Ginevra has the pallor of Parian marble. With all 'the refinement of the dead,'[72] her unearthly beauty suggests a mask, a spirit that has 'not flesh and bones.' Her look is waxen, like that of the Munich youths laid out behind glass. The old Florentine records describe a sculptor as 'a master of live stone.' With her half-closed eyes and imperturbable gaze, she appears carved out of living stone. She is the Pygmalion myth in reverse, not art awakening to life, but life metamorphosed back into the deathless stillness of art. She resembles Mona Lisa only in the pose of the figure and the gaze that seems to follow her viewer. In all else they are contraries. Mona Lisa's nose is a little too long, her forehead too high; she has no visible eyebrows; her plump, stubby hands, if flexed, might lift weights; her torso could move furniture. Leonardo divinizes not her beauty but her ambiguity. Neither young nor old, fair nor foul, she is the subtlest of Leonardo's androgynous figures, a smiling image, Pater tells us (and Freud picks this up), that had defined itself on the very 'fabric' of Leonardo's dreams.[73] Had Marcel Duchamp drawn a moustache on the face of Ginevra de' Benci he would have committed a schoolboy act of obscene vandalism. But the moustache that he affixed to the face of Mona Lisa is both a put-down of the epitome of high bourgeoisie culture and a witty comment on her implied androgyny. In Pater's celebrated description she also manages to be antique and modern, Pagan and Christian, Madonna and femme fatale, as she smiles her polite, Paterian smile:

The presence that rose thus so strangely beside the waters, is expressive of what in the ways of a thousand years men had come to desire. Hers is

the head upon which all 'the ends of the world are come,' and the eyelids
are a little weary. It is a beauty wrought out from within upon the flesh,
the deposit, little cell by cell, of strange thoughts and fantastic reveries
and exquisite passions. Set it for a moment beside one of those white
Greek goddesses or beautiful women of antiquity, and how would they
be troubled by this beauty, into which the soul with all its maladies has
passed! All the thoughts and experience of the world have etched and
moulded there, in that which they have of power to refine and make
expressive the outward form, the animalism of Greece, the lust of Rome,
the mysticism of the middle age with its spiritual ambition and
imaginative loves, the return of the Pagan world, the sins of the Borgias.
(*The Renaissance,* pp. 95–6)

I have broken Pater's paragraph at the point where Yeats picks it up, reprinting
the remainder as free verse at the start of his edition of *The Oxford Book of
English Verse* (1936):

She is older than the rocks among which she sits;
Like the Vampire,
She has been dead many times,
And learned the secrets of the grave;
And has been a diver in deep seas,
And keeps their fallen day about her;
And trafficked for strange webs with Eastern merchants;
And, as Leda,
Was the mother of Helen of Troy,
And, as St Anne,
Was the mother of Mary;
And all this has been to her but as the sound of Lyres and flutes,
And lives
Only in the delicacy
With which it has moulded the changing lineaments,
And tinged the eyelids and the hands. (Hill, p. 96)

For the New Critics, this passage marked the nadir of an impudent
impressionism. For Yeats, it was of 'revolutionary importance' and 'dominated'
his generation.[74] Among its many indeterminacies, Yeats saw that the passage
hovered between poetry and prose. One phrase – 'as Leda, / Was the mother
of Helen of Troy' – must have lingered especially in his mind, for in time it
engendered the finest sonnet of the twentieth century: 'Leda and the Swan.'

The first to be composed and by far the longest chapter in *The Renaissance,*
'Winckelmann' (1867), is also the boldest. Pater's portrait of the great Hellenist

who 'fingers those pagan marbles...with no sense of shame'[75] is also at bottom a self-portrait. An aesthete, a homosexual, and art-critic, Winckelmann lives the life that Pater advocates in the 'Conclusion': he burns with a hard, gem-like flame; he is the spiritual begetter of Walter Pater, as Pater is of Oscar Wilde.

Less a polemic than a plea, the Winckelmann essay attempts to extend into the sphere of sexual behavior the political freedoms that Mill was soon to advocate in *On Liberty* (1869). Pater applauds Winckelmann's 'more liberal mode of life' and his 'fervid, romantic friendships with young men.'[76] He virtually invites the assumption that he, too, shares the same tastes.[77] And he shares with Winckelmann a heterodox preference for the Greek worship of beauty over the Christian 'worship of sorrow,' with its 'crucifixion of the senses....'[78] Pater's brief biography of Winckelmann presages the myth, familiar to us in Thomas Mann's 'Death in Venice,' of the frigid, cramped Teutonic temperament coming to a fatal encounter with the torrid sexuality of the Mediterranean.[79] Released in Rome from the somber 'repressions' of his native Germany,[80] Winckelmann recognizes his 'affinity with Hellenism' and forms friendships with young men more beautiful than Guido Reni's Archangel Michael. In the moments before his death at the hands of Arcangeli, Winckelmann 'beguiled' his time with a youth from Trieste. I like to think that the boy bore a family resemblance to Aschenbach's Tadzio.

Winckelmann's extravagant raptures over the male figure appear a little odd in Pater's pages, but the Winckelmann who wrote the *History of Ancient Art* is even stranger than the Winckelmann of *The Renaissance*. In one of his several rhapsodies over the Apollo Belvedere he acquires the voice of a prophet and the breasts of a woman:

> An eternal spring, as in the happy fields of Elysium, clothes with the charms of youth the graceful manliness of ripened years, and plays with softness and tenderness about the proud shape of his limbs.... In the presence of this miracle of art I forget all else.... My breast seems to enlarge and swell with reverence, like the breasts of those who were filled with the spirit of prophecy...for my image seems to receive life and motion, like the beautiful creation of Pygmalion.[81]

Winckelmann himself becomes an androgynous work of art, like the softly featured Apollo he depicts, a composite of 'graceful manliness' and the 'tenderness' of a woman – a Pygmalion-Galatea in the image of Winckelmann himself. His writing evokes the divine afflatus of the Christian mystics, but it daringly fuses, as Pater fuses, the religious, the sexual, and the aesthetic in a way that recalls Apollo's ravishing of Daphne or Bernini's St. Teresa in open-mouthed ecstasy, about to receive the arrow of the Seraph. Pater introduces Winckelmann into high Victorian culture in a way calculated to disorient and to subvert.

Because the hard, gem-like flame of Beauty is cool to the touch – in Yeats's phrase, 'An agony of flame that cannot singe a sleeve' – Winckelmann can handle the pagan marbles 'with unsinged hands.'[82] The sensuousness of the ancient Greeks does not 'fever the conscience: it is shameless and childlike.'[83] For an instant the reader takes 'shameless' to mean *brazen*, but *childlike* tones down the meaning to *without guilt*.

At the heart of the Winckelmann essay is an erotics of negation[*] that makes white more evocative than crimson, the slender, bronze 'Boy at Prayer' more attractive than the gendered beauty of the Venus de Milo, the taste of water that has no taste at all the most delicious to the palate. Beauty, Winckelmann wrote, should be like the purest water, drawn from the spring itself, free of all 'foreign admixture.'[84] Perhaps recalling Winckelmann's praise of purity, Pater writes in a magical passage from *Marius the Epicurean* of the healing waters of the Well of Aesculapius, water so entirely free of organic matter, so salubrious, that it 'was more like a draft of wonderfully pure air.'[85]

Such beauty is at once desexualized and highly erotic. It is 'a colourless, unclassified purity,' like that of a child awakening from sleep, and it arouses in the beholder a corresponding aesthetic of 'passionate coldness':[86]

> The beauty of the Greek statues was a sexless beauty: the statues of the gods had the least traces of sex. Here there is a moral sexlessness, a kind of ineffectual wholeness of nature…. This serenity is, perhaps, in great measure, a negative quality: it is the absence of any sense of want, or corruption, or shame. (*The Renaissance*, p. 176)[87]

Nowhere else in Pater's writings are paradox and indirection asked to accomplish so much. 'Sexless beauty' is a seeming contradiction. The 'absence of want' is a double negative, signifying the lack of any deficiency or the lack of sexual desire. The most striking phrase – *moral sexlessness* – is Pater's code for *sexually pubescent*, when a boy's body most resembles a girl's, an idealized figure of an androgynous, pre-potent (sexually 'ineffectual') wholeness. Such

---

[*] Pater personifies the erotics of negation in the character of 'Sebastian van Stork,' one of his most successful *Imaginary Portraits*. The handsome Sebastian is in love with none of his buxom 'suitors' (Pater's term for the young women who pursue him) but with the beatific calm of non-being. A sort of aristocratic Bartleby of the Netherlands ('I would prefer not to'), he is enamored of the 'pallid Arctic sun' and the 'dead level of a…barren and absolutely lonely sea.' He luxuriates in the concept of 'zero,' of 'equilibrium, the void,' toward which he and the world are moving. (Buckler, pp. 296–7.) A martyr, as it were, to the Second Law of Thermodynamics, he prefers winter to summer and takes pleasure in contemplating 'the earth beneath our feet cooling down for ever from its old cosmic heat' (Buckler, p. 291). At the end of the story, he achieves an ecstatic vision of negation by drowning himself, in a rapture of nullity, in the shallow flats of the Herder.

a figure displays not the slightest mark of discomposure, indeed bears a cousinly connection to Pater's impassive, waxen dancers at rest in the Munich Morgue. Their antithesis (and I imagine that Winckelmann and Pater would have found them loathsome) is the gallery of recumbent Hermaphrodites in the Louvre, with their voluptuous breasts, rounded thighs, and fully erect penises.

Constrained by a culture at once deeply Christian and homophobic, Pater masks his skepticism and homosexuality in a prose in which *passionless* can mean *passionate*, *sexless* can mean *sexual*, and the worship of Beauty trumps the worship of God. Pater's Greeks, like Winckelmann's, live in a sinless, pre-lapsarian world. St. Paul wrote, 'where no law is, there is no transgression,'[88] and much of the appeal of the Greek Revival in Victorian England lay in its return to a pagan Eden of imagined innocence, perhaps to sweeten harsh memories of homosexual subjugation in the English public schools, certainly to escape an England that for the first time in its history criminalized homosexual acts between males in the Criminal Law Amendment Act of 1885,[89] the law that condemned Oscar Wilde to two years of brutally hard labor, where one of his only comforts was reading his 'Golden Book,' Pater's *Renaissance*.

Pater's homosexuality puts him in a distinct minority, however sizeable, yet he shares with the larger culture certain tastes and predilections. Like much of popular Victorian art, J. W. Waterhouse's 'Hylas and the Nymphs' is an invitation to the titillation of purity. A cluster of naked nymphs reach out to touch a stooping Hylas, their skin not flesh-toned but marble white, their nipples barely budding into pink. They are of an age and pallor, if not the gender, beloved of Winckelmann and Pater. Hiram Powers's *The Greek Slave* – one of the most popular statues displayed at The Great Exhibition of 1851 – seems as if it were sculpted to Pater's direction. Although naked and chained, she is oddly impassive, erotic but also 'curiously frigid.'[90] Mrs. Browning wrote a sonnet in praise of her 'passionless perfection,' a phrase that might have been lifted from *The Renaissance*.

At first blush the once scandalous 'Conclusion' seems a little tame and contrived after the unguarded fervors of 'Winckelmann.' Less personal, more philosophical, this five-paragraph coda to *The Renaissance* is nonetheless at least as radical. Pater takes for his epigraph Heraclitus's 'All things give way; nothing remaineth.' In the first paragraph he dissolves the seeming stability of the material world; in the second, the self that perceives that world. Not only can we not, in Heraclitus's words, step into the same river twice; the self that does the stepping is itself in constant flux. Language invests objects with a solidity that they do not in reality possess. Even in attempting to reach out to others, we are imprisoned within 'a thick wall of personality.'[91] This is solipsism, but a solipsism without a self. We are left with only a 'tremulous wisp' of sensation, a 'continual vanishing away, that strange, perpetual, weaving and unweaving of ourselves.'[92] If this sounds familiar, Virginia Woolf has made it seem so: 'I am made and remade continually' (*The Waves*).[93]

In the original version of the 'Conclusion,' Pater ended the second paragraph with one of the most bleakly beautiful passages in all of his writings:

> Such thoughts seem desolate at first; at times all the bitterness of life seems concentrated in them. They bring the image of one washed out beyond the bar in a sea at ebb, losing even his personality, as the elements of which he is composed pass into new combinations. Struggling, as he must, to save himself, it is himself that he loses at every moment. (*The Renaissance*, p. 273)

In 'Dover Beach' the Sea of Faith has ebbed, but Arnold can still hear 'its melancholy, long, withdrawing roar.' Here, Pater drowns in its shoals. And he does so willingly, taking Scripture along with him. Jesus had said, 'Whosoever will lose his life for my sake shall find it.'[94] Pater chooses instead to immerse himself in the flux. Mortality and mutability are his grim equivalents to the Fortunate Fall, for out of them we wrest and fashion art and achieve the 'supreme artistic view of life.' While 'all melts under our feet,' we burn with a gem-like flame.

At the end of the 'Conclusion,' Pater again draws on Scripture only to subvert it. We are all damned ('condamnes'), yet 'we have an interval, and then our place knows us no more.' But in that interval, we must grasp at experience and love 'art for its own sake.'[95] In the Psalms our 'days are as grass,' in Job he who goes to his grave 'shall come up no more...neither shall his place know him any more.'[96] The brevity and uncertainty of life, traditionally a cause to repent our sins, is for Pater an invitation to a dance of the senses, a seeking after 'strange dyes...and curious odours.' The only sense not invoked in the 'Conclusion' is the sense of hearing, for we are all immured within the thick wall of personality.[97]

## 4

Newman, Arnold and Hopkins had all left Oxford well before the publication of *The Renaissance* in 1873. But the Reverend W. W. Capes, Pater's former tutor, stepped into Newman's old pulpit at St. Mary's to preach a University Sermon inveighing against Pater's 'new Philosophy of Art' and his corrupting lack of 'manhood.'[98] The same charges might equally have been leveled against *Marius the Epicurean* (1885), a philosophical romance in which the hero falls in love – Pater nicely calls it 'friendship at first sight' – with the Pagan Flavian and then with the Christian Cornelius. 'Mr. Pater,' remarked Benjamin Jowett, the formidable Master of Balliol, 'you seem to think that religion is all idolatry.'

Jowett's put-down is perhaps truer than he intended, but it is also wide of the mark. An idolater has found the object of his belief. Pater, like Marius, is in quest of a god who is clothed in human form. As Michael Levey keenly observes, *Marius the Epicurean* has more in common with Newman's *Apologia Pro Vita Sua* than, say, with Bulwer Lytton's *Last Days of Pompei.*[99]

To approach *Marius* expecting the pleasures of a Victorian novel is to ask a sieve to carry water. Pater flagrantly disregards the imperatives of character, dialogue, and plot. Rituals, processions, and ruminations replace action. What Pater slights in action and characterization he gives to the formative importance of place in the shaping of the consciousness of the hero. Marius has no surname – only the epithet Epicurean – perhaps because his father is Walter Pater. He is Pater's Child in the House, but he grows up in the ancient Roman countryside of the second century A.D. All the rest of his life is a longed-for return to his early 'dwelling-place.'[100] A contemporary critic, well ahead of his time, wrote that *Marius the Epicurean* belonged on the 'same shelf as Rousseau's *Confessions.*'[101]

Like most autobiographies – like the *Prelude*, the *Apologia*, and *Praeterita* – *Marius* is never better than in its opening pages. In that dawning of consciousness, the clear distinction between the world within the child and the world outside has not yet grown rigid – a state of consciousness we can later inhabit only in our dreams. Marius is a born animist, his 'own nearer household gods' gathered like toys around his bed. He comes to consciousness in a countryside haunted by the worship of the old gods, 'a religion of usages and sentiments rather than facts and beliefs, and attached to very definite things and places…'[102] In Newman's eyes, a religion without dogma was no religion at all; but for Pater it was the only one in which he ever believed. The young Marius very much resembles what the child Wordsworth would have been, had the Lake District poet been born in a northern province of Antonine Italy. Pater himself makes the connection between the young Marius and Wordsworth at the start of the story. Marius feels 'a native instinct of devotion,' like that of Wordsworth, in passing a spot 'touched of heaven' where a bolt of lightning had struck dead an aged laborer, a 'spot of time' marked by a stone and 'mouldering garlands.'[103] (The word *mouldering* is a favorite in Pater's lexicon because of its hallowed association with earth and with death.)

Were *Marius* in any conventional sense an historical novel, Wordsworth's presence would be a crippling anachronism. But anachronisms of persons and of places are legion in *Marius* not by default but by design. They are the markers of Pater's cultural syncretism, of the 'composite experience of all the ages' that is incarnate in Marius's consciousness, outcroppings of the past or heralds of the future, like the traces of soil still clinging to the ancestral figures the boy Marius worships, or the appearance of Dante, Giotto, Hamlet and Montaigne all in a single chapter. *Marius the Epicurean* is less a novel than a kind of archaeology of human culture set in ancient Italy. Some of its liveliest scenes take place underground, in tombs and catacombs; scenes above ground alternate with those below, breaking the boundaries between waking life and dreams.[104] Shortly before his death, Marius revisits the tomb of his ancestors, breaks the great seal at its entrance, and piously rearranges their graves, re-aligning his past with his present. Beneath the house of the early Christian Cecilia, Marius comes upon the tombs of children, cut into the porous tufa of the catacombs, their toys laid out beside them. In contrast, the live children overhead that Marius hears singing Christian hymns have 'a sort of quaint unreality.'[105] It is as if Marius, now grown up, has read Wordsworth's 'We Are Seven' and taken to heart its lesson of the living presence of the dead. The scenes at Cecilia's early monastic community near the end of the story recall the child Marius at its beginning, going to sleep surrounded by his household gods; all that is absent from his felicity is his mother's kiss. The dream-like architecture of his childhood home – 'White Nights' (the title of the second chapter) – suggests that moment of equilibrium in summer when day and night, waking and sleeping, can scarcely be distinguished.

The adolescent Marius leaves White Nights for school at Pisa, where he meets the young aesthete Flavian. Like a 'carved figure in motion,' Flavian is decadence incarnate, a prototype of Oscar Wilde's Dorian Gray.[106] The relationship between the adoring Marius and the imperious Flavian looks back to that between Raoul and Jasmin in *Gaston de Latour*. But that was a case study in the erotics of sado-masochism; this is a celebration of friendship at first sight. The experience that turns the young friends into lovers is the reading of a book in a shuttered granary, the story of Cupid and Psyche in Apuleius's *Golden Ass*. Marius and Flavian are seduced by a book, as *The Renaissance* is said to have seduced a generation of Oxford undergraduates. For fifteen pages the narrative grinds to a halt as Pater retells the story of Psyche's trials in pursuit of the God of Love. But Pater's thematic intention is clear: Marius, too, is in quest of the God of Love, a quest that first leads him to the person of Flavian, then to his austere, early Christian counterpart, the Roman soldier Cornelius. (Proper names in Pater's fiction are often transgendered: Marius/ Marie, Flavian/Flavia, Cornelius/Cornelia.)

Sexual love in Pater almost always comes to an untimely end. Flavian's end comes in the form of the plague. His death is portrayed as a chaste Victorian *Liebestod*. Marius nurses Flavian, then enters his bed:

> It seemed that the light of the lamp distressed the patient, and Marius extinguished it. The thunder which had sounded all day among the hills, with a heat not unwelcome to Flavian, had given way at nightfall to steady rain; and in the darkness Marius lay down beside him, faintly shivering now in the sudden cold, to lend him his own warmth, undeterred by the fear of contagion which had kept other people from

passing near the house. At length about daybreak he perceived that the last effort had come with a revival of mental clearness, as Marius understood by the contact, light as it was, in recognition of him there. 'Is it a comfort,' he whispered then, 'that I shall often come and weep over you?' – 'Not unless I be aware, and hear you weeping!' (*Marius*, p. 101)*

The faint, spasmodic shivering in bed may be the most discreet orgasm in English literature. The fear of contagion that causes passersby to shun the lovers' house is Pater's sly swipe at the homophobia of his contemporaries. The bleak words spoken at the end of the paragraph resolutely deny the words of 2 Samuel: 'and in their death they were not divided' (1: 23). They are also an implicit refutation of the climactic ninety-fifth Section of *In Memoriam*, in which the souls of Tennyson and Hallam are each 'wound' in the other. Here, a corpse poised on the brink of dissolution is hastily burned (it is a time of plague), and Marius is left alone by the roadside holding a handful of ashes.

I pass lightly over the philosophical disquisitions interpolated throughout Marius – on Epicureanism, Cyrenaicism, the Stoicism of Marcus Aurelius – for they seem to me far from the vital center of the book. The first requisite to interesting one's readers, Pater writes in *Marius*, is to know what interests oneself.[107] Pater is most interested in arresting the perception of beauty and the, for him, inextricably linked experience of pain. With no evident pertinence

---

* It is remarkable how much sexual liberty the Victorians could take despite the pruderies of the period. In his *Confessions* the adolescent De Quincey, down and out in London, shares a deserted house with a ten-year-old waif. They bed together on the floor with a bundle of rags to fend off the cold:

> The poor child crept close to me for warmth and for security against her ghostly enemies. When I was not more than usually ill, I took her into my arms so that, in general, she was tolerably warm and often slept when I could not.... But my sleep distressed me more than my watching, for besides the tumultuousness of my dreams (which were only not so awful as those which I shall have to describe hereafter as produced by opium), my sleep was never more than what is called *dog sleep*; so that I could hear myself moaning and was often, as it seemed to me, awakened suddenly by my own voice; and, about this time, a hideous sensation began to haunt me as soon as I fell into a slumber, which has since returned upon me, at different periods of my life, namely, a sort of twitching (I know not where, but apparently about the region of the stomach), which compelled me violently to throw out my feet for the sake of relieving it.

The narrator's moaning, twitching, and violent spasm of the legs all suggest an orgasm. Yet the scene, like that between Marius and Flavian, seems to me utterly unprurient, indeed quite touching in the protective concern of the stronger partner for the weaker.

to the plot, Marius comes upon a handsome racehorse, crippled and being led to the slaughterhouse. The 'mad appeal' in the horse's eyes puts Pater in mind of 'our poor humanity,' with its mute, unheard cries for fellowship in its pain.[108] These sudden surges of engaged concern appear throughout *Marius*, as in Pater's gruesomely graphic depiction of the martyrdom of the early Christians in Rome. But the tortures of the martyrs, like the slaughter of the horse, are acts inflicted by men. What most persistently compels the imagination of Marius and of his creator is the inexplicable pain inherent in the very nature of experience itself. The title of the chapter in which the crippled horse makes its mute appeal is 'Sunt Lacrimae Rerum' – the tears inherent in things, a phrase from Virgil's most famous line, which Pater quotes in full immediately after describing the doomed horse.[109] The line haunted Pater, as it haunts Gaston de Latour, who, upon hearing the tremor in an aged voice, or picking up a forgotten toy, 'became suddenly aware of the great stream of human tears falling always through the shadows of the world.'[110] Experience for Pater is inevitably retrospective and can be fully known only in the aftermath of memory, like 'some strange second flowering after date.'[111] All memory is the memory of loss. *Marius* is an intensely personal *memento mori* disguised as an historical novel.

Only twice in the course of three hundred pages does Marius come close to arresting time – in the secular epiphany he experiences in an olive garden and on his death bed. The scene of Marius alone in a garden, desperate with a will to believe, inevitably recalls the conversion of St. Augustine. But it also recalls Wordsworth's mystical moment in an Alpine gorge in the *Prelude*, where a roaring waterfall, ever changing yet ever changeless, puts him in mind of 'Eternity.'[112] So, too, Marius hears the roar of a nearby 'immemorial waterfall' that plunges with an 'unchanging' motion and that suggests 'an image of unalterable rest.'[113] Yet Marius's 'privileged hour' is less memorable for what it affirms than for what it denies. For the hour brings not a revelation but a 'fair' hope, a tortured skepticism that ends in a feeble joy:

> The purely material world, that close, impassable prison-wall, seemed just then the unreal thing...and he felt a quiet hope, a quiet joy dawning faintly, in the dawning of this doctrine upon him as a really credible opinion. (*Marius*, p. 212)

I find a touching integrity in this crippled sentence that concludes Marius's failed epiphany. A *really credible opinion* is disarmingly inept. Pater's prose is hobbled because he cannot in conscience carry Marius further along the path to conversion than he himself could go.

The agent who brings Marius to the brink of conversion is Cornelius, a Roman legionnaire and covert Christian. The 'straight' counterpart of the flamboyantly decadent Flavian, Cornelius is a 'military-knight,' an exemplar of the refined asceticism that Pater always found irresistible. Through Cornelius, Marius reaches the clandestine Christian community in Rome, where he dies after contracting the plague, laying down his life to save his friend Cornelius.

The presiding deity of that community is the virginally beautiful, statuesque Cecilia, a wealthy Roman matron whose 'temperate beauty brought reminiscence of the serious and virile character of the best female statuary of Greece.'[114] A widowed Madonna, she walks among the freshly converted with an 'antique severity' as she holds a little child in her arms.[115] In the heady days of his leadership of the Oxford Movement, Newman had personified the early Church as his vigorous 'Spiritual Mother,' whom he recognized by 'the joyous swing of her advance.' Surprisingly, he quotes the words of the pagan Virgil – 'Incessu patuit Dea' ('By her step she revealed herself a goddess'[116]) – to suggest her empowered grace. I cannot recall Newman or Pater ever warming to the figure and movement of a woman, except for Newman's 'Spiritual Mother' and Pater's Demeter-like Cecilia. They bear a striking sisterly resemblance, perhaps because Newman's image of his 'Spiritual Mother' lingered in Pater's mind, Newman having exerted as powerful a sway over Pater as over Arnold and Hopkins, a remarkable quartet of Victorian Oxonians.

Newman would have been appalled at my associating his Church with a pagan goddess. Pater *intends* the association, his only quarrel with Christianity being its claim to possess the exclusive Truth. A decade before *Marius*, Pater wrote a highly perceptive and sympathetic essay on the myth of Demeter and Persephone, whose continuing hold on our imagination is 'akin to the influence of cool places, quiet houses, subdued light, tranquilising voices.'[117] A print of the Cnidian Demeter was very likely before his eyes as he wrote the essay. Her full, stately form and features seem expressly to animate his later description of the Christian Cecilia.[118] The rituals of early Christianity – the bread, the wine, the oil – are the old rituals poured into new vessels, for a 'new organism' is not conceived by 'sudden and abrupt creation' but by the gradual action of new principles upon older elements, 'all of which in truth already lived and died many times.'[119] The very architecture of Cecilia's house, like her body itself, materially expresses this idea of accretive hybridism – ancient Roman on the way to becoming Romanesque:

> The fragments of the older architecture, the mosaics, the spiral columns, the precious corner-stones of immemorial building, had put on, by such juxtaposition, a new and singular expressiveness... (*Marius*, p. 228)

*Marius the Epicurean* was published in the last decade of Pater's life. As a child Pater adored 'playing at priests,' dressing in a nightgown for a surplice and preaching to his mother and his admiring Aunt Bessie.[120] As an Oxford undergraduate he had lost his faith in Christianity, a loss everywhere apparent in *The Renaissance*, but most memorably in the image in the 'Conclusion' of being washed away in an ebbing sea, losing his life even as he tries to save it. Sometime after the publication of *The Renaissance* and before composing *Marius*, the Sea of Faith began imperceptibly but steadily to wash back over Pater. He was occasionally seen at worship at the Reverend Hopkins's St. Aloysius in Oxford. He took part in the Requiem Mass for Cardinal Newman in 1890, four years before his own death. He was a frequent attendant at the High Anglican Church of St. Albans in London. There, as the author of *Marius the Epicurean*, he could not have failed to notice that the celebrant of the Mass wore 'the formal evening dress of a Roman gentleman of the second century.'[121] The boy Marius, like his creator when a boy, plays solemnly 'at priests,' Marius conducting household ceremonies in the absence of his deceased father (Pater's father died when Walter was four). Near the end of the story, Pater tells us that 'the boy-priest survived' in the adult Marius, who in his last days is welcomed into the devout monastic community of Cecilia.

*Marius* had opened with a child slipping into sleep with his household gods at his bedside. It closes with the same child, now a middle-aged adult, lying on his back in a dream-like delirium. The scene is at once erotic and deeply religious. The tablet of Marius's mind awaits whatever 'the divine fingers might choose to write there.'[122] He is suspended in a kind of ecstasy, open-mouthed and expectant, hovering in perfect passivity between sleep and death. For the God of Love is about to enter Marius's mouth, the Bridegroom, as it were, taking his bride in the form of a wafer placed on his lips:

> The people around his bed were praying fervently – *Abi! Abi Anima Christiana.* In the moments of his extreme helplessness their mystic bread had been placed, had descended like a snow-flake from the sky, between his lips. (*Marius*, p. 296)

Marius receives not the Eucharist but 'mystic bread,' sacred both to Christians and to Demeter. Pater ends on a note of perfect equivocation: the bread is placed between Marius's lips, not in his mouth. Pater's disciple Oscar Wilde always went further than his master: on his death bed in Paris he received the Eucharist and became a baptized Catholic. Pater died at home in the arms of his sister Clara. Neither Walter nor Clara nor Hester ever married. They all lived together, adult children in the same house, and they are entombed in a single grave in Oxford.

# VARIETIES OF INFERNAL EXPERIENCE: THE FALL OF THE CITY IN VICTORIAN LITERATURE

The city is at once an organism and an idea. As an organism, it flourishes and fades, presenting a different aspect to the beholder at each moment in its history. As an idea, the city has haunted the human imagination with a fixity equaled perhaps only by the idea of time or of God. The new industrial towns of the nineteenth century were probably as unlike the early cities of the Fertile Crescent as hell is from heaven, yet we still apprehend and describe cities in archetypal patterns that predate ancient Babylon or Tyre. Even the literature of the modern city, like modern man himself, is haunted by recollections of the gods and by the ghosts of the fallen cities they once founded.

The earliest cities were believed to be sacred in origin and to have come into being as the terrestrial counterpart of a celestial model. The golden city that the Evangelist sees at the end of the Apocalypse might stand as the type of all urban foundations: 'And I John saw the holy city, new Jerusalem, coming down from God out of heaven, prepared as a bride adorned for her husband' (21:2). The vision still dazzles, but the mode of thought is elementally archaic. For early man recognized as real only those places or events which, by analogy, he could fit into a divine prototype.[1] Like the New Jerusalem, the ancient cities of Egypt and Babylon, of India and the Orient, came down from God out of the heavens and were ruled by His surrogates on earth – kings and priests. To found a city was to create a cosmos out of chaos, to duplicate in miniature the act of Creation itself. Hence it is that Troy was built to the music of Apollo's lyre and that the Egyptian god Ptah, the generative force of the world, was described as he who 'founded cities' and 'put the gods in their shrines.' The medieval city, dominated by the cathedral enshrining its patron saint, retains the idea of the city as sacred center, an *axis mundi* where heaven, earth and hell intersect.[2]

From the perspective of the secularized modern city and its rootless suburban extensions, it is virtually impossible to appreciate the supernatural aura associated with cities until recent times. Yet it was credible to an earlier period that the gods themselves fought over the fate of Troy and the founding of Rome. The destiny of Jerusalem lay in the hands of Jehovah himself, and when He decreed its fall and the Israelites became captives in Babylon, their survival depended on remembering their sacred city in a strange land. No subject seems more to have moved the ancient imagination than the fate of a great city. Although Troy falls in our minds only, Homer everywhere anticipating but never describing its collapse, that doom weighs more heavily upon the *Iliad* than the sum of its countless individual deaths. As Simone Weil writes, the poem 'lies under the shadow of the greatest calamity the human race can experience – the destruction of a city.'[3] Second only to language as the producer, transmitter and preserver of human culture, the city in its continuity defies individual mortality and, perhaps in so doing, struck the ancient mind as necessarily divine, an embodiment on earth of an immortal order.

If the *Iliad* is burdened with the fall of Troy, the *Aeneid* labors under the equal weight of its second founding as Rome. In the most pictorial scene in the entire epic, Aeneas, fleeing through the burning streets of Troy and followed by his wife, bears his aged father on his back and holds his son by the hand, carrying the city's past upon his shoulders and guiding its future beside him. Virgil's vignette of this elemental human family in flight is completed by Aeneas' putting on the tawny pelt of a lion, emblematic of man's reversion to the semi-savage with the loss of his city. Yet, however primitive, they remain a *holy* family, for Aeneas takes with him the sacred relics of the city and his household gods. Only with these in hand can he hope for an answer to his prayer:

> Grant us a walled home of our own, a place for tired men,
> A future, and a continuing city! Ensure for us few,
> Left by the Greeks and relentless Achilles, a second Troy!
> (III, 85–7, trans. C. Day-Lewis)

The earliest cities descended out of the heavens from God; by a curious reverse movement, as the great earthly cities fell into captivity or decay, they were projected back into the heavens in idealized versions reminiscent of their origins. Rome had resisted invasion for nearly a thousand years when it was finally sacked by Alaric in 410; out of its earthly ashes arose St. Augustine's *City of God*. The New Jerusalem became an obsessive motif with the Hebrew prophets and psalmists upon the destruction of the old, and Plato wrote his ideal *Republic* after he had seen Athens surrender her empire to Sparta, Socrates martyred, and the city fall prey to tyrants and demagogues. Plato's attitude toward the earthly city is essentially that of St. Paul in the Epistle to the Hebrews: 'For here have we no continuing city, but we seek one to come' (13:14). At the close of the ninth book of the *Republic*, Socrates remarks that the pattern of his ideal commonwealth is 'set up in the heavens for one who desires to see it and, seeing it, to found one in himself. But whether it exists anywhere or ever will exist is no matter; for this is the only commonwealth in whose politics he can ever take part.' Plato's utopia, like St. Augustine's, is a profoundly religious vision of perfection grounded in the experience of despair. In this regard, the *Republic* differs from the tradition of secular utopias, such as Bacon's *New Atlantis* or William Morris's *News from Nowhere*, which are patterned on no celestial archetype, deny original sin, and suppose that man unaided can build his own earthly paradise. It is a lugubrious comment on our own urban experience that the utopian tradition has given way to the inverted utopias of Orwell's *1984* and Anthony Burgess's *A Clockwork Orange*, secular versions of Dante's Hell.[4]

The city as New Jerusalem is only a few paces removed in the human imagination from the city as Inferno – no further, indeed, than the thin sculptural line separating the hosts of the saved from the damned in a Romanesque tympanum. Ptah may have installed the gods in cities, but Milton's lewd Belial walks their darkened streets. And Mulciber, the architect of Milton's Heaven, is the same angel who, fallen, builds Pandemonium. Like all human experience – indeed, like heaven and hell themselves – the city has a peculiarly dual quality; it liberates and confines the human spirit; it enriches and deforms, protects and menaces, draws men together and plunges them into the terrible solitude of the crowd. The literature of the city thus runs to rhetorical extremes, straining to encompass the radical disparities it describes. A mid-nineteenth-century observer praised Manchester as 'the very symbol of civilization…a grand incarnation of progress.' Another contemporary peered through the soot and saw 'the chimney of the world…the entrance to hell realized!'[5]

This ambivalence toward cities is as old as the myth of the Fall. The only art perfected in our primal paradise was gardening, and if on leaving Eden man took with him the curse of mortality, he also took the knowledge of good and evil, and the seeds of civilization. At the end of *Paradise Lost*, Adam and Eve shed a few 'natural tears,' soon wiped away, for on leaving Eden they found 'the World was all before them.'

*The Epic of Gilgamesh*, which predates the earliest written books of the Bible by at least one thousand years, contains an even more ambivalent account of man's evolution from a creature of nature to an inhabitant of cities. Gilgamesh, the semi-divine hero, builds the great ramparts surrounding ancient Uruk and rules with a demonic energy that keeps his people in terror. They pray to the goddess Aruru to create a companion for Gilgamesh who will hold his energies in check. Out of clay she shapes Enkidu, a naked primitive man with matted hair who forages with wild beasts and drinks at their water holes. He and Gilgamesh grapple 'like bulls,' but each subdues the other and they embrace in friendship. Before their encounter, and prerequisite to it, another embrace had occurred, that between the wild Enkidu and a hired harlot from the city who seduces him. At that moment, Enkidu's animal companions flee from him, and, Samson-like, he loses his strength and swiftness of foot; but 'wisdom was [now] in him, and the thoughts of man were in his heart.' The harlot serves him as a kind of nourishing mother, clothing him, teaching him to herd sheep, to eat human food. Finally, she leads him to great Uruk, where men and women dress 'in gorgeous robes.... He rubbed down the matted hair of his body and anointed himself with oil. Enkidu had become a man.'[6]

## 2

The harlot-tutor personifies the city in its dual role as corrupter and civilizer of man. These dual aspects of the city persist, but sometime in the early nineteenth century the scales began to tip under the pressures of chaotic industrial growth and social dislocation, and the city as a possible paradise became an actual inferno. Of course, there has always been a literature highly critical of the city and quick to point out that, if God built the first garden, Cain founded the first city.[7] In this predominantly Puritan tradition, the city figures as Sodom or, in its Anglicized version, as the Vanity Fair of John Bunyan. But it is in Dr. Johnson's celebrated pronouncement on London that we find the predominant attitude toward the city through the eighteenth century: 'When a man is tired of London, he is tired of life; for there is in London all that life can afford.' The gentleman retired to the country for refreshment, for choice 'views,' perhaps for contemplation; but he returned to the city as the rational, agreeable arena of human activity. I want now to concentrate on the transition from Dr. Johnson's London to the menacing, smoking labyrinth of the Victorians.

William Blake comes at the very beginning of the transition, or rather serves as its prophet, for the English countryside he knew was still largely the countryside of Chaucer, and the English town had not yet become 'the entrance to hell realized.' His *Songs of Innocence* (1789) are set in a natural paradise, and even in the *Songs of Experience* (1794) the city is scarcely glimpsed, with the remarkable exception of 'London.' The poem foreshadows the moral nightmare the city is to become in Victorian literature. Seen at night by the solitary poet, London serves as the ghostly, darkened frame for the human wrecks he encounters:

> I wander thro' each charter'd street,
> Near where the charter'd Thames does flow,

And mark in every face I meet
Marks of weakness, marks of woe.

In every cry of every Man,
In every Infant's cry of fear,
In every voice, in every ban,
The mind-forg'd manacles I hear.

How the Chimney-sweepers cry
Every black'ning Church appalls;
And the hapless Soldier's sigh
Runs in blood down Palace walls.

But most thro' midnight streets I hear
How the youthful Harlot's curse
Blasts the new born Infant's tear,
And blights with plagues the Marriage hearse.

The key to the poem is the reiterated 'charter'd,' with its sense of confined menace, an unnatural constriction intensified by the 'mind-forg'd manacles' of the second stanza. For the poem is less about the actual city of London than about the moral condition it induces. The essence of that condition is its total and imprisoning isolation. The Infant, the Soldier, the Sweep, the Harlot are so removed from one another and from the poet that they are never actually *seen* but merely heard as disembodied voices, whose cries or curses imply their presence: the cry of the Sweep indicts the institution of the Church, the curse of the Harlot diseases the institution of marriage. A half-century later Dickens was to trace through the three volumes of *Bleak House* the connection between the diseases of the slums and the moral disease of the entire society that tolerated them. In 'London,' with phantasmagoric compression, Blake negotiates the same leap of the moral imagination in sixteen lines.

'London' is Blake's vision of the fallen city. The same darkness seems to threaten the countryside in the famous lyric in which he asks,

And did the Countenance Divine
Shine forth upon our clouded hills?
And was Jerusalem builded here
Among these dark Satanic Mills? ('Preface,' *Milton*)

The poem was written in the first years of the nineteenth century, when the Satanic Mills began to spread through the Midlands.[8] One cannot, I think, overestimate the impact this blight had upon the English imagination. The desecration of the countryside produced, on the one hand, a magnificent literature of protest, and, on the other, a nostalgic return to a remembered Eden as industrial England was becoming a slag heap.

Seen from this perspective, the Gothic Revival, like Blake's New Jerusalem, represents one of the ageless evocations of the City of God called into being when the earthly city becomes intolerable. In the pre-industrial period, the Revival had been a romantic toying with the picturesque, such as Horace Walpole's 'Strawberry Hill,' a Gothic jest in stone. But in the nineteenth century, the Revival ceased to be a refuge from neoclassicism and became a serious attempt to rebuild Jerusalem 'in England's green and pleasant land.'

Published in 1836, Augustus Welby Pugin's *Contrasts* was a brilliant piece of visual propaganda for the Revival. Pugin, a convert to Catholicism, worked himself to premature death trying to restore in England the faith and architecture of the Middle Ages. His book consists of a prefatory essay followed by paired plates, each contrasting an example of medieval architecture with its nineteenth-century counterpart. In one, an idealized Catholic town in 1440, we see a broad stream flowing past a city of exquisitely delicate spires and high-gabled houses, behind which rises a rolling, idyllic landscape that frames a lost urban paradise. In the same town in 1840, the spires have been replaced by smoke-stacks, a gas-works stands on the site of a ruined abbey, and the once open foreground is dominated by a huge, octagonal, windowless jail.

The motif of the two cities reappears in Carlyle's *Past and Present* (1843), in which twelfth-century St. Edmundsbury figures as another medieval Eden, and nineteenth-century Manchester as Hell. The opening chapter of *Past and Present* is written in a style of astonished incredulity, as if the conditions Carlyle reports were the product of a nightmare. He enters a workhouse and sees some fifty able-bodied men sunken in idle torpor. 'There was something,' he writes, 'that reminded me of Dante's Hell in the look of all this; and I rode swiftly away.'[9] Carlyle rides, as it were, into the England of Coeur de Lion and St. Edmund's Abbey. History in Carlyle's pages is transmuted into elegy for a vanished world of monks and sheep, matins and miracles. Within the cohesive, organic community of Abbot Samson and his monks, he finds the antithesis of the atomized society of industrial England, in which the only bond between men is the 'cash nexus' and the only liberty the worker has won is the liberty to starve.

Carlyle typifies the shift in the uses to which the nineteenth century put the Middle Ages. For the Romantics, they were an inviting source of nostalgia; for the Victorians, the Middle Ages became an instrument of radical social criticism. Carlyle, Pugin, Ruskin, and Morris all construct their medieval utopias in the spirit of urban planners who would change not merely the architecture of the city but the very quality of its life.

To trace the motif of the two cities in the writings of John Ruskin would require an essay in itself; we will rest with a single, striking example. In 1859 Ruskin lectured in the heart of the industrial Midlands on 'Modern Manufacture and Design.' The theme of the lecture is that beautiful design can be created only by 'people who have beautiful things about them, and leisure to look at them.' But in the north of England the environmental conditions of fine design were becoming impossible. Ruskin illustrates his point by describing what he had just seen of Rochdale on his way to the lecture hall:

> Just outside the town I came upon an old English cottage...with mullioned windows and a low arched porch; round which, in the little triangular garden, one can imagine the family as they used to sit in old summer times, the ripple of the river heard faintly through the sweetbrier hedge, and the sheep on the far-off wolds shining in the evening sunlight. There, uninhabited for many and many a year, it had been left in unregarded havoc of ruin; the garden-gate still swung loose to its latch; the garden, blighted utterly into a field of ashes, not even a weed taking root there; the roof torn into shapeless rents; the shutters hanging about the windows in rags of rotten wood; before its gate, the stream which had gladdened it now soaking slowly by, black as ebony, and thick with curdling scum; the bank above it trodden into unctuous, sooty slime: far in front of it, between it and the old hills, the furnaces of the city foaming forth perpetual plague of sulphurous darkness; the volumes of their storm clouds coiling low over a waste of grassless fields, fenced from each other, not by hedges, but by slabs of square stone, like gravestones, riveted together with iron.[10]

The flourishing of human life in harmony with nature has vanished, and in its place stands, or rather ferments, the modern industrial wasteland, unpeopled, petrifying, Satanic.[11] To this hellscape, Ruskin juxtaposes the prospect of Pisa as it might have appeared to the medieval artist. A glittering river replaces the polluted stream. Instead of furnaces and grassless fields, one sees a dome and bell tower, vine-clad hills, troops of knights, and, rising above them, the 'untroubled and sacred sky' which opened upon 'a heaven in which every cloud that passed was literally the chariot of an angel, and every ray of its Evening and Morning streamed from the throne of God.'

One is moved to remark, along with one of King Arthur's knights on first seeing the distant spires of Camelot,

> Lord, there is no such city anywhere,
> But all a vision. ('Gareth and Lynette,' ll. 203–4).

Camelot is the classic nineteenth-century urban Eden, but its essence, as Tennyson makes clear from the very start of the *Idylls of the King*, lies in its passing. King Arthur clears the wilderness and, for a brief time, made 'a realm and reigned.' But he founds no continuing city. The vows of his knights are all broken, the marriage bond breaks, and 'the realm reels back into the beast.'

The light that bathes Camelot at Arthur's coming fades into the dim, sinister gloom of his passing. And 'the city built to music' dissolves into the aboriginal wasteland of his final battle,

> A land of old upheaven from the abyss
> By fire, to sink into the abyss again;
> Where fragments of forgotten peoples dwelt,
> And the long mountains ended in a coast
> Of ever-shifting sand, and far away
> The phantom circle of a moaning sea.
>
> ('The Passing of Arthur,' ll. 82–7)

Displacement in time was only one nineteenth-century mode of creating the ideal city, and the movement was not always backward to the Middle Ages. William Morris' socialist utopia in *News from Nowhere* (1891) is set in the year 2200, after a bloody class-war is fought in the streets of London. But once the revolution succeeds, Morris lapses from the Marxist realism of the opening and creates a post-industrial England of idyllic villages scattered throughout a garden paradise. His solution to the problem of the modern city is to abolish it and build instead a second Eden. *News from Nowhere* is less compelling as a social program than as testimony to the enduring power of myth. One is reminded of Ruskin's St. George's Guild, a legally chartered corporation whose quixotic aim was to found agrarian communities on which there was to be no industry, no railroads, 'none wretched but the sick; none idle but the dead.' Morris wrote his *News from Nowhere* as an admitted fantasy; Ruskin's venture was totally in earnest, and failed almost totally.

Of all the ideal cities in nineteenth-century English literature, the most difficult to place is Wordsworth's sonnet 'Composed Upon Westminster Bridge.' The difficulty is twofold, for Wordsworth is preeminently the poet of nature's superiority to the city, and the London he portrays in the sonnet is not an idealized construction. It is actual London, seen from the roof of a coach just after dawn on September 3, 1802. Wordsworth succeeds in portraying the city in majesty not by displacing it in time but by putting it to sleep and half-assimilating it back to nature:

> Earth has not anything to show more fair:
> Dull would he be of soul who could pass by
> A sight so touching in its majesty:
> This City now doth, like a garment, wear
> The beauty of the morning; silent, bare,
> Ships, towers, domes, theatres, and temples lie
> Open unto the fields, and to the sky;
> All bright and glittering in the smokeless air.

> Never did sun more beautifully steep
> In his first splendor valley, rock, or hill;
> Ne'er saw I, never felt, a calm so deep!
> The river glideth at his own sweet will:
> Dear God! The very houses seem asleep;
> And all that mighty heart is lying still!

The sense of latent, quiescent power stems less from the tumultuous life which is soon to rise from the houses, crowd the streets and cloud the 'smokeless air' than from the fields which environ the city and the river which glides through its 'mighty heart' – more mighty because 'still.' Neither the city nor the river is ever named; the inhabitants are unseen; the city's only garment is 'the beauty of the morning.' The very bareness and anonymity is charged with a kind of natural holiness. Wordsworth has created a new genre, urban pastoral, in which the city is lovelier than any valley, rock, or hill. But the power of Wordsworth's vision of London at sunrise lies in its very evanescence. The sonnet is a proleptic elegy for a 'majesty' that in a moment will be shattered by a rude awakening to tumult and smoke.

An attitude toward the city more typical of Wordsworth appears in 'Tintern Abbey,' where the poet leaves the lonely urban setting in order to recover

> that blessed mood,
> In which the burthen of the mystery,
> In which the heavy and the weary weight
> Of all this unintelligent world,
> Is lightened. ...      (ll. 37–41)

And for the denouement of the long pastoral idyll 'Michael,' Wordsworth assumes a stereotypic, negative response to the city. Michael's son, on whom the father's whole life hinges, leaves the Lake District and 'in the dissolute city' gives himself 'to evil courses.' No more need be said. The aged Michael dies, and Wordsworth abruptly ends his tale where the modern novelist would eagerly pick it up.

A much fuller portrait of the city appears in Book VII of The Prelude, 'Residence in London.' Wordsworth's stance is that of the solitary spectator, the one fixed point in 'a thickening hubbub' of 'men and moving things.' Minstrels, prostitutes, dancing dogs, a Turk, a 'travelling cripple' cut off up to the trunk, form a gallery of grotesques, at once gaudy and secretive. Not yet an Inferno, Wordsworth's London is a kind of cosmopolitan Vanity Fair,

> a phantasma,
> Monstrous in colour, motion, shape, sight, sound!
>                     (ll. 687–8, 1850 version)

For all its diseased vitality, the city is seen only in bits and pieces of local color that form no overriding metaphoric pattern. It is as if Wordsworth's imagination is locked in an earlier mode, and he cannot bring the city into literary focus, as Dickens was to do a half-century later. He remains the outsider, the 'transient visitant,' more repelled than fascinated by what he sees.[12] Yet his very alienation from the city made him feel with especial keenness what another outsider, Friedrich Engels, was to observe of London in his *Condition of the Working Class in England in 1844*: the 'brutal indifference'[13] and unfeeling isolation of those who rush regardlessly past one another. For Wordsworth, the mystery of London resided not in its vastness or even its variety, but in the self-enclosed solitude of its inhabitants:

> How oft, amid those overflowing streets,
> Have I gone forward with the crowd, and said
> Unto myself, 'The face of every one
> That passes by me is a mystery!' (ll. 626–9)

That mystery is incarnate in the figure of a blind beggar whose story is told not in his own words but by a placard that hangs from his chest. Solitary, speechless, he is the very type of the unintelligibility of the city. Wordsworth's London rings not with speech but with the din and anarchic hubbub of Babel, a cacophony at once 'Barbarian and infernal' (l. 661). Street vendors scream out their shrill cries but no two human beings converse, for this is a city without community, as Dante's hell is a city without citizens.

No contrast could be starker than that afforded, half a century later, by the astonishingly vocal and articulate street people in Henry Mayhew's *London Labour and the London Poor* (1851–61), the first and possibly greatest sociological study in English. Mayhew's London, like Dickens', is a teeming metropolis of verbal virtuosi, vociferous relics of an older England. Desperately impoverished, they are nonetheless as articulate as the rustics in Shakespearian comedy or the gravedigger in *Hamlet*. Mayhew is the memorialist of an ancient underclass, many of whom were half-starved migrants from the rural counties of southern England.

The image of London that emerges from Mayhew's pages is that of a vast, ingeniously balanced mechanism in which each class subsists on the drippings and droppings of the stratum above, all the way from the rich, whom we scarcely glimpse, down to the deformed and starving, whom we see groping for bits of salvageable bone or decaying vegetables in the markets. Such extreme conditions bred weird extremities of adaptation, a remarkably diverse yet cohesive subculture of poverty. Ragged, fantastic armies, each with its distinctive jargon and implements, roamed the streets: 'pure-finders' with bucket and glove, picking up dog dung and selling it to tanners; rag-gatherers, themselves dressed in the rotted cloth they salvage, armed with pointed sticks; bent, slime-soiled 'mud-larks,' groping at low tide in the ooze of the Thames for bits of coal, chips of wood, or copper nails dropped from the sheathing of barges, a regiment of three hundred who subsisted on average earnings of threepence a day.

The remarkable first-person narratives in *London Labour and the London Poor* validate Mayhew's claim in the Preface that his is the first book to publish the history of a people, from the lips of the people themselves – giving a literal description of their labour, their earnings, their trials, and their sufferings, in their own 'unvarnished' language. Mayhew invented 'oral history' a century before the term was coined. He is also the explorer, as he puts it, of a class of whom 'the public had less knowledge than of the most distant tribes.' The rapid, wrenching industrialization of England (London's population trebled between 1800 and 1850) was breeding a new species of humanity, a rootless generation entirely environed by brick, smoke, work and want.

Yet poverty, however it curtails their lives, does not, except for the dying, suppress their speech. Consider, for example, this excerpt from a 'running patterer,' a man who hawks and at times *invents* narratives of murders, rapes, and the like:

> There's nothing beats a stunning good murder after all. Why, there was Rush [a homicidal farmer] – lived on him for a month or more. When I commenced with Rush, I was 14s. in debt for rent, and in less than fourteen days I astonished the wise men in the east by paying my landlord all I owed him.... Why, I went down to Norwich expressly to work the execution. I worked my way down there with '*a sorrowful lamentation*' of his own composing, which I'd got written by the blind man expressly for the occasion. On the morning of the execution we beat all the regular newspapers out of the field; for we had the full, true, and particular account down, you see, by our own express, and that can beat anything that ever they can publish; for we gets it printed several days afore it comes off, and goes and stands with it right under the drop; and many's the penny I've turned away when I've been asked for an account of the whole business *before* it happened. (I, 223–4)

The patterer is indistinguishable from a character out of Dickens. Although he is a bona fide 'case-history,' he belongs as much to literature as to journalism, criminology, or sociology. Reading *London Labour and the London Poor*, with its brave abundance of life, its vast scope yet minuteness of detail, its celebration of the intricate, dense, eccentric texture of Victorian London, its moral outrage and grotesque wit, brings us closer to the feel of Dickens than does anything else in our literature. To pass from Mayhew's case-histories to Dickens's inventions is merely to cross sides of the same street; only the point of view shifts, not the landscape. Knowledge of Mayhew persuades us that Dickens the comic-caricaturist is in essence a great *realist*, just as reading Dickens persuades us that Mayhew was not merely a fine reporter but also a superb artist. Both Dickens and Mayhew are collateral descendants of Wordsworth, memorializers in prose of the 'real language' not of rural derelicts but of urban outcasts and eccentrics.

The whole subsequent history of our subject is epitomized in the contrasting views from two bridges. In T. S. Eliot's *The Waste Land*, the tranquil London of Wordsworth's 'Westminster Bridge' awakens to nightmarish life:

> Unreal City,
> Under the brown fog of a winter dawn,
> A crowd flowed over London Bridge, so many,
> I had not thought death had undone so many.
> Sighs, short and infrequent, were exhaled,
> And each man fixed his eyes before his feet.
> Flowed up the hill and down King William Street,
> To where Saint Mary Woolnoth kept the hours
> With a dead sound on the final stroke of nine. (ll. 60–8)

The crowd that flows in a ghostly stream over the bridge is a procession of living specters whom a spiritual death has undone. The fourth line – 'I had not thought death had undone so many' – is a direct quotation from Canto III of the *Inferno*, and the sighs of the solitary walkers recall the damned in Canto IV whose sighs keep the air forever trembling. The church bell no longer summons the living to worship but the defunct to their daily toil. This is the totally secularized city, soiled, fragmented, phantasmagoric. It is as though the dormant houses of Wordsworth's London awoke, and one saw

> all the hands
> That are raising dingy shades
> In a thousand furnished rooms. ('Preludes: II,' ll. 21–3)

And in place of the towers, domes, and temples lying open to the fields,

> The morning comes to consciousness
> Of faint stale smells of beer. ... ('Preludes: II,' ll. 14–15)

The peculiar hallmark of Eliot's city is its leveling of both the celestial and the sinister to a sleazy ennui. Horror is dissipated into vague half-ludicrous guilts, and

> Streets that follow like a tedious argument
> Of insidious intent
> To lead you to an overwhelming question...
>                                    ('The Love Song of J. Alfred Prufrock,' ll. 8–10)

...evade the question, trailing off into 'sawdust restaurants' and tawdry places of assignation. For the Romantics, the city is a moral blemish; for its Victorian critics, the city is a formidable adversary filled with the stalking terrors of James Thomson's *City of Dreadful Night*; for Eliot, the battle has been lost, and the energy remaining after the struggle spills over into irony, the squalor of immortal longings spent in 'one-night cheap hotels.'

3

The city as wasteland is not Eliot's invention but part of his Victorian heritage, a heritage that looms larger with each year since his death. For in the lives of the Victorians the physical city had already emerged as the symbol *par excellence* of the spiritual condition of modern man. As labyrinth or prison, as morgue, madhouse, wasteland or inferno, the city dominates a body of writing as sprawling and various as the phenomenon it describes. This literature reflects a radical dislocation not only in the physical environment but in the world of values as well. The problem of analysis is further complicated by the fact that the writing descriptive of London differs markedly from the writing descriptive of the new industrial cities, and even they differed widely among themselves, and from decade to decade as well as from observer to observer. A drawing of the industrial quarter of Leeds in 1885 shows, rising over the soot-encrusted slums in the foreground, at least one hundred factory chimneys belching blackly into the sky. Yet a contemporary enthusiast of Leeds describes the city as 'an effusion of the Eternal Mind.'[14] The best writers, however, described the indescribable worst, and it is to them that I now wish to turn.

The topography of hell has always been rendered more graphically in literature than the topography of heaven; England's manufacturing centers afforded the additional literary advantage of imitating the topography of hell so closely that one's symbols, as it were, lay before one's very eyes and ears and nose.[15] A writer in 1862 describes the River Irwell, which oozed through Manchester like the fecal pool in Dante's Malebolge, as 'a flood of liquid manure.' And the canal at Bradford emitted gases so noxious that it 'took fire.'[16]

But literature is more than a topographic rendering, and in the novels and social criticism of the 1840s and 1850s we find a larger vision of the social consequences of this urban setting. In Dickens's Coketown, in the Manchester of *Past and Present* and Mrs. Gaskell's *Mary Barton*, the blighted cityscape serves as the physical counterpart of the moral blight of an entire society. For the city, whose end is the enhancement of human life, had become a mere container of machines. 'The great cry that rises from all our manufacturing cities, louder than their furnace blast,' Ruskin wrote, is 'that we manufacture everything there except men; we blanch cotton, and strengthen steel, and refine sugar, and shape pottery; but to brighten, to strengthen, to refine, or to form a single living spirit never enters into our estimate of advantages.'[17]

Two decades before Ruskin, Alexis de Tocqueville observed the same perversion of the ends of the city during his journey through the Midlands in the 1830s. He describes Birmingham as 'an immense workshop, a huge forge...black, dirty and obscure,' where men work 'as if they must get rich by the evening and die the next day.' He is struck above all by the anarchic energy of the industrial centers; everything he sees attests to 'the individual powers of man; nothing [to] the directing powers of society.'[18] His eyewitness description of Manchester deserves the classic status of Engels's more familiar account of the identical site a decade later. Here is one of the earliest verbal portraits of the industrial inferno, complete with River Styx:

> Thirty or forty factories rise on the tops of the hills I have just described. Their six stories tower up; their huge enclosures give notice from afar of the centralisation of industry. The wretched dwellings of the poor are scattered haphazard around them.... The roads which connect the still-disjointed limbs of the great city, show, like the rest, every sign of hurried and unfinished work; the incidental activity of a population bent on gain, which seeks to amass gold so as to have everything else all at once.... Heaps of dung, rubble from buildings, putrid stagnant pools are found here and there amongst the houses...whose ill-fitting planks and broken windows show them up, even from a distance, as the last refuge a man might find between poverty and death. None-the-less the wretched people reduced to living in them can still inspire jealousy of their fellow beings. Below some of their miserable dwellings is a row of cellars to which a sunken corridor leads. Twelve to fifteen human beings are crowded pell-mell into each of these damp, repulsive holes.
>
> The fetid, muddy waters, stained with a thousand colours by the factories they pass...wander slowly round this refuge of poverty.... It is the Styx of this new Hades....
>
> From this foul drain the greatest stream of human industry flows out to fertilise the whole world. From this filthy sewer pure gold flows. Here humanity attains its most complete development and its most brutish; here civilisation works its miracles, and civilised man is turned back into a savage.[19]

Tocqueville's description of Manchester appears in the journal of his visit to England in 1835. The journal is in the form of unrevised notes, unlike Engels's more studied account of the same scene. Yet the two versions of what Engels calls 'this hell on earth' are virtually interchangeable. Engels places the reader on Ducie Bridge, overlooking the slums that line the 'coal-black, stinking'

River Irk. Barrack-like factories rise in the distance near the workhouse and the paupers' cemetery, a trinity that requires no commentary. The workhouse is literally the high point of the scene. Its battlement and high walls seem 'to threaten the whole adjacent working-class quarter like a fortress.' Recessed below, in the lowest circle of Engels's hell and sprawling over a no-man's-land between city and suburb, are the slums of Little Ireland, where

> A horde of ragged women and children swarm about the streets and they are just as dirty as the pigs which wallow...in the pools of filth.... The creatures who inhabit [the dilapidated cottages] and even their dark, wet cellars, and who live confined amidst all this filth and foul air – which cannot be dissipated because of the surrounding lofty buildings – must surely have sunk to the lowest level of humanity.[20]

The transition from these documentary accounts to their counterparts in Victorian fiction is so slight that it is hardly perceptible. Dickens's characters, distorted by the fragmenting pressures of the city into severed quirks of humanity, often strike us as caricatures; his places do not. The horror of Coketown is that it is *not* a satire but a deadly accurate composite of the industrial Inferno.[21] So too, the melodrama and thin characters in Disraeli's *Sybil; or, The Two Nations* (1845) obscure the accuracy of his portrait of the savagely squalid town of Wodgate, where the apprentice steel-grinders are worked for sixteen hours a day, sold by one master to another, fed on carrion, and lodged in cellars. Like the Communist Engels, the Tory Disraeli drew many of his facts directly from Parliamentary Commissions of Inquiry into the condition of the mines, factories, and manufacturing towns. Some attempt to explain how such conditions arose and the horror they evoked is indispensable to an understanding of the literature of the Victorian city, which is above all a literature of social analysis and protest.

Perhaps the most far-reaching source of change was the breakdown of the ancient boundaries that had given shape to the city and to the social relations within it. One thinks of the medieval city, with its lucid division between walled town and open field, a division of life into two spheres as crisply defined as the lines in Ambrogio Lorenzetti's allegorical fresco of Good Government. The 'destructive dynamism'[22] of capitalism blew those walls apart, and a kind of formless organism – 'enlarg'd without dimension, terrible,' in Blake's phrase[23] – spread out from the urban centers.

We think of suburbia as a typically American, twentieth-century phenomenon, but it is a nineteenth-century invention and nothing is more characteristic of the Victorian literature of the city than a loathing of suburbia, as of some uncontrolled, cancerous growth. Ruskin writes that cities are no longer crystallized about a coherent center but rather 'clotted and coagulated; spots of dreadful mildew, spreading by patches and blotches over the country they consume.'[24] The same revulsion from formlessness figures in a remarkable passage from Ruskin's *The Seven Lamps of Architecture*. Its force derives from something far deeper than aesthetic disgust. For the metaphors of decay throughout the passage apply not only to the jerry-built houses but to the crumbling national values they embody:

> I look upon those pitiful concretions of lime and clay which spring up, in mildewed forwardness, out of the kneaded fields about our capital – upon those thin, tottering, foundationless shells of splintered wood and imitated stone – upon those gloomy rows of formalised minuteness, alike without difference and without fellowship, as solitary as similar – not merely with the careless disgust of an offended eye, not merely with sorrow for a desecrated landscape, but with a painful foreboding that the roots of our national greatness must be deeply cankered when they are thus loosely struck in their native ground.[25]

In a single alliterating phrase – houses 'as solitary as similar' – Ruskin diagnoses the defining dreariness and vacuity of suburbia, its achievement of conformity without community.

Of course the suburbs of London, a capital city and commercial and cultural center, wore a less sinister aspect than the excrescences of the industrial cities. But they shared the same lack of local government and municipal services as the New Towns. Manchester and Birmingham, for example, were not incorporated until 1838, and neither achieved the status of a city until the second half of the century. The growth of the industrial centers was at once wildly chaotic and, as it were, extra-legal. Their inhabitants were largely outside the ancient communion of the national Church and illiterate to the degree that sixty per cent of those in the district described by Engels could not even sign their own names. Brutalized by an economic system which virtually enslaved them, degraded by a physical environment that scarcely supported life, the industrial proletariat of early Victorian England was, as Tocqueville wrote, 'turned back almost into a savage.' This whole noxious complex is epitomized by Dickens in a passage from *The Old Curiosity Shop* (1840–1): Nell and her grandfather come upon

> a long, flat, straggling suburb...where not a blade of grass was seen to grow; where not a bud put forth its promise in the spring....
>
> On mounds of ashes by the wayside, sheltered only by a few rough boards, or rotten pent-house roofs, strange engines spun and writhed like tortured creatures; clanking their iron chains, shrieking in their rapid whirl from time to time as though in torment unendurable, and making the ground tremble with their agonies. Dismantled houses here and there appeared, tottering to the earth, propped up by fragments of others that

had fallen down, unroofed, windowless, blackened, desolate, but yet inhabited. Men, women, children, wan in their looks and ragged in attire, tended the engines, fed their tributary fires, begged upon the road, or scowled half-naked from the doorless houses...and still, before, behind, and to the right and left, was the same interminable perspective of brick towers, never ceasing in their black vomit, blasting all things living or inanimate, shutting out the face of day, and closing in on all these horrors with a dense dark cloud. (Chapter 45)

The horror of such a scene, quite apart from its human wrecks, stems from its monotonous featurelessness, which Dickens compares to 'the horror of oppressive dreams.' Browning depicts virtually the same landscape of amorphous menace in 'Childe Roland to the Dark Tower Came' (1852). The grass grows 'scant as hair / In leprosy' (ll. 73–4) and an ominous engine of torture stands alone in the center of a surreal wasteland.[26] In *The Image of the City*, Kevin Lynch stresses the connection between an ill-defined cityscape and the anxious sense of disorientation it engenders. The absence of landmarks, of places of historic association or of natural features such as the line of a river – in short, a visually 'illegible' city – can produce a confusion akin to the terror of being lost in a maze. So deep, apparently, is the need for points of orientation that in a maze experiment the human subjects 'developed affection for such simple landmarks as a rough board.'[27] In this context, the Victorian archetype of the city as labyrinth takes on profounder meaning than that of a mere literary conceit. Cities not only spread out in formless limbs, but their familiar historic core was being gutted to make room for railway terminals, factories, warehouses, and all the accoutrements of a growing industrial economy, including a vastly expanded urban population crowded into less and less viable space.[28] The nightmarish flight of Little Nell through the desolate industrial maze in the passage I just quoted, conveys the horror of an 'oppressive dream,' but like all of Dickens's dreams, it is grounded in the firmest reality. The same menacing corridors and blind alleys figure in James Thomson's *The City of Dreadful Night*. The solitary narrator wanders through unending streets, which merge and cross and are 'black as subterranean lairs.' Like Dickens, Thomson was an obsessive haunter of London's streets at night, but in Thomson's poem the city has lost all the hard actuality of Dickens's London and become surreal, a city of the mind without definition and without escape. Even the orienting points of the stars are absent from the night sky, and in this metropolis-turned-necropolis, the houses are 'dark and still as tombs.' Time, which moves with spastic rapidity in Dickens's novels, here 'crawleth like a monstrous snake,/ Wounded and slow and very venomous.' Like Dante's Hell, Thomson's city admits of no exit, either in time or place; the night is dreadful because it is endless. The urban labyrinth of Dickens here becomes a labyrinth of the spirit from which all transcendence has fled. Infinite ennui replaces the classical torments of hell, for in this unending City of Man even the desired torments of God are beyond reach:

> I reached the portal common spirits fear,
> And read the words above it, dark yet clear,
> 'Leave hope behind, all ye who enter here':
>
> And would have passed in, gratified to gain
> That positive eternity of pain,
> Instead of this insufferable inane. (ll. 355–60)

The Victorian literature of the city, then, reflects a psychological and spiritual displacement which parallels the chaos wrought in the physical environment. Anxiety over an anarchic present – the title of Arnold's *Culture and Anarchy* (1869) comes to mind – intensified the longing for a past order. Nor is it surprising that the economic forces which changed the face of England produced radical changes in values and social relationships. Utilitarian ethics in alliance with laissez-faire economics effectively broke up the traditional allegiances to community and to an older order in which men believed themselves bound to the land, to each other, and to God. The sense of neighborhood, which is the urban equivalent to natural features in a landscape, became increasingly blurred as rural populations drifted into cities that were themselves in the process of explosive change. As the countryside was being ripped up, the benevolent nature that the Romantics worshipped began to seem 'red in tooth and claw.'

Even the concept of time was taking on a more frightening aspect. Representing the traditionalist view, the historian George Rawlinson contended, in the same year that Darwin published *The Origin of Species* (1859), that Moses lived only a few generations after Adam and might actually have heard 'of the Temptation and Fall at fifth hand.'[29] A decade later, *The City of Dreadful Night* (1874) reflects the shift from comfortably measurable Biblical time to the bleak temporal vistas of evolution. The narrator comes upon a hideous, aged, half-human creature who crawls on all fours 'through vast wastes of horror-haunted time' and vainly seeks an irrecoverable Eden. While the past seemed to recede indefinitely, the railroad and the increased tempo of urban life brought a sense of dizzying acceleration to the present. One of Thackeray's characters contrasts the coaching world of 'only yesterday' with the new era of railroads and describes himself as a survivor out of the ancient world, 'like Father Noah and his family out of the Ark.'[30] And Dickens's Mr. Dombey rides with hallucinatory speed,

> Away, with a shriek, and a roar, and a rattle, from the town, burrowing among the dwellings of men and making the streets hum, flashing out

into the meadows for a moment, mining in through the damp earth, booming on in darkness and heavy air, bursting out again into the sunny day so bright and wide; away, with a shriek, and a roar, and a rattle...through the chalk, through the mould, through the clay, through the rock, among objects close at hand and almost in the grasp, ever flying from the traveller, and a deceitful distance ever moving slowly within him – like as in the track of the remorseless monster, Death![31]

If Dickens's appeal lay in his actualizing the tempo and feel of the city, the novels of George Eliot and Thomas Hardy offered the nostalgic appeal of escape to the older, slower rhythms of provincial life and rural setting. The town of Middlemarch serves as a rich, communal nexus in which people grow and change and interact. The flow of time is dense and steady, as stable as the mores of the community, as solid as the furnishings of its homes. In Dickens's London, time flows in spurts; the pace is cinematic; people do not grow and interact, but remain fixed centers of consciousness, suspended as it were in an unstable medium in which objects can never be relied on to remain safely inanimate and people are often locked into mannerisms as unchanging as stones.

## 4

All of the multiple changes that I have been tracing – the desecration of nature, the blurring of traditional boundaries between town and country, the physical chaos and social dislocation in the cities, the shock to religious faith produced by evolution and the vistas of 'horror-haunted time' that it opened up – intensified the attachment to place at the very moment that the physical and spiritual environment seemed most in flux. The lost orphan is a stock character in Victorian fiction not merely for sentimental reasons but because, as a figure wrenched from the elemental unit of the human family, he symbolized the sense of displacement the Victorians felt so keenly. In this connection, it is worth noting that the author of The City of Dreadful Night was in fact an orphan, and the young Dickens felt himself outrageously thrust into that role by his father's imprisonment for debt in the Marshalsea. A literature of nightmare on the one hand, and of nostalgia on the other, grew out of this intensified awareness of place. Dickens's city streets are fearful, but his old country inns, with roaring fires and tables piled with Gargantuan joints, provide the coziest rooms in English fiction. And the most moving passages in Ruskin's Praeterita are elegies to the world that had vanished with his childhood.

The destruction of that childhood Eden and its bearing upon the novel of the city form the subject of Ruskin's remarkable essay entitled 'Fiction, Fair and Foul' (1880–1). The essay opens with an idyllic picture of the hawthorn hedges and crystal stream by which Ruskin had played near his home in

suburban London. He revisits the scene to find the ground gashed to pieces
and littered with 'mixed dust of every unclean thing that can crumble in
drought, and mildew of every unclean thing that can rot or rust in damp:
ashes and rags, beer-bottles and old shoes, battered pans, smashed crockery,
shreds of nameless clothes...bones, and ordure indescribable,' all kneaded
together in 'pits of stinking dust and mortal slime.' The modern sensibility is
formed on this kind of desolate nastiness and develops by default an affinity for
modes of decay, physical and psychological. This taste is further whetted by

> the hot fermentation and unwholesome secrecy of the population
> crowded in large cities, each mote in the misery lighter, as an individual
> soul, than a dead leaf, but becoming oppressive and infectious each to
> his neighbour, in the smoking mass of decay. The resulting modes of
> mental ruin and distress are continually new; and in a certain sense,
> worth study in their monstrosity; they have accordingly developed a
> corresponding science of fiction, concerned mainly with the description
> of such forms of disease, like the botany of leaf-lichens.

In 'Fiction, Fair and Foul' Ruskin defines a new genre, the novel of the city,
the pathological violence of which he attributes to a kind of death-wish
engendered by the monotony, dehumanization and imprisoning solitude of
urban life. Even the relieving variety of the seasons has vanished from the city,
where the utmost power of a storm 'is to choke the gutters, and the finest
magic of spring, to change mud into dust.' To drive home his point, Ruskin
compiles from *Bleak House* a Homeric catalogue of deaths by violent or strange
causes, including assassination, madness, paralysis, starvation, chagrin and,
most grotesque of all, the spontaneous combustion of Mr. Krook.[32]

The affinity for aberration and criminality that has drawn modern critics to
Dickens revolted Ruskin. Yet despite his disgust, Ruskin remains one of the
earliest Victorians to have understood 'our' Dickens, the dark symbolist and
social critic, at a time when he was praised for his caricatures and sentimental
death-scenes. The nostalgic journey of Mr. Pickwick through a pastoral
countryside recapitulates the 'rural ride' taken by English literature through
Fielding's *Tom Jones* and into the nineteenth century. In a way that was to
presage all his future work, as well as the future of English fiction, Dickens
leads Mr. Pickwick from the country to the city, from nostalgia to nightmare,
where his eyes are opened to the 'wretched dungeon' of London's Fleet Prison.
In *Oliver Twist* and *The Old Curiosity Shop*, the movement is reversed – from
the terrors of the city to the tranquil refuge of the country. But the repose that
the countryside offers Oliver is repeatedly associated with the repose of death,[33]
and Nell's flight from London only takes her deeper into the industrial inferno
and ends in actual death. In the great sequence of novels that follow, the city

dominates Dickens's imagination and becomes for the first time in English literature what our own experience confirms it to be.

To appreciate Dickens's achievement we have only to consider the unmanageableness of his subject. The city is more complex, mobile and vast than the power of our senses to take in at any given moment. Our perception of the city is necessarily local, fragmentary, intermittent; to see it panoramically, we must withdraw ourselves and lose in immediacy what we gain in clarity. The vogue for 'balloon views' of London no doubt gratified a desire to perceive what no eye had previously seen in its totality. But such views, however artfully transcribed in words, achieved their comprehensiveness at the cost of concreteness. 'It was a wonderful sight,' two aerial observers of London wrote in 1862,

> to behold that vast bricken mass of churches and hospitals, banks and prisons, palaces and workhouses…to contemplate from afar that strange conglomeration of vice and avarice and low cunning, of noble aspirations and humble heroism, and to grasp it in the eye, in all its incongruous integrity, at one single glance—to take, as it were, an angel's view of that huge town where, perhaps, there is more virtue and more iniquity, more wealth and more want, brought together into one dense focus than in any other part of the earth.[34]

This is not Victorian London, but reflections that the panorama of the city evoked. It captures extraordinarily well the moral ambiguity of all cities; yet it remains essentially an 'angel's view,' not Dickens's. The early Soviet poet Mayakovski approaches the city from street level, a perspective remarkably close to Dickens's own:

> The city itself is becoming an element from whose womb a new urban man is being born. We city dwellers don't know the forests, fields and flowers – we are acquainted with the tunnels of the streets, their movement, noise, rumbling, flickering, eternal circulation…. Everything has become lightning-fast, swift as it is on motion picture films. The flowing, calm, unhurried rhythms of the old poetry don't correspond to the psyche of the modern city dweller…. There are no flowing, measured, curved lines. The picture of the city is one characterized by corners, fractures, zigzags.[35]

Dickens's novels are full of the surprising corners and zigzags that characterize one's experience of the city street; his tempo is set to the kaleidoscopic pace of passing crowds, and his people seem to soliloquize into the busy void. The improbable coincidences in his plots convey the sense of a sudden, chance encounter, collisions between people or events that propel themselves with frightening freedom through a world whose traditional social bonds have broken to pieces. The child – lost, exploited, or pursued – in the city streets is the perfect subject to let loose in this void. Totally immersed in the totally unintelligible, he perceives the city with all the sensory closeness of childhood, yet cannot comprehend it. His very incomprehension is the most rational possible response to a society which is, as Dickens sees it, in essence irrational.

Thus Dickens's novels mimic the very modes in which we perceive the city. The criss-crossing strands of his plots are appropriate to his labyrinthine subject, and the very profusion of his characters, each imprisoned in his own exuberant vitality, reflects the vitality and mystery of the streets. But this narrative and psychological fragmentation would by itself produce chaos. And so what Dickens disjoins in plot and character, he puts together through symbol and fable. The result is a sense of wholeness, like that of the 'balloon view' of the city, achieved without the remoteness and unnatural stillness of such views. For example, not a scene, character or event in *Little Dorrit* is unrelated to the overriding symbol of the prison, first rendered literally in the opening scene; then transferred to the tomb-like tottering house of the deathly Mrs. Clenham; then shifted to the Marshalsea in which Mr. Dorrit is imprisoned; extended to the labyrinthine operation of the government's Circumlocution Office, into which men disappear for years; rendered again in the mansion of the magnate Mr. Merdle, who is the prisoner of his own butler and of the bejewelled, frigid bosom of his wife; and yet again in the paranoid Miss Wade, who escapes the Prison of Society only to become more firmly locked in her own obsessions.

The underlying role of fable in Dickens is harder to define than that of symbol and seems to run counter to the vivid actuality of his urban settings. In the category of fable I would include the capacity of his characters to gather around themselves a kind of demonic force, either for good or evil, a demonism that often spills over into objects which take on a furious animation of their own, like the ostentatious Podsnap silver that boasts aloud, 'Wouldn't you like to melt me down?' One cannot read Dickens very long without coming upon these animated objects in improbable stories about improbable characters who are never far removed from those in a fairy tale – witches like Good Mrs. Brown, devils like Fagin, demons like Quilp, or secular saints like Little Dorrit. Even in the 'mature' novels of social criticism, these inhabitants of a lost world lie close to the surface, and one of the most queerly Dickensian of incongruities is his transplanting of these ancient motifs and characters from their traditionally rural setting to the modern commercial metropolis. No house could be more stolidly prosaic than the house of the stolid Mr. Dombey. Yet for his daughter Florence, who is virtually buried alive within it, 'no magic dwelling-place in magic story, shut up in the heart of a thick wood, was ever more solitary and deserted to the fancy than was her father's mansion in its grim reality, as it stood lowering on the street' (Chapter 23). Dickens's novels simultaneously inhabit two worlds, the urban world we know of brick and pavement, and the forgotten one of demons and 'thick woods' and saints. The two elements combine in the unique Dickensian fusion of moral fable and superbly observed novel of the city. Finally, through fable Dickens restores to the city a sense of lost transcendence. For fable serves him as the equivalent of the nature that had been bricked out of the city and as a link to the supernatural, vestiges of Wordsworth's rural England transposed into Victorian London.

The Victorians never felt more cut off from the transcendent than in their cities. The bleakest moment in Tennyson's great elegy to Arthur Hallam occurs as the poet stands vigil by the dark house of his dead friend, waiting in 'the long unlovely street' as '…ghastly thro' the drizzling rain / On the bald street breaks the blank day' (*In Memoriam*, Section 7). Ruskin draws no starker contrast than that between St. Mark's Cathedral, ruling over the splendour of fifteenth-century Venice, and St. Paul's, overlooking the slums of nineteenth-century London.[36] In *Bleak House*, in the fermenting center of those slums, Joe the half-starved crossing-sweep, the last and lowliest of our elegists, looks up at the Cross of St. Paul's and sees only 'the crowning confusion of the great, confused city; so golden, so high up, so far out of his reach' (Chapter 19). Yet if the gods seem to withdraw from the Victorian city, they never wholly vanish; Joe still gazes up, however unavailingly, at St. Paul's Cross, unlike Eliot's sepulchral clerks who cross London Bridge with eyes cast down, like Dante's damned. In the century of literature we have surveyed, the city seems to undergo a second Fall, and in place of the promised Jerusalem arises the modern Inferno.

# Notes

## Chapter 1: The Age of Elegy

1 The phrase is from the opening lines of 'The Spirit of the Age' (1834).

2
>                            The days gone by
> Come back upon me from the dawn almost
> Of life; the hiding-places of my power
> Seem open, I approach, and then they close;
> I see by glimpses now, when age comes on
> May scarcely see at all... (Bk. 11, ll. 333–8; 1805 version)

Wordsworth's anxiety over the eventual loss of his creative powers can be felt as a kind of heavy breathing in the five internal stops within the last four lines.

3 Charles Tennyson, *Alfred Tennyson* (London: Macmillan, 1950), p. 49.

4 *Table Talk*, October 23, 1833.

5 '...I wrote the book very quickly; and when it was written, I ceased to be obsessed by my mother. I no longer hear her voice; I do not see her.' 'A Sketch of the Past,' in *Moments of Being*, ed. Jeanne Schulkind, 2nd ed. (New York: Harcourt Brace Jovanovich, 1976), p. 81.

6 *The Diary of Virginia Woolf*, ed. Anne Olivier Bell (New York: Harcourt Brace, 1981), p. 34, entry of June 18, 1925.

7 Unmistakable in the light of Mr. Ramsay's repeated quotation from Tennyson, cited below, and the textual parallels I cite here.

8 *Fraser's Magazine*, June 1839, cited in Martin Butlin and Evelyn Joll, *The Paintings of J.M.W. Turner*, rev. ed. (New Haven and London: Yale University Press, 1984), p. 203.

9 *The Works of John Ruskin*, eds. E.T. Cook and Alexander Wedderburn, 39 vols. (London: George Allen, 1903–12), 35:383, 13:170–1.

10 Herman Melville took only a mild poetic license when he wrote

> The fighting Temeraire
>    Built of a thousand trees,
> Lunging out her lightnings,
>    And beetling o'er the seas... ('The Temeraire,' 1866)

Like Turner, Melville does not use accents in the ship's title. He borrowed the epithet *fighting* from the artist, who was the first to apply it to the ship. See Judy Egerton, *The Fighting Temeraire* (London: National Gallery Publications, 1995), pp. 22, 32.

11    'The Passing of Arthur,' l. 408. The line first occurs in 'The Coming of Arthur,' l. 508. The earliest version of 'The Coming' appeared as the 'Mort d'Arthur' in 1842.

12    The title in its full Victorian amplitude is *Contrasts; or, A Parallel between the Noble Edifices of the Fourteenth and Fifteenth Centuries, and Similar Buildings of the Present Day; Shewing the Present Decay of Taste: Accompanied by Appropriate Text.*

13    See my *Carlyle and the Burden of History* (Cambridge, Mass.: Harvard University Press, 1985), pp. 121 and 188, n. 17.

14    'Prologue' to *Oliver Cromwell's Letters and Speeches* (1845).

15    See Basil Willey, *Nineteenth Century Studies* (London: Chatto & Windus, 1949), p. 105.

16    Walter Pater, *The Renaissance: Studies in Art and Poetry*, ed. Donald. L. Mill (Berkley: University of California Press, 1980), p. 187.

17    'A Sketch of the Past,' cited above, pp. 70, 142.

## Chapter 2: Carlyle: History and the Human Voice

1    *Reminiscences*, ed. Charles Eliot Norton (1932; rpt. London: J. M. Dent, 1972), p. 3.

2    Charles Richard Sanders, et al., eds, *The Collected Letters of Thomas and Jane Welsh Carlyle* (Durham, N.C. Duke University Press, 1970), 8:67, fn. 1.

3    Cited in Louise Merwin Young, *Thomas Carlyle and the Art of History* (Philadelphia: University of Pennsylvania Press, 1939), p. 143.

4    'Well said, old mole! Canst work I'th'earth so fast?' Hamlet exclaims (I.v.162). His last words are, 'The rest is silence.'

5    August 29, 1842, Joseph Slater, ed. *The Correspondence of Emerson and Carlyle* (New York: Columbia University Press, 1964), p. 328; cf. p. 357.

6    *Ibid.* p. 278; September 26, 1840.

7    *Ibid.* p. 325; July 19, 1842.

8    *The Works of Thomas Carlyle*, ed. H. D. Traill, 30 vols. (Chapman and Hall, 1896–1901). Unless otherwise specified, all subsequent citations from Carlyle's works will be to this edition and appear parenthetically in the text.

9    The phrase is from 'My Heart Leaps Up', the last three lines of which Wordsworth used as the epigram to the Immortality Ode:

> The Child is Father of the Man;
> And I could wish my days to be
> Bound each to each by natural piety.

10    *Iliad*, 5:58, the death of Skamandrios, in the Lattimore translation. The formula recurs with minor variations in dozens of instances.

11    James Anthony Froude, *Thomas Carlyle: A History of His Life in London*, 1834–1881, 2 vols. (New York: Charles Scribner, 1910). I, 172. December 26, 1840.

12    *Ibid. London*, I:45–6. Summer 1835. Cf. Psalm 120:5.

13    Sanders, *Collected Letters*, 8:209; September 23, 1835.

14    Slater, *Correspondence*, pp. 144,145; April 29, 1836.

15    Sanders, *Collected Letters*, 8:253–4; November 2, 1835.

16    *Ibid.* 9:267–8; July 28, 1837.

17    Fred Kaplan, *Thomas Carlyle: A Biography* (Ithaca: Cornell University Press, 1983), p. 395.

18  In tracing the motif of cannibalism in *The French Revolution* I am indebted to Lee Sterrenburg's essay, 'Psychoanalysis and the Iconography of Revolution,' *Victorian Studies*, 19 (1975), 241–64.

19  See Luke 4:1–2 and Matthew 26:36.

20  It is possible, but unlikely, that Robespierre was shot by one of his guards. See Carlyle's footnote, 4:284. Georges Lefebvre assumes an attempted suicide: *The French Revolution*, 2:135–6.

21  Mark 15:16–20.

22  See Matthew 27:12, 14; Mark 15:3–5; Luke 23:9.

23  The unnamed woman is a clear antitype of Veronica, who, in 'The Gospel of Nicodemus,' wipes Jesus's brow as he approaches Calvary.

24  See Matthew 27:28, 31; Mark 15:17, 20.

25  Slater, *Correspondence*, p. 104; August 12, 1834. Compare Carlyle's praise of Emerson's 'The American Scholar' as a kind of sacred music:

> It was long decades of years that I heard nothing but the infinite jangling and jabbering and inarticulate twittering and screeching, and my soul had sunk down sorrowful, and said there is no articulate speaking them any more, and thou art solitary among stranger-creatures?—and lo, out of the West, comes a clear utterance, clearly recognizable as a m[an's] voice, and I have a kinsmen and brother: God be thanked for it! I coul[d have]wept to read that speech; the clear high melody of it went tingling thro' my heart... (*Ibid.*, p. 173).

26  Matthew 27:50; cf. Mark 15:37 and Luke 23:46.

## Chapter 3: Stopping for Death: Tennyson's *In Memoriam*

1  Hallam Tennyson, *Alfred Lord Tennyson: A Memoir* (London: Macmillan, 1897), 1:72–3. Hereafter cited as *Memoir*. Tennyson was twenty-one years old when his father died.

2  William Allingham's *Diary* (August 7, 1884), cited in Christopher Ricks, *Tennyson* (New York: Macmillan, 1972), p. 28n.

3  Robert B. Martin, *Tennyson: The Unquiet Heart* (Oxford: Oxford University Press, 1980), p. 73.

4  Charles Tennyson, *Alfred Tennyson* (Hamden, Connecticut: Archon, 1968), p. 145.

5  Jack Kolb, 'Morte d'Arthur: The Death of Arthur Henry Hallam,' *Biography* 9 (1986): 38–9.

6  Tennyson told James Knowles that Section 9 was 'the first written,' and in the Heath MS it is dated October 6, 1833. See *In Memoriam*, ed. Susan Shatto and Marion Shaw (Oxford University Press 1982), pp. 172–3. All quotations from *In Memoriam* are taken from the Shatto and Shaw edition, hereafter referred to as *S&S*. Quotations from all other Tennyson poems are from the Ricks three-volume *Poems* (London: Longmans, 1969). I am much indebted to this magisterial edition, as I am to the commentary of Shatto and Shaw.

7  A minor touch in this most tactile of poems: of the many repetitions of 'calm,' only this last one is modified by an adjective. The preceding line, describing the swaying of the waves, is regularly iambic. But here Tennyson breaks the rhythm, the stress falls on 'dead,' and the resulting spondee reads like a compound –'dead

and calm' – with equal weight going to noun and adjective. The poet has given eerie life to a cliché.

8   Cf. Alan Sinfield, *The Language of Tennyson's* In Memoriam (New York, Bames & Noble, 1971), p. 128: 'The tree is almost embracing the dead, as the poet would wish to do.'

9   T.S. Eliot, 'In Memoriam' (1936), in *Selected Essays* (London: Faber & Faber, 1951), pp. 333–4.

10   *Memoir*, 1:304–5.

11   'The last three months of 1833 saw a series of storms, of uncharacteristic vehemence, sweep across England and the Continent. Shipping records recounted vessels lost at sea or wrecked upon various coasts' (Kolb, p. 41).

12   Cited in *S&S*, p. 170.

13   They never join, that is, in Section 7. The 3000 lines of *In Memoriam* are about the closing of the gap, which occurs in the companion poem, Section 119: 'And in my thoughts with scarce a sigh / I take the pressure of thine hand' (ll. 11–12).

14   *S&S*, p. 169.

15   Ricks, 2:312.

16   Sinfield writes perceptively of the poet's frustration at Hallam's 'inability to respond' in Section 7. 'Behold me, he says, but no one is listening and he is compelled to recognize the awful fact of death in the flat statement, "He is not here"' (p. 81).

17   I.11.153–4. Wordsworth echoes the same phrase in the ninth stanza of the Immortality Ode: 'our mortal Nature / Did tremble like a guilty Thing surprised.' In addition to the common phrasing, *In Memoriam* shares with the Immortality Ode a common concern with death, loss, and pain.

18   For the remarkably high opinion of Hallam retained by his Cambridge friends, including Gladstone, see Martin, pp. 73–4, and Ricks, 2:306.

19   Cited in Buck McMullen and James Kincaid, 'Tennyson, Hallam's Death, Milton's Murder, and Poetic Exhibitionism,' *Nineteenth Century Literature*, 45 (1990), p. 179.

20   Peter Sacks, *The English Elegy: Studies in the Genre from Spenser to Yeats* (Baltimore: Johns Hopkins University Press, 1985), p. 351. I am indebted to Sacks's eloquent chapter on *In Memoriam*. See also Martin, p. 187, and Kolb, pp. 42–3.

21   Cited in Ricks, *Tennyson*, p. 221.

22   'Infant' means, literally, 'unable to speak' (in = not + 'fans,' the present participle of 'fa-ri,' to speak). Tennyson's infant cries with piercing urgency and monotony. The stanza contains a remarkable number of repeated words and virtually only one rhyming sound. The central rhyme 'night' / 'light' all but rhymes with the end rhyme 'I' / 'cry,' which in turn is twice repeated by the 'crying' in the middle of the middle lines.

23   2 Kings 4, 31; see Ricks, 2:337.

24   I much admire Professor Martin's *Tennyson: The Unquiet Heart*, but here we disagree. Professor Martin quotes a remark of Elizabeth Barrett Browning that Tennyson's poetry 'has not flesh and blood enough to be sensual,' and he adds that Browning had 'accurately sensed the deep lack of sexuality that sometimes made Tennyson's poetry seem a touch pallid' (pp. 266–7). On the contrary, I find Tennyson's poetry profoundly sexual and have argued, in *The Fall of Camelot*, that *Idylls of the King* is virtually sex-obsessed. True, Tennyson wrote a number of pallid 'Airy, fairy, Lilian' poems – 'early girly poems,' Ricks calls them (*Tennyson*, p. 52) – but these 'Keepsake'

exercises are not examples of failed sexuality but of the idling of a great poetic engine, mere doodles. Tennyson's greatest poetry is charged with sexuality, but it often lurks in strange places, like tropical landscapes and mossy flower pots, asserts itself by default, is deflected into nostalgia or awakens into regret. It is almost never fulfilled (once or twice Lancelot and Guinevere reveal in their language or their gait the lineaments of gratified desire) but manifests itself in the frustrations of an Oenone or a Mariana ('O God, that I were dead!') or in the insistently phallic vision of a nun in *The Holy Grail*. It manifests itself in the maternal passion of a poem composed in Tennyson's old age, 'Rizpah,' about a mad crone who gathers up the bleached bones of her hanged son, 'bones that had sucked me.... They had moved in my side.' The last six words, Swinburne said, 'give perfect proof once more of the deep truth that great poets are bisexual' (Ricks, *Tennyson*, p. 218). Finally and most movingly, sexual passion manifests itself in the pathos of its renunciation by the world's oldest mortal, Tithonus, who craves release from the ever-renewed sexuality of the Dawn. The poem was drafted immediately after Tennyson learned of Hallam's death.

25 See the Duke of Argyll's letter of February 23, 1862 to Tennyson, cited in *S&S*, p. 176.

26 Cf. the sonnet's end: 'But O as to embrace me she enclin'd / I waked, she fled, and day brought back my night.' In voicing their most intimate griefs, both Milton and Tennyson borrow heavily from Ovid. See *S&S*, p. 176, and Ricks, 2:331.

27 *Memoir*, 1:298.

28 For a fuller discussion of Tennyson, homosexuality, and *In Memoriam*, see chap. 1 of Richard Dellamora's occasionally muddled *Masculine Desire: The Sexual Politics of Victorian Aestheticism* (Chapel Hill: University of North Carolina Press, 1990). Dellamora points out the historical inapplicability of the term 'homosexual' to Tennyson if only because it 'refers to the construction of male-male sexuality in the work of late-nineteenth-century sexologists' (p. 19). For a feminist critique of Tennyson and gender, see Marion Shaw, *Alfred Lord Tennyson* (New York: Harrester Wheatsheaf, 1988). Linda M. Shires writes astutely of the 'gender politics' of *In Memoriam* in *Victorian Sages and Cultural Discourse*, ed. Thaïs E. Morgan (New Brunswick: Rutgers University Press, 1990), pp. 57–61. See also Christopher Craft's '"Descend, and Touch, and Enter": Tennyson's Strange Manner of Address,' *Genders* 1 (1988): 83–101. Craft is a highly perceptive reader of the 'homosexual longing' that, he argues, underlies *In Memoriam*.

29 See *Memoir*, 1:71, and *S&S*, p. 254.

30 See Ricks, *Tennyson*, pp. 218–9, and cf. p. 215.

31 Review of November 28, 1851. See *Memoir*, 1:298, and Robert B. Martin, *Gerard Manley Hopkins: A Very Private Life* (New York: G.P. Putnam's Sons, 1991), p. 6.

32 See *S&S*, p. 232. Shatto and Shaw list 15 revisions that 'obscure and make less personal the references to himself and Arthur Hallam.' See pp. 25–6.

33 *S&S*, p. 255.

34 *Ibid.*, p. 255.

35 Trinity MS. See *S&S*, p. 6.

36 *The Writings of Arthur Hallam*, ed. T.S. Vail Motter (New York: Modern Language Association, 1943), p. 203.

37 Charles Tennyson, p. 498. Cf. *Memoir*, 1:320.

38 *Memoir*, 1:321n.

39 I owe this phrase to Timothy Peltason, *Reading* In Memoriam (Princeton: Priceton University Press, 1985), p. 15.

40 I am indebted here to James Eli Adams, 'Woman Red in Tooth and Claw: Nature and the Feminine in Tennyson and Darwin,' *Victorian Studies*, 33 (1989): 7–27. See especially pp. 15 and 17.

41 *Memoir*, 1:485.

42 *De Rerum Natura*, 2.578–80.

43 One recalls T.S. Eliot's gibe that although Tennyson had a brain of sorts, it was 'a large dull brain like a farmhouse clock.' From 'Verse Pleasant and Unpleasant,' in *The Egoist* (March 1918), p. 43. See Louis Menand, 'The Nineteenth Century in Modernist Criticism,' Dissertation, Columbia University (1980), p. 56.

44 The comparison is Tennyson's own. See *Memoir*, 1: 304–5.

45 *S&S*, pp. 13–14.

46 Peltason, p. 4.

47 Martin, pp. 149–50.

48 *Ibid.*, pp. 324–5.

49 See Martin, p. 274 and Chapter XVIII: 'Emotional Breakdown, 1844–1845.'

50 Ricks, 2:312.

51 I italicize the phrase because of its telling superfluity. Of course Odysseus knew the great Achilles – as Tennyson knew the great Arthur. 'Ulysses' always seems longer in memory than its mere seventy lines. But not a word is wasted. These four words are pointless, unless they bear the meaning I find in them. Tennyson was particularly fond of reciting the line, and Thackeray remarked on how the poet 'went through the streets, screaming about his great Achilles, whom we knew, as if we had all made the acquaintance of that gentleman, and were very proud of it' (Martin, p. 190).

52 Tennyson's words to Knowles, cited in Ricks, 2:312.

53 See Ricks, 2:20, and *Memoir*, 2:466.

54 *S&S*, p. 10. Letter of February 14, 1834.

55 See Ricks, *Tennyson*, pp. 103–4.

56 The phrase is not mine but Walter Pater's, coined for the meeting of Marius and Flavian in *Marius the Epicurean*. The fascination of *Marius* for the modern reader lies in its encoded homoeroticism, secreted like a musk on every page; the fascination of *In Memoriam* is quite different, a love story between males that is *not* erotic.

57 R. J. Tennant. See Martin, p. 187.

58 Tennyson induced such 'waking trances' by 'repeating my own name to myself silently, till all at once as it were out of the intensity of consciousness of individuality the individuality itself seemed to dissolve and fade away into boundless being – & this not a confused state but the clearest of the clearest, the surest of the surest, utterly beyond words – where Death was an almost laughable impossibility – the loss of personality (if so it were) seeming no extinction but the only true life.' Cited in Martin, pp. 28–9. See also pp. 83–95, 278–80, 347.

59 I read Section 95 and the Epilogue as celebrations of Tennyson's 'first' or spiritual marriage to Hallam. Martin writes that Emily proposed the visit to Hallam's tomb – 'apparently Tennyson's first' – on their honeymoon: '"It seemed a kind of consecration to go there," she said' (Martin, p. 338).

60    Martin, pp. 538–9.

61    That Tennyson intends the dark arms to work in this way is evident from an exactly analogous usage in 'The Kraken.' Line 10 in the juvenile version of the poem depicts submerged polypi winnowing 'with giant fins the slumbering green.' But the mythic Kraken inhabits two worlds, the vegetable-primordial and the human apocalyptic; and so Tennyson alters the 'fins' of 1830 to read 'arms' in 1872.

62    Sacks, p. 200.

63    See Epilogue, ll. 34–7 and S&S, p. 294.

64    'The peace of God came into my life before the altar when I wedded her.' Cited in Martin, p. 334. For the title of In Memoriam, see pp. 332–3.

65    Ricks, 2:312.

66    S&S, p. 248.

67    Memoir, 1:44–5.

68    For Dante's influence on Hallam and on the design of In Memoriam, see the dissertation of the late Elizabeth Wheeler, 'No Second Friend: The Idea of Friendship in Mill, Carlyle, and Tennyson,' Columbia University (1985), pp. 229–31. See also Ward Hellstrom, On the Poems of Tennyson (Gainesville: University of Florida Press, 1972), p. 41; Gerhard Joseph, Tennysonian Love: The Strange Diagonal (Minneapolis: University of Minnesota Press, 1969), pp. 59–63; Gordon Hirsch, 'Tennyson's Commedia,' VP, 8 (1970): 93–106.

69    See S&S, p. 293, for twenty-five specific parallels.


## Chapter 4: Tennyson and the Passing of Arthur

1    All quotations of Tennyson's poetry are from The Poems of Tennyson, ed. Christopher Ricks (London: Longmans, 1969) and cited in the text. Titles of individual idylls will be abbreviated as follows: 'The Coming of Arthur,' CA; 'Gareth and Lynette,' GL; 'Balin and Balan,' BB; 'Lancelot and Elaine,' LE; 'The Last Tournament,' LT; 'Guinevere,' G; and 'The Passing of Arthur,' PA.

2    See Morte d'Arthur, ed. R. Wilks (London, 1816), III, chap. 50; and David Staines, Tennyson's Camelot: The Idylls of the King and its Medieval Sources (Waterloo, Canada, 1982), p. 173.

3    The lines first appeared in Tennyson's 'Morte d'Arthur' (1842). Hopkins surely had them in mind when he composed the first quatrain of 'Heaven-Haven' in 1864:

                    HEAVEN-HAVEN
                    A nun takes the veil

              I HAVE desired to go
                    Where springs not fail,
              To fields where flies no sharp and sided hail
                    And a few lilies blow.

              And I have asked to be
                    Where no storms come,
              Where the green swell is in the havens dumb,
                    And out of the swing of the sea.

4   See Eliot L. Gilbert, 'The Female King: Tennyson's Arthurian Apocalypse,' *PMLA*, 98 (1983), 868.

5   See Hallam Tennyson, *Alfred Tennyson: A Memoir*, 2 vols. (London: Macmillan, 1897), I:109.

6   See 'The Ancient Sage,' ll. 217–19.

7   See 'To Virgil,' Tennyson's tribute to the
> 'Wielder of the stateliest measure
>     ever moulded by the lips of man.'

8   Quoted by Sir James Knowles, 'Aspects of Tennyson,' *Nineteenth Century*, 33 (1893), 170.

9   See Ricks, pp. 598–9 and 1082. In addition to the links with *In Memoriam*, Ricks notes the resemblance of the lines to the Middle English lyric,

> Westron winde, when wilt thou blow,
> The smalle raine downe can raine?
> Christ if my love were in my armes,
> And I in my bed againe.

10   *The Table Talk and Omniana of Samuel Taylor Coleridge*, ed. T. Ashe (London, 1923), p. 279.


## Chapter 5: Ruskin's Benediction: A Reading of *Fors Clavigera*

1   Ruskin first drew Santa Maria della Spina, with the Arno in the background, in 1840. The close-up drawing used as the frontispiece of Letter 20 (in *The Works of John Ruskin*, ed. by E.T. Cook and Alexander Wedderburn (London: George Allen, 1903–12), Vol. IV, plate 4) is of the eastern end of the chapel and was made from a daguerreotype he commisioned in 1845. In the Library Edition, Cook and Wedderburn shift the drawing to the end of the letter, where it faces Ruskin's description of the destruction of the chapel. They also delete, perhaps distressed by what they took to be hyperbole, Ruskin's dramatic 'Now in Ruins.' The chapel survives, or rather in its stead now stands a meticulous but chilling replica of the early-thirteenth and fourteenth-century church Ruskin saw knocked to pieces, stone by stone, in 1872. Centuries of neglect, followed by severe flooding, led to the 'restoration' of the chapel, along with raising it three feet and shifting it from its ancient position overhanging the buttressed banks of the Arno. Letter 20 records Ruskin's appalled witness to the early stages of this reconstruction, with its needless smashing of many of the old stones (38:274). In reading the letter we are reminded that Ruskin was an early advocate of architectural preservation, arguing that 'restoration' was a lie often more devastating, because more subtle in its obliteration of the past, than outright destruction. Two years after the reconstruction of Santa Maria della Spina he wrote to Sir Gilbert Scott, President of the Royal Institute of Architects, declining the award of its Gold Medal. While Europe's architectural heritage was being devastated, as at Pisa, through neglect and ruinous restoration, he wrote, we must not 'play at adjudging medals to each other' (34:514). Today the visitor to Pisa reads in the guidebooks of this 'gem of Pisan-Gothic architecture' and is given no clue – other than the strange lifelessness of the chapel itself – that he is gazing at a late nineteenth-century replica.

2   'I don't *anger* my soul,' he wrote to a reader of *Fors,* 'I relieve it, by all violent language.... I *live* in chronic fury...only to be at all relieved in its bad fits by studied expression' (37:371).

3   All citations of Letter 20 are from the Library Edition (27:334–51).

4   The striking phrase is Cardinal Manning's (see 36:lxxxvi).

5   See Letter 5 (27:95–7). For a fuller discussion of the Guild's aims and its limited success, see John. D. Rosenberg, *The Darkening Glass* (New York: Columbia University Press, 1961), pp. 188, 195–9.

6   Ruskin so narrates the event that the reader's perception of it exactly mirrors the successive stages of Ruskin's own experience. Hence, while still stationed at the window in the first sentence, Ruskin cannot see, nor does he permit the reader to realize, that the boy is selling figs. Rather he describes only the figure of a boy 'selling something black' from a basket; only when on the quay in the second sentence can he (or we) distinctly hear the cry of 'Fighiaie' or clearly see the half-rotten figs. Similarly, the syntactically acrobatic account of the boy bending and rising as he cries 'Fighiaie' mimics the action it describes.

7   Paul Sawyer uses the phrase to characterize the confessional elements of *Fors* through which Ruskin 'records a private quest for a lost Eden, a Paradise within,' and contrasts it to the related but more public myth of St. George, through which Ruskin seeks the spiritual rescue and rebirth of England. See 'Ruskin and St. George: The Dragon-Killing Myth in *Fors Clavigera,*' *Victorian Studies,* 23 (Autumn 1979), pp. 7, 15. Sawyer's essay is one of the first important studies of *Fors.*

8   The thumbing gesture of 'giving the figs' would of course have been familiar to Ruskin from the streets of Italy and from Dante, whom he explicates throughout *Fors.* The fig-gesture serves Dante as a supremely shocking instance of blasphemy at the start of Canto XXV of the *Inferno,* where Vanni Fucci directs it at God Himself. For Ruskin's invective against the obscene shoutings and gesturings he had witnessed in the streets of Venice and Florence, see *The Darkening Glass,* pp. 181–5.

9   At the end of the paragraph Ruskin appends this footnote: 'And the stars of heaven fell unto the earth, even as a fig-tree casteth her untimely figs, when she is shaken of a mighty wind. – Rev. 6:13; compare Jerem. xxiv. 8, and Amos viii. 1 and 2.'

10  (28:207). The force of this excerpt cannot be appreciated apart from its context in 'Advent Collect,' one of the most moving letters in all of *Fors.* The autograph manuscript, owned by the Pierpont Morgan Library (MA 2285), has relatively few revisions and is written in a rapid, even hand, as are the other draft letters of *Fors* for 1874 bound in the same notebook. One is astonished that under such stress Ruskin could compose with such apparent ease.

11  Luke 10:23; Isaiah 35:6.

12  Scarcely a phrase in the *Capo d'Istria* paragraph is without similar allusive force. For example, the fiercely-smoking English warship is a kind of iron-clad Leviathan clearly akin to the flaming monster in Job 41:19–21. Ruskin's translation of Canto XXI appeared in the June 1872 issue of *Fors* (27:313).

13  One of Ruskin's copies of the *Dream of St. Ursula* is reproduced in Letter 27, plate 8, and faces his analysis of the painting in 'Benediction.' In Letters 71 and 72 of *Fors* he transcribes at length the legend of St. Ursula and further analyses Carpaccio's painting. For the profile sketch of Rose and the drawing of the head of Ilaria di Caretto, see Letters 35, plate C, and 23, plate 19. The family resemblance among Ruskin's 'sleeping beauties' is striking. For the importance he attached to

Jacopo della Quercia's tomb of Ilaria di Caretto in his aesthetic development, see 35.347, 349, and 4.122, 347. For a fuller account of his association of Rose with St. Ursula, see Derrick Leon, *Ruskin: The Great Victorian* (London: Routledge & Kegan Paul, 1949), pp. 507–10, and *The Darkening Glass*, pp. 204–6.

14   Leon, op. cit., p. 496.

15   'For in the resurrection they neither marry, nor are given in marriage, but are as the angels of God in heaven' (Matthew 22:30).


## Chapter 6: Water into Wine: The Miracle of Ruskin's *Praeterita*

1   An abbreviated version of this essay was presented as the Mikimoto Memorial Lecture at the International Ruskin Symposium, Lancaster University, 19 July 2000.

2   All citations from *Praeterita* are from the Library Edition of *The Works of John Ruskin*, eds. E.T. Cook and Alexander Wedderburn, 39 vols (London: George Allen, 1903–12). Volume and page references appear in parentheses.

3   There are exceptions, of course, the most celebrated of which is John Stuart Mill's *Autobiography*. The child of his father's eighteenth-century rationalism, Mills writes an unrelentingly linear narrative. But his reading of Wordsworth figures centrally in his story. In the chapter on his mental breakdown, Wordsworth's poetry serves Mill as a kind of psychological tonic ('medicine' is Mill's term) that cures his depression. Wordsworth, who had been banished from James Mill's library, teaches Mill the culture of feelings and brings him belatedly into the nineteenth century.

4   For an excellent account of typological elements embedded in the structure of *Praeterita*, see Heather Henderson, *The Victorian Self: Autobiography and Biblical Narrative* (Ithaca: Cornell University Press, 1989), 65–115. In writing this essay, I realize that I have learned much about Ruskin from the published works of three others of my former doctoral students: Professors Jay Fellows (*The Failing Distance: The Autobiographical Impulse in John Ruskin*, Baltimore: Johns Hopkins University Press, 1975); Elizabeth K. Helsinger (*Ruskin and the Art of the Beholder*, Cambridge: Harvard University Press, 1982); and Paul Sawyer (*Ruskin's Poetic Argument*, Ithaca: Cornell University Press, 1985). For important analyses of the 'circuitous structure' of *The Prelude* and of typology in Ruskin, see M. H. Abrams, *Natural Supernaturalism* (New York: Norton, 1973) and George P. Landow, *The Aesthetic and Critical Theories of John Ruskin* (Princeton: Princeton University Press, 1971).

5   All citations from Wordsworth's *The Prelude* are from the 1805 version. See William Wordsworth, *The Prelude: 1799, 1805, 1850*, eds. Jonathan Wordsworth, M. H. Abrams and Stephen Gill (New York: W. W. Norton, 1979).

6   The point is made conclusively by Elizabeth K. Helsinger in her important essay on 'The Structure of Ruskin's *Praeterita*,' in George P. Landow, ed., *Approaches to Victorian Autobiography* (Ohio University Press, 1979), 87–108. To borrow a term from psychoanalysis, Ruskin's visionary moments in *Praeterita* are 'overdetermined.' They include Ruskin's experiences at Schaffhausen in 1833 (35:115–6), at the Col de la Faucille in 1835 (35:167–8), at Lans-le-Bourg in 1841 (35:297); on the open road in 1842 while drawing a sprig of ivy at Norwood and an aspen at Fontainebleau (35:311, 314–15); standing before the tomb of the sleeping Ilaria di Caretto in Lucca (35:349), the frescoes in the Campo Santa at Pisa, the

Tintorettos in the Scuola di San Rocco in Venice in 1845, and Veronese's 'Solomon and the Queen of Sheba' at Turin in 1858: and on further occasions too numerous to specify, while resident in Rouen, Geneva, Chamounix, Pisa, Venice, Assisi, and Siena.

7    Ruskin cites the line 'We live by Admiration, Hope, and Love' (*Excursion*, IV, 763) at least ten times throughout his works. Wordworth placed his most famous line – 'The Child is father of the Man,' borrowed from his earlier 'My Heart Leaps Up' – at the head of his Immortality Ode, as if the Ode, like the poet himself, were self-begotten. But if the child fathers the man, who is the father of Wordsworth's child? The answer comes in Stanza 5, with the myth of pre-existence. We arrive on earth '...not in utter nakedness, / But trailing clouds of glory...' from our celestial home. The voyage is necessarily circular.

8    Proust was Ruskin's first translator into French, and he was so drawn to *Praeterita* that he claimed to know it by heart. For his early discipleship to Ruskin, see John D. Rosenberg, *The Darkening Glass: A Portait of Ruskin's Genius* (New York: Columbia University Press, 1961), 55, 208f., 221–2.

9    These lines from the opening of *The Prelude* (I, 59–64), in which the poet assumes the mantle of the priest and prophet, are virtually repeated in Book IV. At dawn, in sight of mountains and the distant sea, Wordsworth exchanges vows with an unnamed presence and becomes 'a dedicated Spirit' who walks on 'in thankful blessedness' (IV, 337–8).

10   See 35:317, 560, for Ruskin's experiments with 'water-works,' domestic and foreign. The finest of all tracings of the continuities between Ruskin's earliest and later writings, including *Harry and Lucy*, is Sheila Emerson's *Ruskin: The Genesis of Invention* (Cambridge: Cambridge University Press, 1993). In an unpublished essay of 1988, Emily Elliot writes of some two hundred and thirty passages in *Praeterita* describing water as it flows, gathers, gushes, pools, leaps, cascades, springs, glistens and glows.

11   Ruskin's footnote is pertinent here: 'I always think of Tay as a goddess river, as Greta a nymph one' (35:67n).

12   Tim Hilton, Ruskin's most important modern biographer, persuausively corrects earlier depictions of the elder Ruskins as distant and aloof. See *John Ruskin: The Early Years, 1819–1859* (New Haven: Yale University Press, 1985).

13   My tutor in all metrical matters is Dr. Elliott Zuckerman, of St. John's College, who was with me on my first Ruskin outing nearly half a century ago.

14   'The Simplon' is the seventeenth of a projected thirty-six chapters. See 35:liv.

15   See 35:xxxiv.

16   See *The Darkening Glass*, 223, 250, and Fontaney 356, n. 17. Joan Evans misdates the passage on p. 100 of her 1954 biography of Ruskin; Kenneth Clark repeats the error on p. 42 of his 1964 anthology of Ruskin, then silently corrects himself in the fine Introduction to his 1978 edition of *Praeterita*.

17   My depiction of Mr. Bautte's Geneva is indebted to Pierre Fontaney, 'Ruskin and Paradise Regained' and to Elizabeth K. Helsinger, 'The Structure of Ruskin's *Praeterita*' in Landow 101–3.

18                                    [Harry] soon
                                 observed a rainbow and a-
                                 rising mist under it which

> his fancy soon transform
> ed into a female form. He
> then remembered the witch of
> the waters at the Alps who
> was raised from them by-
> takeing some water in the-
> hand and throwing it into
> the air pronouncing some
> unintelligable words (35:55).

19   See *The Winter's Tale*, IV, iv, 140–2.

20   The best commentary I know on Ruskin's Rhone passage is a story Henry Adams tells in *Mont-Saint-Michel and Chartres* of a shy and lowly tumbler who expresses his gratitude and devotion to the Virgin in the only way he can, by going down to the crypt of Clairvaux and pirouetting on her altar with miraculous acrobatic virtuosity and grace. The Rhone passage is Ruskin's pirouette.

21   The sentence comes from two alternative conclusions to the chapter, neither of which was published in Ruskin's lifetime.

22   Song of Songs 4:12, cited in Fleischman 179.

23   See *The Darkening Glass*, 203.

24   Letter of September 2, 1861 to John James Ruskin (35:1xvii).

25   Ruskin uses the word in the title of *Fors Clavigera*, a wide-ranging series of public letters on the state of Europe's soul and his own begun in 1871 and terminated in 1884, the year before he began *Praeterita*. The first two chapters of *Praeterita* originally appeared in *Fors Clavigera*. For the many meanings of the title, see *The Darkening Glass*, 186n.

26   'Imagine all that any of these men had seen or heard in the whole course of their lives, laid up accurately in their memories as in vast storehouses, extending, with the poets, even to the slightest intonations of syllables heard in the beginning of their lives, and with the painters, down to minute folds of drapery, and shapes of leaves or stones; and over all this unindexed and immeasurable mass of treasure, the imagination brooding and wandering, but dream-gifted, so as to summon at any moment exactly such groups of ideas as shall fit each other: this I conceive to be the real nature of the imaginative mind' (*Modern Painters* IV, 'Of Turnerian Topography,' 6:41–42).

27   See *The Darkening Glass*, 172, fn. 14.

28   My source for the 'crystal' water and the 'rainbow' arc is William Sharp, who had seen the painting in Severn's studio: the painting 'evinced a touch of genius in representing the transformed water poured from one pitcher at first transparent as crystal, but changing colour in its arc, like a rainbow, and descending red into the other pitcher.' *The Life and Letters of Joseph Severn*, ed. William Sharp (New York: Scribners, 1892), 303. The painting itself has proven as elusive to me as Ruskin's corncrake and I have been unable to track it down.

29   See Arrowsmith, 209.

30   Letter of June 19, 1872, cited in Leon, 487–8. Ruskin was never given the letter, but there is no doubt that he got its message, through mutual friends and subsequent letters from Rose decrying his 'sins against God.'

31   See *The Darkening Glass*, 203.

32   My calling Norton Ruskin's Virgilian guide would be a bit of a stretch, were it not that only a few pages earlier Ruskin had written that Norton, though younger, saw all of Ruskin's 'weaknesses...and, from the first, took serenely, and it seemed of necessity, a kind of paternal authority over me, and a right of guidance...' (35:522).

33   See Helsinger, 104.

34   'Ruskin's Fireflies.' *The Ruskin Polygon*. Eds. John Dixon Hunt and Faith M. Holland (Manchester: Manchester University Press, 1982), p. 209.

35   *Paradiso*. trans. Allen Mandelbaum (Berkeley: University of California Press, 1984): XIV, 67–72. The subsequent citation from *The Divine Comedy* is also from the Mandelbaum translation.

36   See *Inferno* XXX, 58–78. Ruskin writes of Adamo and the Fonte Branda in *Val D'Arno* (22:28).

37   *The Life of John Ruskin*. 2 vols (London: George Allen & Co., 1911) II, p. 498.

38   The cigar-smoking girls, anti-types of 'Little Joanie,' appear in a footnote, usually cut by Ruskin's editors, immediately preceding the final two paragraphs. Ruskin describes a pantomime performance at Covent Garden of *Ali Baba and the Forty Thieves* at the end of which the forty girl thieves all light up cigars to the applause of the audience and to Ruskin's disgust. The passage first appeared in *Time and Tide*. In these closing lines Ruskin has also overcome his phobia of spots of bright light against dark backgrounds. All of his adult life, perhaps due to extraordinary sensitivity to light, he was disturbed by such high contrasts in nature or in art. This hypersensitivity perhaps accounts for his intemperate attacks on chiaroscuro in Rembrandt, who could paint only 'the lamplight upon the hair of a costermonger's ass' (17:109–12) and his libelous attack on Whistler's *The Falling Rocket* in 1878 (29:160), the year of his first unequivocal attack of madness. But here in his final moment as a writer he transforms pathology into great art.

39   Arrowsmith p. 226.

40   An autograph facsimile of 'The Last Words of *Praeterita*' faces page 562 of vol. 35 of the Library Edition. Apparently Ruskin first dictated the chapter to Joan Severn in May of 1889 and later revised it in his own hand. But the Cook and Wedderburn facsimile departs in a few instances from the version they set up in type. For example, the drawing that hangs in Joanie's *nursery* in the facsimile hangs in her *schoolroom* in the printed version.

41   I use Ruskin's translation. See 23:27.

## Chapter 7: Mr. Darwin Collects Himself

1   *The Autobiography of Charles Darwin*, ed. Nora Barlow (New York: Norton, 1958), p. 21. Hereafter referred to as *Autobiography*.

2   *Ibid*., p. 21.

3   The title appears at the head of the autograph manuscript. Of the approximately one hundred editions in at least twenty-two languages, only one – that of the Soviet Academy of Sciences in 1957 – gets Darwin's title right. See R. B. Freeman, *The Works of Charles Darwin: an Annotated Bibliographical Handlist*, 2nd ed. (Hamden, CT: Dawson-Archon, 1977), pp. 172–80.

4   Ralph Colp, Jr., M.D., 'Notes on Charles Darwin's *Autobiography*,' *Journal of the History of Biography*, 18.3 (Fall, 1985), p. 361.

5   *Autobiography*, p. 21.

6   'When 110 days old he was exceedingly amused by a pinafore being thrown over his
    face and then suddenly withdrawn; and so he was when I suddenly uncovered my
    own face and then suddenly approached his. He then uttered a little noise which was
    an incipient laugh. Here surprise was the chief cause of amusement, as is the case to
    a large extent with the wit of grown-up persons. I believe that for three or four weeks
    before the time when he was amused by a face being suddenly uncovered, he received
    a little pinch on his nose as a good joke. I was at first surprised at humour being
    appreciated by an infant only a little above three months old, but we should remember
    how very early puppies and kittens begin to play...' (In *Metaphysics, Materialism,
    and the Evolution of Mind: Early Writings of Charles Darwin*, ed. Paul H. Barrett,
    commentary by Howard E. Gruber (Chicago: University of Chicago Press, 1980), p.
    209.

    The paper first appeared in *Mind* in 1877 but was based on Darwin's much earlier
    notes of 1839–41. A 38-year interval between inception of an idea and its publication
    was not unusual for Darwin. His early research on worms produced papers in 1838
    and 1840, but he worked at a pace mimetic of the creature in whose humble work-
    habits and intelligence he delighted, and who wrought such mighty effects from such
    minute causes, ultimately altering and fructifying the surface of the earth with each
    of its myriad and remembered turns. Darwin's four decades of worm-research
    culminated in 1881 in his last, highly popular work, *The Formation of Vegetable
    Mould, through the Action of Worms, with Observations on their Habits*. Darwin
    rehabilitates worms in the world of the lower animals as Wordsworth had rehabilitated
    Cumberland beggars and leech-gatherers in the human world. The suggestion of
    memory, and hence a degree of intelligence and even of shared culture, is implicit in
    the word *Habits*.

7   The work was published by Francis Darwin in 1887, five years after his father's
    death, in *Life and Letters of Charles Darwin, Including an Autobiographical Chapter*.
    In deference to family opinion but in violation of his own, Francis deleted nearly
    six thousand words, most importantly those expressing disbelief in the truth of
    Revelation and hostility to the 'damnable doctrine' of eternal punishment for
    disbelievers (*Autobiography*, Preface, pp. 11–3, 86–7).

8   For Darwin's identification of the third beetle, see the anecdote, recounted fifty
    years after the fact, by Frederick Watkins, Archdeacon of York and undergraduate
    friend of Darwin, in *The Life and Letters of Charles Darwin*, ed. Francis Darwin
    (New York: Appleton, 1896), I, 144. Darwin gives an account of the loss of the
    'sacred' *Panagaeus crux major* almost identical to the one in the *Recollections* in a
    letter of 1846 to the naturalist Leonard Jenyns. See *Life and Letters*, I, 396.

9   *Life and Letters*, I, 143; *Autobiography*, p. 54.

10  Letter of 8 September, 1830 to William Fox, *The Correspondence of Charles Darwin*,
    eds. Frederick Burkhardt and Sydney Smith. (Cambridge: Cambridge University
    Press, 1983–2001), I, 106.

11  I owe this point, as I owe so much else, to my graduate school mentor, Jerome
    Hamilton Buckley. 'The ideal autobiography,' Buckley writes in *The Turning Key:
    Autobiography and the Subjective Impulse since 1800*, 'describes a voyage of self-
    discovery, a life journey...' (Cambridge: Harvard University Press, 1984, p. 39).

12  *Autobiography*, p. 79. Darwin set sail in December 1831 and returned in October
    1836.

13   *Ibid.*, p. 32.

14   *Ibid.*, p. 76.

15   Josiah Wedgwood II, son of the founder of the pottery works and father of Emma, Darwin's first cousin and wife. Maer Hall, in Staffordshire, was only twenty miles from The Mount, the late-Georgian house in Shrewsbury built by Darwin's father. There was much traffic between the establishments and much intermarriage among the inhabitants.

16   *Autobiography*, p. 55.

17   Entry of 26–27 September 1835, ed. Nora Barlow (Cambridge: Cambridge University Press, 1933), p. 336.

18   *Correspondence*, I, 386, 525. The *Beagle* hoard ultimately yielded for Darwin nine volumes of geological and zoological research, in addition to *The Origin of Species* and various collaborative publications by others on fossil mammalia, fish, birds, reptiles, flowers, plants, beetles, spiders, corals, crustacia, and so forth. A considerable number of specimens remain to be described after more than a century and a half of work in museums and laboratories all over the world. See *Correspondence*, II, xv, xvii, xxi.

19   'Throughout the voyage Darwin collected only a few specimens (usually a male and a female) of each species....' See Frank J. Sulloway, 'Darwin's Conversion: The *Beagle* Voyage and Its Aftermath,' *Journal of the History of Biography*, 15.3 (Fall 1982), p. 387.

20   (London: Henry Colburn, 1839), II, 671–2.

21   *W. B. Yeats and T. Sturge Moore: Their Correspondence 1901–1937*, ed. Ursula Bridge (London: Routledge, 1953), p. 154.

22   *Autobiography*, p. 79.

23   Letter of 24 October–24 November 1832, *Correspondence*, I, 278.

24   Letter of 8 February 1858, *Life and Letters*, I, 467–8.

25   'Darwin's Reading and the Fictions of Development,' in *The Darwinian Heritage*, ed. David Kohn (Princeton: Princeton University Press, 1985), p. 558.

26   Dr. Edward Kempf, one of the more inventive analysts of Darwin's behavior, speculates in the *Psychoanalytic Review* that Darwin fancied he could alter the color of the flowers 'after he had repeatedly urinated on them (not an uncommon experiment of boys).... The urinating on the flowers probably had the value of being a fertilization curiosity.' Dr. Kempf further speculates that Darwin suffered from repressed homosexuality, a surmise based on a misreading of the passage in the *Recollections* in which Darwin describes his uneasiness at dining alone in the same cabin with Captain Fitz-Roy, a man of irritable temper. Fitz-Roy was 'extremely kind to me,' Darwin writes, but 'very difficult to live with on the intimate terms which necessarily followed from our messing by ourselves in the same cabin' (*Autobiography*, p. 73). Dr. Kempf appears to mistake *messing* for *groping*. See 'Charles Darwin – The Affective Sources of His Inspiration and Anxiety Neurosis,' *Psychoanalytic Review*, 5 (1918), pp. 156, 166–7. For an excellent discussion of Darwin's health, physical and mental, see Dr. Ralph Colp's *To Be an Invalid* (Chicago: University of Chicago Press, 1977).

27   *Autobiography*, p. 24.

28   *Autobiography*, p. 23n. Leighton later became an Anglican clergyman and botanist. The careers of many of Darwin's classmates and mentors combined in easy harmony

the roles of cleric and naturalist. Darwin's Cambridge mentor, the Rev. John Stevens Henslow, Professor of Mineralogy and Botany, comes to mind, as do William Fox and Leonard Jenyns. If to us the vocations of scientist and clergyman seem at cross-purposes, to the early Victorians they were complementary callings. As cleric, one was an exegete of God's 'First Book,' the Bible; on weekdays, as naturalist, one celebrated the intricate design of God's 'Second Book,' Nature. Darwin planned to pursue the tandem career of cleric-naturalist until quite late in the voyage of the *Beagle*.

29   Written in answer to a questionnaire on 'English Men of Science, their Nature and Nurture.' See letter of 28 May 1873 to Francis Galton, cited in Colp, 'Notes on Charles Darwin's *Autobiography*,' p. 364, n. 28. See also *Autobiography*, pp. 22, 24; 'An Autobiographical Fragment' (1838), in *Correspondence*, II, 439; *Life and Letters*, II, 355.

30   Letter of 23 March 1842, *Correspondence*, II, 315–16. A year later Darwin wrote to the still-devastated Fox that he had had no comparable experience of losing a 'cherished one' (*ibid.*, p. 352).

31   'Granny' was his pet name for his older sister Susan. His older sisters served in place of his mother at the Mount in the last stages of her illness and after her death.

32   Even on her tombstone she remains elusive. As if in token of her abbreviated life, her name is truncated to 'Susan.'

33   Painted 'in or about' 1780, after George Stubbs. Reproduced in *Emma Darwin: A Century of Family Letters 1792–1896*, ed. Henrietta Litchfield (New York: Appleton, 1915), I, facing p. 8; and in Alan Moorehead, *Darwin and the Beagle* (New York: Harper & Row, 1969), p. 29. See also the miniature of Susannah of 1792 by Peter Paillou, reproduced in Julian Huxley and H.B.D. Kettlewell, *Charles Darwin and His World* (New York: Viking, 1965), p. 9; and in Peter Brent, *Charles Darwin* (London: Heinemann, 1981), facing p. 120. Francis Darwin describes a miniature of Susannah with a 'remarkably sweet and happy face,' but if he writes of the Paillou portrait, the expression is more notable for its strength and intelligence than for its sweetness. See *Life and Letters*, I, 9.

34   Letter of June 1807, in Eliza Meteyard, *A Group of Englishmen* (London: Longmans, 1871), p. 357. The phrase 'prognosticating sigh' is Meteyard's.

35   Brent, p. 24.

36   For her interest in pigeon-breeding and in flowers, see Meteyard, pp. 260–1. Francis Darwin (*Life and Letters*, I, 9) casts doubt on Meteyard's account of 'the Mount pigeons,' but Meteyard quotes letters of some length of 1807 and 1808 from Susannah to her brother Josiah promising him a gift of doves she has been breeding.

37   See *Life and Letters*, II, 533–41; and Freeman, *The Works of Charles Darwin*, pp. 194–207.

38   *Life and Letters*, I, 10.

39   The most astute comment on Darwin's health appears in one of his own letters: 'I hope I may be able to work on right hard during the next three years...but I find the noddle [*sic*] & the stomach are antagonist powers.... What thought has to do with digesting roast beef, — I cannot say, but they are brother faculties' (*Correspondence*, II, 85). His 'Journal' shows a clear correlation between periods of illness and periods of stress associated with his work or, more rarely, with family calamities. Persistent vomiting and weakness reduced his normal workday to three or four hours, but within those hours his accomplishment was prodigious. His

assorted illnesses were 'adaptive,' not in the sense of being imaginary or invented, but in sparing him, as he points out in the *Recollections*, 'from the distractions of society and amusement' (*Autobiography*, p. 144). For Darwin's own litany of the maladies that plagued him for most of his adult life, see his 'Medical Notes' of 1865 cited in Colp, *To Be an Invalid*, pp. 83–4. Colp surveys every scrap of medical evidence and speculation, ranging from arsenic poisoning to 'neurotic hands' to 'suppressed gout,' and concludes that no single cause accounts for Darwin's many symptoms, although most 'are indicative of psychic (as opposed to organic) causes' (p. 142). Darwin continued to work productively into old age and died of coronary insufficiency at the age of 73.

40   'The Life of the Shawl,' *Lancet*, 9 (January 1954), p. 106. Dr. Good's ingenious thesis of patricide through publication has been frequently reiterated, among others by Ernest Jones in *Free Associations* and by Phyllis Greenacre in *The Quest for the Father*. In addition to 'anxiety neurosis...much complicated by genius,' Dr. Greenacre attributes to Darwin (without foundation) 'severe attacks of malaria' (New York: International University Press, 1963, pp. 32–3).

41   Letter of 20–31 December 1831, *Correspondence*, I, 187.

42   Brent, p. 32. The incident is recounted by Darwin's son George, as told to him by his father.

43   *Life and Letters*, II, 355.

44   'I do not think I gained much from him intellectually' (*Autobiography*, p. 42). Yet Robert Darwin's observations are cited more frequently in Darwin's early notebooks and manuscripts than those of any author except Charles Lyell. The intellectual interaction between father and son was especially intense during the most creative years of Darwin's life, those immediately following his return from the *Beagle*. Charles considered his father an authoritative observer of mental processes, especially of pathological states, and frequent queries to Robert find their answers in Charles's notebooks. See Edward Manier, *The Young Darwin and His Cultural Circle* (Boston: Reidel, 1978), p. 18; and *Metaphysics, Materialism, passim*.

45   *Autobiography*, p. 52. Darwin applies the analogy to his later becoming an honorary member of various royal societies.

46   See T.H. Huxley, Obituary Notice, *Proceedings of the Royal Society of London*, 44 (April 12, 1888–June 21, 1888 [London: Harrison, 1888]), p. xii, n. i.

47   Letter of May 1838, *Correspondence*, II, 85.

48   Letter of 4 February 1861, *Life and Letters*, II, 153.

49   Letter of 21–2 November 1838, *Correspondence*, II, 123.

50   *The Philosophy of the Inductive Sciences* (1840), I, 113. Cited in the *Oxford English Dictionary*.

51   The most striking instance is the last sentence of the *Recollections*:

With such moderate abilities as I possess, it is truly surprising that thus I should have influenced to a considerable extent the beliefs of scientific men on some important points.

It is not clear in this flattest of all valedictions if Darwin presumes to include himself in the genus of 'scientific men.' His surprise at the extent of his influence strikes me as wholly genuine – the dual consequence of his having been intellectually slandered as a child and self-educated as an adult.

52   See James R. Moore, 'Darwin of Down: The Evolutionist as Squarson-Naturalist,' in *The Darwinian Heritage*, pp. 435–81.

53   *Autobiography*, pp. 47–8.

54   *Ibid.*, p. 51. For the identity of the taxidermist, see R.B. Freeman's engaging *Charles Darwin: A Companion* (Hamden, CT: Dawson-Archon, 1978), p. 133.

55   Ronald W. Clark, *The Survival of Charles Darwin: A Biography of a Man and an Idea* (London: Weidenfeld and Nicolson, 1984), p. 11.

56   The full title of Paley's book is *Natural Theology; or, Evidences of the Existence and Attributes of the Deity, Collected from the Appearances of Nature*.

57   For Paley, see *Autobiography*, p. 59; for Humboldt, pp. 67–8. In 1845 he wrote to Hooker, '[m]y whole course of life is due to having read and re-read as a youth his (Personal Narrative)' (*Life and Letters*, I, 305).

58   Entry of 21 March 1835, *Charles Darwin and the Voyage of the Beagle*, ed. Nora Barlow (New York: Philosophical Library, 1946), p. 234.

59   Dr. Douglas Hubble, 'The Life of the Shawl,' *Lancet* (26 December 1953), p. 1352. Cf. '...his father was always autocratic' (Huxley and Kettlewell, p. 66).

60   See letter of 30 August 1831 to Henslow, *Correspondence*, I, 131. Darwin actually wrote two letters of declination, one to Henslow and one to George Peacock, with whom the offer had originated. Further, he asked Henslow to send a second note to Peacock 'in the chance of his not getting my letter.' Temptation loomed so large, it seems, that Darwin felt compelled to burn his bridges twice over, for he also asked Peacock to notify Captian Fitz-Roy of his decision.

61   'Young Darwin in Love and At Work,' review of *Correspondence*, I, in *The New York Times Book Review*, 21 April 1985, p. 28.

62   *Life and Letters*, I, 117.

63   *Collected Letters* I, p. 570, from the *Beagle diary*, ed. Nora Barlow, p. 400.

64   Letter of November 1879, *Life and Letters*, II, 414.

65   'He is the most open, transparent man I ever saw,' Emma wrote on the eve of her marriage (*Emma Darwin*, II, 6).

66   Compare Einstein's 'Autobiographical Notes,' begun at exactly the same age Darwin began his: 'Here I sit in order to write, at the age of 67, something like my own obituary.' Cited in James Olney, *Metaphors of Self: The Meaning of Autobiography* (Princeton: Princeton University Press, 1972), p. 183, n. 3.

67   *Autobiography*, p. 139. The same self-reification attaches to his description of the huge portfolios into which he gathered and cross-indexed a lifetime's hoard of facts. Stacked high on shelves in an alcove adjacent to his study at Down, the portfolios served him as a kind of external brain (*Autobiography*, pp. 137–8).

68   Letter of 5 September 1831, *Correspondence*, I, 142.

69   *Life and Letters*, II, 511–2.

## Chapter 8: The Oxford Elegists: Newman, Arnold, Hopkins

1   Letter to R.W. Dixon of 1879, *The Correspondence of Gerard Manley Hopkins and Richard Watson Dixon*, ed. Claude Colleer Abbott (London: Oxford University Press, 1935), p. 20.

2   Peter Snow, *Oxford Observed* (London: John Murray, 1991), p. 237.

3   'Gareth and Lynette,' ll. 203–4.

4   I have drawn details on the Church and on Newman's preaching from David J. DeLaura's 'O, Unforgettable Voice: The Memory of Newman in the Nineteenth

Century' and from R.D. Middleton's 'The Vicar of St. Mary's' in *Sources for Reinterpretation...Essays in Honor of C.L. Cline* (University of Texas at Austin, 1975). The quotes immediately following the reference to Darwin's father are from DeLaura, pp. 28, 41.

5   *The Autobiography of Charles Darwin*, ed. Nora Barlow (New York and London, 1958), p. 96.

6   Over a decade earlier Arnold had written expressing his indebtedness to Newman's 'influence and writings...the impression of which is so profound, and so mixed up with all that is most essential in what I do and say.' (Cited in Ian Ker, *John Henry Newman* (Oxford: Clarendon Press, 1988), p. 666. For Newman as the embodied spirit of Oxford, see Arnold's 'Literary Influence of Academies' (1864): '...a man who alone in Oxford of his generation, alone of many generations, conveyed to us in his genius that same charm, that same ineffable sentiment which this exquisite place itself conveys, — I mean Dr. Newman....' See David DeLaura's keenly informative account of the effect of Newman's preaching in *Sources for Reinterpretation*. 'We are dealing,' DeLaura writes, in 'O Unforgettable Voice,' 'with a phenomenon so powerful, so widespread and long continued, so awash with the deepest cross-currents of thought and feeling, that it fully deserves the term myth.' (p. 28).

7   The same imputation appears in an 1851 letter of Kingsley's on the Oxford Movement: 'In...all that school, there is an element of foppery – even in dress and manner; a fastidious, maundering, die-away effeminacy, which is mistaken for purity and refinement...' Cited in Oliver S. Buckton, 'An Unnatural State: Gender, Perversion and Newman's *Apologia Pro Vita Sua*,' *Victorian Studies*, 35 (1992), p. 372.

8   *John Henry Newman: Autobiographical Writings*, ed. Henry Tristman (London, 1956), p. 143.

9   *Apologia Pro Vita Sua*, ed. David J. DeLaura (New York: Norton, 1968), p. 16. Cited as *Apologia* below.

10   Cited in Ker, p. 544.

11   'Mr. Kingsley's Method of Disputation,' Pamphlet 2 of the *Apologia*, 1864 edition.

12   *Apologia*, p. 360.

13   John Henry Newman, 'The Tamworth Reading Room,' Discourse 6, in *Discussions and Arguments on Various Subjects* (London: Longmans, 1874–1921).

14   *Ibid.*, pp. 15–16.

15   Ker, p. 11.

16   'Memorial Verses,' ll. 43–4.

17   'The Scholar-Gipsy,' l. 69; 'Thyrsis,' l. 19.

18   In 1866 rioters agitated in Hyde Park over the Reform Bill, which extended the franchise and was passed in 1871.

19   Matthew 5:48. Arnold chose this verse as the epigraph of *Culture and Anarchy*: 'Estote ergo vos perfecti.'

20   1 Corinthians 13:4–5; *Culture and Anarchy*, ed. Samuel Lipman (New Haven and London: Yale University Press, 1994), p. 47.

21   For an excellent analysis of the complex relations between Newman and Arnold, see David J. DeLaura's *Hebrew and Hellene in Victorian England* (Austin: University of Texas Press, 1969).

22 Cited in Robert Bernard Martin, *Gerard Manley Hopkins: A Very Private Life* (1991), p. 309.

23 *Ibid.*, p. 32.

24 In the fourteenth century (and later) the Mayor of Oxford made an annual circuit of the city by boat, claiming its boundaries, starting at Magdalen Bridge and proceeding down the Cherwell, to Folly Bridge, 'following rivers and streams round the "island" of Binsey to Godstow...' See Norman MacKenzie, *A Reader's Guide to Gerard Manley Hopkins* (1981), p. 111.

25 Letter cited in Norman White, *Hopkins: A Literary Biography* (Oxford: Clarendon Press, 1992), p. 305.

26 Abbott, *Correspondence*, p. 20.

27 'Binsey Poplars' invites comparison with Hopkins's other woodland elegy, 'Spring and Fall' (1880). A young girl, Margaret (*regret* is encoded in her name) grieves over the falling of leaves in an autumnal grove ('Goldengrove unleaving'), presaging her own mortality. Composed in a moment of equipoise between the Sonnets of Rapture and the Sonnets of Desolation, 'Spring and Fall' strikes a rare middle-note among Hopkins's poems.

28 Martin, p. 212, from *Journals*, p. 230.

29 For Ruskin as Hopkins's visual master, see White, *Hopkins*, pp. 70–9, 81–2, 89, 163, and the paired plates, 12 and 14, showing Hopkins's 'Sketches in a Ruskinese point of view.'

30 Cited in White, *Hopkins*, p. 435.

31 According to a beautifully printed and illustrated guide that appeared in Oxford bookstalls in 1817, shortly after Newman matriculated, St. Margaret's Well was a site 'of great resort in popish times.' The hallowed spring near Binsey attracted countless pilgrims. See W.M. Wade, *Walks in Oxford: Comprising an Original, Historical, and Descriptive Account of the Colleges...* (Oxford: Law and Whittaber), p. 336.

32 See Snow, *Oxford Observed*, p. 174.

33 *Poems and Prose of Gerard Manley Hopkins*, ed. W.H. Gardner (Harmondsworth: Penguin, 1953), pp. 145–6.

34 See Martin, *Hopkins*, illustration 13a.

35 See White, *Hopkins*, pp. 370, 404–5, 410.

36 See Daniel A. Harris, *Inspirations Unbidden: The 'Terrible Sonnets' of Gerard Manley Hopkins* (Berkeley: University of California Press, 1982), p. xiii.

37 Letters of 17 February 1887, 1 April and 8 May 1885, cited in White, *Hopkins*, pp. 429, 392, 394.

38 See White, p. 235.

39 White, p. 459.

40 White, p. 273.

41 Martin, p. 413.

42 The Church never really knew what to do with her two most greatly gifted English converts of the nineteenth century, a point finely made in Jill Muller's *Gerard Manley Hopkins and Victorian Catholicism: A Heart in Hiding* (New York: Routledge, 2003), p. 13.

43 'Righteous *art* thou, O Lord, when I plead with thee: yet let me talk with thee of *thy* judgments: Wherefore doth the way of the wicked prosper? Wherefore are all they happy that deal very treacherously?' (Jeremiah 12:1).

44 *The Letters of Gerard Manley Hopkins to Robert Bridges*, ed. Claude Colleer Abbott (London: Oxford University Press, 1935), pp. 222, 270.

45 See MacKenzie, *Guide*, p. 203.

46 Letter of 29–30 July, 1888, cited in Abbott, *Correspondence*, p. 157; my italics.

47 Quoted in White, p. 126.

48 *Journal* 4 May, 3 June, 1866, cited in White, *Hopkins*, p. 131.

## Chapter 9: Swinburne and the Ravages of Time

1 Cf. George Lafourcade's comment: 'Il y a, dans ses plus pures inspirations, une sorte de simplicité négative d'expression, une...sobriété presque puritaine' (*La Jeunesse de Swinburne* (Strasbourg, 1928), II, 536–7).

2 *The Novels of A.C. Swinburne*, with an Introduction by Edmund Wilson (New York, 1962), pp. 24–5.

3 'Matthew Arnold's New Poems,' *The Complete Works of Algernon Charles Swinburne* (Bonchurch Edition) (London, 1927), XV, 77. All italics in quoted poems are my own.

4 'Swinburne as Poet,' *Selected Essays* (London, 1951), p. 326.

5 *The Complete Works of Algernon Charles Swinburne*, eds. Edmund Gosse and T.J. Wise (London: Heineman, 1925–7), XIII, p. 421.

6 A hero-worshipper and perfect mimic, Swinburne pays silent tribute to Browning in 'The Leper.' In Browning's 'Porphyria's Lover' (1836), an early dramatic monologue, the mad, naïve speaker strangles his beautiful, high-born lady.

7 Cf. the remarkable ninth stanza of 'The Garden of Proserpine,' in which *all* of the thirteen nouns are plural:

> There go the loves that wither,
>   The old loves with wearier wings;
> And all dead years draw thither,
>   And all disastrous things;
> Dead dreams of days forsaken,
> Blind buds that snows have shaken,
> Wild leaves that winds have taken,
>   Red strays of ruined springs.

The poem illustrates Swinburne's mastery of the music of enervation; the blurring, generic plurals, the muted imagery, and the rhymes all evoke the pause of being 'when the spirit, without fear or hope...thirsts only after the perfect sleep' (Swinburne's note).

8 When Swinburne began the poem in 1869, in emulation of what he liked to call Tennyson's 'Morte d'Albert,' he wrote to Edward Burne-Jones that the thought of Wagner's music 'ought to abash but does stimulate me' *The Swinburne Letters*, ed. Cecil Y. Lang (New Haven, 1959), II, 51. He also planned to write a poem in French on the Prelude to *Tristan* some ten years before the English premier of the opera (see Letters, II, 183). Two excellent discussions of the Wagnerian elements

in Swinburne occur in Elliott Zuckerman's *The First Hundred Years of Wagner's Tristan* (New York, 1964), and Samuel Chew's *Swinburne* (Boston, 1929).

9    *Letters*, III, 51. Cecil Lang has shown that Swinburne's disappointment in love occurred sometime between 1862–5, when he was in his mid-twenties, and that the probable cause was the marriage of his cousin Mary Gordon, with whom he was much in love, to Colonel Disney Leith. See 'Swinburne's Lost Love,' *PMLA*, LXXIV (1959), 123–30.

10   See Mario Praz's *The Romantic Agony*, 2nd ed. (London, 1951), pp. 225–6. Atalanta is indirectly, Althaea directly, responsible for Meleager's death, the play offering the unusual spectacle of both mistress and mother in the roles of *femmes fatales*. Convinced Freudians might take something of the added fact that when Meleager presents Atalanta with the hairy spoil of the wild boar, she laughs in his face. Cf. Swinburne's self-description in 'Thalassius' as 'a manchild with an ungrown God's desire.'

11   *Letters*, VI, 231. Cf. Thomas Hardy's description, in 'A Singer Asleep,' of the first effects of Swinburne's poetry upon high Victorian culture:

> It was as though a garland of red roses
> Had fallen about the hood of some smug nun
> When irresponsibly dropped as from the sun,
> In fulth of numbers freaked with musical closes,
> Upon Victoria's formal middle time
>     His leaves of rhythm and rhyme.

12   A few lines of Reginald Harewood, the autobiographical hero of *Love's Cross-Currents*, illuminate the connection in Swinburne's poetry between his sado-masochism and his hero-worship; the passage is patterned on the – for Swinburne – voluptuous metaphor of a flogging on all fours: 'When I fall in with a nature and powers above me, I cannot help going down before it. I do like admiring; service of one's masters must be good for one, it is so perfectly pleasant…I feel my betters in my blood; they send a heat and sting through one at first sight. And the delight of feeling small and giving in when one does get sight of them is beyond words…' (*Novels*, pp. 162–3).

13   *Letters*, VI, 245, 248.

14   'Failure' is too harsh a term. There are at least a dozen distinguished poems in the volume, among them 'Super Flumina Babylonis,' 'Hertha,' 'Before a Crucifix,' 'Hymn of Man,' 'Genesis,' 'Christmas Antiphones,' 'Siena,' 'Cor Cordium,' 'Tiresias,' 'On the Downs,' 'Messidor,' and 'Non Dolet'. But none of these reaches the standard set in *Poems and Ballads*, 1866, by 'The Leper,' 'Laus Veneris,' and 'The Triumph of Time,' and attained again in *Poems and Ballads*, 1878, by 'A Forsaken Garden,' 'Ave Atque Vale,' and 'A Vision of Spring in Winter.'

15   *Letters*, I, 268.

16   'Les Noyades,' set in the French Revolution, is a special case within a special case: the lovers are roped together, limb to limb, then drowned. The reader can find in the fourteenth and sixteenth stanzas the strong links in theme and diction between this apparently impersonal ballad and the autobiographical 'Triumph of Time.'

17   *Letters*, III, 12; V, 275.

18   The setting recurs a third time, with the same macabre beauty, in 'By the North Sea,' in which Swinburne describes the sterile, salt wastes along the Dunwich coast,

where whole towns have lapsed into the marshes and time bears its pasturage of spires and graves into the sea:

> Now displaced, devoured and desecrated,
> Now by Time's hands darkly disinterred,
> These poor dead that sleeping here awaited
> Long the archangel's re-creating word,
> Closed about with roofs and walls high-gated
> Till the blast of judgement should be heard,
>
> Naked, shamed, cast out of consecration,
> Corpse and coffin, yea the very graves,
> Scoffed at, scattered shaken from their station,
> Spurned and scourged of wind and sea like slaves,
> Desolate beyond man's desolation,
> Shrink and sink into the wastes of waves. (ll. 277–88)

19  For Swinburne's admiration of Turner – 'I was brought up on him…and simply revel in everything of his' – see *Letters*, III, 11; V, 216, 254, 258; VI, 72, 118 and 152n.

20  'Notes on the Text of Shelley,' *Works*, XV, 380.

21  For the archaic and hieratic quality of 'Ave Atque Vale,' see Peter Sacks's fine essay on Swinburne in *The English Elegy* (Baltimore and London: Johns Hopkins University Press, 1985), pp. 204–26.

22  Swinburne has been poorly served by anthologists. In glancing through a dozen selections of his poems, I have come across only one which includes 'A Nympholept' – the greatest and strangest of his later lyrics. To read it is to experience the terror and 'splendid oppression of nature at noon which found utterance of old in words of such singular and everlasting significance as panic and nympholepsy' (Swinburne's note). Nowhere else does the pagan purity of Swinburne's apprehension of nature come across so starkly. The poem *embodies* the pantheism for which Swinburne expounds the theologic and philosophic basis in 'Hertha,' the 'Hymn of Man,' and 'Genesis.'

23  *Letters*, I, 122.


## Chapter 10: Walter Pater and the Art of Evanescence

1  William E. Buckler (ed.), *Walter Pater: Three Major Texts* (New York: New York University Press, 1986), p. 262; hereafter cited as Buckler.

2  *Ibid.*, p. 321.

3  R.M. Seiler (ed.), *Walter Pater: A Life Remembered* (Calgary, Canada: University of Calgary Press, 1987), p. 108.

4  Hester and Clara. Clara, the younger of the two, was quite distinguished in mind and person. She taught the young Virginia Woolf Latin and Greek and was the first tutor in classics at Somerville College, Oxford.

5  Seiler, pp. 2–3, 103, 148. Seiler cites Thomas Wright's *The Life of Walter Pater* (New York: Haskell House, 1969), but Wright is often unreliable; others corroborate that Pater was 'rather hump-backed.'

6  Letter of 13 December 1894, cited in Denis Donoghue, *Walter Pater: Lover of Strange Souls* (New York: Alfred A. Knopf, 1995), p. 14.

7  Seiler, p. 162.

8    For the frog, see Michael Levey's *The Case of Walter Pater* (London: Thames and Hudson, 1978), p. 201. For the carp, see Gerald C. Monsman's *Walter Pater's Art of Autobiography* (New Haven: Yale University Press, 1980), p. 31. To this bestiary, I might add that of bulldog. The novelist Paul Bourget compared Pater to 'un amant de Circe transforme en dogue.' Cited in Kenneth Clark (ed.), *The Renaissance: Studies in Art and Poetry* (Limited Editions Club, 1976), Introduction, p. ix. The cruelest comment of all is Lionel Johnson's: 'An ugly pig, though learned and charming too.' Cited in Donoghue, p. 77.

9    Levey, pp. 170–1.

10   Walter Pater, *Marius the Epicurean*, ed. Michael Levey (Penguin, 1985), p. 184. Hereafer cited as *Marius*.

11   'Overtures to Salome,' in *Golden Codgers* (New York and London: Oxford University Press, 1973), p. 53.

12   From a review of *Imaginary Portraits*, in the *Pall Mall Gazette*, 11 June 1887, cited in Seiler, *Walter Pater: The Critical Heritage* (London and Boston: Routledge, 1980), p. 165.

13   'Poems by William Morris,' *Westminster Review*, 1868, pp. 303, 309.

14   'Diminuendo,' from *The Incomparable Max: A Selection*, introduced by S.C. Roberts (London: Heinemann, 1962), p. 59.

15   See Gerald Monsman's exemplary edition (Greensboro: ELT Press, 1995), p. 109.

16   'The Age of Athletic Prizemen,' from *Greek Studies*, ed. Charles L. Shadwell (New York: Macmillan, 1897), p. 307. Pater, on his first tour of Italy in 1865, was accompanied by Shadwell, then a strikingly handsome Oxford undergraduate.

17   *Gaston*, p. 101.

18   *Ibid.*, p. 107.

19   *Ibid.*, p. 106.

20   *Ibid.*, pp. 108–9.

21   Donoghue, pp. 6–7. For an excellent set of essays touching on themes I discuss in this chapter, see *Comparative Criticism* vol. 17. Ed. E. S. Shaffer. (Cambridge: Cambridge University Press, 1995).

22   Cited in Lawrence Evans (ed.), *Letters of Walter Pater* (Oxford: Clarendon Press, 1970), p. xxix.

23   'Child in the House,' from *Imaginary Portraits*, Eugene J. Brzenk ed., (New York: Harper & Row, 1964), p. 20. All references from 'Child in the House' are from this edition, hereafter cited as Brzenk.

24   *Ibid.*, p. 17.

25   In 1842 Pater's widowed mother moved from London's Commercial Road to the village of Enfield, eleven miles north of the city, where the family lived for ten years. This is the idealized house in 'The Child in the House' that Flavian, like Pater, sadly leaves at the age of twelve.

26   For the definitive study of Pater's influence on Woolf, see Perry Meisel, *The Absent Father: Virginia Woolf and Walter Pater* (New Haven and London: Yale University Press, 1980).

27   'I grew up / Foster'd alike by beauty and by fear.' Book I, 305–6, 1805 version.

28   The strangely speaking wind blows *through* (not *in*) his ears, as through a mountain crevasse, for he has become a kind of animated natural object. Only Wordsworth could create great poetry out of the bald redundance of the closing lines ('sky...sky...motion moved').

29  *Gaston*, p. 109.

30  Walter Pater, 'Preface,' *The Renaissance: Studies in Art and Poetry* ed. by Donald L. Hill (Berkeley: University of California Press, 1980), p. xxiii. Hereafter cited as *The Renaissance*.

31  *Ibid.*, pp. 85–6.

32  'Poems by William Morris' (1868), *The Westminster Review*, p. 302. Pater softens the sentence in the 1889 reprint in *Appreciations*, then drops it altogether in later editions.

33  Brzenk, p. 20.

34  *Ibid.*, p. 21.

35  'My Heart Leaps Up.'

36  *The Renaissance*, p. 160.

37  *Ibid.*, pp. 160–1.

38  *Ibid.*, p. 83.

39  Once assumed to be by Leonardo but actually by Caravaggio. See Levey, *The Case of Walter Pater*, p. 130.

40  *The Renaissance*, p. 81.

41  *Romantic Image* (New York: Vintage Books, 1957), pp. 64–5.

42  *The Renaissance*, p. 183.

43  *Ibid.*, p. 106.

44  *Suspiria de Profundis*, in *Confessions of an English Opium Eater and Other Writings*, ed. Aileen Ward (New York: Signet, 1966), pp. 129–33.

45  I am indebted to Alexandra Mullen for several details in this paragraph. See her Columbia University dissertation, 'The Dead Child and the Victorian Conscience' (1994), p. 4. For Dickens's 'insatiability,' see Levey, *The Case of Walter Pater*, p. 129.

46  Devout Christians were not the only readers who recoiled from *The Renaissance*. George Eliot found it 'quite poisonous in its false principles of criticism and false conceptions of life' (*The Renaissance*, p. 446). But Pater was genuinely surprised and distressed by the hostile response in journals and from pulpits. In this he resembles Darwin, who had been dismayed by the much greater storm aroused by *The Origin of Species*. Much has been written in recent years on the homophobic reaction to *The Renaissance* and its thwarting of Pater's career at Oxford. See especially essays by Billie Andrew Inman and Laurel Brake in *Pater in the 1990s*, eds. Laurel Brake and Ian Small (Greensboro, NC: ELT Press, 1991).

47  *The Renaissance*, p. 90.

48  2 Samuel 1: 23.

49  *The Renaissance* pp. xix–xx.

50  *Ibid.*, pp. xix–xx.

51  *Ibid.*, p. 3.

52  *Modern Painters* I, 'Definition of Greatness in Art.'

53  'The School of Giorgione,' *The Renaissance*, p. 104.

54  Cited in Ellmann, *Golden Codgers*, p. 46.

55  *The Renaissance*, p. 49.

56  *Ibid.*, p. 50.

57  *Ibid.*, p. 136.

58  *Ibid.*, p. 138.

59    *Ibid.*, p. 104.

60    *Ibid.*, p. 113.

61    'All art constantly aspires towards the condition of music.' *Ibid.*, p. 106.

62    *Ibid.*, p. 82.

63    *Ibid.*, p. 93.

64    *Ibid.*, p. 93.

65    'Aesthetic Poetry.' Originally published as 'Poems by William Morris,' *Westminster Review* (October 1868), p. 307.

66    *New Library Edition of the Works of Walter Pater*, 10 vols (London Macmillan, 1910), vol. 6, pp. 72–3.

67    Pater, like Darwin, lacked the term *gene*. But Pater's 'laws...of heredity' in part points to the concept.

68    The painting, not a true fresco, is on the refectory wall of Sta. Maria della Grazie in Milan. Pater points out that Leonardo used oils on damp plaster, a mixture doomed to impermanence.

69    *The Renaissance*, p. 77, italics mine. Pater actually tones down Vasari's sentence in the first (1550) edition of *Le vite de' più eccellenti pittori...*: 'His cast of mind was so heretical that he did not adhere to any religion, deeming perhaps that it was better to be a philosopher than a Christian.'

70    *Ibid.*, p. 77.

71    *Ibid.*, pp. 95, 233. I have restored the last two sentences, which Pater cut from the 1893 text. For Pater's play on the word Host, see Carolyn Williams's keen analysis in *Transfigured World: Walter Pater's Aesthetic Historicism* (Ithaca, NY: Cornell University Press, 1989), p. 98.

72    *Ibid.*, p. 65.

73    *Ibid.*, p. 98.

74    See Introduction, *The Oxford Book of English Verse*, p. viii. Yeats makes three trivial errors in his transcription that I have let stand.

75    *The Renaissance*, p. 177.

76    *Ibid.*, pp. 146, 152. Pater tones down *fervid* to *fervent* in the book version of the essay.

77    Michael Levey makes this point in *The Case of Walter Pater*, p. 133.

78    *The Renaissance*, p. 197.

79    Cf. this passage from Mme. de Staël: '[Winckelmann] felt in himself an ardent attraction toward the south. In German imaginations even now traces are to be found of that love of the sun, that weariness of the north...' Cited by Pater in *ibid.*, p. 142.

80    *Ibid.*, p. 152.

81    Winckelmann, *History of Ancient Art*, trans. G. Henry Lodge (New York: Frederick Ungar, 1968), II, 312–13. From Vol. IV, Bk. 11, 'Greek Art Among the Romans.'

82    *The Renaissance*, p. 177. The Yeats quotation is from 'Byzantium,' l. 32.

83    *Ibid.*, p. 177.

84    'Winckelmann,' I, 201, #23.

85    *Marius*, p. 55.

86    *The Renaissance*, pp. 174, 183.

87    Much of this passage is a verbatim borrowing from Pater's first work, 'Diaphaneite,' which he read to Old Mortality, an Oxford literary society, in 1864.

88 Romans 4:15.

89 For centuries first the Church, then the State, punished homosexual acts not as such but under the general rubric of Sodomy. Same-sex sex was not a separate category of crime but a sin against the Biblical injunction to be fruitful and multiply. The Criminal Law Amendment Act criminalized all male homosexual acts – the Queen is said to have been incredulous that homosexual acts might be committed between women – in public or private. The law was not revoked until 1967. Pater wrote in the tense interim just before the criminalization of homosexual acts and their subsequent treatment as a 'disease.' This conceptual shift from the sin of Sodomy to the sickness of homosexuality finds its counterpart in our designating as a 'nervous breakdown' or 'personality disorder' what the early Victorians called a 'spiritual crisis.'

90 I borrow this phrase from Richard Jenkyns's discussion of the statue in his deeply learned and witty *The Victorians and Ancient Greece* (Cambridge: Harvard University Press, 1980), p. 136, where Jenkyns also cites the phrase I quote from Mrs. Browning.

91 *The Renaissance*, p. 187.

92 *Ibid.*, p. 188.

93 Compare Pater's 'thick wall of personality' to this sentence from 'A Sketch of the Past': 'we are sealed vessels afloat upon what it is convenient to call reality.' *Virginia Woolf: Moments of Being*, ed. Jeanne Schulkind (New York: Harcourt Brace Jovanovich, 1985), p. 142.

94 Matthew 16:25.

95 *The Renaissance*, pp. 189–90.

96 Psalms 103; Job 7: 9–10.

97 Barbara Charlesworth makes this point in Dark Passages (Madison: University of Wisconsin Press, 1965); see pp. 34–35, 39–40.

98 Cited in *The Renaissance*, pp. 447–48.

99 Levey, 'Introduction', *Marius*, p. 7.

100 *Marius*, p. 48.

101 Levey, *Marius*, Introduction, p. 11. See pp. 18–19 for numerous parallels between the biographies of Pater and Marius.

102 *Marius*, p. 2.

103 *Marius*, p. 38.

104 The late Jay Fellows brilliantly explored this shadowy region in *Tombs, Despoiled and Haunted: 'Under-Textures' and 'After-Thoughts' in Walter Pater* (Stanford: Stanford University Press, 1991).

105 *Marius*, pp. 228, 231.

106 See Levey, *Marius*, p. 52.

107 *Marius*, p. 93.

108 *Marius*, p. 270.

109       ...they weep here
For how the world goes, and our life that passes
Touches their hearts.

                  (*Aeneid*, Bk. I, ll. 628–30, trans. Fitzgerald)

110 *Gaston*, pp. 11–12.

111   'Poems by William Morris,' p. 300.

112   *Prelude*, VI, 556–73 (1805 ed).

113   *Marius*, p. 209.

114   *Marius*, p. 233.

115   *Marius*, p. 233.

116   *Apologia*, ed. David J. DeLaura (New York: W. W. Norton, 1968), p. 37; *Aeneid* I, 405.

117   *Fortnightly Review*, Part II, Feb. 1876, p. 276.

118   See Linda Dowling's fine article on 'Walter Pater and Archaeology: the Reconciliation with Earth,' *Victorian Studies*, 31 (1987), pp. 209–31.

119   *Marius*, p. 228. Cf. Mona Lisa, 'who has been dead many times.'

120   See Wright, I, 21 and Seiler, *Life*, p. 226.

121   Ian Fletcher, Walter Pater (London: Longmans, 1959), p. 24. This brief monograph, along with Graham Hough's essay on Pater in *The Last Romantics* (London: Duckworth, 1949), remains indispensable.

122   *Marius*, p. 294.


## Chapter 11: Varieties of Infernal Experience: The Fall of the City in Victorian Literature

1   See Mircea Eliade, *The Myth of the Eternal Return*, trans. Willard R. Trask (New York, 1954), p. 10.

2   See Eliade, Chapter I, *passim*; also, Lewis Mumford, *The City in History* (New York, 1961), pp. 31, 35, 48, 69, 87; Sigfried Giedion, *The Eternal Present: The Beginnings of Architecture* (New York, 1963), p. 217.

3   'The *Iliad* or the Poem of Force,' in *The Proper Study*, ed. Quentin Anderson and Joseph A. Mazzeo (New York, 1962), p. 25.

4   For the shift from utopia to dystopia, see Chad Walsh, *From Utopia to Nightmare* (New York, 1963), p. 14.

5   *Chambers' Edinburgh Journal*, 1858, and General Napier, writing in 1839, both quoted in Asa Briggs, *Victorian Cities* (London, 1963), pp. 83, 131.

6   Prologue and Chapter I, *The Epic of Gilgamesh*, trans. N. K. Sandars (Baltimore [Penguin Classics], 1960), pp. 59–67. The wild man consorting with animals, like the naked Adam, recalls the primal state when man could 'talk' to the animals, not because he knew their language, but because he *was* an animal. From this point of view, the exchange of innocence for wisdom associated with the Fall symbolizes that astounding modification of mind from animal pre-consciousness to human self-consciousness.

7   'And Cain went out from the presence of the Lord...and builded a city, and called the name of the city, after the name of his son, Enoch' (Genesis 4:16–17).

8   I am aware of other plausible readings of 'Satanic Mills.' See Harold Bloom and David Erdman, *The Poetry and Prose of William Blake* (New York: Doubleday, 1965), pp. 823–4.

9   Thomas Carlyle, *Past and Present* ed. Richard D. Altick (New York: New York University Press, 1977), p. 8.

10   *The Genius of John Ruskin: Selections*, ed. John D. Rosenberg (New York, 1963), p. 224. For the description of Pisa that follows, see pp. 225–6.

11 Gerard Manley Hopkins's private terrors of soul have so interested us that we forget that he, too, lived and preached in areas such as Ruskin describes. Cf. this quatrain from 'God's Grandeur':

> Generations have trod, have trod, have trod;
> And all is seared with trade; bleared, smeared with toil;
> And wears man's smudge and shares man's smell; the soil
> Is bare now, nor can foot feel, being shod.

12 Charles Lamb, the most urbanized of Romantics, typifies the insider's view of London. 'I was born…in a crowd,' he writes; 'this has begot in me an entire affection for that way of life, amounting to an almost insurmountable aversion from solitude and rural scenes.' Lamb's London is as teeming and strange as Wordsworth's, but its frenzied vitality tickled his grotesque fancy: 'Humour, Interest, Curiosity, suck at her measureless breasts without a possibility of being satiated.' ('The Londoner,' in *Miscellaneous Essays and Sketches* [London, 1929], pp. 7–8).

13 Trans. W.O. Henderson and W. H. Chaloner (Oxford, 1958), p. 31.

14 The drawing is reproduced in Joan Evans's *The Victorians* (Cambridge, 1966), Plate 89. Asa Briggs cites the 'Eternal Mind' quotation in *Victorian Cities* (Harmondsworth: Penguin, 1968). But he also cites Dickens's description of Leeds as 'a beastly place, one of the nastiest places I know' (p. 87).

15 The descriptions of the Black Country that follow are very nearly incredible, yet strangely familiar. The familiarity perhaps stems from a sense of *déjà vu*, as of Milton's Hell revisited:

> The dismal Situation waste and wilde,
> A Dungeon horrible, on all sides round
> As one great Furnace flam'd, yet from those flames
> No light, but rather darkness visible
> Serv'd only to discover sights of woe,
> Regions of sorrow, doleful shades, where peace
> And rest can never dwell, hope never comes
> That comes to all…   (Book I, ll. 60–7)

16 See Mumford, pp. 459–60; Briggs, p. 147.

17 'The Nature of Gothic,' in *The Genius of John Ruskin*, p. 180.

18 *Journeys to England and Ireland*, ed. J. P. Mayer (New Haven, 1958), pp. 94, 105.

19 *Journeys*, pp. 106–8.

20 *Condition of the Working Class*, pp. 60–1, 64, 71.

21 See *Hard Times*, Book I, Chap. V: 'It was a town of machinery and tall chimneys, out of which interminable serpents of smoke trailed themselves for ever and ever, and never got uncoiled. It had a black canal in it, and a river that ran purple with ill-smelling dye, and vast piles of building full of windows where there was a rattling and a trembling all day long, and where the piston of the steam-engine worked monotonously up and down, like the head of an elephant in a state of melancholy madness. It contained several large streets all very like one another, and many small streets still more like one another, inhabited by people equally like one another, who all went in and out at the same hours, with the same sound upon the same pavements, to do the same work, and to whom every day was the same as yesterday and to-morrow, and every year the counterpart of the last and the next.'

22    The quotation is from Lewis Mumford's *The City in History*, p. 413. The chapter, ironically entitled 'Paleotechnic Paradise: Coketown,' paints a bleak and potent picture indeed, corrected in detail but not in substance by Asa Briggs's *Victorian Cities*.

23    *Jerusalem*, Chapter I, Plate 5, l. 5.

24    *The Works of John Ruskin*, ed. E.T. Cook and Alexander Wedderburn (London, 1903–12), XX, 113.

25    'The Lamp of Memory,' in *The Genius of John Ruskin*, p. 132.

26    When asked for the source of 'Childe Roland,' Browning replied that he was aware of none and that the poem 'came upon me as a kind of dream,' a curious parallel to Dickens' comparison of the landscape in *The Old Curiosity Shop* to a nightmare. For Browning's dream-like source for 'Childe Roland,' see William Clyde DeVane, *A Browning Handbook* (New York: Appleton-Century-Crofts, 1955), p. 29; for the engine of torture, see stanza xxiv.

27    Lynch (Cambridge, Mass., 1960), p. 125. Cf. the account on p. 126 of a scene from a contemporary Italian novel in which the Florentines in their daily walks continue to follow the outlines of non-existent streets through a war-ravaged section of their city.

28    Hence Ruskin argued in *The Seven Lamps of Architecture* for the preservation of ancient buildings not as an antiquarian luxury but as a civic and psychological necessity. Cf. the end of 'The Lamp of Memory':

> The very quietness of nature is gradually withdrawn from us; thousands who once in their necessarily prolonged travel were subjected to an influence, from the silent sky and slumbering fields, more effectual than known or confessed, now bear with them even there the ceaseless fever of their life; and along the iron veins that traverse the frame of our country, beat and flow the fiery pulses of its exertion, hotter and faster every hour. All vitality is concentrated through those throbbing arteries into the central cities; the country is passed over like a green sea by narrow bridges, and we are thrown back in continually closer crowds upon the city gates. The only influence which can in any wise there take the place of that of the woods and fields, is the power of ancient Architecture.

29    See R.A. Forsyth, 'The Victorian Self-Image and the Emergent City Sensibility,' *University of Toronto Quarterly*, XXXIII (1963), pp. 61–77.

30    Briggs, p. 14.

31    Chapter 20. Of course such new experiences produced radically differing responses in different temperaments. The actress Fanny Kemble (1809–93), for example, described her first railroad journey as follows: 'You can't imagine how strange it seemed to be journeying on thus, without any visible cause of progress other than the magical machine, with the flying white breath and rhythmical unvarying pace.... When I closed my eyes this sensation of flying was quite delightful.... I had a perfect sense of security and not the slightest fear' (*Early Victorian England*, ed. G.M. Young [Oxford, 1934], II, 290). And Tennyson's ride on the first Liverpool-Manchester run in 1830 resulted in this celebrated couplet from 'Locksley Hall':

> Not in vain the distance beacons. Forward, forward let us range,
> Let the great world spin forever down the ringing grooves of change.

John Stuart Mill points out in his essay on 'The Spirit of the Age' that the unique quality of the moment was its extreme self-consciousness of change, and that to men who identified with the present, such change was 'a subject of exultation'; to men still bound to the past, it was a source 'of terror.' Hence it is that the Victorian period appears to us in two contradictory guises, as The Age of Progress, and The Age of Anxiety. Almost all of the writers on the city with whom I am dealing greeted the new period with apprehension, but I would be guilty of distortion were I not to acknowledge an opposing tradition, best exemplified by the brilliant Philistine Macaulay, for whom an acre of crowded Middlesex was 'worth a principality in Utopia.' (Review of Southey's *Colloquies*). For an excellent analysis of Victorian attitudes toward time and change, see Jerome H. Buckley's *The Triumph of Time* (Cambridge, Mass., 1966).

32    *The Genius of John Ruskin*, pp. 435–40.

33    See J. Hillis Miller's *Charles Dickens: The World of His Novels* (Cambridge, Mass., 1965), pp. 78–9. Miller persuasively demonstrates the connection between 'any beautiful landscape' in *Oliver Twist* and a desire for a 'prenatal paradise' linked with death.

34    Henry Mayhew and John Binny, *The Criminal Prisons of London* (London, 1862), p. 143.

35    Cited in unpubl. Diss. (Columbia, 1967) by Elizabeth Beaujour, 'The Invisible Land: A Study of the Imagination of Iurii Olesha,' p. 164.

36    'The Two Boyhoods,' *The Genius of John Ruskin*, pp. 114–15.

# Bibliography

Abrams, M. H. *Natural Supernaturalism*. New York: Norton, 1973.

Adams, James Eli. 'Woman Red in Tooth and Claw: Nature and the Feminine in Tennyson and Darwin.' *Victorian Studies*, 33 (1989): 7–27.

Arnold, Matthew. *Matthew Arnold (Oxford Poetry Library)*. Ed. Miriam Allot. London: Oxford University Press, 1995.

Arrowsmith, William. 'Ruskin's Fireflies.' *The Ruskin Polygon*. Ed. John Dixon Hunt and Faith M. Holland. Manchester: Manchester University Press, 1982.

Beaujour, Elizabeth. 'The Invisible Land: A Study of the Imagination of Iurii Olesha.' Dissertation, Columbia University, 1967.

Beer, Gillian. 'Darwin's Reading and the Fictions of Development.' *The Darwinian Heritage*. Ed. David Kohn. Princeton: Princeton University Press, 1985.

Beerbohm, Max. 'Diminuendo.' *The Incomparable Max: A Selection, Introduced by S. C. Roberts*. London: Heinemann, 1962.

———. *The Poet's Corner*. London: William Heinemann, 1904.

Blake, William. *The Poetry & Prose of William Blake*. Ed. Harold Bloom & David Erdman. New York: Doubleday, 1965.

Boas, George. 'Mona Lisa in the History of Taste.' *Journal of the History of Ideas*, 1 (1940): 207–24.

Brake, Laurel and Ian Small, eds. *Pater in the 1990s*. Greensboro, NC: ELT Press, 1991.

Brent, Peter. *Charles Darwin*. London: Heinemann, 1981.

Bridge, Ursula, ed. *W.B. Yeats and T. Sturge Moore: Their Correspondence 1901–1937*. London: Routledge, 1953.

Briggs, Asa. *Victorian Cities*. London: Penguin Books, 1963.

Buckley, Jerome H. *The Triumph of Time*. Cambridge: Harvard University Press, 1966.

———. *The Turning Key: Autobiography & the Subjective Impulse Since 1800*. Cambridge: Harvard University Press, 1984.

Butlin, Martin and Evelyn Joll. *The Paintings of J.M.W. Turner*, Rev. Ed. New Haven and London: Yale University Press, 1984.

Carlyle, Thomas. *The Collected Letters of Thomas and Jane Welsh Carlyle*. Ed. Charles Richard Sanders, et.al. Durham, N.C.: Duke University Press, 1970.

———. *The French Revolution: A History*. Ed. John D. Rosenberg. New York: Random House, 2002.

———. *Past and Present*. Ed. Richard Altick. New York: New York University Press, 1977.

———. *Reminiscences*. Ed. Charles Eliot Norton. 1932. London: Dent, 1972.

———. *Sartor Resartus*. Ed. Charles F. Harrold. New York: Odyssey Press, 1937.

————. *The Works of Thomas Carlyle*. 30 vols. Ed. H. D. Traill. Chapman & Hall, 1896–1901.

Clark, Kenneth, ed. 'Introduction.' *The Renaissance: Studies in Art and Poetry*. By Walter Pater. New York: Limited Editions Club, 1976.

Clark, Ronald W. *The Survival of Charles Darwin: A Biography of a Man and an Idea*. London: Weidenfeld & Nicholson, 1984.

Coleridge, Samuel Taylor. *The Table Talk and Omniana of Samuel Taylor Coleridge*. Ed. Coventry Patmore. London: Oxford University Press, 1917.

Colp, Ralph. 'Notes on Charles Darwin's Autobiography.' *Journal of the History of Biology* 18 (1985): 357–401.

————. *To Be An Invalid: The Illness of Charles Darwin*. Chicago: University of Chicago Press, 1977.

Cook, E.T. *The Life of John Ruskin*. 2 vols. London: George Allen, 1911.

Craft, Christopher. '"Descend, and Touch, and Enter": Tennyson's Strange Manner of Address.' *Genders* 1 (1988): 83–101.

Dante Alighieri. *Inferno*. Trans. Allen Mandelbaum. Berkeley: University of California Press, 1980.

————. *Paradiso*. Trans. Allen Mandelbaum. Berkeley: University of California Press, 1984.

Darwin, Charles. *The Autobiography of Charles Darwin*. Ed. Nora Barlow. New York: Norton, 1958.

————. *The Correspondence of Charles Darwin*. 12 vols. Ed. Frederick Burkhardt and Sydney Smith. Cambridge: Cambridge University Press, 1983–2001.

————. *The Formation of Vegetable Mould Through the Action of Worms, with Observations on Their Habits*. London: Murray, 1881.

————. *Metaphysics, Materialism, and the Evolution of Mind: Early Writings of Charles Darwin*. Ed. Paul H. Barrett, with commentary by Howard E. Gruber. Chicago: University of Chicago Press, 1980.

————. *The Origin of Species*. Intro. Ernst Mayr. Boston: Harvard University Press, 1975.

Darwin, Francis. *Life and Letters of Charles Darwin, Including an Autobiographical Chapter*. 2 vols. New York: Appleton, 1896.

Dellamora, Richard. *Masculine Desire: The Sexual Politics of Victorian Aestheticism*. Chapel Hill, NC: University of North Carolina Press, 1990.

De Quincey, Thomas. *Confessions of an English Opium-Eater and Other Writings*. Ed. Aileen Ward. New York: Signet, 1966.

DeVane, William Clyde. *A Browning Handbook*. New York: Appleton, 1955.

Dickens, Charles. *Bleak House (Penguin Classics)*. New York: Penguin USA, 2003.

————. *Dombey and Son (Penguin Classics)*. London: Penguin Books, 2002.

————. *Hard Times (Penguin Classics)*. London: Penguin Books, 2003.

Donoghue, Denis. *Walter Pater: Lover of Strange Souls*. New York: Knopf, 1995.

Dowling, Linda. 'Walter Pater and Archaeology: The Reconciliation with Earth.' *Victorian Studies*, 31 (1987): 209–31.

Egerton, Judy. *The Fighting Temeraire*. London: National Gallery, 1995.

Eliade, Mircea. *The Myth of the Eternal Return*. Trans. Willard R. Trask. Princeton: Princeton University Press, 1954.

Eliot, T.S. 'In Memoriam.' *Selected Essays*. London: Faber and Faber, 1951.

————. 'Swinburne as Poet.' *Selected Essays*. London: Faber and Faber, 1951.

_____. *The Waste Land and Other Poems*. Mineola, New York: Dover Publications, 1998.

Ellmann, Richard. 'Overtures to Salome.' *Golden Codgers*. New York: Oxford University Press, 1973.

Emerson, Sheila. *Ruskin: The Genesis of Invention*. Cambridge: Cambridge University Press, 1993.

Engels, Friedrich. *The Condition of the Working Class in England in 1844*. Trans and ed. W. O. Henderson & W. H. Chaloner. Oxford: Blackwells, 1958.

*Epic of Gilgamesh*. Trans. N. K. Sanders. Baltimore: Penguin, 1960.

Fellows, Jay. *Tombs, Despoiled and Haunted: Under-Textures and After-Thoughts in Walter Pater*. Stanford: Stanford University Press, 1991.

Fleischman, Avrom. 'Ruskin's *Praeterita*: The Enclosed Garden.' *Figures of Autobiography*. Berkeley: University of California Press, 1983.

Fletcher, Ian. *Walter Pater*. London: Longmans, 1959.

Fontaney, Pierre. 'Ruskin and Paradise Regained.' *Victorian Studies*, 12 (1969): 347–56.

Forsyth, R. A. 'The Victorian Self-Image & The Emergent City Sensibility.' *University of Toronto Quarterly*, 33 (1963): 61–77.

Freeman, R. B. *The Works of Charles Darwin: an Annotated Handlist*. 2$^{nd}$ ed. Hamden, CT: Dawson-Archon, 1977.

Freud, Sigmund. *Leonardo da Vinci and a Memory of His Childhood*. Trans. Alan Tyson. New York: Norton, 1961.

_____. 'The Sexual Aberrations.' *Three Essays on the Theory of Sexuality*. New York: Basic Books, 1962.

Froude, James Anthony. *Thomas Carlyle: A History of His Life in London, 1834–1881*. 2 vols. New York: Scribner, 1910.

Gelpi, Barbara Charlesworth. *Dark Passages: the Decadent Consciousness in Victorian Literature*. Madison, WI: University of Wisconsin Press, 1965.

Giedion, Sigfried. *The Eternal Present: The Beginnings of Architecture*. New York: Pantheon Books, 1963.

Gilbert, Eliot L. 'The Female King: Tennyson's Arthurian Apocalypse.' *PMLA*, 98 (1983): 863–78.

Good, Rankine. 'The Life of the Shawl.' *Lancet*, 9 (January, 1954): 106–7.

Gould, Stephen Jay. 'Young Darwin in Love and at Work.' *New York Times Book Review*, 21 April, 1985: 27–8.

Greenacre, Phyllis. *The Quest for the Father*. New York: International University Press, 1963.

Hallam, Arthur. *The Writings of Arthur Hallam*. Ed. T. H. Vail Motter. New York: MLA, 1943.

Helsinger, Elizabeth K. 'The Structure of Ruskin's *Praeterita*.' *Approaches to Victorian Autobiography*. Ed. George P. Landow. Athens, OH: Ohio University Press, 1979.

Henderson, Heather. 'Revelation and Recurrence in Ruskin's *Praeterita*.' *The Victorian Self: Autobiography and Biblical Narrative*. Ithaca, New York: Cornell University Press, 1989.

Hilton, Tim. *John Ruskin: The Early Years: 1819–1859*. New Haven: Yale University Press, 1985.

_____. *John Ruskin: The Later Years: 1860–1900*. New Haven: Yale University Press, 2000.

Holroyd, Michael. *Lytton Strachey: A Biography*. London: Heinemann, 1970.

Hough, Graham. *The Last Romantics*. London: Ducksworth, 1949.

Hubble, Douglas. 'The Life of the Shawl.' *Lancet.*, 8 (December, 1953): 1351–4.

Humboldt, Alexander Friedrich von. *Personal Narrative of Travels to the Equinoctial Regions of the New Continent During the Years 1799–1804*. Trans. Helen Maria Williams. 7 vols. London: Longman, 1814–29.

Huxley, Julian and H. B. D. Kettlewell. *Charles Darwin and His World*. New York: Viking, 1965.

Huxley, T. H. 'Obituary Notice' [of Charles Darwin]. *Proceedings of the Royal Society of London* 44 (12 April 1888–21 June 1888). London: Harrison, 1888.

Jenkyns, Richard. *The Victorians and Ancient Greece*. Cambridge: Harvard University Press, 1980.

Kaplan, Fred. *Thomas Carlyle: A Biography*. Ithaca, New York: Cornell University Press, 1983.

Kempf, Edward J. 'Charles Darwin – The Affective Sources of His Inspiration and Anxiety Neurosis.' *Psychoanalytic Review*, 5 (1918): 151–92.

Ker, Ian *John Henry Newman* Oxford: Clarendon Press, 1998.

Kermode, Frank. *Romantic Image*. New York: Vintage Books, 1957.

Kolb, Jack. 'Morte d'Arthur: The Death of Arthur Henry Hallam.' *Biography*, 9 (1986): 37–58.

Lafourcade, George. *La Jeunesse de Swinburne*. 2 vols. London: Oxford University Press, 1928.

Lamb, Charles. 'The Londoner.' *The Collected Essays of Charles Lamb. Vol. 2, Miscellaneous Essays and Sketches*. London: J. M. Dent & Sons, 1929.

Lang, Cecil Y. *The Swinburne Letters*. 6 vols. New Haven: Yale University Press, 1959.

————. 'Swinburne's Lost Love.' *PMLA*, 74 (1959): 123–130.

Lefebvre, Georges. *The French Revolution From 1793 to 1799, Vol.2*. Trans. John Hall Stewart & James Friguglietti. New York: Columbia University Press, 1964.

Leon, Derrick. *Ruskin: The Great Victorian*. London: Routledge, 1949.

Levey, Michael. *The Case of Walter Pater*. London: Thames, 1978.

Litchfield, Henrietta, ed. *Emma Darwin: A Century of Family Letters 1792–1896*. New York: Appleton, 1915.

Lynch, Kevin. *The Image of the City*. Cambridge: MIT University Press, 1960.

Malory, Thomas. *Le Morte d'Arthur*. Ed. Joseph Haslewood. 3 vols. London: R. Wilks, 1816.

Mannier, Edward. *The Young Darwin and His Cultural Circle*. Boston: Reidel, 1978.

Martin, Robert B. *Tennyson: The Unquiet Heart*. London: Oxford University Press, 1980.

Mayhew, Henry. *London Labour and the London Poor*. 4 vols. (1851–62). Intro. John D. Rosenberg. New York: Dover, 1968.

Mayhew, Henry and John Binny. *The Criminal Prisons of London*. London: Bohn & Company, 1862.

McMullen, Buck and James R. Kincaid. 'Tennyson, Hallam's Corpse, Milton's Murder, and Poetic Exhibitionism.' *Nineteenth Century Literature*, 45 (September, 1990).

Meisel, Perry. *The Absent Father: Virginia Woolf and Walter Pater*. New Haven: Yale University Press, 1980.

Meteyard, Eliza. *A Group of Englishmen*. London: Longmans, 1871.

Mill, John Stuart. *Autobiography and Other Writings*. Ed. Jack Stillinger. Boston: Houghton Mifflin, 1969.

————. 'The Spirit of the Age.' *Mill: The Spirit of the Age, On Liberty, The Subjection of Woman*. Ed. Alan Ryan. New York: W. W. Norton & Company, 1996.

Miller, J. Hillis. *Charles Dickens: The World of His Novels*. Cambridge: Harvard University Press, 1965.

Monsman, Gerald C. *Walter Pater's Art of Autobiography*. New Haven: Yale University Press, 1980.

Morris, William. *News From Nowhere*. Vol.16 in *The Collected Works of William Morris*. 24 vols. Ed. May Morris. London: Longmans, Green, 1910–15.

Mullen, Alexandra. 'The Dead Child and the Victorian Conscience.' Dissertation, Columbia University, 1994.

Muller, Jill. *Gerard Manley Hopkins and Victorian Catholicism: A Heart in Hiding*. New York: Routledge, 2003.

Mumford, Lewis. *The City in History: Its Origins, Its Transformations, and Its Prospects*. New York: Harcourt, Brace & World, 1961.

Newman, John Henry. *Apologia Pro Vita Sua*. Ed. David J. De Laura. New York: Norton, 1968.

Olney, James. *Metaphors of Self: The Meaning of Autobiography*. Princeton: Princeton University Press, 1972.

Paley, William. *Natural Theology; or Evidences of the Existence & Attributes of the Deity, Collected From the Appearances of Nature*. Philadelphia: John Morgan by H. Maxwell, 1802.

Pater, Walter. 'The Age of Athletic Prizemen.' *Greek Studies*. Ed. Charles L. Shadwell. New York: Macmillan, 1897.

————. 'The Child in the House.' *Imaginary Portraits*. Ed. Eugene J. Brzenk. New York: Harper & Row, 1964.

————. *Gaston de Latour*. Ed. Gerald Monsman. Greensboro, NC: ELT Press, 1995.

————. *Letters of Walter Pater*. Ed. Lawrence Evans. Oxford: Clarendon Press, 1970.

————. *Marius the Epicurean*. Ed. Michael Levey. Hammondsworth: Penguin, 1985.

————. *New Library Edition of the Works of Walter Pater*. 10 vols. London: MacMillan, 1910.

————. 'Poems by William Morris.' *The Westminster Review* 90 n.s.34 (1868): 300–12.

————. *The Renaissance: Studies in Art and Poetry*. Ed. Donald L. Hill. Berkeley: University of California Press, 1980.

————. *Walter Pater: Three Major Texts*. Ed. William E. Buckler. New York: New York University Press, 1986.

Peltason, Timothy. *Reading 'In Memoriam.'* Princeton: Princeton University Press, 1985.

————. "Ruskin's Finale: Vision and Imagination in *Praeterita*." *English Literary History* 57 (1990): 665–84.

Praz, Mario. *The Romantic Agony*. 2nd ed. London: Oxford University Press, 1951.

Pugin, A.W.N. *Contrasts; or, A Parallel Between the Noble Edifices of the Fourteenth and Fifteenth Centuries, and Similar Buildings of the Present Day; Shewing the Decay of Taste: Accompanied by Appropriate Text*. London, 1836.

Ricks, Christopher. *Tennyson*. New York: Macmillan, 1972.

Rosenberg, John D. *Carlyle and the Burden of History*. Cambridge: Harvard University Press, 1985.

————.*The Darkening Glass: A Portrait of Ruskin's Genius*. New York: Columbia University Press, 1961.

————. *The Fall of Camelot: A Study of Tennyson's 'Idylls of the King.'* Cambridge: Harvard University Press, 1972.

Ruskin, John. *The Genius of John Ruskin: Selections From His Writing.* Ed. John D. Rosenberg. Charlottesville: Virginia University Press, 1997.

———. *The Works of John Ruskin.* 39 vols. Ed. E.T. Cook and Alexander Wedderburn. London: George Allen, 1903–12.

Sacks, Peter. *The English Elegy: Studies in the Genre from Spenser to Yeats.* Baltimore: Johns Hopkins University Press, 1985.

Sanders, Charles R., ed. *Collected Letters of Thomas and Jane Welsh Carlyle.* Durham, NC: Duke University Press, Duke-Edinburgh edition, 1970.

Sawyer, Paul. 'Ruskin and St. George: The Dragon-Killing Myth in *Fors Clavigera*.' *Victorian Studies,* 23 (1979): 5–8.

Seiler, R. M., ed. *Walter Pater: A Life Remembered.* Calgary: University of Calgary Press, 1987.

Shaffer, Elinore, ed. *Comparative Criticism,* vol. 17: 'Walter Pater and the Culture of the Fin-de-Siécle,' Cambridge: Cambridge University Press, 1995.

Sharp, William, ed. *The Life and Letters of Joseph Severn.* New York: Scribners, 1892.

Shaw, W. David. *Elegy and Paradox: Testing the Conventions.* Baltimore: Johns Hopkins Press, 1990.

Sinfield, Alan. *The Language of Tennyson's 'In Memoriam.'* New York: Barnes & Noble, 1971.

Slater, Joseph D., ed. *The Correspondence of Emerson and Carlyle.* New York: Columbia University Press, 1964.

Sterrenburg, Lee. 'Psychoanalysis and the Iconography of Revolution.' *Victorian Studies,* 19 (1975): 241–64.

Swinburne, Algernon C. 'Matthew Arnold's New Poems.' *The Complete Works of Algernon Charles Swinburne.* 20 vols. Ed. Sir Edmund Gosse and Thomas James Wise. London: William Heinemann Ltd., 1925–7.

Sulloway, Frank J. 'Darwin's Conversion: The *Beagle* Voyage & Its Aftermath.' *Journal of the History of Biology* 15 (1982): 1–53.

Taylor. A. J. P. 'Macaulay and Carlyle.' *Essays in English History.* Hamondsworth, Middlesex: Penguin, 1976.

Tennyson, Alfred. *In Memoriam.* Ed. Susan Shatto and Marion Shaw. London: Oxford University Press, 1981.

———. *The Poems of Tennyson.* 3 Vols. 2$^{nd}$ ed. Ed. Christopher Ricks. Berkeley: University of California Press, 1987.

Tennyson, Charles. *Alfred Tennyson.* London: Macmillan, 1950.

Tennyson, Hallam. *Alfred, Lord Tennyson: A Memoir.* 2 vols. London: Macmillan, 1897.

Thomson, James. 'The City of Dreadful Night.' *The Poetical Works of James Thomson.* St. Clair Shores, MI: Scholarly Press, 1971.

Toqueville, Alexis de. *Journeys to England and Ireland.* Ed. J. P. Mayer. New Haven: Yale University Press, 1958.

Virgil. *Aeneid.* Trans. Robert Fitzgerald. New York: Vintage Books, 1983.

Walsh, Chad. *From Utopia to Nightmare.* New York: Harper, 1962.

Weil, Simone. 'The *Iliad* or The Poem of Force.' *The Proper Study: Essays on Western Classics.* Ed. Quentin Anderson and Joseph A. Mazzeo. New York: St. Martin's Press, 1962.

Wheeler, Michael. *Death and the Future Life in Victorian Literature and Theology.* Cambridge: Cambridge University Press, 1990.

Willey, Basil. *Nineteenth Century Studies.* London: Chatto, 1949.

Williams, Carolyn. *Transfigured World: Walter Pater's Aesthetic Historicism*. Ithaca, New York: Cornell University Press, 1989.

Wilson, Edmund. 'Introduction.' *The Novels of A. C. Swinburne: Love's Cross-Currents; Lesbia Brandon. With an Introduction by Edmund Wilson*. New York: The Noonday Press, 1962.

Winckelmann, Johann Joachim. *History of Ancient Art*. 4 vols. Trans. G. Henry Lodge. New York: Ungar, 1968.

Woolf, Virginia. *The Diary of Virginia Woolf*. Ed. Anne Olivier Bell. New York: Harcourt, 1981.

_____. 'A Sketch of the Past.' *Moments of Being*. 2nd ed. Ed. Jeanne Schulkind. New York: Harcourt, 1976.

Wordsworth, William. *Selected Poems and Prefaces*. Ed. Jack Stillinger. Boston: Houghton Mifflin, 1965.

_____. *The Prelude: 1799, 1805, 1850*. Eds. Jonathan Wordsworth, M. H. Abrams, and Stephen Gill. New York: Norton, 1979.

Wright, Thomas. *The Life of Walter Pater*. New York: Haskell, 1969. (Reprint of the 1907 edition in 2 vols.)

Yeats, William Butler, ed. 'Introduction.' *The Oxford Book of English Verse*. London: Oxford University Press, 1936.

_____. 'The Tragic Generation.' *Autobiography*. New York: Macmillan, 1965.

Young, G. M., ed. *Early Victorian England: 1830–1865*. 2 vols. London: Oxford University Press, 1934.

Young, Louise Merwin. *Thomas Carlyle and the Art of History*. Philadelphia: University of Pennsylvania Press, 1939.

Zuckerman, Elliott. *The First Hundred Years of Wagner's 'Tristan.'* New York: Columbia University Press, 1964.

# Index